EVALUATION OF LEASE FINANCING

About the Author

E. Chandraiah, M. Com., M. Phil., Ph.D., is a faculty in Commerce at Dr. B.R. Ambedkar Open University, Hyderabad. Earlier, he was a lecturer at Badruka Degree College, Hyderabad. He has been associated with the course planning and design of different academic programmes offered by the Faculty of Commerce of the university. He has also written course lessons, radio and audio lessons for distance learners.

A resource person for many television lessons and teleconferencing programmes, Chandraiah has to his credit two books and 10 research papers. He has also presented papers at national and international seminars and conferences.

EVALUATION OF LEASE FINANCING

by

E. CHANDRAIAH

CONCEPT PUBLISHING COMPANY, NEW DELHI-110059

ISBN : 81-8069-035-0

First Published 2004

Published and Printed by
Ashok Kumar Mittal
Concept Publishing Company
A/15-16, Commercial Block, Mohan Garden,
New Delhi-110059

Phones : 25351460, 25351794
Fax : 091-11-25357103
Email : publishing@conceptpub.com

FOREWORD

The Indian financial system comprises an impressive network of financial markets, financial institutions and financial services. Leasing companies, which have been considered Non-Banking Financial Companies (NBFCs), constitute a part of financial system.

Financial services sector assumes strategic role in the increasingly turbulent and uncertain business environment in the era of liberalisation. The growth of NBFCs has been rapid especially during early 1990s, which has broadened the leasing and financial services markets in the financial system.

NBFCs, in general, have recorded accelerated growth in mobilisation of public deposits and some of them indulged in indiscriminate deployment of funds without concomitant care for the interests of the depositors, which led to certain disquieting developments in this sector. Consequently, the RBI Act was amended by an Ordinance on January 9, 1997, which has since been affecting comprehensive changes in the statutory provisions for regulation of NBFCs.

The operations of leasing companies received a setback because of inadequate understanding of the implications of lease financing and absence of long-term strategy or direction.

The introduction of mandatory credit rating system from January 2, 1998, for NBFCs and its linking with the acceptance of public deposits has adversely affected the liquidity and profitability position, thereby resulting in liquidation of many leasing and finance companies, which had negligible net owned funds.

The study, "Evaluation of Lease Financing", attempts at an analysis of performance of leasing companies in the context of regulatory requirements. The study also makes an attempt to find out the extent to which subdued market conditions and associated non-performing assets have adversely affected the lease market. Further, the study evaluates lessees' point of view the extent of reliance on leasing to finance capital assets required and reasons for leasing.

Though it is essential that the financial services industry should be regulated to avoid defaults in refunding public deposits, the present regulatory measures taken by RBI seem to be very stringent and deserve some relaxation. Further, there has been absence of proper policy regarding recovery mechanism.

On the whole, as it was the absence of well-planned and phased mechanism for regulation of NBFCs in general and leasing in particular, there was significant incidence of failures of these institutions.

This study is an eye opener for policy makers as to how reformatory measures are to be initiated without adversely affecting the fortunes of the really genuine and good finance companies, which have become a casualty because of installation of sudden regulatory mechanism.

The findings of the study would be of interest to researchers, academics, concerned industrialists and policy makers to know as to how far the regulatory provisions being planned and implemented would make the leasing and finance companies run on sound lines and result in healthy growth of the sector.

Hyderabad

Prof. J. Satyanarayana
Adviser and Head, Research and Monitoring Wing for Essential Commodities in Andhra Pradesh, Hyderabad and formerly Emeritus Professor, Faculty of Commerce, Osmania University, Hyderabad.

ACKNOWLEDGEMENTS

No words would be adequate to express the debt of gratitude that I owe to my Research Supervisor, Prof. V. Nagaraja Naidu, for the rich guidance, insightful comments, constant encouragement and help given to me in the successful completion of the research work. My debt of gratitude will remain for ever for him.

I feel fortunate on having the incisive advice and encouragement of Prof. J. Satyanarayana, Adviser and Head, Research and Monitoring Wing for Essential Commodities in A.P., Hyderabad and formerly Emeritus Professor, Osmania University, Hyderabad. I express my profound gratitude to him for going through the chapters and offering astute and perceptive comments. I am also extremely grateful to him for writing the foreword.

I owe my sincere thanks to Prof. V. Venkaiah, Executive Director; Prof. G. Ram Reddy, Research Academy of Distance Education (GRADE) and formerly Rector; Dr. B. R. Ambedkar Open University, Hyderabad, for his generous suggestions and constant encouragement in my research and writing efforts.

I am thankful to Prof. S. Mahindra Dev, Director, Centre for Economic and Social Studies (CESS); Prof. G. K. Mitra; Dr. C. Ramchandraiah, Programme Co-ordinator; Sri K. Venkataiah, Asst. Programme Co-ordinator, Dr. S. Sudhakar Reddy; Sri Vijayakumar (Librarian) and the other staff of CESS, Hyderabad for their constant support and providing me the necessary research facilities. My thanks are also due to the authorities of Dr. B. R. Ambedkar Open University, Hyderabad, particularly the Vice Chancellor and Registrar for allowing me to pursue my research and granting me the publication grant.

I thank Prof A. Shankaraiah, Prof. K. Rajeshwara Rao, Prof. G. Krishna Murthy, Prof. V. Gangadhar, and Prof. Narsimha Murthy, Senior Faculty members, Department of Commerce and Management, Kakatiya University, Warangal, for their inspiration in completion of the research work.

I am also thankful to my colleagues Prof. K. Koteswara Rao, Prof. Y. S. Kiranmayi, Dr. K. Swamy, Dr. A. Sudhakar, Sri G. Malla Reddy, Dr. E. Sudha Rani, Sri Venkataiah and friends, Dr. K. Shankaraiah, Dr. S. Kamaleswara Rao, Dr. P. Rajalingam and Sri K. Narsimlu for their great help and encouragement in completion of my research.

I wish to place on record the help I received from authorities and staff of lessor and lessee companies selected for the study for their wholehearted cooperation in providing the necessary data.

My thanks are also due to Mr. V. Nagabhaskar Rao, Mr. M. V. Suresh, Mrs. Rushendramani, Mr. D. Srinivasa Rao, Sri M. Vijayakumar, Mr. Ramu and Mr. S. Aditya for their committed assistance.

Finally, I thank the Concept Publishing Company, New Delhi for bringing out this book in record time.

Hyderabad **E. Chandraiah**

CONTENTS

Page No.

Foreword *v*
Acknowledgements *vii*
List of Tables *x*
List of Figures and Charts *xiv*

1. Introduction 1
2. Leasing Business in India 34
3. Impact of Policy Framework on Lease Financing 79
4. Performance of Lessor Companies 142
5. Evaluation of Lessee Companies 222
6. Conclusions and Suggestions 294

Bibliography 326

Index 335

LIST OF TABLES

1.1	Company-wise Capital, Turnover, Net Profit and Leased Out Assets of Select Lessor Companies	22
1.2	Capital Turnover, Net Profit and Leased Assets of Select Lessee Companies	24
2.1	Equipment Leasing Activity in the United States	45
2.2	State-wise Growth of Leasing Companies in India	49
2.3	Sources of Funds of Member Companies of ALFS	53
2.4	Application of Funds of Member Companies of ALFS	54
2.5	Composition of Sources of Funds of Member Companies of ALFS	56
2.6	Component Analysis of Borrowings of Member Companies of ALFS	57
2.7	Proportion of Plant & Machinery to Total Leased Assets of Member Companies of ALFS	59
2.8	Composition of Income of Member Companies of ALFS	60
2.9	Some Important Ratios	63
2.10	Leasing by All India Financial Institutions	68
2.11	Financial Assistance to Leasing Companies by All India Financial Institutions	69
2.12	Gross State Domestic Product of Major States and Gross Domestic Product of All India at Constant (1993-94) Prices	73
2.13	Sector-wise Gross State Domestic Product of Andhra Pradesh and Percentage Distribution at Constant (1993-94) Prices	73
2.14	Per Capita Income of Major States and All India at Constant (1993-94) Prices	74

2.15	Proportion of Leased Assets of Select Lessee Companies to Total Industrial Investment in Andhra Pradesh	75
3.1	Bank Borrowings to Net Worth	90
3.2	Bank Borrowings and Institutional Borrowings to Net Worth	90
3.3	Borrowings of Select Leasing Companies in Andhra Pradesh	91
3.4	Bank and Institutional Borrowings and Net Worth (Company-wise)	92
3.5	Bank Borrowing and Institutional Borrowing to Net Worth	92
3.6	Provision against NPAs of Select Lessor Companies in Andhra Pradesh	98
3.7	Provision for Substandard/Doubtful/Loss Assets (NPAs) of Select Lessor Companies	99
3.8	Calculation of Risk Adjusted Value of Assets (RAVA)	101
3.9	Deposit Rates announced by NBFCs during 1996	113
3.10	Fixed Deposits and Net Worth of Select Lessor Companies	124
3.11	Ratio of Fixed Deposits to Net Worth	124
3.12	Increased Cost of a 5-year Lease due to Sales Tax	129
4.1	Sources and Application of Funds of Select Lessor Companies Sources of Funds	145
4.2	Proportion of Each Component of Sources and Application of Funds of Select Lessor Companies	148
4.3	Component Analysis of Aggregate Borrowings of Select Lessor Companies	148
4.4	Average Proportions of Owned Funds and Borrowings of Select Lessor Companies	149
4.5	Types of Assets Leased Out by Select Lessor Companies	155

4.6	Share of each Component of Leased Assets of Select Lessor Companies	155
4.7	Growth and Share of Plant & Machinery of Select Lessor Companies	156
4.8	Growth and Share of Vehicle Leasing of Select Lessor Companies	157
4.9	Growth and Share of Office Equipment of Select Lessor Companies	160
4.10	Growth and Share of Assets other than Plant & Machinery, Vehicles and Office Equipment of Select Lessor Companies	160
4.11	Component Analysis of Income of Select Lessor Companies	164
4.12	The Share of Each Component of Expenditure to Total Income of Select Lessor Companies	165
4.13	Provision for Non-Performing Assets and Lease Equalisation	168
4.14	Return on Capital Employed of Select Lessor Companies	170
4.15	Earning Per Share of Select Lessor Companies	170
4.16	Income and Costs of Three Lessor Companies	175
4.17	Debt-Equity Ratio of Select Lessor Companies	178
4.18	Interest Coverage Ratio	181
4.19	Consolidated Cash Flow Statement of Select Lessor Companies	185
4.20	Cash Flow Statement of NFL	187
4.21	Cash Flow Statement of PPL	191
4.22	Cash Flow Statement of LFL	193
4.23	Cash Flow statement of DCL	197
4.24	Cash Flow statement of MWL	199
4.25	Cash Flow Statement of SCFSL	203
4.26	Share of Fixed Deposits by Each Select Company	209

4.27 Fixed Deposits as a Percentage of Total Borrowings of Select Lessor Companies 210
5.1 Types of Assets taken on Lease by Lessee Companies 228
5.2 Types of Total Assets taken on Lease by Lessee Companies 229
5.3 Total Leased Assets taken on Lease by Lessee Companies 230
5.4 Plant and Machinery taken on Lease by Lessee Companies 231
5.5 Sub-Classification of Vehicle taken on Lease by Lessee Companies 240
5.6 Company-wise Analysis of Vehicles taken on Lease by Lessee Companies 241
5.7 Computers and Office Equipments taken by Lessee Companies on Lease 243
5.8 Volume of Leased Assets by Type of Lease Agreement 1990-91 to 1996-97 252
5.9 Year-wise Leased Assets and Investments in other than Leased Assets of Lessee Companies 256
5.10 Volume of Leased Assets falling under Different Rates of Depreciation 264
5.11 Leasing Rates [Leasing rates per month per thousand (pmpt)] 266
5.12 Lease Agreements of Lessee Companies from 1990-91 to 1996-97 266
5.13 Leasing Rates and Equivalent Interest Rates for 5 Years Lease Agreement 268
5.14 Component Analysis of Expenses (Aggregate) of Select Lessee Companies 280
5.15 Component Analysis of Expenses (Company-wise) of Select Lessee Companies 281
5.16 Reasons cited for Leasing by 16 Lessee Companies 286
5.17 Matrix of Preferences of Executives of 16 Lessee Companies for Reasons for Leasing 286

LIST OF FIGURES AND CHARTS

5.1 The Propportion, of each Assets to Total Assets taken on Lease 244
5.2 Tripartite Agreement under Sale and Lease back method 253
5.3 Step Leases 285

CHARTS

2.1 Lease Arrangement 35
3.1 Clossification of Non-Baning Companies 80
3.2 Rating Syambols of CRISIL, ICRA and CARE Debt 106
3.3 Minimum Credit Rating 107
3.4 Ceiling Limits 115
3.5 Revised Limits 117
3.6 Credit Rating of Fixed Deposits of Select Lessor Companies (1996-97 and 1997-98) 123
3.7 Concessions/Exemptions and Rate of Tax 130

1

INTRODUCTION

SECTION A

The benefits of equipment leasing were not realised until severe financial constraints in the procurement of capital equipment forced organisations to explore new avenues. When leasing business grew and met with initial success there was a mushroom growth of institutions offering leasing services in India. But, there was an absence of long-term strategy or direction.

Need for and the Importance of the Study

Leasing has been contributing significantly to the capital formation in developed and developing countries. Globally, leasing is the second most powerful source of financing, next to that of banks. This is in spite of the fact that bank financing is some centuries old, whereas leasing is only about 40 years old in developed countries and 20 years old in developing countries. The global penetration of leased assets as a percentage of total industrial assets is around 21%; which means, roughly one-fifth of all assets bought by industrial undertakings are actually bought by leasing industry and passed on for industrial use.

According to the "Survey of Industry Activity (SIA) 1986" published by the American Association of Equipment Lessors, the assets leased represent about 28% of all business investments in capital equipment in USA as against 19% in the U.K. In India it accounts for a meagre 4% to 5% of the total industrial investment. At present, especially after 1997, the potential for growth of leasing business in India is not encouraging. The leasing industry today is mainly composed of the Non-Banking Financial Companies and hence leasing companies are treated as NBFCs. Banks, which were involved in leasing through their subsidiaries since 1984, were permitted to do so directly from February 1994. The all India Financial Institutions are directly engaged in leasing. Almost every state level Financing Corporation has entered the leasing market.

Thus, we have had a large number of players in this industry – such as NBFCs, Financial Institutions, Banks and even manufacturing companies.

Leasing, in particular has gained greater recognition as an innovative means of industrial equipment financing and also as an important vehicle in the economic development of a country in general.

According to the reports of Association of Leasing and Financial Services, the assets growth of 216 NBFCs in India is as follows:

Year	*Rs. crore*
1994-95	26,573.3
1995-96	36,158.1
1996-97	43,833.1

The fixed deposits growth of 216 NBFCs in India is as follows:

Year	*Rs. crore*
1994-95	4,404.3
1995-96	7,017.6
1996-97	10,309.8

The survival of finance companies or NBFCs depends upon the effective mobilisation of required resources from the public as well as banks and other financial institutions. The above trend of growth of NBFCs and the growth of fixed deposits indicates that leasing has become an increasingly important mode of financing asset acquisition in India.

In India, until the first half of 1980's companies in the private sector transacted leasing business. The second half of 1980s saw the emergence of wholly owned subsidiaries of major government owned banks and financial institutions entering the leasing market with a big bang.

Thus over a period of more than 20 years of its existence, especially up to 1997, leasing played an important role in India's financial sector.

The VIII Five-Year Plan (1992-97) aimed at a 5.6% annual growth in the Gross Domestic Product (GDP) with a total proposed outlay of Rs. 7,92,000 crores. The emphasis in this plan period was resource mobilisation.

Users of Lease Financing

In addition to big, medium and small-scale companies and entrepreneurs, the Government owned enterprises such as – Department of Telecommunications, Coal India, Indian Railways, etc., have been resorting to use of leasing for quite some time. The contribution of leasing to infrastructure financing, particularly to State Electricity Boards, is notable.

Hence, it is of interest to study and evaluate the different aspects of lease financing from the point of view of the lessor and the lessee to know the performance of Lessor Companies, the use of leasing to finance capital assets and its impact on quantity of lessee's investment behaviour and the reasons for why lessees prefer leasing.

Objectives of the Study

The study specifically aims at:

(i) the study of the leasing business in India and its contribution to industrial finance;
(ii) evaluating the impact of policy framework on lease financing;
(iii) analysing the financial performance of select lessor companies by using cash flow technique;
(iv) evaluating the select lessee companies in terms of assets leased, cost of leasing, the use of leasing to finance capital assets and its impact on quantity of lessee's investment behaviour and reasons for leasing.

Scope and Period of Study

The study pertains to the evaluation of lessor and lessee companies with respect to certain select companies in Andhra Pradesh. Broadly, it covers the performance of lessor companies and the impact of the using lease financing to finance capital asset on industrial investment. Further, it covers the impact of policy framework on lease financing. It may be mentioned that the macro level growth perspectives are derived from secondary data and covered at all-India level. The study covers a period of 7 years from 1990-91 to 1996-97. As most of the leasing companies have diversified into other activities and some of the selected lessor companies have closed down their business during the years 1997 and 1998, the study also covers the data pertaining to the year 1997-98, wherever it is necessary.

Methodology

The study is based on survey method. The data has been collected from both primary and secondary sources. The primary data has been collected from the sample units in three stages. The first stage consists of semi-structured interviews with 12 Executive level Managers – such as Managers (Finance), Financial Advisers, Managers (Marketing), Senior Managers (Accounts) from lessor and lessee companies. Based on this, the problem of the study was identified and structured questionnaires were designed from the lessor and the lessee points of view. The secondary stage of primary data collection involved observational fieldwork, which consisted of giving questionnaires to top and middle level executives of both lessor and lessee companies and collection of Annual Reports of select companies. The third stage of primary data collection was collecting the questionnaires personally, which were earlier given to the executives of select companies and ascertain information pertaining to leasing and reasons for leasing and other related information.

The secondary data has been collected from:

(i) Annual Reports of select companies; Reports of Equipment leasing Association Madras and Association of Leasing and Financial Services, Bombay;
(ii) Reports of Centre for Monitoring Indian Economy (CMIE). The CMIE is India's leading Economic and Business Research Enterprise;
(iii) Reserve Bank of India Bulletins and Reports on currency and finance, published by RBI;
(iv) IDBI Reports on Development Banking in India;
(v) Stock Exchange Official Directory, Bombay;

(vi) The Annual Survey of Industries, New Delhi;
(vii) Report on the Annual Survey of Industries, Government of AP;
(viii) Journals, Standard Magazines, and Dailies;
(ix) All other relevant reports and publications.

Data Analysis

The data ascertained through these questionnaires and reports are analysed and interpreted with the help of appropriate accounting and statistical tools.

The ratios such as debt-equity, return on investment, interest coverage; common size statements, etc. are used to evaluate the companies financial performance, operating results and growth prospects.

The technique of cash flow analysis is used by preparing cash flow statement, which reveals the sources from which cash has come into the business and the activities on which the cash has been spent. The net result is reflected in the balance of the cash account as on a certain point of time, and the reasons for changes in cash position in select lessor companies.

The statistical tools such as averages, compound growth rates, Standard Deviation, x^2 (chi square) test, etc. are used in appropriate contexts. Further, paired comparison method is used to convert the rank order data for the preferences of reasons for taking assets on lease into the matrices of preferences to indicate the relative importance of each response of the select lessee companies.

In the analysis of the structured data and interviews, care has been taken to relate comments and observations to draw unbiased inference on the facts revealed by the study.

Selection of Sample Companies

The addresses of AP based leasing and finance companies were obtained from the Registrar of Companies. The total number of leasing and finance companies registered with the Registrar of Companies in AP was 123 as on 31-3-1995. These companies were engaged in leasing, hire purchase financing and other related activities. Out of these 123, 54 are public limited companies and the remaining 69 are private limited companies.

After ascertaining the information from the Registrar of Companies a sample of 18 (33%) leasing companies was drawn based on authorised capital of having Rs. 200 lakhs and above as on 31-3-1991. Out of the 18 leasing companies, nine companies responded and all of them were given questionnaires and interviews. Three of the nine companies were manufacturing companies and were found to be largely irrelevant to the study as they did very little leasing business meant specially for tax planning purpose. Consequently, for the purpose of quantitative analysis, the following three companies were ignored (i) Raasi Cements Ltd., (ii) ITC Bhadrachalam Ltd., and (iii) Pennar Steels Limited. The latter two are included in select lessee companies, as they have taken assets on lease. However, for the purpose of qualitative analysis, the opinion of the executives of these three companies were taken into account in order to have a broader perspective in terms of volume of leasing business and performance of lessor companies. It may be pointed out that the selected six lessor companies are large companies. And it is ascertained that the volume of leasing business done by these six companies constitutes more than 85% of total leasing business done by all leasing companies in A.P.

Initially, the addresses of 40 lessee companies were obtained from lessor companies for the study out of which 20 A.P. based companies were selected at random. Out of the 20 companies, 9 companies responded and the remaining 11 companies have declined to give quantitative information, when approached. However, qualitative information was obtained from 16 top level Executives, including 9 companies who responded to questionnaires and discussions. The structured questionnaires and interviews conducted at different levels of executives in the lessee companies provided considerable insight into the types and volume of leased assets, use of leasing to finance capital asset and its impact on the quantity of investment, reasons for leasing and other related aspects.

The names of selected lessor companies are:

(i) Nagarjuna Finance Limited,
(ii) Pennar Paterson Securities Limited,
(iii) Laxmi Finance Limited,
(iv) DCL Finance Limited,

(v) Midwest Leasing Limited, and
(vi) Srichakra Financial Services Limited.

The names of selected lessee companies are :

1. AP State Electricity Board,
2. AP Rayons Limited,
3. AP State Road Transport Corporation Limited,
4. Coromandal Limited,
5. ITC Bhadrachalam Limited,
6. Pennar Aluminium Limited,
7. Pennar Steels Limited,
8. PSM Spinning Mills Limited, and
9. VST Limited.

Limitations of the Study

The following are the limitations of the study :

1. The evaluation pertaining to performance of lessor companies and the use of leasing to finance capital assets, its impact on lessee's investment and reasons for leasing is restricted to lessor and lessee companies registered and located in Andhra Pradesh.
2. Leasing companies in A.P. do not exclusively engage in leasing business. They undertake other activities such as hire purchase business, bill discounting, merchant banking, etc simultaneously. Hence, ratios and other statistical methods calculated here might not be applicable exclusively to leasing business but both to leasing and other finance business activities as well.
3. Though sufficient care was taken to get accurate information, some select companies might not have provided complete or totally accurate data.
4. The lease rental fixation could not be included in the present study as it is a vast area and deserve separate treatment and study.
5. It is found that most of the private limited leasing companies have diverted to other activities. Some have been dormant and some companies have been closed; and hence, to maintain consistency, the study of private limited leasing companies is

excluded. And the public limited leasing companies established after 1991, were not considered for the study in order to maintain consistency.

Plan of the Study

Based on the objectives, the study is organised into six chapters including introduction and conclusions and suggestions.

Chapter 1: Introduction

The first chapter is introductory in nature. It dealt with the need and importance and conceptual analysis of leasing. It also covers the objectives, scope and period of study, methodology including sample design and profile of select companies and limitations of the study. In addition to this, the past literature on the subject is also reviewed.

Chapter 2 : Leasing Business in India

This chapter presents the origin and evolution of leasing and examines the volume of leasing business in India and A.P. Further, it examines the contribution of leasing to industrial finance in A.P. and in India as a whole.

Chapter 3 : Impact of Policy Framework on Lease Financing

The policy framework broadly consists of RBI guidelines, prudential norms, credit rating and sales tax Act, etc. This chapter evaluates the impact of policy framework on leasing.

Chapter 4: Performance of Lessor Companies

This chapter attempts to study the sources and application of funds. It evaluates the performance of lessor companies by using the cash flow technique and relevant ratios.

Chapter 5 : Evaluation of Lessee Companies

This chapter makes an attempt to evaluate the selected lessee companies in terms of assets leased, cost of leasing, the use of leasing to finance capital assets and its impact on quantity of lessee's investment behaviour and reasons for leasing.

Chapter 6 : Conclusions and Suggestions

This chapter summarises the study and presents the conclusions arrived at.

In addition, the study also attempts to offer a few suggestions, which may be useful to lessor and lessee companies, policy makers and academics.

SECTION B

Review of Literature

There has not been much of research work carried out on Indian Leasing since the concept itself is of recent origin. There is not even a single study, which attempted to study the "Evaluation of Lease Financing" both from lessor and lessee points of view. It is in this context, that the present study examines the impact of policy framework on leasing, performance of lessor companies and use of leasing to finance capital assets and its impact on lessee's investment behaviour and reasons for leasing. However, the relevant studies, having direct and indirect impact on the present work have been bifurcated, for the purpose of review and the research work done on lease financing, into two parts:

1. Conceptual Studies, and
2. Research Studies.

Conceptual Studies

The studies of this sort provide theoretical and conceptual foundation for equipment leasing. Conceptual studies are again categorised into two types, viz., Inclusive and Exclusive conceptual studies.

The inclusive studies are books, which deal with concepts and techniques of leasing as a part of the study of Financial Management. The text books that belong to this category were authored by the writers like, John J. Hampton;[1] Van Horne and Wachowicz;[2] I.M. Pandey;[3] Gupta, N.C. (edited);[4] Prasanna Chandra;[5] Srivastava, R.M.;[6] Bierman and Smidt;[7] and Kuchhal, S.C.[8]

The existing *exclusive* studies on equipment leasing belong to the other category of conceptual studies, dealt with the conceptual framework of leasing, problems of leasing, evaluation of leasing, etc. The exclusive studies authored by writers like Vinod Kothari[9], Verma, J.C.;[10] Kamath, K.V. *et al.*;[11] Premlal Joshi;[12] Rajas Purchure and Ashok Kumar, N.;[13] Rajas Purchure;[14] Gosh, P.K., and Gupta, G.S.;[15] Henry, S. Beers, Jr.;[16] Mathur B.L. (edited);[17] Nagaraja Naidu, V., *et al.*[18] (edited); Tom Clark; [19] John Williamson.[20]

Research Studies

Research studies on Equipment Leasing are found to be very limited in India compared to developed countries like USA, UK, West Germany, etc. The research studies on equipment leasing are again classified into two:

(i) Indian Studies, and
(ii) Studies Abroad.

All research studies in India and abroad can be broadly classified as:

1. Studies focusing on the growth of leasing and the factors, which influenced the growth of leasing.
2. Studies pin-pointing towards accounting practices and procedures.
3. Studies analysing lease or borrow decision.
4. Studies, which perform an empirical analysis of lease, contracts to focus on the rates of return and cost of leasing.

Indian Studies

Satyanarayana Murthy [21] in his unpublished Doctoral dissertation analysed the role of leasing industry in equipment leasing decisions of business firms in the private corporate sector of India. The study examines the growth patterns of leasing industry and the design of lease contracts and determinants of lease rentals. Accordingly, an in-depth analysis has been made of 211 contracts signed by the three Hyderabad based leasing companies. Some of the main findings of the study are:

(i) Information pertaining to the maturity period disclosed that 99 of the contracts constituting 47 per cent of the total number of contracts had a maturity period ranging from 4 to 7 years and another 75 contracts represent the class ranging from 2 years to 4 years. These two maturity groups, therefore, accounted for the vast majority of the total contracts.

(ii) Lease contracts entered by the three companies have been broadly categorised into six asset categories, viz., (i) autos and trucks, (ii) medical and health, (iii) office, (iv) manufacturing, (v) construction, and (vi) miscellaneous. Manufacturing equipment constituted the bulk of the lease contracts accounted for around 40% of the total contracts.

Narayana Swamy[22], in his research study analysed the issues in accounting for leases by lessees and by lessors. This study is purely a piece of academic research.

The questionnaire survey covered the capitalisation of lease by lessees, recovery of cost of leased asset by lessor in primary lease period.

The questionnaire was posted to 146 leasing companies. Usable responses were received from 72 companies yielding a response rate of 49%. Detailed interviews were conducted with some lessors, Chartered Accountants, and other concerned officers. Some findings of the study are:

(i) Of the respondents, 66 had over 30% of their turnover or gross revenue from finance leases.
(ii) Lessors like lessees to disclose their lease obligations in footnotes to lessee's accounts but opposed to lease capitalisation by lessees in view of uncertain tax consequences.
(iii) Lessors support recovery of asset cost in primary lease period but do not support showing leased assets as receivables, presumably for tax reasons. Sreenivasa Murthy[23] in his study of 130 Indian lessee companies reported the factors influencing the decision to lease and not to lease, leasing activities and lease purchase decision practices. The important findings of the study are:

    (i) Availability, working capital, tax benefits, and off-balance sheet financing are important factors in the decision to lease.
    (ii) Companies used different forms of acquisition methods

to acquire different types of assets. Finance lease was mainly used to acquire computers, air conditioners, passenger vehicles, etc.

(iii) The step-wise multiple regression results showed that liquidity factor (independent variable) influences the volume of leasing (dependent variable) to a great extent.

(iv) Majority of select companies preferred private leasing companies while others preferred public financial institutions and banks for lease financing.

Brahmaiah[24] conducted a study on the accounting practices of 60 leasing companies. The study reveals the following:

(i) There is no uniformity in the accounting practices of lessee companies. Lessees show their leased assets in their balance sheets neither as assets nor as liabilities in view of their future rental obligations, making the lease transaction as 'off the balance sheet' transaction. Similarly, lessors do not show the lease rental to be received as receivables in their balance sheet.

(ii) Only a few companies showed owned assets and leased assets separately under the head 'fixed assets'. Further, the method of depreciation followed for leased assets is different from those of owned assets. Leasing companies follow written down value method (WDV) of depreciation for owned assets and straight-line method (SLM) for leased assets.

Ms. Sharmila Dayal's[25] study on "Lease Financing in India—Problems and Prospects" focused on the growth and development of leasing companies in India, bringing out the multifarious causes of their mushrooming. Some of the important factors that were found by this researcher were:

(i) Tendency of profit flooding of early companies,
(ii) Trend of share market price,
(iii) Activity and operational levels of leasing business in India,
(iv) Future expectations etc.

Investors' interaction with leasing companies has been elaborately discussed by the author quoting the statements of shareholders of leasing companies. She has also paid a sincere attention towards the existing vacuum in the standardised accounting treatment of leasing in India. A critical appraisal of financial resources and dividend policies of leasing companies in India has been analysed by the researcher with the help of various financial ratios. Further, legal aspects of lease financing have been comprehensively discussed with emphasis on the impact of various relevant Acts on the working of these leasing companies.

Studies Abroad

An extensive survey was conducted by Mayes, D.G., and Nicholas, C.S.,[26] on "The Economic Impact of Leasing" focusing on the effects of leasing on the investment behaviour of lessee firms and its macro economic implications.

A sample of 25 leasing companies in the Southwest was drawn from lessors operating in the UK to get a considerable insight into the leasing activity and the role of leasing in relation to the investment behaviour.

Two samples of lessee companies in the South-West Economic Planning Region (SWEPR) and in the National Institute of Economic and Social Research (NIESR) representing a range of commerce and industry were drawn to investigate the past behaviour of firms with respect to leasing and the effects of leasing on the level and timing of investment and to assess the general impact of the 1984 Budget on the use of leasing.

Questionnaires were sent to 1000 companies in the South West Economic Planning Region and 406 (40.6%) companies replied. Questionnaires were also sent to 85 companies on the National Institute of Economic and Social Research Survey Panel and 30 companies replied giving a response rate of 35.3 per cent, a little lower than that in South West Survey.

Some findings of the study are:

(i) The lessor survey indicated that the majority of the interviewees considered that leasing had in fact increased the level of investment and the tax advantage had played an important role in this process, but they were unable to quantify the effect of leasing on investment.

(ii) Of the 406 companies that replied to the questionnaire in the

South West Economic Planning Region (SWEPR) 268 (66%) had in fact used leasing and 138 (34%) had not. While, of the 30 respondent companies from the NIESR survey panel, 26 (86.7%) had used leasing and 4 (13.3%) had not.

(iii) The survey indicated some behavioural differences in the two samples. The South-West survey (of generally smaller companies) avoiding large capital outlay appears to be the most significant factor influencing leasing decision. Whereas in the NIESR survey (of generally larger companies) tax advantage is more obviously a predominant factor in leasing decision.

(iv) In the South West sample, there was quite a marked preference towards ownership of assets rather than leasing. A large number of companies have indicated that they were able to take direct advantage of capital allowances if they purchase the asset and leasing was too expensive compared to other sources of funds.

Fawthrop and Terry[27], in their study of debt management and the use of lease financing found that companies did not consider tax implications to be particularly relevant in their use of leasing. The survey was based on the responses of senior financial executives of 54 major corporations located in the UK. Many respondents agreed that leasing is a part of a planned financing mix and rejected the point that leasing is an emerging mode of financing.

Sykes[28] examined leasing practices in 202 BIM (British Institute of Management) member companies. Some of the results of the study are:

(i) 65% of the numbers answering felt the immediate availability of tax allowances through leasing to be relatively or totally unimportant,

(ii) All the companies with an annual turnover of over $100 million considered tax allowances to be important in leasing decisions.

(iii) It was found that there was no correlation between rate of sales, growth and tendency to lease.

Hull and Hubbard[29] examined the attitudes and behaviour of lessees in the UK leasing industry. The survey found that 48% of sample companies, which had been liable to tax over the previous two years, had in fact leased assets during that period. Finally, Hull and Hubbard concluded from their study that the rationale for leasing is not totally based on tax advantage but dependent on many factors. The important factors for leasing were conserved cash flow; the fact that leasing is cheaper than hire purchase; additional form of finances; etc. Other marginal factors are assistance in having a mixed financing strategy, safeguard against obsolescence, certainty of fixed payments etc.

An extensive survey on "Lease *vs*. Purchase decision making" was conducted by Ferrara, Thies and Dirsmith.[30] The survey was based on American and Canadian companies. The questionnaires were mailed to 925 industrial firms and the responses were received from 541 (58.5%). The results of this study are:

(i) The factors which have an impact on lease purchase decision are listed as: implicit rate, threat of obsolescence, income taxes, maintain flexibility, conserve working capital, less restrictive financing, and off-balance sheet financing.
Dr. Jur. Alfred W. Fink's[31] research is based on an ongoing research project started by Leaseurope in 1990. The aim of the project is to study and report on the similarities and differences of the leasing industry in the various countries represented by Leaseurope. The survey up to 1992 covers, *inter alia*, lease accounting in Austria, Belgium, The Republic of Ireland, The Netherlands, Portugal and Switzerland.

(ii) The survey traces a clear positive correlation between the extent of leasing and leverage and a clear positive correlation between the extent of leasing and income coverage for fixed charges.

(iii) The survey also indicated that computers, vehicles, duplicating equipment, and buildings (including office space) were substantially leased assets in both Canada and US. The above assets are ranked in that order.

(iv) For financially strong firms, leasing becomes a costly method of financing but that the higher cost may be considered worth while by some firms considering the executor services offered by the lessors and the obsolescence factor.

The principal controversy relates to the accounting of finance lease, whether it is legitimate to prepare financial statements to consider the commercial substance of lease transactions (disclosure of leased asset in the books of the lessee) rather than in their legal form (disclosure of leased asset in the books of the lessor). There was considerable divergence of views on the question of lease capitalisation.

Dr. Jur. Alfred W. Fink observed the general position taken in selected countries with regard to the capitalisation of leased assets as mentioned hereunder.

Legal Form Countries	*Commercial Substance Countries*
Austria	Belgium
Portugal (Until 1994)	The Republic of Ireland
Switzerland	The Netherlands
	Portugal
	(From 1-1-1994)

Presently in India, the accounting for lease is followed according to legal form. The accounting standard for leasing is yet to be framed.

SECTION C

Profile of Select Companies

A. Brief Profile of Lessor Companies

1. NFL

This company was established in 1982. It is one of the leading integrated finance companies in India and belongs to the rapidly growing group company. It offers a wide range of quick and efficient financial services to accelerate trade, commerce, and industrial growth. The company's regular activities have been in the areas of leasing, hire purchase financing, consumer financing, portfolio management, trade financing, etc.

The company's main strength is its innovative methods. As part of its innovation, the company has diversified into (i) Stock markets, (ii) Real estate, (iii) Software development, (iv) Merchant banking, and (v) Mutual funds.

Thus, the NFL has consolidated its position in the financial services market through information. The authorised capital of the company has increased from Rs.1,000 lakhs in 1990-91 to Rs. 5000 lakhs in 1996-97, while the capital employed has increased from Rs.6,338.41 lakhs in 1990-91 to Rs.19,425.63 lakhs in 1996-97. The volume of lease business done by NFL has increased from Rs. 2,050.50 lakhs in 1990-91 to Rs.17,387.75 lakhs (more than 8 times increase is recorded) in 1996-97. The net profit increased from Rs. 225.72 lakhs in 1990-91 to Rs. 1,025.48 lakhs in 1995-96 and decreased to Rs. 610.12 lakhs in 1996-97.

The economy in general and financial services in particular experienced a rather difficult year during 1996-97 that resulted in decelerated growth. The situation was further aggravated with the entry of a good number of multi-national companies into Indian non-banking financial sector. Because of these prevailing circumstances, the NFL entered the crop protection business by acquiring the undertaking comprising the business of manufacture and sale of insecticides at Ethakota, Andhra Pradesh from Vijaya Lakshmi Insecticides & Pesticides Ltd. for total consideration of Rs. 684.00 lakhs.

2. PPL

The PPL company was established in 1987 to transact the business in financial services. The main activities include – security market, leasing and hire purchase financing, bill discounting etc. The authorised capital of the company has increased from Rs. 500.00 lakhs in 1990-91 to Rs. 3,000.00 lakhs in 1996-97.

During the year 1995-96, this company has expanded its branch network to Delhi, Bangalore, Pune and other centres in Andhra Pradesh. The volume of leased out assets has increased to Rs. 4,332.93 lakhs in 1996-97 from Rs. 81.23 lakhs in 1990-91. The performance of the company has been remarkable from 1990-91 to 1994-95. The income rose from Rs. 64.7 lakhs in 1990-91 to Rs. 3,604.9 lakhs in 1996-97.

The net profit also rose from Rs. 19.9 lakhs in 1990-91 to Rs. 901.79 lakhs in 1994-95 but decreased to Rs. 373.5 lakhs in 1996-97 due to unprecedented decline in the economy in general and linking of credit rating to acceptance of public deposits.

With this result, the year 1997-98 was a difficult one and the net availability of funds to the company showed a decline. The regulatory guidelines restricted the borrowings of non-banking finance companies, which in turn caused a decline in the growth of the asset base and led to default in payment of public deposits as and when matured. Presently this company is in the liquidation process.

3. LFL

The LFL company was established in 1985. The authorised capital of the company has increased from Rs.200.00 lakhs in 1990-91 to Rs. 300.00 lakhs in 1996-97. The main activities of the company are securities market, bill discounting, leasing and hire purchase, etc.

The company has issued bonus shares in the ratio of one bonus share for two existing equity shares and declared dividend of 25% during the year 1991. Further, the company has undertaken the expanded activity of manufacturing of plastic moulded articles during the year 1991. The net profit increased substantially from Rs. 52.37 lakhs in 1993-94 to Rs. 141.26 lakhs in 1994-95 resulting in a growth rate of 170%. This is mainly due to the increase in leasing activities and the Directors were pleased to recommend a dividend at the rate of 40% per equity share of Rs.100 each subject to deduction of tax at source for the year ended 31st March, 1995. The company also issued bonus shares in the ratio of one bonus share for every two equity shares held. As a result, the paid up equity capital of the company increased to Rs. 225 lakhs from Rs. 150 lakhs.

During the year 1996-97, the financial operations of the company received a set-back mainly on account of high cost of funds and subdued market conditions for leasing and hire purchase activities and associated recovery problems. As a result, the net profit of the company came down to Rs. 40.76 lakhs in 1996-97 from Rs. 109.06 lakhs in 1995-96. Consequently, the company has declared a low dividend of 15% (i.e., Rs. 1.50 per equity share of Rs. 10 each).

The problems have been compounded on account of the RBI

policy changes with respect to the provisioning norms, income recognition, and acceptance of public deposits by NBFCs. Consequently, the financial operations of the company have been severely affected and the company has not taken up new business in the field of leasing and hire purchase and concentrated in a limited way in the area of short term financing, viz., Inter-corporate Deposits and Bill Discounting.

4. DCL

The DCL company was established in 1982 with the main objective of providing fund based financial services. Its authorised capital increased from Rs. 600.00 lakhs in 1990-91 to Rs. 1,000.00 lakhs in 1996-97 and capital employed was Rs. 2,944.7 lakhs in 1996-97 as against Rs. 1,167.5 lakhs in 1990-91 indicating 152.2% increase over a period of seven years.

Its main activities include leasing, hire purchase finance and bill discounting. The company provided different kinds of assets—such as plant and machinery, vehicles and other assets on leasing.

Encouraged by the liberalisation measures of the government, the company has expanded its business to fee based activities by undertaking merchant banking in 1992-93. As such the company has undertaken the fee based activities of underwriting issues of other companies. During the year 1993-94, the company has successfully underwritten as many as 41 companies' issues for an amount aggregating to Rs. 571.55 lakhs and the company has made a profit of Rs. 9.08 lakhs on the above activity. In order to establish the presence in other regions of the country, the company has opened its branches at Indore and New Delhi during the year 1993-94.

The net profit of the company increased from Rs. 44.96 lakhs in 1990-91 to a high Rs. 425.89 lakhs in 1994-95 indicating an increase by 9.47 fold. But thereafter it has decreased to Rs. 265.73 lakhs in 1995-96 and further dropped to Rs. 148.46 lakhs in 1996-97. Consequently, the payment of dividends to the shareholders is also reduced from 20% (in 1994 to 96) to 12% (in 1996-97).

The drop in profits for the years mentioned was due to high competition in the financial services sector and strict adherence to the prudential norms prescribed by the RBI.

The year 1997-98 witnessed a sea change in the fortunes of the financial services Industry. The DCL was no exception to these changes.

As this company was facing the accumulation of Non-performing Assets (NPA), it initiated timely and appropriate steps, both legal and conciliatory methods for recovery of outstanding amount. A number of non-viable branches have been closed and staff reduced to the desired levels.

5. MWL

This company was established in 1983, with an objective to provide financial services of leasing, hire purchase and bill discounting. The authorised capital of the company increased from Rs. 500.00 lakhs to Rs. 2,500.00 lakhs.

The company made significant progress in offering leasing services at the beginning and the company maintained a comparatively good result up to 1993-94. The net profit of the company increased from Rs.103.39 lakhs in 1990-91 to Rs.178.67 lakhs in 1993-94 indicating 1.73 times increase. But the subsequent year 1994-95 witnessed a declining trend and the year 1996-97 recorded a loss of Rs. 392.08 lakhs, mainly because of Non-performing Assets. With the result, though the company declared dividends at the rate of 15% in 1991-92, 12% in 1993-94, no dividend was declared during the year 1994-95. The bad debts written off amounting to Rs. 187.78 lakhs and loss on sale of assets amounting to Rs. 28.27 lakhs were recorded during the year 1995. The liquidity crunch and the reluctance on the part of the banks in lending to NBFCs had an adverse impact on the operations and profitability of the company.

Further, the economy was passing through difficult times and the severe liquidity crisis prevalent in the corporate sector resulted in the accumulation of non-performing assets and the company faced many setbacks. Though it initiated appropriate steps for the recovery of outstanding amount, the company was in default for making payments of public deposits. As such the company was in liquidation process during the year 1997-98 at the instance of public complaint.

6. SCFSL

This company was established in 1983. The main activities of the company were hire purchase, lease financing, and bill discounting. The authorised capital of the company increased from Rs. 350.00 lakhs in 1990-91 to Rs. 900.00 lakhs in 1996-97. The capital employed increased from Rs. 496.1 lakhs in 1990-91 to Rs. 741.6 lakhs in 1996-97. The company opened its branch offices at Vijayawada, Rajahmundry, Visakhapatnam and Madras.

The total income of the company during 1991-92 was higher at Rs. 261.31 lakhs as against Rs. 103.22 lakhs in 1990-91. The net profit also rose from Rs. 21.47 lakhs in 1990-91 to Rs. 107.22 lakhs in 1991-92. The company declared dividend of 18% in 1991-92 as against 14% in previous year, subject to deduction of tax at source.

The total income during the year had marginally dropped to Rs. 238.49 lakhs in 1992-93 as against Rs. 261.31 lakhs in 1991-92. The net profit had also come down abnormally to Rs.50.87 lakhs in 1992-93 from Rs. 107.22 lakhs in 1991-92. Subsequently, the net profit further reduced to Rs. 26.52 lakhs in 1993-94 and the net loss recorded at Rs. 55.10 lakhs and further, the net loss increased to Rs. 219.06 lakhs during 1996-97. Thus the company continued to suffer net loss and liquidity crisis due to depressed capital market conditions, stringent RBI guidelines, and lack of trained and qualified manpower.

B. Brief Profile of Lessee Companies

1. APSEB

The APSEB was established in 1959, with an objective of generation and transmission of electric power.

There are 24 Generating Stations in the State, out of which 10 are Thermal and 13 are Hydro and one Wind Station. The operation and maintenance of all these stations including Machkund Hydro Electric (Joint) scheme is under the control of AP State Electricity Board. The Thunga Bhadra Hydroelectric (Joint) Scheme (TB Dam Power House which is a joint project of Government of AP and Government of Karnataka with 80 : 20 of share of power) is managed by Thunga Bhadra Board.

Table 1.1 : Company-wise Capital, Turnover, Net Profit and Leased Out Assets of Select Lessor Companies

(Rs. lakhs)

Lessor Cos.	*Year of Establishment*	*Authorised Capital*		*Capital Employed*		*Turnover (Income)*		*Net Profit*		*Leased Out Assets*	
		1990-91	1996-97	1990-91	1996-97	1990-91	1996-97	1990-91	1996-97	1990-91	1996-97
NFL	1982	1000.0	5000.0	6338.4	19425.6	1095.2	10840.3	225.7	610.1	2050.5	17387.7
PPL	1987	500.0	3000.0	316.4	9682.6	64.7	3604.9	19.9	373.5	81.2	4332.9
LFL	1985	200.0	300.0	877.4	1198.8	252.5	235.2	64.2	40.8	127.8	915.8
DCL	1982	600.0	1000.0	1167.5	2944.7	344.8	2886.9	44.9	148.5	639.9	1447.6
MWL	1983	500.0	2500.0	1977.9	1931.7	609.7	547.3	103.4	(392.1)	1005.1	1016.9
SCFSL	1983	350.0	900.0	496.1	741.6	103.2	267.9	21.5	(219.1)	89.8	449.7

Note: Capital Employed = Owned Capital + Debentures + Term Loans
Source: Annual Reports of Select Lessor Companies

The Government of Andhra Pradesh gave the Reform and Restructuring initiatives of the APSEB in its policy on power sector reforms enunciated on 13-2-1997. The broad objectives envisaged by the State Government are as follows:

1. Promoting private participation of the power sector in the power supply industry.
2. Removing dependence of electricity utilities on Government budgetary assistance.

For achieving these objectives, the State Government intends to restructure the APSEB on functional lines into companies dealing with Generation, Transmission and Distribution functions. The plan is to organise the State's power distribution network into a number of distinct distribution areas, each of which is administered by a viable distribution company. The Government also plans to privatise the entities in gradual steps.

APSEB has taken the assets on lease amounting to Rs. 1,10,500 lakhs as on 31st March 1997. 99% of these leased assets is under "Sale-cum-lease" back agreements. On an average, the leased assets occupied the ratio of 24.64% of year-wise total assets acquired. The leased assets gradually increased from Rs. 2,390 lakhs in 1990-91 to Rs. 15,000 lakhs in 1993-94 and further increased to Rs. 1,10,500.00 lakhs in 1996-97.

The net profit of the company increased from Rs. 2,214.0 lakhs in 1990-91 to Rs. 14,394.8 lakhs in 1996-97 (Table 1.2).

2. APR

The APR company was established during 1978-79 with an objective of paper manufacturing and producing high quality Rayon Grade Pulp.

The procurement of raw material is one of the main concerns of the company. With the State Government not being able to supply suitable pulpable species of wood, the company has been forced to resort to open market purchase both within the State and outside at a considerably higher cost. The company continues its efforts to develop farm forestry resources in Warangal District in order to have an assured source of supply of raw materials in future.

Table 1.2 : Capital Turnover, Net Profit and Leased Assets of Select Lessee Companies

(Rs. Lakhs)

Lessee Companies	*Year of Establishment*	*Authorised Capital*		*Capital Employed*		*Turnover (Income)*		*Net Profit*		*Volume of Assets taken on lease*	
		1990-91	1996-97	1990-91	1996-97	1990-91	1996-97	1990-91	1996-97	1990-91	1996-97
1. APSEB	1959	19913*	27949*	145004.0	786010.6	123033.1	434080.7	2214.0	14394.8	—	115500.0
2. APR	1979	1600	7500	4582.1	42644.9	5322.4	21766.1	642.5	2073.9	350.5	3860.5
3. APSRTC	1958	19520*	20127*	79200.7	24511.0	78564.5	165928.7	(11.92)	631.7	—	1186.0
4. CML	1962	2500	2500	24066.2	26359.5	20962.5	37623.6	3393.1	2922.5	40.9	451.8
5. ITC	1978	2700	7700	12714.5	78910.2	13856.9	23878.4	1547.5	1671.6	918.7	1270.1
6. PAL	1989	5000	12000	31.6	22003.4	Operations started	20064.2	Operations started	(8889.3)	—	91.7
7. PSL	1987	1000	3500	2705.3	10539.9	3296.8	11729.4	160.0	620.4	50.0	190.0
8. PSM	1981	600	2000	2289.6	8761.3	4033.6	12190.3	373.4	397.9	46.0	397.0
9. VST	1930	1000	5000	7390.3	20083.4	44613.9	57681.5	2455.0	1993.9	374.3	1218.6

Note: *Share Capital from Government.

Source: Annual Reports of Select Lessee Companies.

The net profit of the company increased from Rs. 642.5 lakhs in 1990-91 to Rs. 2,073.9 lakhs in 1996-97 (Table 1.2).

APR Limited took assets on lease worth Rs. 350.48 lakhs in 1990-91, and increased to Rs. 3,860.5 lakhs in 1996-97. On an average the company's leased assets represent 24.47% of its total assets. The leased assets of ClO_2 Plant alone costs Rs. 18.00 crore. This asset was commissioned in early 1997. Besides, the APR has acquired the chemical recovery boiler through leasing, the latest air pollution control systems to ensure a cleaner atmosphere.

Though the APR was a sick company in 1990, it successfully navigated through difficult times. In spite of tight liquidity position, the company was able to complete its borrowing programme for funding the expansion successfully, re-affirming the confidence of the lending Banks/Institutions. Based on the borrowing programme, the company had also taken assets on lease as required. The company had received full support from leasing companies in getting the assets on lease.

3. APSRTC

The APSRTC was established in 1958 with an objective to provide mass transport system in A.P. The corporation had a total fleet strength of 16,879 buses as on 31-3-1996. During the year 1996-97, 1761 new buses were added and 1144 buses were scrapped, the net addition of fleet being 617 buses. As on 31-3-1996, 194 depots were under operation. As many as 437 bus stations had been constructed and brought under use by the end of 1995-96. And, 1363 bus shelters have been provided to facilitate passengers waiting at the bus stops.

The traffic earnings increased from Rs. 1315.21 crores in 1994-95 to Rs. 1,529.61 crores during 1995-96. The growth in earnings being 16.30%, APSRTC earned net profit of Rs. 631.7 lakhs during 1996-97 (Table 1.2).

The capital contribution is provided by the State and Central Governments as per Section 23(1) of Road Transport Corporation Act, 1950 in the ratio of 2:1. Capital requirement of the corporation was however mainly met from internal reserves generated in the form of retained profits, if any, Depreciation Fund, and also loans from LIC, IDBI, Commercial Banks etc. The total capital of the corporation increased from Rs. 19,520.0 lakhs in 1990-91 to Rs. 20,127.0 lakhs in 1996-97 (Table 1.2).

The long-term loans outstanding amounted to Rs. 3,672 lakhs in 1996-97. Further, the APSRTC had taken assets on lease twice over the period of study. In the year 1991-92, it had taken 34 buses costing Rs.193 lakhs and in 1995-96 wind mills costing Rs. 993 lakhs. On an average the leased assets cover 8.04% of its total assets. In the year 1995-96, the leased assets share was recorded at 54.88% of its total assets acquired during that year.

The corporation, realising the need for effective public relations, established a Public Relations Department at the corporate level, Public Relation Cell at 6 Zonal Offices, 23 Regional Offices and 194 Depot Offices with a view to educate the public on the proper usage of passenger bus services, bus stations, and to motivate the workers to adopt courteous and helpful behaviour towards the passengers.

As far as the Corporation Tax is concerned, the Supreme Court, in its judgement dated 7-3-1986 has affirmed the decision of A.P. High Court treating APSRTC as a Charitable Institution and exempted from corporation tax. The amount of tax paid from the Assessment year 1958-59 to 1972-73 amounting to Rs.197.37 lakhs is due from the Income Tax Department. The APSRTC has filed Annual Returns of Income from assessment year 1990-91 to 1996-97 after completion of Tax Audit under Section 12A (b) as well as 44AB of the Income Tax Act 1961. The Income tax Department had passed NIL Assessment Orders up to Assessment year 1995-96. For Assessment year 1996-97 provisional NIL Return was submitted by APSRTC.

4. CML

The CML company was established in 1962 with the main objective of production of fertilizers. The authorised capital was Rs. 2,500 lakhs in 1990-91 and there was no change up to 1996-97. The turnover of the company has increased from Rs. 20,962.5 lakhs in 1990-91 to Rs. 37,623.6 lakhs in 1996-97. However the net profit decreased from Rs. 3,393.1 lakhs to Rs. 2,922.5 lakhs in 1996-97 (Table 1.2) due to adverse market conditions.

As the CML is a high tax paying company, the proportion of leased assets to total cash outflow in each year towards acquisition of fixed assets is very less. On an average the proportion of leased assets to year-wise investment was 6.05%. The highest proportion of leased assets was recorded at 28.42%, which was Rs. 291.53 lakhs in 1993-94. The company had not taken any assets on lease in the years 1991-92, 1994-95 and 1996-97. Due to high tax payment, the company preferred to borrow the amount and purchase the assets and claim the depreciation rather than taking the assets on lease.

Production of fertilizers at 3,95,493 MT during 1996-97 as against 3,69,080 MT last year was the best production record ever achieved by the plant. Product optimisation through linear programming techniques and modernisation of plant operations through upgradation of instrumentation and process control systems have been initiated with significant improvements and these will be carried through in the years to come. Further, as a part of this programme, following a study made by Jacobs, USA, a revamp of Ammonia was taken up involving a capital outlay of Rs. 16 crores.

5. ITC

The ITC company was established in 1978 with the main objective of manufacturing paper. The authorised capital of the company increased from Rs. 2,700 lakhs in 1990-91 to Rs. 7,700 lakhs in 1996-97. The capital employed by the company increased to Rs. 23,878.4 lakhs in 1996-97 from Rs. 13,856.9 lakhs in 1990-91 (Table 1.2).

The ITC Bhadrachalam maintained its lead as the largest exporter of paper and paperboards. It had been exporting about half of the country's total exports of paper and paper boards. The value of exports was Rs. 31.09 crores during 1994-95 as against Rs. 23.70 crores in the previous year registering a growth of 31%. The foreign exchange earned amounted to US $9.4 million during 1994-95 as against US $ 7.1 million in the previous year.

The performance of the company during 1996-97 was adversely affected due to the severe recession in the paper industry both in the international and home markets. The production, at 86,041 tonnes during 1996-97 was lower than 89,057 tonnes in the previous year on account of difficult market conditions.

The domestic paper industry was affected by the severe recession caused due to

- — the slow down in industrial growth and exports,
- — increase in imports of value added grades on account of lower, duties and surplus in international markets, and
- — tight liquidity conditions.

The ITC Bhadrachalam acted as both the lessor and the lessee. The company had given assets on lease to APSEB in 1992-93 worth Rs. 499 lakhs. It had taken assets on lease worth Rs. 1,270.1 lakhs during 1990-91 to 1994-95. The average share of leased assets to its total assets recorded at 5.41%.

6. PAL

PAL was incorporated in 1989 with an authorised capital of Rs. 5,000 lakhs. The main objective of the company was to manufacture aluminium and aluminium alloy products. Its actual operations were started during 1991-92. The company had taken assets on lease worth Rs. 91.7 lakhs during 1991-92 to 1994-95. After 1995 it could not take assets on lease.

The company was declared sick by December 1993 and at the instance of Financial Institutions, the company management was taken over by Pennar Group. The sales volume of this company improved three-fold in just two years after it was taken over and the company turned from loss making unit to a profit making company.

During the year 1996-97, the company had gone into financial difficulties and incurred heavy losses of Rs. 8,889.3 lakhs (Table 1.2). There had been a significant reduction in the demand for aluminium rolled products due to unfavourable economic conditions and recession in the country as a whole. The frequent fluctuations in metal price in the domestic market have also affected the demand growth. The reduction in import duty on rolled products from 105% to 20% during the year 1996-97 had also created unfavourable conditions of competing with imports of rolled products. Upon making a reference to the Board for Industrial & Financial Reconstruction (BIFR) under the provision to sub-section (1) of section 15 of Sick Industrial Companies (Special Provisions) Act ,1985, the BIFR at the hearing held on 27 April, 1998 declared the company "SICK" as the company's losses at the end of financial year 1997 exceeded its net worth. BIFR had appointed IDBI as the operating agency to prepare and submit a report for rehabilitation of the company.

7. PSL

The PSL was established in 1987. The authorised capital of the company increased from Rs. 1,000 lakhs in 1990-91 to Rs. 3,500 lakhs in 1996-97. The PSL is a part of Pennar Group Companies.

The PSL Company's products of steel find extensive application in the domestic and industrial appliances—automotive, engineering, steel furniture, and construction industries. This company had also promoted a Joint Venture with M/s. Thomas & Betts of USA for the manufacture of Electronic and Electrical Components.

During 1994-95, the company had diversified its operations to turn it into a multi-product and multi-location company. The plan includes setting up of Wind Energy Farm in Tamil Nadu to manufacture metal components and to manufacture compressor shells and components, automobile components and recycling of scrap and slag. In view of these growth plans, the company raised additional funds through various sources including lease-financing facility. The company had taken assets on lease worth Rs. 190.0 lakhs during 1990-91 to 1994-95. After 1995, the company had not taken any asset on lease. On an average, the leased assets represent 12.97% of its total assets.

During 1997-98, the PSL Company was merged with NSL (Nagarjuna Steels Limited). The combined entity now stands as one of the leading companies in the cold rolled and cold-formed steel business. As a merged entity the company is positioning itself to achieve economies of scale and improve operational efficiencies to enable it to face the increasing competition both from within the company and from overseas. Further, the company has been positioning itself as a specialised supplier of engineered steel with the focus on technology structures, storage and logistics solutions, all of which find use in the upcoming and developing industrial sectors of the economy.

8. PSM

This company was established in 1981 with the main objective of manufacturing yarn and fabric.

The company has invested Rs. 1 crore in IBIZA Industries Ltd., a Joint Venture with Mafatlal group to manufacture premium fabrics during 1994-95. The commercial production of the IBIZA Industries Ltd. is well accepted in the market. The capital employed increased to Rs. 8,761.3 lakhs in 1996-97 as against Rs. 2,287.60 lakhs in 1990-91 (Table 1.2).

During 1996-97, the company exported yarn and fabric to the tune of Rs. 2,549.79 lakhs as against the previous year's exports of Rs. 1,703.76 lakhs.

The PSM is a low tax paying company and the average proportion of leased assets to total fixed assets is maintained at 7.43%. The highest volume of plant and machinery worth Rs. 230 lakhs was taken in 1992-93 and commissioned in I phase at Unit-II near Ongole which has gone into production and contributes to the increase in turnover. The turnover touched Rs. 12,190.3 lakhs in 1996-97 as against Rs. 4,033.6 lakhs in 1990-91(Table 1.2).

9. VST

This company was established in 1930 with the main objective of manufacturing and selling cigarettes. On 10th November, 1990, the company completed 60 years since its incorporation and celebrated its Diamond Jubilee. The company's Diamond Jubilee also coincides with the 400 Anniversary of the foundation of the city of Hyderabad, of which the company has been proud to be an integral part.

The company's authorised capital has increased from Rs. 1,000.0 lakhs in 1990-91 to Rs. 5,000.0 lakhs in 1996-97 indicating five-fold increase over the study period. The capital employed of the company increased from Rs. 7,390.30 lakhs in 1990-91 to Rs. 20,083.40 lakhs in 1996-97 (Table 1.2).

The VST has made major investments in the upgradation and packaging of two important brands – CHARMINAR and CHARMS VIRGINIA FILTER. The pack designs of two other brands—CHARMS MINI KINGS and CHARMINAR GOLD FILTER—have been contemporised in line with the changing consumer needs. These packaging improvements have been well received by the consumer. The company attained a good measure of success in the field of tobacco exports, and has achieved international standards in terms of the quality of processed tobacco by plant modernisation and innovation.

The company has taken assets of PMD Machinery, Energy saving Equipment, Vehicles, Computers, etc. on lease in order to improve the production.

The company has enjoyed the highest credit rating of FAAA for its fixed deposit schemes and P1+ for issue of commercial paper from the CRISIL from 1991 to 1996. However, the fixed deposit scheme has been downgraded from FAAA to FAA+ by CRISIL during 1996-97 in view of the company's decline in net profit from Rs. 2,455.0 lakhs in 1990-91 to Rs. 1,993.98 lakhs in 1996-97.

However, during the year 1997, the company has issued 18.5% secured redeemable Non-Convertible Debentures amounting to Rs. 18.00 crores to strengthen the company.

REFERENCES

1. John J. Hampton, *Financial Decision-Making – Concepts, Problems and Cases,* Prentice-Hall of India Private Limited, New Delhi, 1994, pp.484- 510.
2. Van Horne, J.C., and Wachowicz, J.M. Jr., *Fundamentals of Financial Management,* Prentice-Hall of India Private Limited, New Delhi, 1994, pp.630 - 657.
3. Pandey, I.M., *Financial Management*, Vikas Publishing House Private Limited, New Delhi, 1990, pp.842-858.
4. Gupta, N.C. *et al.*, (edited) *Corporate Financing – Emerging Options,* Anmol Publications, New Delhi, 1991, pp.109-129.
5. Prasanna Chandra, *Financial Management – Theory and Practice*, Tata McGraw Hill Publishing Company Ltd., New Delhi, 1994.

6. Srivastava, R.M., *Financial Decision Making – Text, Problems and Cases*, Sterling Publishers Private Limited, New Delhi, 1984.
7. Bierman, H. Jr., and Seymone Smidt, *The Capital Budgeting Decision – Economic Analysis of Investment Projects*, MacMillan Publishing Company, New York, 1984, pp.254-278.
8. Kuchhal, S.C., *Financial Management*, Chaitanya Publishing House, Allahabad, 1993, pp.440-477.
9. Vinod Kothari, *Lease Financing and Hire-Purchase*, Wadhwa and Company Private Limited, Law Publishers, Dantoli, Nagpur, 1996.
10. Verma, J.C., *Lease Financing – Concept, Law and Procedure*, Bharat Law House, New Delhi, 1994.
11. Kamath, K.V., *et al.*, *The Principles and Practice of Leasing*, Lease Asia, Croydon CROZPU, Surrey, England, 1990.
12. Premlal Joshi, *Leasing Comes of Age – Indian Scene*, Chembur, Bombay, 1986.
13. Rajas Purchure and N. Ashok Kumar, *Introduction to Lease Financing*, The Times Research Foundation, Pune, 1985.
14. Rajas Purchure, *Lease Financing*, The Times Research Foundation, Pune, 1983.
15. Gosh, P.K., and Gupta, G.S., *Fundamentals of Leasing and Lease Financing*, Vision Books Private Limited, New Delhi, 1985.
16. Henry S. Beera, Jr., *Computer Leasing*, Life Time Learning Publications, California London, 1983.
17. Mathur, B.L., (Edited), *Readings in Lease Financing*, Arihant Publishers, Jaipur, 1990.
18. Nagaraja Naidu, V., *et al.*, (edited) *Lease Financing in India*, Delta Publishing House, Hyderabad, 1995.
19. Tom Clark, *Leasing Finance*, Euromoney Publications Ltd., Nestor House, Playhouse Yard, London, 1985.
20. John Williamson, *Leasing and Finance Companies*, The Institute of Chartered Accountants in England and Wales, Moorgata Place, London, i991.
21. Satyanarayana Murthy, P., *Leasing Industry in India: A Study of Selected Equipment Lease Contracts,* Unpublished thesis submitted to Osmania University for the award of the Degree of Doctor of Philosophy in Business Management, 1992.
22. Narayana Swamy, R., *Accounting for Leases by Lessors – A Research Study*, Indian Institute of Management, Bangalore, 1990 (This study was sponsored by SBI Capital Markets Limited).
23. Srinivasa Murthy, S., *Lease Purchase Decisions in the Indian Corporate Sector,* Unpublished thesis submitted to the University of Madras for the award of Degree of Doctor of Philosophy in Commerce, 1994.
24. Brahmaiah, B., "Leasing – A Growing Industry," *The Indian Management*, January 1990.
25. Sharmila Dayal, *Lease Financing in India – Problems and Prospects*, Sarup & Sons, New Delhi, 1994.
26. David G. Mayes and Clive S. Nicholas, *The Economic Impact of Leasing*, The MacMillan Press Limited, London, 1988.
27. Fawthrop, R.A., and Terry, B., "Debt Management and the Use of Leasing

Finance in U.K., Corporate Financing Strategies," *Journal of Business Finance and Accounting*, Autumn, 1975, pp.295-314.

28. Sykes, A., "The Lease – Buy Decision: A Survey of Current Practices in 202 Companies," *Management Survey Report No. 29*, British Institute of Management, 1976.
29. Hull, J.C., and Hubbard, GL., "Lease Evaluation in the U.K. Current Theory and Practice," *Journal of Business Finance and Accounting,* Winter, 1980, pp. 619-637.
30. Ferrare, W.L., Thies, J.B., and Dirsmith, M.W., *The Lease Purchase Decision*, National Association of Accountants (USA), 1980.
31. Dr. Jur. Alfred W. Fink, *A Practical Guide to Leasing*, McGraw Hill Book Company, England, 1994.

2

LEASING BUSINESS IN INDIA

Leasing, as a source of finance, is an alternative to borrowings from financial institutions or from banks. It is an alternative to loan financing and is somewhat akin to hire-purchase transaction. The major point of difference between hire purchase and lease financing is that in case of the former, the contract provides for automatic transfer of ownership of an asset to the hirer (purchaser) from hiree (financier) at the end of the stipulated period. Whereas in the case of the lease financing, the ownership rests with the financier and the ownership never transfers to the user. As such, the hirer claims the depreciation in case of hire purchase and financier claims the depreciation benefit in case of lease financing, as they are owners of the asset.

Concept of Lease Financing

The concept of "Lease Financing" comes under the general title of "instalment credit". Leasing of an asset, in layman's language, means renting of an asset to a business entity or to another party, for use on rental basis. Thus, leasing is essentially a mode of asset based financing. In leasing, the first rule to be followed is that the ownership of an asset being financed is vested in the financier, and the right to use is vested in the user. The financier is called the *Lessor*; the user is called the *Lessee*.[1]

According to the *Dictionary of Commerce* : "Lease is an agreement whereby the legal owner of real property gives another person the possession of that property with freedom to use it as he/she wishes, though possibly under certain conditions, in return for regular specified payments referred to as rent"[2].

The Cholamandalam Investment & Finance Company Limited, Madras,[3] one of the reputed leasing companies in India, has defined "Leasing" in its preamble as follows:

"Lease Financing is an arrangement whereby the asset required by the 'User Company' is let on lease over a period, on terms and rentals mutually agreed between them. Various agreements are possible at the end of the lease tenure:

(i) the lessee may surrender the asset to the lessor soon after the lease period is over;
(ii) the lessee may renew the lease on a perpetual basis or for a definite period;
(iii) the lessor may take the asset back from the lessee soon after the lease period and sell it to a third party; or
(iv) the lessor may sell it to the lessee through a third party.

The choice of a specific alternative is the function of the lease package offered by the lessor at the beginning of the lease tenure."

The International Accounting Standards Committee (IASC) has defined lease as "an agreement whereby the lessor conveys to the lessee in return for rent the right to use an asset for an agreed period of time."

A typical lease arrangement is shown in Chart 2.1.

Chart 2.1 : Lease Arrangement

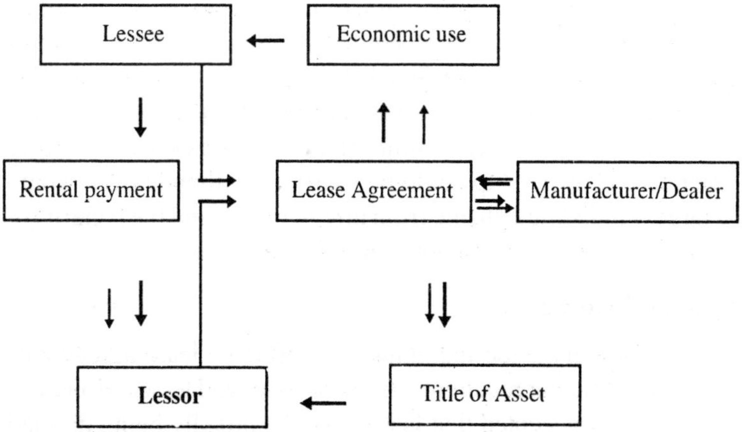

The lessee pays the lease rental as regular fixed payments over a period of time at the beginning or at the end of a month, quarter, half-year, or year as per the lease agreement. Although generally fixed, the amount and timing of lease rental payment can be tailored to the Lessee's profits or cash flows. In up fronted lease, more rentals are charged in the initial years and less in the later years of the contract. The opposite happens in back ended leases. At the end of the lease contract, the asset reverts back to the lessor, who is the legal owner of the asset. As the legal owner, the lessor claims the depreciation (and investment allowance if it is available) on the leased asset.

Although the lessor is the legal owner of a leased asset, the lessee bears the risk and enjoys the returns. Leasing separates ownership and use as two economic activities and facilitates asset use without ownership.[4]

This separation of "ownership" from "use" of an asset led to a dramatic development of leasing in India. A business entity requires only the use of required assets, which need not necessarily entail their ownership. This fundamental fact as the basis of lease financing has made Donald B. Grant, an expert on business finance, to metaphorically observe, "why own a cow when the milk is so cheap? All you really need is the Milk and not the Cow".[5]

Leasing is thus, the separation of the use and ownership of an asset into distinct legal and economic activities. The lessor remains the legal owner, while the lessee has the right to economic use. This distinction makes leasing a unique form of financial instrument and from which the economic effects of leasing are largely generated. If ownership could be transferred, then leasing would be largely indistinguishable from hire purchase and the benefits of capital allowances would not accrue to the lessor.

Types of Leasing

It is common in the leasing industry to structure lease agreements to suit the particular requirements of the lessor and lessee. However, it is generally accepted that leases may be broadly being divided into two categories—finance leases and operating leases. Finance leasing and operating leasing differ widely both in practice and in underlying economic rationale.[6]

Though there are several types of lease agreements/contracts, virtually all lease financing arrangements fall into one of these two categories for accounting purpose. However, the leasing arrangements in India and abroad are classified as follows:

1. Financial Lease
2. Operating Lease
3. Other Types of Leases

    3.1 Leveraged Lease
    3.2 Sale and Lease back method
    3.3 Percentage Lease
    3.4 Cross Border Lease
    3.5 Wet and Dry Lease
    3.6 Swap Lease

Financial Lease

The financial lease is also known as capital lease, long term lease, full payout lease and net lease. The financial lease is the most popular form and all lessor companies in India provide the facility of financial leases in addition to other leases. Under finance lease, the lessor merely finances the asset for the acquisition but does not provide the services of repairs and maintenance, and bears no insurance or other expenses in relation to the asset. Except the title (ownership), the lessor transfers all the risks and rewards/benefits of ownership of an asset to the lessee. It means, the lessee has to bear all the expenses of maintenance, repairs, etc.

The International Accounting Standards-17 (IAS-17) has defined a finance lease as "a lease that transfers substantially all the risks and rewards incident to ownership of an asset. The title may or may not eventually be transferred".

The term of the lease depends upon the type of the asset. The lease period usually coincides with the economic life of the asset (it may extend from 5 years to 15 years or more) and may be categorised into primary and secondary lease periods.

During the primary lease period (the desired pay back period), the lease rates are so fixed as to repay the Lessor's principal as well as interest. The secondary lease period is for the balance of the life of the asset, when only nominal rentals are charged to continue the agreement till the lease period is over. The lease rental in the secondary period may be even fixed at Re.1 per instalment to continue the lease agreement.

The residual scrap then reverts back to the lessor soon after the lease agreement is over. During the primary lease period, unless both the parties agree, the lease contract is non-cancelable by either party.

The cost of the equipment is fully amortised during the lease period and the salvage value of the asset is expected to be negligible.

The financial lease could also be arranged with purchase option to the lessee—not directly but through a third party. The lease rental is adjusted accordingly. Thus, the asset in finance lease is specially tailored for the lessees without remarket value.

High cost equipments such as –Aircrafts, Satellites, Plants & Machinery, Earth moving equipments, Pollution control equipments, Ships, Industrial equipments, etc., are frequently leased under financial leases.

Operating or Service Lease

The operating lease is also known as short-term or maintenance lease. It is concerned with the provision of a complete service to the lessee rather than a simple financial arrangement. The asset is purchased, maintained and insured by the lessor. Unlike finance leasing, the lessor does not recover the asset cost over a single lease period. Profit may be derived from leasing the asset over a number of relatively short periods to successive lessees, from ancillary arrangements, or from the sale of the asset[7]. It means, the maturity of the lease contract is considerably lower than the useful economic life of the asset. The period of lease can be for one month, six months, one year or for three years.

Therefore, in an operating lease, substantially all the risks and rewards incidental to ownership are not transferred to the lessee from the lessor. Under this type of lease agreement, the lessee has the right to cancel or return the leased equipment before the expiry of the lease period.

Under this type of lease agreement, the assets usually leased are of the latest technological developments such as computers, office equipments, Data Processing Machines, Copy Machines, Vehicles, etc., are leased.

Since operating lease provides services such as maintenance, repairs, technical advice, etc., it involves higher payment of rentals.

Thus, the main difference between financial lease and operating lease is the term of the agreement and service function.

Other Types of Leases

Leveraged Lease

The leveraged lease system is more complex than the ordinary lease in terms of size, number of parties involved and the relative advantages to all the parties. Leveraged lease belongs to the class of financial lease but is used mainly to finance assets, which requires huge capital outlay (big-ticket lease). This outlay for the purchase of assets generally varies from Rs. 50 lakhs to Rs. 2 crores or more,[8] which the lessor may be unable to finance from its own funds. The lessor provides only a percentage of the equipment cost and borrows the balance from institutional investors. The lessor in a leveraged lease is called as an equity investor and the investors or financiers are called debt-participants. The leasing company invests its equity contribution to the 'TRUST', which may range from 20% to 30% of the lease. The debt participants take up the balance of the lease. The asset to be leased is acquired out of Trust proceeds and lease rentals may be payable to the Trust itself. The main advantage from a leveraged lease is that lessor company enjoys 100% depreciation benefits despite the fact that only a small percentage of the leased asset is financed by the lessor company through its own funds. Added to this, the lessor recovers his investment in a much shorter time than the full lease term. The lessor can, therefore, pass on a part of these benefits to the lessee in the form of lower lease cost.

Sale and Lease Back

This is a special type of leasing. Under "sale and lease back arrangement", a firm sells an asset, which it already owns, to another party and takes it back on lease from the buyer (Lessor). That is, the seller (Owner) becomes the lessee and the purchasing company becomes the lessor. The asset is usually sold at its market value to the leasing company and the seller firm (lessee) receives the sale price in cash, and continues the use of the same asset by acquiring it on lease. These funds can be used in the business for working capital or for further expansion purpose. The firm, in turn, has to make periodic lease payments, as per the agreement to the Lessor Company. Thus, sale and lease back transactions have become a popular source of working capital.

The "sale and lease back" is especially attractive for those companies whose liquidity position is not sound. Such companies can restore their liquidity position by selling their assets to lessors who can obtain the tax benefits of depreciation and investment allowance. The lease rental payments are allowed as tax-deductible expense for the lessee. Further, if the sale value of asset is less than written-down value, the loss may be claimed as terminal depreciation. On the other hand, if the sale value is more than the written-down value, then the Lessee Company will have to pay tax for capital gains as per the provisions of the Income Tax Act.

Sale and lease back transactions have become exceedingly popular in the U.S., after the introduction of the Economic Recovery Tax Act where companies with low profits were encouraged to sell and lease back their assets, thereby infusing them with cash without losing the right to use of these assets.[9] The same sort of scenario was seen in India especially from 1991 to 1996. After 1996, the sale and lease back mode of lease finance is not very much in use as taxation laws and RBI guidelines are quite restrictive for such type of deals.

Further, as per the RBI guidelines, bank finance is not available to leasing companies for sale and lease back transactions, as bank finance would cover purchases of new equipment only.[10]

Percentage Lease

Under this percentage lease, the lessee is required to pay a fixed amount of rent in each period plus a percentage of gross revenue received during the previous period.

Usually, the additional percentage rent is calculated as a percentage of revenue received above minimum base amount. Such lease arrangements are to compensate in part for the effects of inflation. Percentage leases are generally structured for a long-term use.

Cross Border Lease

Cross Border Lease is international leasing. A Cross-Border Leasing comes into existence when the lessor and lessee reside in different countries. Cross border lease originated in the USA in the early 1950s. Aircraft, ships, oil-drilling equipment etc., were leased to lessees located outside the country.[11] Later the practice gained popularity in the UK and Europe and in Asia.

Wet and Dry Lease

The terms wet and dry leases originated with aircraft industry. A dry lease provides finance as well as fuel and servicing. With respect to lessor service, the provisions of a wet lease are similar to those of an operating lease.[12]

Swap Lease

Swap lease allows the lessee to exchange the equipment in need of major repair with properly working, replacement equipment to avoid costly maintenance and repair delays.[13]

The demand for leasing has created a status of industry as more and more of the world's capital equipment needs are being met through this unique form of financing. Leasing is multi-disciplinary industry—with all taxes, accounting and finance, playing an integral role in virtually every transaction.

In order to provide a perspective of this interesting industry, an attempt is made in this chapter to analyse the following aspects:

- Evolution of Leasing
- Leasing Business world over
- Leasing Business in India
- Leasing Business in AP
- Future of Leasing Business

Evolution of Leasing

(A) *Early History*

Although the exact date of the first leasing transaction is not known, the earlier records of leasing reveal that the primitive form of leasing was practiced worldwide as early as 6000 BC.[14] From about 3000 BC, documentary leasing was developed in "Sumer" (Southern Iraq) in the City State of Uruk. Agriculture was the predominant occupation in Sumer.[15] A major source of income for the Sumerians was leasing fields for agriculture, usually combined with lease for the supply of irrigated water, animals, mostly oxen, as well as ploughs and other equipments. In addition to this, tenants (lessees) might obtain operation credits, e.g., for seeds, oxen fodder, and wages for ploughmen, etc. Thus, it was possible for penniless Sumerians to start agricultural operations on their own.[16]

Other ancient civilizations, including the Greeks, Romans and Egyptians, found leasing attractive, affordable and viable method of financing equipment, land and livestock. Many short-term charters or engagements were provided for use of the crew as well as the ship. Long-term charters or engagements were also written for periods covering the estimated economic life of the ships and required the lessee to assume most of the benefits and obligations of ownership. Many of the same kind of negotiating issues that today's lessors and lessees face, were addressed in these ancient ship charters or engagements.[17]

Finance leasing of land and buildings became popular in Europe in the Middle Ages because of the rigid system of land law and the restrictions on inheriting freehold property. The technique was quickly taken up in the United States.[18]

Leasing of Railway Wagons in the United Kingdom in the 1840s is the first example of a full pay out or finance lease facility for commercial or industrial equipment. Leasing companies, known at the time as wagon companies, were among the first to be incorporated and taken advantage of the general production of limited liability in the 1850s. The world's first registered leasing company, the Birmingham Wagon Company, was constituted on March 20, 1855, which immediately began leasing Railway Wagons to coal and other mineral proprietors for fixed terms of between five and eight years.[19]

(B) *Modern Development*

In May 1952, Henry Schoenfeld set up the first modern leasing company, United States Leasing Corporation, now United States Leasing International Inc. Subsequently, leasing grew rapidly offering 100% financing, tax benefits, off balance sheet treatment, etc. By the end of 1950s, leasing was sufficiently developed in the United States for leading leasing companies to turn their attention to foreign markets.[20]

In June 1959, United States Leasing International set up a Canadian Subsidiary, Canada Dominion Leasing Corporation; a year later, with the UK finance house, Mercantile Credit Company, established Mercantile Leasing Company in London. Leasing companies were established in France and Italy in 1961, in Germany in 1962, and by 1966 throughout Europe. Orient leasing company, the first Japanese Leasing Company, was formed in 1963 and several Australian Finance Companies began marketing leasing facilities in the early 1960s.[21]

In India, the feudal system itself was based on leasing of land (method of holding land by paying rent to the owner). The 'Pattidari' system of agricultural land became a feature of the feudal system, in which the tenant (cultivator) never became the owner. The landlord enjoys rental profits from land held mostly by customary tenants. There are similarities between the Indian Pattidari system and today's concept of leasing. We are familiar with the lease of factory; lease of land etc. The purpose of mentioning these types of lease is not merely to highlight them, but to indicate how leasing has developed in modern times. The rapid growth of equipment leasing has now steadied itself in most of the countries where leasing was established early, simply because the business is maturing. Recent years have also seen leasing business gaining much more importance in developing countries.

Thus, leasing can be traced back to thousands of years, although it has evolved considerably during the last 45 years. The industry evolved from being a manufacturer's selling technique into a specialised financial service, with the formation of the first independent leasing company in 1952 in the United States. The industry extended to Europe and Japan in the 1960s and has been spreading through developing countries since the mid-1970s.[22] By 1994, leasing had been established in more than 80 countries including 50 odd developing economies.[23]

It is now pertinent to examine the volume and development of leasing business in various countries including India.

Leasing World Over

Globally, leasing is the second most powerful source of financing. This is in spite of the fact that bank financing is centuries old, whereas leasing is only about 45 years old.

The global penetration of equipment leasing, i.e., the extent of leased assets as a percentage of total industrial assets, is estimated at around 21% of all assets bought by industrial undertakings. These are actually bought by leasing companies and passed on to lessee companies for use.

Leasing exists in developed markets as well as in developing markets. In most countries, equipment leasing has grown with distinct support from the regulators.

The comparative data collected by London Financial Group (LFG) on the volume, rate of growth and market penetration of the World's top 50 national leasing concerns has been published in the World's Leasing Year Book—1996, according to which equipment-leasing volume grew in 41 of the top 50 countries. The analysis of LFG shows that during 1993-94, the growth pushed total world leasing volume to a record of US $356.4 bn. However, contraction took place in 1993 when volume felt to US $309.6 bn.[24]

Japan's leasing industry's growth in 1994 remains by far the largest in the Asian Region, with a volume of US $ 73.7 bn. Korea is the second largest national leasing industry in Asia. In 1994 Korean Volume exceeded US $ 13.2 bn. Since the mid-1970s when leasing first started in Korea, the industry has achieved a compounded annual growth rate of nearly 30%.[25]

Australia has a robust and creative leasing industry, which has performed very well with a growth rate of 26.3%, and a market penetration of 21.0% of capital assets during the year 1993-94. Brazil's 22.7% volume increase to US $ 8.1 bn was typical of the robust 1994 growth. Chile and Columbia grew by 24.7% and 28.7% respectively, while Peru's industry grew by 91.7%. The Venezuelan industry was the only major South American leasing industry to report a volume decline in 1994 by 11.3%.[26]

The U.S. leasing industry is the largest and the most developed in the world. The North America's share of the world leasing market was registered at 42.8% in 1993 and 41.5% in 1994. U.S. has contributed nearly 95% of the total regions. The balance comes from Canada and Mexico, which contributed just over 3% and 2% respectively.[27] Equipment leasing activity in the United States recorded US $85.0 bn in 1986 and recorded an increasing trend up to 1989 registering $125.4 bn. Later, it registered a declining trend till 1991 with $120.2 bn. Again, the leasing activity increased from 1991 to1994. In 1994, it reached a record volume of $ 140.2bn., an increase of 7.4% over the previous year (Table 2.1).

Table 2.1: Equipment Leasing Activity in the United States (yearwise figures)

(US $ bn)

	1986	1987	1988	1989	1990	1991	1992	1993	1994
Equipment Leasing	85.0	98.0	112.7	125.4	124.3	120.2	121.7	130.5	140.2
Business Investment in Equipment	296.2	311.2	348.4	365.7	388.3	375.5	376.2	443.9	466.1
Leasing as a percentage of Business Investment	28.7	31.5	32.3	34.3	32.0	32.0	32.3	29.4	30.1

Source : World Lease Year Book—1996.

Though the leasing market penetration in the US declined to 29.4%, in 1993, growth in leasing increased the market penetration to 30.1% in 1994 (Table 2.1). The US leasing industry and their levels of investment are the benchmarks. The US has enjoyed relatively steady growth both in business investment and in the leasing activity from 1986 to 1994, except in 1991 and 1992 when

Corporation observed at the sixth World Leasing Convention that in United States and in many countries of the world, about one-fourth of all business equipment is financed by leases. Peter Nevitt further observed that in the United States, the leasing is by far the most popular method of financing automobiles for both individuals and for businesses. About one-third of all automobiles sold in the United States are leased. In dollar terms, the market size is in the range of $40 to 50 billion, which is over and above the $100 billion in the equipment annually leased in the United States.[29] The US leasing business, which still appears to be growing, represents about half the total world's leasing. North America accounts for 41.5% of worldwide leasing in 1994, followed by Asia region (27.8%), Europe region (24.5%), South America (3.1%), Australia (1.8%), and Africa (1.3%).

Thus, United States is a clear leader both in terms of volume (with US $ 140 billion of leases written in 1994) and market penetration (with 30.1% plant and equipment leases).

Leasing exists both in developed countries as well as in developing countries. But, its growth in developing economies has been most remarkable.

The growth of leasing business in UK was remarkable and the equipment leasing industry had built up dramatically on the basis of the available capital allowances to equipment lessors. Leasing accounts for around 19% of all United Kingdom investment in capital equipment.[30]

Looking beyond the US and the UK, the growing importance of leasing can also be seen elsewhere in the world.

The concept of modern lease financing has been popularly recognized as an innovative method of equipment financing right from the start of its introduction to Asia in 1960s. By the early 1980s, almost all the Asian Nations were being served by a network of leasing companies. The 1980s proved to be the decade of internationalisation of equipment leasing. The leading leasing companies foresaw the need for an organisation and formed the Asian Leasing Association (Asia Lease) in 1982. Almost all nations in East Asia are represented in Asia Lease with members coming from Hong Kong, India, Indonesia, Japan, Korea, Malaysia,

Pakistan, the Philippines, Sri Lanka, Taiwan and Thailand. Hong Kong is a major commercial and financial centre in South East Asia, and is the regional head office for many international financial institutions. It is also a major centre for the leasing industry and other asset based financing operations. Leasing business has grown at a remarkably fast rate in Japan. The first leasing company in Japan was established in 1963. The rapid growth of industry attracted the attention of smaller banking institutions including regional banks.

Many of these developing nations have followed the US and UK examples in matters of tax and accounting techniques. However, both the US and UK have a strong base and have coped well with the tax changes through highly sophisticated innovation.

It is now pertinent to analyse the leasing business and its status in India.

Leasing Business in India

Until 1973, the concept of 'leasing' in India was mainly restricted to real estate (immovable property) only. The modern concept of equipment leasing is a recent development and emerged for the first time in Madras in 1973.

For almost 7 years, the first leasing company of India Limited was the sole leasing company in India. The leasing transactions were quite limited until 1980s. In 1980 another leasing company, the 20th Century Leasing Company (TCL), was promoted in Bombay as a wholly owned subsidiary of the 20th Century Finance Limited.

The success of these two leasing companies attracted many entrepreneurs into the leasing field and set the tone for the growth of leasing business in India.

By 1981, four other finance companies namely, Shetty Investment and Finance, Jaybharat Credit and Investment, Motor and General Finance and Sundaram Finance entered the leasing field. By 1982, leasing business picked up momentum. A new dimension to the leasing industry was the entry of financial institutions and banks. Thus, this initial growth has led to a mushroom growth of finance companies, offering leasing services.

Now it is pertinent to analyse the types of lessor companies that have undertaken the leasing activity.

Types of Lessor Companies

In 1993, the number of leasing companies registered was 1722 (Table 2.2). The leasing companies can be classified as follows:

1. Independent Leasing companies
2. Finance and Investment companies in leasing business
3. Leasing subsidiaries of Manufacturing of captive or in-house companies
4. Financial Institutions with leasing business
5. Subsidiaries of Commercial Banks

Independent Leasing Companies

These companies are independent ones like any other manufacturers and specialise in leasing business as their main object. They purchase equipment required by the lessees from various manufacturers and lease the equipment to the end users or lessees. Independent leasing companies are often referred to as third party lessors. The three parties are the lessor, the unrelated manufacturer and the lessee. First Leasing company of India Limited, 20th Century Leasing Company Limited, Grover Leasing Limited, etc., can be cited as examples of independent leasing companies. They have also entered into other financial services such as Merchant Banking, Bill Discounting, Corporate Advisory Services, etc. At present all leasing companies in India are engaged not only in fund based activities but also in fee-based activities—such as merchant banking, corporate advisory services, management of issues, under writing of shares, etc.

Finance and Investment Companies

Many investment, finance and hire-purchase companies also enter leasing business. Prominent among them are Sundaram Finance Limited, Motor and General Finance Limited, DCL Finance Limited, Nagarjuna Finance Limited, Cholamandalam Investment and Finance Company Limited, Jai Bharat Credit and Investment Company Limited, etc. As such there are a number of finance and investment companies, which are into leasing business in India because of the tax advantages available to them. Leasing is not

Table 2.2 : State-wise Growth of Leasing Companies in India

State/Union Territory	*Public Ltd. Companies*	*Private Ltd. Companies*	*Total Companies*
1. Andhra Pradesh	48	57	105
2. Assam	5	4	9
3. Chandigarh	4	13	17
4. Delhi	244	234	478
5. Gujarat	17	80	97
6. Haryana	–	4	4
7. Karnataka	41	51	92
8. Kerala	10	24	34
9. Madhya Pradesh	8	50	58
10. Maharashtra	148	297	445
11. Punjab	4	42	46
12. Tamil Nadu	36	117	153
13. Uttar Pradesh	17	35	52
14. West Bengal	42	57	99
15. Others	13	20	33
Total:	637	1085	1722

Source : Corporate News, Company Law Board, New Delhi, 1990.

their regular business and in fact they normally opt for lease finance of 100% depreciable items[31] so as to reduce or avoid tax liability.

Leasing Subsidiaries of Manufacturing Companies

When manufacturing companies or dealers employ leasing as a means of selling their products, it is known as vendor leasing or sales aid leasing, as it promotes sale of their own products.

When a manufacturer or dealer establishes a wholly owned subsidiary to perform the leasing function, it is referred to as captive leasing company. If this subsidiary leasing company is promoted by group companies, it is known as 'in-house' leasing company. These companies predominantly cater to the needs of the house or group companies to which they belong. Examples are: Ashok Leasing & Hire Purchase Limited of Ashok Leyland Limited, Enfield Leasing Finance Company Limited at Madras, etc. The industrial houses, which are having their own leasing subsidiaries, are: Tatas, Birlas, Kirloskar, Modi of U.P., J.K. group of Kanpur, Kotharis of Madras, etc.

Financial Institutions with Leasing Business

A number of financial institutions both at all India and State level are providing leasing facilities. The all India level financial institutions include:

(i) Industrial Reconstruction Bank of India (IRBI)
(ii) Industrial Credit and Investment Corporation of India (ICICI)
(iii) Industrial Development Bank of India (IDBI)
(iv) Industrial Finance Corporation of India (IFCI)
(v) Small Industries Development Bank of India (SIDBI)
(vi) Shipping Credit and Investment Corporation of India (SCICI), etc.

The State Level financial institutions include:

(i) Gujarat Industrial and Investment Corporation (GIIC)
(ii) Karnataka State Industrial Development Corporation (KSIDC)
(iii) State Industrial and Investment Corporation of Maharashtra (SICOM)
(iv) Pradeshiya Industrial and Investment Corporation of Uttar Pradesh (PIICUP)
(v) Rajasthan Industrial and Investment Corporation Limited (RIICO), etc. and many more State financial institutions are taking up leasing activity.

Subsidiaries of Commercial Banks

With the amendment of Banking Regulation Act of 1949 by the Government in August 1984, commercial banks were allowed to undertake the business of equipment leasing by setting up their own subsidiaries with not less than 51% of shareholding. Such a subsidiary, however, is prohibited from transacting hire-purchase business and financing other companies or concerns engaged in equipment leasing.[32] It meant that commercial banks were not eligible to engage in lease directly, but were allowed to start a subsidiary of a financial services institution to do the leasing business.

The subsidiaries of commercial banks include:

(i) SBI Capital Markets Limited of SBI

(ii) Canbank Financial Services Limited of Canara Bank
(iii) PNB Capital Services Limited of Punjab National Bank
(iv) Infrastructure Finance and Leasing Company Limited of Central Bank of India and Unit Trust of India
(v) BOI Financial Services Limited of Bank of India
(vi) BOB Fiscal Services Limited of Bank of Baroda, etc.

Recently, in August 1994, the RBI announced new norms, according to which the commercial banks were allowed to engage in lease business on their own without establishing subsidiaries up to 10% of their total advances portfolio.

The International Finance Corporation (IFC) collaborated in forming four joint ventures in four regions of the country, each with a commercial bank and a private sector company as partners. These are:

(i) IFC, Bank of India, and Twentieth Century Leasing;
(ii) IFC, State Bank of India, and TVS Group Sundaram Finance;
(iii) IFC, National Insulated Cables, and United Commercial Bank;
(iv) IFC, Motor and General Finance Company, and Punjab National Bank.

The IFC contributes 15% of the equity contributions, commercial bank 30% and the private sector company contributes the balance 55%.

Thus, the entry of financial institutions as early as 1983 and the banks later in 1984 into the leasing field has brought a certain amount of respectability and credibility to the leasing industry.

The number of leasing companies grew from 2 in 1980 to 60 in 1982 and to 150 in 1983, 500 in 1985 and further to 1722 in 1990 (Table 2.2).

There has been an explosive growth of financial innovations in the Indian financial system from the early seventies. New financial institutions – such as leasing companies, merchant banks, mutual funds, factoring, venture capital, etc. have come up and were quite active in the financial market. All these come under the Non-Banking Financial Companies (NBFCs). Over the period, the non-banking financial companies (NBFCs) sector has grown exponentially and become an integral part of the Indian financial system.

The NBFC industry has witnessed a major upsurge during early nineties.

The NBFC industry has been a prime beneficiary of the liberalisation drive. Since the reforms launched in June 1991, there have been far reaching changes in the financial system. In the rapidly changing scenario in the financial sector, NBFCs have emerged as important players in the financial market. Majority of the companies has recorded rapid growth in mobilisation and deployment of funds without concomitant care for quality of the assets and interest of the depositors due to the liberalisation drive. As a result, the NBFCs were overcrowded and the number of NBFCs has increased from 7,063 in 1981 to 31,258 in 1992 and to 41,361 in 1994.[33] Such proliferation of NBFCs is no indication of the industry's well-being. According to a recent survey by RBI, barely 700 of these companies are active in the financial market. The rest are essentially front outfits of corporate or small private limited companies with negligible net owned capital or fund.

The leasing industry in India has had its own ups and downs measured in terms of number of fly by night operators who were there in the competitive arena only for a short while. Now, because of the progressive doses of liberalisation that the Government has been administering to the sector, the ultimate test of the "survival of the fittest" has been operating in the market.

This would lead to a healthy and constructive competition amongst the leasing companies and promote steady industrial growth in India. However, while competition in any industry is an economic phenomenon, the existing leasing companies would continue to have their usual share of business owing to the personalised services they offer.

We shall now analyse the contribution of lease finance to the industrial or business finance in India.

Leasing Industry and its Role in Promoting Industrial Investment in India

Leasing is a mode of financing capital assets. This is comparable to the role of oxygen in human life. Participating aggressively and innovatively in the financial system, leasing companies carry out

Table 2.3 : Sources of Funds of Member Companies of ALFS (Cumulative Figures)

(Rs. crores)

Composition of funds	*1991-92*	*1992-93*	*1993-94*	*1994-95*	*1995-96*	*1996-97*	*C.G.R (%)*
Owned Funds (Net Worth)	404.19	1054.65	2678.57	6912.6	8932.30	9532.00	93.81
	–	(160.93)	(153.98)	(158.07)	(29.22)	(6.71)	
Borrowed Funds	815	1868.48	3966.34	8627.08	14209.0	15530.3	85.35
	–	(129.17)	(112.28)	(117.51)	(64.70)	(9.30)	
Fixed Deposits	407.39	1147.03	2176.10	4642.70	7017.60	10309.8	89.36
	–	(181.56)	(89.72)	(113.35)	(51.15)	(46.91)	
Depreciation	239.06	658.48	1195.63	2168.50	2978.10	4101.10	73.74
	–	(175.45)	(81.57)	(81.37)	(37.33)	(37.71)	
Total	1865.96	4728.64	10016.64	22350.88	33137.00	39473.2	86.97
	–	(153.42)	(111.83)	(123.14)	(48.26)	(19.12)	

Note : CGR = Compound Growth Rate.

Source : Compiled from India Leasing Year Books 1994, 1996 and 1998.

Table 2.4 : Application of Funds of Member Companies of ALFS (Cumulative Figures)

(Rs.crores)

Composition of Assets	*1991-92*	*1992-93*	*1993-94*	*1994-95*	*1995-96*	*1996-97*	*C.G.R. (%)*
Leased assets	716.43	1725.88	3189.78	6403.00	8959.10	10425.00	72.22
	–	(140.90)	(84.82)	(100.73)	(39.92)	(16.36)	
Stock on Hire	828.59	2119.58	3831.50	7812.35	11265.60	12956.00	74.35
	–	(155.81)	(80.77)	(103.89)	(43.43)	(15.62)	
Owned Assets	182.57	339.25	725.34	1564.75	1972.90	2588.30	73.62
	–	(85.82)	(113.81)	(115.73)	(26.08)	(31.19)	
Investments	111.23	376.96	1088.32	3131.71	4119.30	6271.20	125.06
	–	(238.90)	(188.71)	(187.76)	(31.54)	(52.24)	
Other Assets (Net Working Capital)	27.14	166.97	1181.70	3439.07	6880.10	7232.50	214.92
	–	(515.22)	(607.73)	(191.02)	(100.10)	(5.12)	
Total	1865.96	4728.64	10016.64	22350.88	33137.00	39473.20	86.97
	–	(153.42)	(111.83)	(123.14)	(48.26)	(19.12)	
No.of Cos.	34	67	157	320	216	216	–

Note: CGR = Compound Growth Rate.

Source : Compiled from India Leasing Year Books – 1994, 1996 and 1998.

the financial intermediary function by mobilising funds from various sources for investment in capital assets.

The details regarding the sources and application of funds of member companies of Association of Leasing and Financial Services are presented in Table 2.4. The table reveals that the total sources and application of funds of member companies of Association of Leasing and Financial Services (ALFS) have recorded a commendable growth of 153.42% in 1992-93, 111.83% in 1993-94 and 123.14% in 1994-95. Later this growth rate came down to 48.26% in 1995-96 and to 19.12% in 1996-97. This is due to increase in number of member companies from 67 in 1992-93 to 157 in 1993-94 and to 320 in 1994-95 and other favourable conditions of capital market.

"Borrowings" that include fixed deposits are the major component constituting 63.25% of the total sources of funds. The remaining of 36.75% is shared by owned funds (25.46%) and depreciation 11.29% (Table 2.5).

Resource mobilisation by way of fixed deposits grew up to Rs.1147.03 crores in 1992-93 from Rs. 407.39 crores representing a commendable growth rate at 181.56%. Almost the same trend is maintained up to 1994-95. Later, this growth rate slowed down to 51.15% representing Rs. 7017.60 crores in 1995-96 and 46.91% constituting Rs. 10309.80 crores in 1996-97, mainly due to RBI Guidelines. The compound growth rate of fixed deposits is recorded at 89.36% (Table 2.4).

The borrowed funds including fixed deposits represent 63.25% of total sources of funds followed by owned funds representing 25.46% and depreciation at 11.29% (Table 2.5). Thus on an average, the leasing industry depends upon owned funds including depreciation to the extent of 36.75% and borrowed funds including public deposits to the extent of 63.25%.

Among the borrowings, the average proportion of fixed deposits is higher registering 35.79%, followed by bank borrowings (22.51%), Institutional borrowing (17.69%) and other borrowings (17.08%). Debentures registered at the lowest of 6.93% (Table 2.6). Further, the higher average compound growth rate is recorded by fixed deposits registering at 89.36% (Table 2.6).

Table 2.5 : Composition of Sources of Funds of Member Companies of ALFS *(Per cent)*

Composition of funds	*1991-92*	*1992-93*	*1993-94*	*1994-95*	*1995-96*	*1996-97*	*Average*
Owned funds (networth)	21.66	22.30	26.74	30.93	26.96	24.15	25.46
Borrowed funds	43.69	39.51	39.60	38.60	42.88	39.34	40.60
Fixed deposits	21.83	24.26	21.72	20.77	21.18	26.12	22.65
Depreciation	12.82	13.93	11.94	9.70	8.98	10.39	11.29
Total	100	100	100	100	100	100	100
No. of companies	34	67	157	320	216	216	–

Composition of Application of Funds of Member Companies of ALFS *(Per cent)*

Composition of Assets	*1991-92*	*1992-93*	*1993-94*	*1994-95*	*1995-96*	*1996-97*	*Average*
Leased Assets	38.39	36.50	31.84	28.65	27.04	26.41	31.47
Stock on Hire	44.42	44.82	38.25	34.95	33.82	32.82	38.18
Owned Assets	9.78	7.17	7.24	7.00	5.95	6.56	7.28
Investments	5.96	7.98	10.87	14.01	12.43	15.89	11.19
Other Assets (Net Working Capital)	1.45	3.53	11.80	15.39	20.76	18.32	11.88
Total	100	100	100	100	100	100	100
No. of Companies	34	67	157	320	216	216	–

Source : Compiled from published Reports of Association of Leasing and Financial Services Companies.

Table 2.6 : Component Analysis of Borrowings of Member Companies of ALFS (Cumulative Figures) *(Rs. crores)*

Borrowings	*1991-92*	*1992-93*	*1993-94*	*1994-95*	*1995-96*	*1996-97*	*C.G.R (%).*	$\bar{X}$
	(21.48)	(23.43)	(22.12)	(25.99)	(22.75)	(19.31)		
Bank Borrowings	262.62	706.64	1358.98	3448.75	4829.30	4989.30	84.41	22.51
	—	(169.07)	(92.32)	(153.77)	(40.02)	(3.32)		
	(17.06)	(18.38)	(15.79)	(14.66)	(21.16)	(19.10)		
Institutional Borrowings	208.58	554.40	969.94	1945.83	4491.30	4934.20	91.78	17.69
	—	(165.80)	(74.95)	(100.61)	(130.82)	(9.86)		
	(33.32)	(38.04)	(35.43)	(34.99)	(33.06)	(39.90)		
Fixed Deposits	407.39	1147.03	2176.10	4642.70	7017.60	10309.80	89.36	35.79
	—	(181.56)	(89.72)	(113.35)	(51.15)	(46.91)		
	(8.68)	(7.77)	(5.79)	(4.68)	(7.15)	(7.50)		
Debentures	106.19	234.42	355.50	620.84	1517.00	1938.30	80.56	6.93
	—	(120.76)	(51.65)	(74.64)	(144.35)	(27.77)		
	(19.46)	(12.38)	(20.87)	(19.68)	(15.88)	(14.19)		
Other borrowings including inter-corporate loans	237.93	373.02	1281.92	2611.66	3371.70	3668.50	82.18	17.08
		(56.78)	(243.65)	(103.73)	(29.10)	(8.80)		
	(100)	(100)	(100)	(100)	(100)	(100)		
Total	1222.71	3015.51	6142.44	13269.78	21226.60	25840.10	86.85	100.0
	—	(146.62)	(103.69)	(116.03)	(59.96)	(21.73)		

Note : (i) C.G.R. = Compound Growth Rate. (ii) $\bar{X}$ = Arithmetic Mean. (iii) Figures in upper brackets indicate the per cent of each component to total. (iv) Figures in lower brackets indicate growth rates.

Source: Compiled from *India Leasing Year Books* – 1994, 1996 and 1998.

The leasing and finance companies are allowed to borrow 10 times the net owned funds. The borrowings from banks are limited to 3 to 4 times within the overall ceiling of 10 times depending upon their income. The total debt i.e. total borrowings, including fixed deposits, to networth of member companies of ALFS was 3.03 times in 1991-92, 2.29 times in 1993-94, 2.38 times in 1995-96 and 2.71 times in 1996-97 (Table 2.9). This indicates that the leasing and finance companies were not able to mobilise the required funds as per permissibility within the norms stipulated by the RBI, which led to the lack of funds for leasing and finance companies and the leasing business was, therefore, adversely affected.

On the application (uses) side, Table 2.4 reveals that the leased assets and hire-purchased assets have recorded almost the same trend. Leased assets have registered a growth rate of 100.73% (Rs. 6403.00 crores) in 1994-95 over the previous year. Similarly, hire-purchased assets (Stock on hire) have increased to Rs. 7812.35 crores representing a growth rate of 103.89% over previous year. After 1994-95, the growth rates of both leased assets and hire-purchased assets have slowed down to 39.92% and 43.43% respectively in 1995-96. The growth rate further decreased to 16.36% for leased assets and 15.62% for hire-purchased assets in 1996-97.

Further, Table 2.5 reveals that the composition of leased assets and hire-purchased assets have had a declining trend from 1991-92 to 1996-97 and on an average the proportion of leased assets and hire-purchased assets put together accounted for 69.65% of all assets. The average leased assets share comes to 31.47%, while the share of hire-purchased assets represent 38.18%, investments accounted for 11.19% of all assets. The lowest percentage (7.28%) is recorded by owned assets.

It is evident from Table 2.5 that out of the total sources of funds, an average of about 31.47% per cent of funds are deployed for leasing business and around 38.18% per cent of funds are deployed for hire-purchase business. Among leased assets, plant and machinery has more demand in the lease market. The average proportion of plant and machinery is at 70.60% and others 29.40% (Table 2.7).

Table 2.7 : Proportion of Plant & Machinery to Total Leased Assets of Member Companies of ALFS .

(Rs. lakhs)

Leased Assets	*1991-92*	*1992-93*	*1993-94*	*1994-95*	*1995-96*	*1996-97*	*C.G.R. (%)*	$\bar{X}$
	(64.87)	(64.85)	(71.86)	(72.99)	(75.31)	(73.70)		
Plant & Machinery	464.76	1119.4	2292.18	4673.80	8799.0	10874.1	91.07	70.60
	—	(140.85)	(104.77)	(104.03)	(88.29)	(23.58)		
	(35.13)	(35.15)	(28.14)	(27.01)	(24.69)	(26.30)		
Other Assets	251.67	606.74	897.6	1729.2	2884.3	3881.0	72.15	29.40
	—	(141.09)	(47.94)	(92.65)	(66.80)	(26.30)		
	(100)	(100)	(100)	(100)	(100)	(100)		
Total	716.43	1726.14	3189.78	6403.0	11683.3	14755.1	85.15	100.0
	—	(140.93)	(84.79)	(100.73)	(82.47)	(26.29)		
No. of Companies	34	67	157	320	216	216	–	–

Note: (i) C.G.R. = Compound Growth Rate; (ii) Figures in lower brackets indicate growth rate; (iii) Figures in upper brackets indicate the proportion of each component of asset to total volume of assets leased; (iv) $\bar{X}$ = Arithmetic mean.

Source: Compiled from India Lease Year Books – 1994, 1996 and 1998.

Table 2.8 : Composition of Income of Member Companies of ALFS

(Rs. crores)

Composition of Income	*1991-92*	*1992-93*	*1993-94*	*1994-95*	*1995-96*	*1996-97*	*C.G.R (%).*	$\bar{X}$
	(30.05)	(31.95)	(31.24)	(32.89)	(25.81)	(27.05)		29.83
Lease Income	134.22	373.20	711.88	1531.01	1806.08	2178.03		
	—	(178.05)	(430.38)	(115.07)	(17.98)	(20.59)	74.22	
	(26.92)	(22.77)	(19.50)	(19.89)	(27.04)	(30.51)		24.44
Hire Income	120.23	266.02	444.30	926.16	1892.12	2456.07		
	—	(121.26)	(67.02)	(108.45)	(104.29)	(29.80)	85.92	
	(43.03)	(45.28)	(49.26)	(47.22)	(47.15)	(42.44)		45.73
Other Income	192.21	528.97	1122.72	2198.37	3299.10	3416.80		
	—	(175.20)	(112.25)	(95.81)	(50.07)	(3.56)	79.90	
	(100)	(100)	(100)	(100)	(100)	(100)		100.0
Total	446.66	1168.19	2278.99	4655.54	6997.30	8050.90		
	—	(161.54)	(95.09)	(104.28)	(50.30)	(15.06)	79.85	
Net Profit	94.00	240.91	536.68	1346.49	1326.80	512.00		
	—	(156.29)	(122.77)	(150.90)	(1.46)	(61.41)	51.39	—
No. of Cos.	34	67	157	320	216	216	—	—

Note: (i) Figures in upper brackets indicate the per cent to total. (ii) Figures in lower brackets indicate growth rates. (iii) X = Arithmetic mean..

Source: Compiled from India Lease Year Books – 1994, 1996 and 1998.

It is also evident from Table 2.7 that the leasing business and hire-purchase business showed a declining growth trend during 1996-97 due to lack of demand and general market conditions.

Composition of Income

The income and Net Profit particulars pertaining to member companies of the Association of Leasing and Financial Services Companies were analysed and presented in Table 2.8. The table shows that the average growth rate of hire-purchase income was higher than lease income. However, almost the same trend was recorded for hire purchase business and leasing business. The average proportion of hire-purchase income and lease income both put together was at 54.27%. The remaining proportion of income (45.73%) was shared by others such as bill discounting, inter-corporate deposits, merchant banking, securities transactions and others.

The net profit shows increasing trend up to 1994-95 registering 150.90%, constituting Rs. 1346.49 crores over the previous year. Later, it declined by 1.46% in 1995-96 and 61.41% in 1996-97 due to the rise in costs, RBI's stringent guidelines (the implications of RBI guidelines are analysed in Chapter 3), and general capital market conditions. The increase in expenditure may perhaps be due to the increase in provisioning for non-performing assets as per RBI guidelines imposed in the year 1996. This is evident from the following break-up (figures in percentages) pertaining to income and expenditure.

As per the reports of the Association of Leasing and Financial Services Companies, the income and expenditure in percentage for the years 1994-95 and 1996-97 are mentioned hereunder:

	Income in per cent	
	1995-96	*1996-97*
Leasing & Hire purchase	52.8	57.6
Securities Transactions	7.4	2.0
Dividend	3.9	2.8
Interest	19.2	19.3
Others	16.7	18.3
	100.0	100.0

	Expenditure in per cent	
	1994-95	*1996-97*
Interest	42.0	50.0
Operating Expenditure	16.0	22.0
Depreciation	16.0	19.0
Tax	2.0	3.0
Net Profit (PAT)	24.0	6.0
	100.0	100.0
No. of Companies	320	216

Source: India Leasing Year Book – 1998.

The share of income from leasing and hire purchase operations has moved from 52.8% in 1994-95 to 57.6% in 1996-97. The share of income from securities business and investments have dropped sharply from 7.4% in 1994-95 to 2% in 1996-97 evincing sluggish capital market operations.

The operating expenditure has increased to 22.0% in 1996-97 from 16.0% in 1994-95 due to the increase in provisioning for non-performing assets and increased operating costs. This rise in costs has resulted in the decline of net profit to 6% in 1996-97 from 24% in 1994-95.

Table 2.9 shows that the Return on net worth has recorded a continued declining trend starting from 1991-92 (23.25%) to 1996-97 (5.37%). The Return on net worth has dropped from 14.85% in 1995-96 to 5.37% in 1996-97. This decline indicates poor earnings and tough business environment. Further, Table 2.9 presents that the Return on Capital Employed (ROCE) has increased from 5.03% in 1991-92 to 6.02% in 1994-95. But it has dropped from 4% in 1995-96 to 1.29% in 1996-97, which indicates poor performance of the companies. Increase in non-performing assets could have been a significant cause to this 2.71% fall.

In addition to the specific reasons, the general reasons for the considerably steady increasing growth trend from 1990-91 to 1994-95 and decreasing trend after 1995 both in respect of sources of funds and application of funds are mentioned below:

(i) The Government's New Industrial Policy of 1991-92 and the bold and pragmatic policy pronouncements liberalising most

Table 2.9 : Some Important Ratios

Type of Ratio	*1991-92*	*1992-93*	*1993-94*	*1994-95*	*1995-96*	*1996-97*	$\bar{X}$
Debt-Equity (No. of times)	3.03	2.86	2.29	1.92	2.38	2.71	2.53
Return on Net worth (in %)	23.25	22.84	20.03	19.48	14.85	5.37	17.64
Return on Total Capital Employed or ROA (in %)	5.03	5.09	5.35	6.02	4.00	1.29	4.46
No. of Companies	34	67	157	320	216	216	—

Note : (i) Debt-Equity = Debt (Total Debt) ÷ Equity
(ii) Return on Net worth = Net Profit ÷ Net worth
(iii) ROCE or ROA = Net Profit ÷ Total Capital Employed
(iv) $\bar{X}$ = Arithmetic mean.

Source : Compiled from Reports of Association of Leasing and Financial Service Companies.

segments in the industrial sector from licensing and other controls, positively encouraging direct foreign investment and virtually doing away with the MRTP provisions have predictably been hailed in business and financial circles throughout the country. Thus, the economic reforms introduced by the government from 1991 onwards brought with them vast opportunities for growth and diversification. Leasing business also grew substantially up to 1994-95 as the steady growth trends showed in the Tables from 2.4 to 2.9.

(ii) Capital goods and other requirements of the public sector opened up another vast area of activity for the Non-Banking Finance companies in general and leasing and Hire-Purchase companies in particular. For example, during 1993-94 the leasing requirement of the Department of Telecommunication alone has been estimated during at Rs. 10,000 crores. Similarly, the power sector showing tremendous business opportunities due to its capital-intensive nature and setting up of several power companies in the private sector.

(iii) The Governments of Maharashtra, Tamil Nadu, Punjab, Rajasthan and Andhra Pradesh have exempted the lease tax on lease rentals during 1992-93. This has provided the necessary stimulus to the leasing industry as the effective tax burden on leased goods have come down by 4% to 5%. The Union Budget 1994-95 also reduced corporate tax rates by 5% for widely held companies and 10% for closely held companies. This helped the finance and leasing companies to improve their bottom line.

On the whole, the performance of the member companies was extremely good until 1995. The reasons for slow progress in leasing business after 1995 are discussed below :

(i) The Reserve Bank of India allowed banks during the year 1994 to enter the field of leasing, hire-purchase, factoring and other related activities on their own. Earlier, (i.e., from 1984 onwards) banks could engage in these activities only through subsidiaries. Now they could also departmentally engage in these activities. As the banks have entered into the field of leasing, funding to leasing companies has become a major constraint. Banks on one hand have access to vast funds at low rates of interest and on the other hand may be reluctant to continue lending to leasing companies.

(ii) Almost All State Governments started levying sales tax on lease rentals by which the cost of leasing has increased by 4 to 6%.

(iii) The RBI has announced guidelines in 1994 for NBFCs for prudential norms for accounting and capital adequacy. RBI has also indicated that these guidelines will have to be followed from 31-3-95 and there will be regular reporting to RBI on semi-annual basis.

After 1995, with the entry of banks and financial institutions into the leasing field, most of the leasing companies have diversified into related activities like merchant banking, share broking, securities trading, bill discounting, factoring services, portfolio management, etc. and have started offering a wide range of fund based and fee-based financial services.

Now it is proposed to analyse the leasing business done by All-India Financial Institutions.

Leasing by All-India Financial Institutions

A well-integrated structure of Financial Institutions has evolved over the years providing a variety of financial products and services to suit the varied needs of the corporate. The network comprises 11 institutions at the National level and 46 at the State level. The All-India Financial Institutions (AIFIs) comprise five All India Development Banks (AIDBs), three specialised financial institutions and three investment institutions. At the State level, there are 18 State Financial Corporations (SFCs) and 28 State Industrial Development Corporations (SIDCs).

The All India Development Banks are: Industrial Development Bank of India (IDBI), Industrial Finance Corporation of India Ltd. (IFCI), Industrial Credit and Investment Corporation of India Ltd. (ICICI), Small Industries Development Bank of India (SIDBI) and Industrial Investment Bank of India Ltd. (IIBI). [Erstwhile Industrial Reconstruction Bank of India (IRBI)].

The specialised Financial Institutions are Risk Capital and Technology Finance Corporation Ltd., (RCTC), TDICI Ltd., and Tourism Finance Corporation of India Ltd. (TFCIL). The Investment Institutions are Life Insurance Corporation of India (LIC), Unit Trust of India (UTI), and General Insurance Corporation of India (GIC).

The other institutions consist of National Small Industries Corporation Ltd. (NSIC), State Small Industries Development Corporations (SSIDCs), Stock Holding Corporation of India Ltd. (SHCIL), Commercial Banks (CBs), etc.

Of the above, the All India level financial institutions of ICICI, IDBI, IFCI, NSIC, TFCIL and IIBI are engaged in leasing business in addition to their providing financial assistance to small, medium and large scale industries. They also undertake the promotional and developmental activities.

The data pertaining to volume of leasing done by All India Financial Institutions (sanctions and disbursements) are presented in Tables 2.10 and 2.11.

ICICI is the first All India level financial institution to enter the leasing business in 1983. Later the other financial institutions entered the leasing field. Among all financial institutions, the ICICI has a better record in sanctions, registering a compound growth rate at 55.48% followed by IDBI registering the compound growth rate at 41.88% per annum (Table 2.10).

The sanctions of ICICI under leasing decreased by 38.70% in 1994-95 over the previous year. However, it recorded substantial growth in 1995-96 registering 274.80% (Table 2.10). The disbursements under leasing decreased by 56.50% in 1994-95. However, it has recorded an impressive positive growth in 1995-96 registering 232.80%. It means the sanctions and disbursements have coincided in 1994-95 and 1995-96.

The proportion of volume of cumulative disbursements of leasing done by ICICI is registered at 62.76% which is the highest among all financial institutions followed by IDBI (23.00%), IFCI (11.86%). Whereas NSICL, TFCIL and IIBI have recorded a very lower proportion registering 1.81%, 0.23% and 0.34% respectively (Table 2.10).

During 1996-97, the ICICI has formed a wholly-owned subsidiary called ICICI Credit Corporation Ltd. (I-CREDIT) as a Non-Banking Finance Company to create a country-wide retail net work to enter new areas like financing of automobiles, consumer durables, vendor leasing and factoring services.[34]

In response to the growing needs of various segments of industry and the on-going changes in the financial sector, IDBI has been taking several steps to re-orient its business strategies and expand the range of products and services. Besides providing direct finance by way of term loans to medium and large-scale industries, IDBI also provides merchant banking facilities and undertakes equipment-leasing scheme.

IDBI has entered the leasing field in 1988, and sanctioned finance for acquiring the equipment under leasing scheme for Rs. 1916.20 crores up to end of March 1997 (Table 2.10), while disbursements have recorded at Rs. 1139.50 crores. Overall sanctions of IDBI during 1995-96 for leasing registered an increase by 59.40% to Rs. 694.30 crores while disbursements recorded an increase of 175.4% in the same year of 1995-96 (Table 2.10). However, during 1996-97, the IDBI's overall sanctions and disbursements for leasing declined by 54.20% to Rs. 317.90 crores and 15.50% to Rs. 365.70 crores respectively over previous years due to unfavourable market conditions in the economy.

Further, IDBI also extends loans and makes investments in shares and bonds of various financial intermediaries. Of the 11 All India Financial Institutions, only three viz., IFCI, IDBI, and SIDBI have extended financial assistance to leasing companies (Table 2.11).

The financial assistance extended by SIDBI to leasing companies constitutes Rs. 1978.80 crores cumulative up to end of March 1997 representing 57.39% followed by IDBI representing 23.88% to Rs. 823.3 crores and IFCI representing 18.73% to Rs. 645.70 crores (Table 2.11).

IDBI stopped extending financial assistance to leasing companies from 1995-96, while SIDBI has substantially increased its share of financial assistance to leasing companies from 1993-94 registering an increased growth rate by 362.89% to Rs. 237.0 crores in 1993-94 and by 125.95% to Rs. 535.5 crores (Table 2.11). The reasons could be that the SIDBI, a wholly owned subsidiary of IDBI, commenced its operations on April 2, 1990 by taking over the outstanding portfolio and activities of IDBI pertaining to the small scale sector. Over the years, SIDBI widened its perspective to effectively meet the emerging needs of various industries.

IFCI extends financial assistance to the industrial sector through rupee and foreign currency loans and also financial services through its equipment finance equipment leasing and financial assistance to leasing and hire purchase companies.

As a part of its diversification efforts, IFCI has formed IFCI Financial Services Ltd., for undertaking merchant banking, leasing, stock broking and allied services. It has also set up the Investment Information and Credit Rating Agency (ICRA) to rate various debt instruments of companies.

During 1996-97, leasing sanctions by IFCI declined by 2.60% to Rs. 288.80 crores over the previous year (Table 2.10) while leasing disbursements rose by 200% to Rs. 214.8 crores over the previous year (Table 2.10). Cumulatively, until the end of March 1997, IFCI sanctioned Rs. 1252.30 crores for leasing (Table 2.10)

Table 2.10 : Leasing by All India Financial Institutions (Year-wise Figures) *(Rs. crores)*

Finl. Insts.	*1991-92*	*1992-93*	*1993-94*	*1994-95*	*1995-96*	*1996-97*	*Cumulative up to 1997*	*C.G.R.*
Sanctions								
ICICI	140.7	340.8	634.0	388.4	1455.7	1426.4	(60.01)	
	—	(142.2)	(86.0)	(-38.7)	(274.8)	(-2.0)	4957.9	55.48
IDBI	68.1	209.0	170.6	435.7	694.3	317.9	(23.20)	
	—	(206.9	(-18.4)	(155.4)	(59.4)	(-54.2)	1916.2	41.88
IFCI	85.5	105.7	106.1	9.9	296.4	288.8	(15.16)	
	—	(23.6)	(0.4)	(-90.7)	(1993.9)	(-2.6)	1252.3	21.47
NSICL	9.5	8.1	10.9	14.6	17.1	14.4	(1.08)	
	—	(-14.7)	(34.6)	(33.9)	(17.1)	(-15.8)	89.4	14.09
TFCIL	1.5	3.8	3.1	2.10	12.0	0.20	(0.30)	
	—	(153.3)	(-18.4)	(-32.3)	(471.4)	(-98.3)	24.9	-18.16
IIBI	0.7	2.6					(0.25)	
	—	(271.4)	—	—	—	—	20.8	1
Total	306.0	670.0	924.7	850.7	2475.5	2047.7	(100)	
	—	(118.9	(38.0)	(-8.0)	(190.9)	(-17.3)	8261.5	46.40
Disbursements								
ICICI	78.0	175.0	400.9	174.3	580.0	1194.30	(62.76)	
	—	(124.4)	(129.1)	(-56.5)	(232.8)	(105.9)	3108.9	59.79
IDBI	21.6	68.7	94.4	157.2	432.9	635.7	(23.00)	
	—	(233.5)	(37.4)	(66.5)	(175.4)	(-15.5)	1139.5	79.19
IFCI	33.0	18.5	18.8	9.8	71.6	214.8	(11.86)	
	—	(- 43.9)	(1.6)	(47.1)	(631.6)	(200)	587.6	44.05
NSICL	9.5	8.10	10.9	14.6	17.1	14.4	(1.81)	
	—	(-14.7)	(34.6)	(33.9)	(17.1)	(-15.8)	89.4	14.09

Table 2.10 *(Contd.)*

TFCIL	0.3	1.8	1.8	2.1	3.4	1.6	(0.23)	
	—	(500.0)	(0)	(16.67)	(61.9)	(-52.9)	11.3	34.72
IIBI	4.1	6.5	4.9			0.6	(0.34)	
	—	(58.5)	(-24.6)	—	—	(-87.8)	17.0	—
Total	145.5	278.6	531.7	358.0	1105.0	1791.4	(100)	
	—	(91.50)	(90.90)	(32.70)	(208.7)	(62.1)	4953.7	59.27

Note : (i) Figures in lower brackets indicate growth-rates; (ii) Figures in upper brackets indicate each financial institution's proportion of cumulative leasing to the total.

Source : Computed from IDBI Reports on Development Banking in India from 1991-92 to 1996-97.

Table 2.11 : Financial Assistance to Leasing Companies by All India Financial Institutions (Year-wise Figures) *(Rs. crores)*

Finl. Insts.	*1990-91*	*1991-92*	*1992-93*	*1993-94*	*1994-95*	*1995-96*	*1996-97*	*Cumulative up to 1997*	*C.G.R.(%)*
IFCI	70.8	85.0	76.3	69.2	124.5	74.0	95.0	(18.73)	
	—	(20.06)	(-10.24)	(-9.31)	(79.91)	(-40.56)	(28.38)	645.70	3.98
IDBI	89.90	70.08	85.0	76.30	72.0			(23.88)	
	—	(-22.05)	(21.29)	(-10.24)	(-5.64)	—	—	823.3	—
SIDBI	5.50	26.0	51.20	237.0	535.5	570.5	553.0	(57.39)	
	—	(372.72)	(96.92)	(362.89)	(125.95)	(6.54)	(-3.07)	1978.80	122.20
Total	166.20	181.08	212.50	382.50	732.00	644.50	648.00	(100)	
	—	(8.95)	(17.35)	(70.00)	(91.37)	(-11.95)	(0.54)	3447.80	32.39

Note : (i) Figures in lower brackets indicate growth-rates; (ii) Figures in upper brackets (in cumulative figures column) indicate per cent of assistance by each financial institution to total financial assistance.

Source : Computed from IDBI Reports on Development Banking in India from 1990-91 to 1996-97.

and disbursed for leasing Rs. 587.60 crores, which accounted for 11.86% of all disbursements by all financial institutions (Table 2.10).

NSIC Ltd. provides a wide range of services, predominantly promotional in character to small-scale industries. It supplies machinery, both indigenous and imported on easy hire-purchase terms and on lease basis to industries for expansion, diversification, and modernisation.

Cumulatively, until the end of March 1997, NSIC Ltd. sanctions and disbursements amounted to Rs. 89.40 crores. It has recorded a positive growth trend registering 34.60%, 33.90% and 17.10% in 1993-94, 1994-95 and 1995-96 respectively. This increase is due to the introduction of the scheme, which has been designed to earmark for easier accessibility of latest modern equipment available internationally, so as to enable small-scale industries to compete internationally. But during 1996-97, the growth rate declined by 15.80% (Table 2.10) due to general capital market conditions and low demand for leasing finance.

TFCIL, promoted by IFCI is a specialised All-India Development Financing Institution catering to the needs of Tourism Industry in India. TFCI offers term loans and also the facility equipment leasing for setting up and/or development of tourism-related activities, facilities and services.

Sanctions and disbursements by TFCIL during 1995-96 rose by 471.40% and 61.90% respectively, while sanctions and disbursements during 1996-97 declined by 98.30% and 52.90% respectively (Table 2.10). The entire portion may be due to the lack of demand.

With the corporatisation of the Industrial Reconstruction Bank of India (IRBI) which was set up in 1985 under the IRBI Act, 1984 as the principal Credit and Reconstruction Agency for aiding rehabilitation of sick and closed industrial units, IRBI was converted into a full-fledged all purpose development finance institution and incorporated as Industrial Investment Bank of India Ltd. (IIBI) on March 17, 1997 under the Companies Act, 1956.

IIBI provides financial assistance in form of term loans and also undertakes equipment leasing/hire purchase schemes and merchant banking services.

IIBI has undertaken the leasing activity up to the year 1992-

93. The cumulative disbursements of leasing till March end 1997 amounted to Rs. 17 crore (Table 2.10). This has occupied the 5th place recording 0.30% among all financial institutions pushing TFCIL to 6th place, which recorded a low of 0.20% (Table 2.10).

Industrial Development in Andhra Pradesh

The industrial scenario in Andhra Pradesh is very vibrant and is on the runway to success. The state is strong in the sectors of steel, food and agri-products, chemicals, bulk drugs and pharmaceuticals, textiles, cement, granite, building materials, aquaculture, etc.[35]

The State abounds in first generation entrepreneurs who have built massive empires like K.V.K. Raju (Nagarjuna Group), B.V. Raju (Raasi Group), Nrupender Rao (Pennar Group), Chandrasekhar Reddy (SOL Pharma Group), Harischandra Prasad (Andhra Petro Group), Ravi Sanghi (Sanghi Group) and others.[36]

A.P. has now taken up a new comprehensive industrial policy in software technology to boost up the industrial sector and generate increased employment opportunities to the youth in a big way.

There is perhaps no other industry in the State, which registered such fast progress as the Information Technology industry does. It started with setting up of the Software Technology Park under the Department of Electronics, Government of India at Hyderabad way back in 1991. This was followed by the creation of the necessary conducive environment for this industry to grow in the State.[37]

Software industry in Andhra Pradesh took a quantum jump particularly from 1996-97 with personal initiative of the present Chief Minister, N. Chandrababu Naidu. And Hyderabad is the hub of software industry. It is competing with Bangalore to become India's leading Centre of Information Technology. This effort bore fruit as can be seen from the fact that software exports increased from a mere Rs. 414.59 lakhs in 1992-93 to Rs. 983.81 lakhs in 1993-94, Rs. 2,181.62 lakhs in 1994-95, Rs. 6,037.06 lakhs in 1995-96 and to Rs. 13,325.61 lakhs in 1996-97.[38]

It is now proposed to analyse the industrial status of A.P. compared to other States by considering the GDP and per capita income.

State Domestic Product and Per Capita Income

State Domestic Product (SDP), commonly known as State Income, is one of the important indicators to measure the economic development. It measures in monetary terms the value of all goods and services produced during a given period of time within the geographical boundaries of the State.

The estimates of SDP are prepared at constant prices by evaluating the goods and services of current year with base year prices in order to eliminate the effects of price changes and to measure real growth in the economy. The base year for the preparation of State Income estimates at constant prices has been shifted from 1980-81 to 1993-94.[39]

It can be observed from Table 2.12 that a comparative picture of growth of Gross State Domestic Product (GSDP) in Andhra Pradesh has increased from Rs. 58,227 crores in 1993-94 to Rs. 69,188 crores in 1996-97 recording the growth rates at 5.61% in 1994-95 and 5.65% in 1995-96 and 6.50% in 1996-97. The A.P., annual average growth rate during the 4-year period ending with 1997-98 works out to 4.02% which is less than Tamil Nadu (7.86%), Karnataka (7.72%) and Maharashtra (6.6%), but higher than Madhya Pradesh (3.90%). In terms of volume, the highest GDP was recorded by Maharashtra State registering at Rs. 1,37,688 crores during the year 1997-98, followed by Tamil Nadu registering at Rs. 78,114 crores in 1997-98. A.P. has occupied the third position recording at Rs. 68,015 crores in 1997-98 (Table 2.12).

The growth rate during 1997-98 was negative at 1.70%, which was mainly due to the negative growth rate in primary sector (Table 2.13). The primary sector includes Agriculture, Forestry, Fishing, Mining and Quarrying, etc. The secondary sector has recorded impressive growth rates from 1993-94 to 1997-98. The average annual growth rate is recorded at 8.13%, followed by Tertiary Sector (5.90%). The secondary sector includes registered and unregistered companies, electricity, gas and water supply, construction, etc. The Tertiary Sector includes transport, storage and communication, railways, financing, insurance, real estate and business services, hotels and restaurants, etc.

Further, Table 2.13 reveals the share of primary sector at constant prices has declined over the years from 34.80% in 1993-94 to 27.91% in 1997-98. This decline is more pronounced in 1997-98. The shares of secondary and tertiary sectors have shown an increasing trend. These changes in sectoral pattern reveal that the

Table 2.12 : Gross State Domestic Product of Major States and Gross Domestic Product of All India at Constant (1993-94) Prices

(Rs. crores)

S. No.	*Name of the State*	*1993-94*	*1994-95*	*1995-96*	*1996-97*	*1997-98*	$\bar{X}$
1.	Andhra Pradesh	58227	61491	64966	69188	68015	4.02
		—	(5.61)	(5.65)	(6.50)	(-1.70)	
2.	Karnataka	42739	46209	49574	54784	57508	7.72
		—	(8.12)	(7.28)	(10.51)	(4.97)	
3.	Tamil Nadu	57833	65735	68501	73762	78114	7.86
		—	(13.66)	(4.21)	(7.68)	(5.90)	
4.	Maharashtra	106917	108708	122492	130066	137688	6.6
		—	(1.68)	(12.68)	(6.18)	(5.86)	
5.	Madhya Pradesh	52752	54291	57157	60850	61428	3.90
		—	(2.92)	(5.28)	(6.46)	(0.95)	
All India (GDP at factor cost)		781345	835864	896990	964390	1012816	6.71
		—	(6.98)	(7.31)	(7.51)	(5.02)	

Notes : (i) Figures in brackets indicate growth rates.
(ii) $\bar{X}$ = Arithmetic Mean.

Source : Directorate of Economics & Statistics, Hyderabad, Government of A.P., 1998-99.

Table 2.13 : Sector-wise Gross State Domestic Product of Andhra Pradesh and Percentage Distribution at Constant (1993-94) Prices *(Rs.crores)*

S. No.	*Industry*	*1993-94*	*1994-95*	*1995-96*	*1996-97*	*1997-98*	$\bar{X}$
		(34.80)	(32.49)	(32.66)	(32.55)	(27.91)	
1.	Primary Sector	20262	19975	21216	22521	18980	-4.78
		—	(-1.42)	(6.21)	(6.15)	(-15.72)	
		(21.47)	(23.62)	(23.30)	(23.02)	(25.03)	
2.	Secondary Sector	12504	14525	15135	15929	17026	8.13
		—	(16.16)	(4.20)	(5.25)	(6.89)	
		(43.73)	(43.89)	(44.04)	(44.43)	(47.06)	
3.	Tertiary Sector	25461	26991	28615	30738	32009	5.90
		—	(6.01)	(6.02)	(7.42)	(4.13)	
		(100)	(100)	(100)	(100)	(100)	
Gross Domestic Product		58227	61491	64966	69188	68015	4.02
		—	(5.61)	(5.65)	(6.50)	(-1.70)	

Notes :(i) Figures in upper brackets indicate the proportion of each component to total gross domestic product.
(ii) Figures in lower brackets indicate growth rates. (iii) $\bar{X}$ = Arithmetic Mean.

Source : Directorate of Economics & Statistics, Hyderabad, Government of A.P.

Table 2.14 : Per Capita Income of Major States and All India at Constant (1993-94) Prices *(Rupees)*

S. No.	*Name of the State*	*1993-94*	*1994-95*	*1995-96*	*1996-97*	*1997-98*	$\bar{X}$
1.	Andhra Pradesh	7494	7794	8130	8527	8246	
		—	(4.00)	(4.31)	(4.88)	(-3.3)	2.47
2.	Karnataka	8190	8694	9089	9919	10200	
		—	(6.15)	(4.54)	(9.13)	(2.83)	5.66
3.	Tamil Nadu	9073	10257	10573	11320	11897	
		—	(13.05)	(3.08)	(7.07)	(5.10)	7.08
4.	Maharashtra	12705	12602	13951	14271	14943	
		—	(-0.81)	(10.70)	(2.29)	(4.71)	4.22
5.	Madhya Pradesh	6645	6626	6809	7107	7013	
		—	(-0.29)	(2.76)	(4.38)	(-1.32)	1.38
All India		7698	8069	8479	8987	9271	
		—	(4.82)	(5.08)	(5.99)	(3.16)	4.76

Note : (i) Figures in brackets indicate growth rates.
(ii) $\bar{X}$ = Arithmetic Mean.

Source: Directorate of Economics & Statistics, Hyderabad, Government of AP.

economy of Andhra Pradesh is gradually shifting from agricultural activities to non-agricultural activities, which is a healthy sign.

Table 2.14 analyses the data pertaining to per capita income of major States and of all India at constant prices. Per capita income is one of the indicators to measure the standard of living of the people.

The per capita income at constant prices in A.P. has increased from Rs.7,494 in 1993-94 to Rs. 8,527 in 1996-97. During the year 1997-98, the per capita income has decreased to Rs. 8,246 due to adverse seasonal conditions. In terms of the growth rate, Tamil Nadu stood first recording the average annual growth at 7.08% followed by Karnataka (5.66%) and Maharashtra (4.22%). The A.P. stood fourth in rank recording the average annual growth rate at 2.47% followed by Madhya Pradesh (1.38%).

Thus, A.P. comes under moderate by industrially developed States and is yet to be fully developed. However, the economic reforms have made a fundamental change in the industrial finance scenario. Until then, finance for industry was provided mostly by financial institutions both through equity and debt.

The financial services industry has emerged as a source of industrial finance during early seventies in India and during early eighties in A.P. and has picked up momentum during mid-nineties. There has been a tremendous rush of entrepreneurs, big, medium, and small sized to enter the financial services sector all over India, including Andhra Pradesh.

Contribution of Leasing in Andhra Pradesh

It is now pertinent to see the contribution of lease finance to total industrial investment in A.P. It can be seen from Table 2.15 that there are ups and downs in the increase of productive capital from 1990-91 to 1996-97. Further, it is noticed that there is a constant increase in the industrial investment in AP during 1994-95 and 1995-96 indicating a growth of 9.62% and 9.93% respectively.

With respect to leased assets, a decreasing trend is observed from 1990-91 to 1992-93 representing the proportion of leased assets to A.P. industrial investment at 0.24% in 1990-91, 0.16% in

Table 2.15 : Proportion of Leased Assets of Select Lessee Companies to Total Industrial Investment in Andhra Pradesh

Years	*Industrial Investment at AP Level (Rs. lakhs)*	*Leased Assets by Lessees (Rs. lakhs)*	*Proportion of Leased Assets (in %)*
1990-91	1756485	4171	0.24
	—	—	
1991-92	1964682	3190	0.16
	(11.85)	(-23.52)	
1992-93	2470542	389	0.02
	(25.75)	(-87.81)	
1993-94	2526766	15735	0.62
	(2.28)	(3944.99)	
1994-95	2769918	22430	0.81
	(9.62)	(42.55)	
1995-96	3045090	28546	0.94
	(9.93)	(27.27)	
1996-97	3724636	44705	1.20
	(22.32)	(56.61)	
Total	18258119	119166	0.65

Note : (i) Figures in brackets indicate growth rates.
(ii) It is ascertained that the volume of leased assets of lessee companies cover more than 85% of total volume of leased assets of lessee companies in A.P.

Source: (i) For AP Level Industrial Investment – Reports on annual survey of industries – AP 1990-91 to 1996-97.
(ii) For Leased Assets: Field Survey.

1991-92, and 0.02% in 1992-93. Thereafter, the lease financing contribution to industrial finance in A.P. has substantially increased recording 39.45 times of increase from 1992-93 to 1993-94, but representing only 0.62% of total industrial finance in 1993-94. The contribution of lease financing to total industrial finance is recorded at 0.62% in 1993-94, 0.81% in 1994-95, 0.94% in 1995-96 and 1.20% in 1996-97.

Leasing is thus, an innovative financing device, helping the lessee's credibility, as the lessor looks at the worth of the asset and not merely the financial position of the lessee. As such, leasing promotes industrialisation by permitting industrial units to seek finance based on the value of the assets being acquired. That is why policy makers all over the world encouraged the development of leasing. Most developing countries have, by specific laws, allowed certain privileges and special protection for leasing companies and thus, thereby leasing has grown very impressively over the past decade. The global penetration of leasing, i.e., the extent of leased assets as a percentage of total industrial assets, is estimated at around 21% of all assets bought by industrial undertakings, which are actually bought by a leasing industry and passed on for use.[40] At the national level, the contribution of lease financing constitutes around 3% to 4% and at State level, on an average, it is around 1%. The most remarkable lessees in A.P. are Government owned enterprises. The contribution of leasing to State Electricity Board is notable. The APSEB has taken assets on lease worth Rs.1,10,500 lakhs as on 31-3-1997, representing 92.73% of all assets leased by select lessee companies in A.P.

Thus, industrial development plays an important role and contributes effectively to the overall growth of economy. It is sought as a means of general growth as well as a means of increasing employment opportunities and providing balance to regional development.

In order to achieve the overall growth of economy, there is a need on the part of the Government of AP to encourage Non-Banking Finance Companies in all respects. They have been helping in bridging the credit gaps in several sectors, which the traditional institutions are unable to fulfil. This in turn enables the State Government to accelerate the industrial growth and achieve the desired vision.

In conclusion, it may be inferred that leasing and finance companies in India, by and large, have had a fairly good time in terms of both business growth and profitability during the years 1990-91 to 1994-95. Most of the leasing and finance companies have augmented their financial resources to a significant extent through borrowings from banks and financial institutions, public deposits and, in a few cases through public issues.

A number of leading industrial houses have diversified into leasing, which in turn has resulted in too many players in leasing business.

The year 1991-92 has witnessed a sea change in the economic and industrial policies of the government. The industry has been freed from various controls and these developments set the tone for healthy growth of industry.

Thus, there was a boom period for financial services industry from 1991 to 1995 during which many finance companies have entered the field and witnessed an intense competition amongst the companies. There is a gloom period for NBFCs after 1996-97, and the companies continued to suffer liquidity crisis along with depressed capital market conditions. As such, the financial services industry virtually collapsed. However, a very few larger companies managed to stay afloat for some time, in hope of better times to come.

REFERENCES

1. Osamu Nagano, "The Basic Leasing Concept", *World Leasing Year Book*, Euromony Publications plc. Nester House, London, 1989, p. 48.
2. *Penguin Dictionary of Commerce*, 2nd Ed.
3. Cholamandalam Investments and Finance Company Limited: *Leasing Literature.*
4. Miller, M.H., and C.W. Upton, "Leasing, Buying and the Cost of Capital", *Journal of Finance*, 1976, pp. 761-86.
5. M.N. Kaura and G.L. Sharma, *Corporate Financing : Emerging Options*, Anmol Publications, New Delhi, 1991.
6. David G. Mayes and Clive S. Nicholas, *The Economic Impact of Leasing*, The Macmillan Press Ltd., Hampshire, London, 1988, p. 4.
7. *Op.cit.* p. 5.
8. Premlal Joshi, *Leasing Comes of Age – Indian Scene*, Published by M/s Prakash Kanna, Bombay, 1986, p. 71.

9. Sudhir P. Amembal, *et al., Equipment Leasing*, McGraw-Hill, Inc. New York, 1992.
10. *Lease Finance, Select Readings*, Published by Equipment Leasing Association, p.57.
11. K.V. Kamath, *et al., The Principles and Practice of Leasing, Lease Asia*, Croydon, England, 1990, p. 30.
12. B. Brahmaiah, *Lease Financing : Theory and Practice*, Himalaya Publishing House, Bangalore, 1998, p. 16.
13. *Ibid.*
14. *World Leasing Year Book*, Euromony Publications, Nestor House, London, 1988, p. 43.
15. *Ibid.*
16. *Ibid.*
17. Sudhir, P. Amembal, *et al., Equipment Leasing – A Complete Hand Book*, McGraw Hill, Inc. New York, (1992), p. 4.
18. Tom Clark, *Leasing Finance*, Euromony Publications Ltd. Nestor House, London, (1985) p. 1.
19. *Ibid.*
20. *Ibid.*
21. *Ibid.*
22. T.M. Clark, *Leasing* , McGraw Hill Book Company Ltd. , London, 1978, pp. 3-4
23. *Report on Leasing in Emerging Markets*, Published by the World Bank, Washington, D.C., USA, 1996.
24. *World Leasing Year Book* – Euromony Publications, plc., England, 1996, p. 2.
25. *Ibid.*
26. *Op.cit.* p. 4.
27. *World Leasing Year Book*, Euromony Publications, plc. England, 1996. p. 2.
28. Farouk Irani, *Inside Leasing*, Tata McGraw Hill Publishing Co. Ltd., New Delhi, 1995.
29. *Ibid.*
30. *World Leasing Year Book 1996* – Euromony Publications, Nestor House, England, 1996.
31. Nabhi Kumar Jain (1995). *How to do Lease Financing and Hire Puchase Business,* Nabhi's Publications, New Delhi, p.11.
32. *RBI Report on Trend and Progress of Banking in India* 1985-86.
33. *The Economic Times*, Hyderabad, January 23, 1997.
34. *IDBI Report on Development Banking in India,* IDBI Tower, Mumbai (1996-97), p. 30.
35. *Industrial Directory of Andhra Pradesh*, 1996.
36. *Ibid.*
37. V. Hanumantha Rao, *et al.* (Ed), *Andhra Pradesh at 50 years*, Published by Data News Features, Hyderabad, p. 305.
38. *Ibid.*
39. *New Series on State Domestic Product, Andhra Pradesh 1993-94 to 1998-99*, Directorate of Economics and Statistics, Hyderabad, Govt. of A.P.
40. *Pre-budget Memorandum: 1997-98* by Association of Leasing & Financial Services Companies, Mumbai, 1997-98.

3

IMPACT OF POLICY FRAMEWORK ON LEASE FINANCING

The previous chapter discussed leasing business in India. This chapter examines the business environment influencing the growth and development of leasing industry of India in general and of Andhra Pradesh in particular. The aim of this chapter is to analyse Government policies and RBI Guidelines and their impact on lease financing business.

Leasing companies are treated as Non-Banking Finance companies (NBFCs) and are subject to overall discipline of the Reserve Bank of India. The unprecedented growth of NBFCs particularly the leasing companies, attracted all sorts of entrepreneurs ranging from top industrial houses to new chartered accountants, from banks and financial institutions to stock brokers. Though the NBFCs are registered under the Companies Act, they are also governed by the guidelines of the RBI as regards income recognition norms, capital adequacy requirements, public deposit mobilisation, etc. The leasing/finance companies engaged in merchant banking activities are further subject to scrutiny by the Securities Exchange Board of India (SEBI).

When the concept of Equipment Leasing grew and met with initial success, institutions offering leasing and other allied services increased in large number. But, there was an absence of long-term strategy or direction pertaining to the regulation of leasing companies/NBFCs. The absence of regulations in the beginning of leasing/financial services industry resulted in, at times, contradictory and ambiguous laws governing leasing/financial services. Unfortunately, the regulatory framework of properly defining financial services/leasing services has been slow in evolving.

The word "Regulation" connotes authoritative body of rules specifying details of procedure and conduct to be followed in accordance with such criteria as uniformity, efficiency, control, ethics, and legal considerations.[1]

The working of leasing, hire-purchase and other non-banking finance companies, except Housing Finance Companies (HFCs) is regulated and supervised by the Reserve Bank of India, whereas that of HFC is regulated and supervised by the National Housing Bank (NHB).

A non-disciplinary legal environment has helped the unprecedented growth of leasing industry in particular and financial services industry in general, during early eighties. As there is no specific law governing the leasing business in India, the general law made applicable to all leasing transactions.

The leasing industry came under the Government Regulations only in 1977. The Reserve Bank of India was entrusted with the task of regulating Non-Banking Financial Companies (NBFCs) codified in the form of directions popularly known as NBFCs (Reserve Bank) Directions, 1977. The main objectives of these regulations are: (i) to safeguard public interest; (ii) to enforce discipline in the growth and functioning of NBFCs; and (iii) to separate good companies from bad ones and viable companies from the unviable ones.

According to Reserve Bank Directions, 1977 contained in RBI Notification No. DNBC.38/DG (H)-77 dated June 20, 1977 as amended up to September 24, 1996, Non-Banking Companies are classified as follows:

Chart 3.1 : Classification of Non-Banking Companies

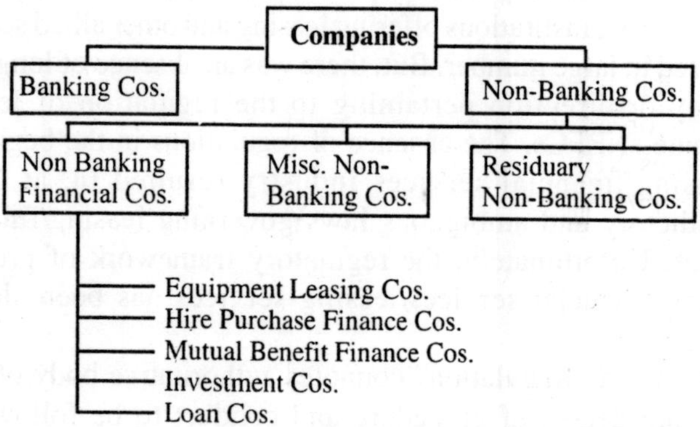

Non-Banking Financial Companies

"Non-Banking Financial Company" includes only non-banking institution, which may be a loan company or an investment company or a hire-purchase finance company or equipment leasing company or a mutual benefit financial company.

(i) "*Loan company*" means any company which is a financial institution carrying on as its principal business, the providing of finance whether by making loans or advances or otherwise for any activity other than its own but does not include an equipment leasing company or a hire-purchase finance company.

(ii) "*Investment Company*" means any company, which is a financial institution carrying on as its principal business, the acquisition of securities.

(iii) "*Hire Purchase Finance Company*" means any company which is a financial institution carrying on as its principal business the activity of hire-purchase transactions.

(iv) "*Equipment Leasing Company*" means any company, which is a financial institution carrying on as its principal business, the activity of leasing equipment.

(v) "*Mutual Benefit Financial Company*" means any company which is a financial institution notified by the Central Government under Section 620A of the Companies Act, 1956 (1 of 1956), e.g., Nidhis.[2]

Miscellaneous Non-Banking Company

Any company carrying on all or any of the following types of business: managing, conducting or supervising as a promoter, foreman or agent of any transaction or arrangement by which the company enters into an agreement with a specified number of subscribers that everyone of them shall subscribe to a certain sum in instalments over a definite period and everyone of such subscribers shall in his turn as determined by a lot or by auction or by tender or in such other manner as may be provided for in the agreement be entitled to the prize amount. Ex: Conducting any other form of Chit or Kuri.

Residuary Non-Banking Company

Any company which receives any deposit under any scheme

arrangements by whatever name called, in one lump sum or in instalments by way of contributions or subscriptions or by sale of units or certificates or other instruments, or in any other manner and which according to the definitions contained in the Non-Banking Financial Companies (Reserve Bank) Directions, 1977, e.g. Peerless Company.

As discussed above, RBI defined the Leasing and Hire-Purchase Companies as Non-Banking Finance Companies; and hence NBFCs include Leasing and Hire Purchase finance companies.

While banking in India even after the entry of the private sector has been closely regulated, non-banking financial companies (NBFCs) which perform para-banking functions have had unregulated functioning over the years. This contributed to a growth momentum far greater than that of the banking sector especially after liberalisation and reforms in the financial sector.

The ICICI, in a study on financial performance of NBFCs for the period 1991-92 to 1994-95, has stated that there has been a mushroom growth of NBFCs in India. From around 7000 companies in the early eighties, their number increased to more than 25,000 by the end of 1980s. By 1995, this figure rose to around 41,000. Of these, only 800 are registered with the RBI and are subject to some degree of control and supervision by the Apex Bank. A preponderant majority is virtually unregulated and is very small in the scale of operations. Further, the ICICI Report has stated that the NBFCs have shown improved performance in terms of profitability margins when compared to banks and manufacturing companies. According to the ICICI Report, "in 1994-95, the ratio of profits to total working funds was 4.73% for NBFCs as compared with 1.04% for private sector banks and 0.24% for public sector banks".

The findings are based on the audited results of a sample of 175 NBFCs while, in 1993-94 the total assets of NBFCs grew by 61.2%, the growth of total assets in 1994-95 was 71%. The total income of NBFCs rose by 69% and other income grew by 83.2% in 1994-95.

During mid-eighties, large number of NBFCs started participating in the intermediate process, thus blurring the distinction between banks and non-banks. Some of them recorded rapid growth in mobilisation and deployment of funds without concomitant care for the quality of the assets and the interest of the depositors. In these circumstances, the existing regulations (Reserve Bank of India –Directions – 1977) for NBFCs proved inadequate and it was realised that the regulatory framework needed to be strengthened.

Having discussed the classification of non-banking companies, it is now pertinent to analyse the regulatory measures for NBFCs in general and leasing companies in particular.

Norms for Lending to Leasing Companies

The Leasing Company plays the role of financier and must, therefore, have adequate finance for financing the capital asset. The sources of funds for leasing companies are equity capital, debentures, term loans from financial institutions and banks, public deposits, intercorporate deposits and retained earnings.

Another major source of funds for leasing companies is bank finance by way of short term and medium term loans, bill rediscounting and cash credits.

No norms/guidelines had been specified with respect to granting credit limits by the banks to leasing companies in the beginning of the leasing business in India. The banks were following their own practices in this regard without any uniformity in sanctioning the loans.

Recognising the concept of leasing as a necessary supplementary source for the development of corporate industry, the Banking Regulation Act was amended in 1984 to enable commercial banks to transact leasing business. In the same year, the Committee of Direction (COD) constituted by the Reserve Bank of India had set up a sub-committee headed by Mr. G.S. Dahotre, the Executive Director, Dena Bank to formulate norms for bank credit to hire-purchase and leasing concerns.

Accepting the recommendations of Dahotre Committee, the Reserve Bank of India issued guidelines in April 1988. The key elements of guidelines in regard to extension of bank credit to leasing companies are as follows[3]:

Maximum Limit for Bank Lending

Banks lending to leasing concerns are linked to their Net Owned

Funds (NOF) and it should not exceed 3 times their NOF, within the prescribed overall ceiling of 10 times their NOF for their total external borrowings including public deposits, debentures/bonds and borrowings from banks, financial institutions, etc., Later this limit was raised 4 times their NOF during 1993. NOF should be computed on the following basis:

NOF = Paid up capital + free reserves (including balance in share premium account, capital and debenture redemption reserve and any other reserve not being created for repayment of any future liability or for depreciation in assets or for bad debts or a reserve created by revaluation of the assets)

LESS

Accumulated balance of loss, balance of deferred revenue expenditure, as also other intangible assets. (Further investments in deposits with and loans/ advances due from subsidiary companies/affiliates is also to be deducted from NOF).

In 1995, the Banks were again advised by the RBI to adopt the following measures with immediate effect.[4]

1. Banks should not grant bridge loans or interim finance against capital/debenture issues and/or in the form of loans of a bridging nature pending, raising of long term funds from the market by way of capital, deposits, etc., to all categories of non-banking financial companies.
2. The extent up to which banks can extend finance to these companies has also been revised with immediate effect as indicated below:

   (a) Bank credit to loan and investment companies and residuary non-banking companies should not exceed twice the net-owned funds of such companies, as against the present limit of three times the net owned funds.
   (b) Banks credit to equipment leasing and hire-purchase finance companies will continue at the present level of four times the net-owned funds of such companies within

the overall ceiling of their borrowing up to 10 times their net owned funds; provided the company is predominantly engaged in Equipment Leasing/Hire-Purchase business. And at least 75% of the company's assets should belong to equipment leasing/hire-purchase business and 75% of the gross income is derived from those two types of activities. Regarding other equipment leasing and hire-purchase finance companies, the limit has been revised to three times the net owned funds from the present level of four times.

The above instructions are issued by the Reserve Bank of India in exercise of powers conferred by Sections 21 and 35A of the Banking Regulation Act, 1949 and came into force with immediate effect.

Nature of Bank Facility

Banks extend finance to leasing companies by way of cash credit facilities. In a few cases, credit has been extended by way of term loans and bill discounting. As bank credit to leasing concerns would primarily be against lease rentals receivable, the credit facility should appropriately be granted by way of cash credit facility alone. Loan drawing limits are regulated within the maximum permissible bank finance on the basis of overall drawing power calculated by applying the formula given at item (iii) below, with respect to individual lease transactions. The facility would be on a revolving basis, allowing leasing concerns to avail of the limit for other lease transactions once the liability/drawing limit for the earlier ones is liquidated or reduced.

(a) Computation of Maximum Permissible Bank Finance (MPBF)

Though the basic methodology of arriving at Maximum Permissible Bank Finance (MPBF) remains the same as in the case of other borrowers, MPBF for leasing concerns is arrived at on the basis of lease rentals due during the period of next 5 years alone. The MPBF may be calculated according to the formula given hereunder, wherein lease rentals due during the period of next five years alone are to be taken into account for the purpose of lending, as a measure of prudent policy:

$$\begin{bmatrix}\text{Outstanding}\\ \text{credit for a}\\ \text{period of 5 years}\\ \text{of each lease}\\ \text{transaction}\end{bmatrix} = \begin{bmatrix}\text{Lease rentals}\\ \text{due during}\\ \text{next 5 years}\end{bmatrix} \div \begin{bmatrix}\text{Total rentals}\\ \text{due under}\\ \text{the}\\ \text{transaction}\end{bmatrix} \times \begin{bmatrix}\text{Cost of the asset}\\ \text{leased}\end{bmatrix}$$

Note : Lease rentals fallen due but not collected should be excluded while computing "outstanding credit".

(b) Drawing Limit

While the outstanding credit is to be arrived at on the basis of the above formula, the drawing power within the credit limit has to be worked out by deducting margin, which should not be less than 25%. It is to be ensured that while the initial disbursement does not exceed 75% of the cost of the leased asset (the margin is 25%), the overall drawing power is to be worked out by applying the following formula to ascertain the entitlement with respect to each lease transaction and aggregating the said amounts:

$$\begin{bmatrix}\text{Drawing}\\ \text{Limit}\end{bmatrix} = \begin{bmatrix}\text{Lease}\\ \text{rental}\\ \text{receivable}\\ \text{for the}\\ \text{next 5}\\ \text{years}\end{bmatrix} \div \begin{bmatrix}\text{Total lease}\\ \text{rentals}\\ \text{receivable}\\ \text{for the}\\ \text{entire lease}\\ \text{period}\end{bmatrix} \times \begin{bmatrix}\text{75\% of the}\\ \text{cost of the}\\ \text{leased}\\ \text{asset}\end{bmatrix}$$

Note : Lease rentals fallen due but not collected are to be excluded while computing "outstanding credit".

Example:

Cost of assets = Rs.20,00,000

Period of lease = 8 years

Lease rentals per annum. = Rs. 4,80,000

Lease rentals due under the transactions i.e., in 8 years = Rs. 38,40,000

Lease rentals due during next 5 years = Rs. 24,00,000

Lease rentals fallen due but not collected = Nil (Presuming it to be a fresh lease).

$$\begin{bmatrix}\text{Outstanding}\\ \text{credit for a}\\ \text{period of 5}\\ \text{years}\end{bmatrix} = 24{,}00{,}000 \div 38{,}40{,}000 \times 20{,}00{,}000 = 12{,}50{,}000$$

Rs.12,50,000 represents outstanding credit for a period of 5 years for the above lease transaction.

$\begin{bmatrix}\text{Drawing}\\\text{Limit}\end{bmatrix}$ = 24,00,000 ÷ 38,40,000 × 15,00,000 (75% of the cost) = Rs. 9,37,500 (this figure constitutes less than 50% cost of the asset)

Here the bank considers rentals due for the next five years (i.e., Rs. 24,00,000) and decides outstanding credit; the amount over the 5 years will be financed by the leasing concern itself. This loan facility is to be within three times of the NOF of leasing company and within the overall ceiling of 10 times to NOF.

However, the Reserve Bank of India clarified in its circular that funds raised from financial institutions need not be included in the ceiling for bank lending. That is, Banks can grant limits upto four times or three times or (two times, as the case may be) of NOF irrespective of the quantum of finance raised by leasing companies from financial institutions.

Supervision and Follow up

As in the case of other advances, it is to be ensured that measures are taken for effective post disbursement supervision. Keeping in view the special features of the leasing business, the following statements are considered appropriate for monitoring purposes:

(a) Banks are to obtain a monthly statement of leased assets and rental receivables within next six months and beyond next 60 months.

In addition, banks are to obtain the following statements:

(b) On a quarterly basis, a summarised position of current assets and current liabilities indicating the estimates at the beginning of each quarter and actuals of the quarter that ended.

(c) On a half-yearly basis, operating and funds flow statements, which contain data relevant to leasing business.

General Guidelines

(a) The leasing concerns are required to maintain a stipulated current ratio of 1.33 not only on the basis of estimates/ projections, but also on the basis of actuals as per the latest audited balance sheet.

(b) The leasing concerns are to furnish their statutory auditor's/ chartered accountant's certificate about the figure of "outstanding credit under lease agreements" to the financing banks.

(c) Some leasing concerns might be entering into secondary and even third lease agreements with respect to the same equipment. However, bank finance is to be restricted only to full payout leases, i.e., those leases where the cost of asset is fully recovered during the primary lease period itself.

(d) The borrowing concerns are required to route the receipt of lease rentals only through the accounts with the lending bank.

(e) Diversion of bank finance obtained for leasing business to other lines of activities, like manufacturing, investment, etc. is to be prevented.

(f) Banks reserve the right to inspect the leasing concerns' records and books of account periodically to ensure the correctness of information furnished by them.

Borrowings Arrangements with More than one bank

In case of borrowers enjoying fund based credit limits aggregating Rs.5 crores or more, from more than one bank, consortium arrangements are obligatory. Compliance of the same is to ensure necessary co-ordination. In other cases where multiple banking arrangements exist without formal consortium, there is a need for periodical exchange of information, amongst the financing banks. Such financing banks are, therefore, to meet at least once in three months to exchange information and share their experience with regard to borrowers' accounts and also to review overdues, if any.

Companies engaged in both Leasing and Hire Purchase Business

In case of a borrowing concern engaged in leasing and hire purchase business, banks are to assess its credit requirements separately for the two categories of business as per the respective norms.

In the absence of any lending norms till now, it is likely that some leasing concerns might have credit limits and/or outstanding in excess of their eligibility for credit in terms of the norms now prescribed. It is therefore necessary for banks to undertake a review of the credit limits sanctioned to all leasing concerns in excess of Rs. 10 lakhs, with a view to verify whether the limits sanctioned to them are within the prescribed norms. Where the limits/outstandings are in excess of borrowing concern's entitlement, banks are to hold discussions with it immediately and ensure that they conform to the present guidelines within a period, not exceeding two years.

VIII. Financing will be available from banks neither for sale and lease back transactions nor for second hand assets.

IX. Finance will not be available from the banks for lease over a period of 60 months, even though leasing companies may enter into such lease agreement/transaction.

The above conditions/guidelines govern the basic credit policy framework within which banks have to lend to the leasing companies.

The reporting requirements that have been stipulated involve a monthly drawing power/limit statement, quarterly statement and half-yearly statement cause undue administrative burden on the leasing companies.

With the above guidelines or norms, it is possible for the larger well established leasing companies to borrow without any significant impact on their drawing power in relation to their total limits. But it is difficult for smaller leasing companies to raise sufficient funds by way of bank borrowings.

Now it is pertinent to examine the ratio of bank borrowings to net worth at all India level and A.P. level and the impact of RBI restrictions on bank borrowings.

Table 3.1 reveals that the finance companies were not able to mobilise bank borrowings, which are not even equal to their net owned funds from 1991-92 to 1996-97, and hence there is no impact of RBI restrictions pertaining to banks lending to leasing and finance companies.

Similarly, it is relevant to examine the ratio of bank borrowing and institutional borrowing to net worth of finance companies to

Table 3.1 : Bank Borrowings to Net Worth

Years	*1991-92*	*1992-93*	*1993-94*	*1994-95*	*1995-96*	*1996-97*
Bank Borrowings (Rs. crores)	262.62	706.64	1358.98	3448.75	4829.0	4989.3
Net Worth (Rs. crores)	404.19	1054.65	2678.57	6912.60	8932.3	9532.0
Ratio of Bank Borrowings to Net Worth	0.65	0.67	0.51	0.50	0.54	0.52
No. of copanies	34	67	157	320	216	216

Source : Compiled from India Lease Year Books – 1995-96 and 1996-97, published by Association of Leasing and Financial Services Companies, Bombay.

find out whether these companies have borrowed three times to their NOF after considering the institutional borrowings.

Table 3.2 : Bank Borrowings and Institutional Borrowings to Net Worth

(Rs. crores)

Years	*1991-92*	*1992-93*	*1993-94*	*1994-95*	*1995-96*	*1996-97*
Bank Borrowings	262.62	706.64	1358.98	3448.75	4829.00	4989.30
Institutional Borrowings	208.58	554.40	969.94	1945.83	4491.30	4934.20
Total	471.20	1261.04	2328.92	5394.58	9320.30	9923.50
Net Worth	401.19	1054.65	2678.57	6912.60	8932.30	9532.00
Ratio	1.17	1.20	0.87	0.78	1.04	1.04
No. of Cos.	34	67	157	320	216	216

Source: Compiled from India Lease Year Books – 1995-96 and 1996-97, published by Association of Leasing and Financial Services Companies, Bombay.

Table 3.2 provides the data pertaining to bank borrowings and institutional borrowings from 1991-92 to 1996-97. It can be observed from the table that the total borrowings of banks and institutional borrowings of finance companies in India put together have not exceeded even two times their net owned funds. Further, these borrowings were reduced to less than one time their net owned funds in 1993-94 and 1994-95, in which period the volume of leasing has been substantially increased. This essentially means the leasing companies have mobilised more from other sources of finance like public deposits compared to bank and institutional loans.

It is now proposed to examine the State level status of leasing companies pertaining to bank and institutional borrowings.

Table 3.3 : Borrowings of Select Leasing Cos. in Andhra Pradesh *(Rs.lakhs)*

Year	*1990-91*	*1991-92*	*1992-93*	*1993-94*	*1994-95*	*1995-96*	*1996-97*
Bank Borrowings	3727.5	4045.7	4960.6	4847.2	11020.5	8488.4	10010.5
Institutional Borrowings	1415.5	1136.3	966.9	1884.3	3014.1	2543.9	2284.2
Total	5143.0	5182.0	5927.5	6731.5	14034.6	11032.3	12294.7
Net Worth	3252.30	4127.60	5684.80	8453.7	12956.9	15668.4	15010.4
Ratios:							
(i) Bank Borrowing to Net Worth	1.2	0.98	0.87	0.57	0.86	0.54	0.67
(ii) Bank and Institutional Borrowings to Net Worth	1.58	1.26	1.04	0.79	1.08	0.70	0.8

Source: Calculated from Annual Reports of Select Leasing Companies.

Table 3.3 provides aggregate data pertaining to borrowings from banks and financial institutions of select leasing companies. A similar trend is found in AP (Table 3.3) as compared to National level of bank and institutional borrowings (Tables 3.1 and 3.2). The restrictions imposed by the RBI from time to time on banks lending to finance/leasing companies have not affected the bank/ institutional borrowings of leasing companies in anyway, as these companies have not borrowed even two times the net owned funds from 1990-91 to 1996-97. It can be deduced that, these companies have greatly depended on other kind of borrowings like public deposits.

Tables 3.4 and 3.5 provide data pertaining to bank borrowings and institutional borrowings and networth, companywise. It is observed that no company was able to mobilise either bank borrowing or institutional borrowing two times its net owned fund. The bank borrowings and institutional borrowings have shown a similar trend for select lessor companies except LFL, which recorded a ratio of less than one for all years from 1990-91 to 1996-97 (Table 3.5). No company exceeded two times its NOF from 1990-91 to 1996-97. Though the finance companies were allowed to borrow funds from banks three times their NOF, no company was able to borrow from banks.

Table 3.4 : Bank and Institutional Borrowings and Net Worth (Companywise)

(Rs. lakhs)

Lessor Cos		*1990-91*	*1991-92*	*1992-93*	*1993-94*	*1994-95*	*1995-96*	*1996-97*
NFL	B.B.	2032.60	2132.60	3049.49	2094.0	5853.6	4489.3	5925.3
	I.B.	515.7	420.80	405.24	957.0	1485.9	1115.2	803.6
	N.W.	1210.9	1461.9	2144.0	3577.9	4572.3	5815.7	5781.7
PPL	B.B.	168.90	425.50	545.90	925.20	2363.6	2044.6	2251.7
	I.B.	–	–	141.90	575.1	1200.5	972.6	1164.1
	N.W.	133.0	261.2	514.5	1345.6	3922.5	5344.9	5568.3
LFL	B.B.	39.60	81.40	162.3	80.5	130.9	75.2	120.0
	I.B.	–	–	–	–	–	–	22.1
	N.W.	837.8	876.7	891.1	890.9	972.2	1018.3	1007.7
DCL	B.B.	304.5	309.5	606.8	1076.8	2042.8	1249.7	1027.2
	I.B.	474.1	463.6	321.8	348.7	327.6	423.2	294.4
	N.W.	280.2	582.4	648.1	1055.4	1310.6	1341.9	1350.4
MWL	B.B.	859.5	807.4	302.6	364.9	308.8	308.8	350.5
	I.B.	425.7	252.0	98.1	3.5	–	–	–
	N.W.	623.6	693.4	1223.9	1310.9	1955.2	1955.2	1370.2
SCFSL	B.B.	322.3	289.4	292.9	305.6	320.8	320.8	335.8
	I.B.	–	–	–	–	–	–	–
	N.W.	166.8	252.1	263.2	272.9	224.2	192.5	(-67.7)

B.B. = Bank Borrowing. I.B. = Institutional Borrowing. N.W.= Net Worth

Source : Annual Reports of Select Lessor companies.

Table 3.5 Bank Borrowing and Institutional Borrowing to Net Worth(Companywise)

Lessor Cos		*1990-91*	*1991-92*	*1992-93*	*1993-94*	*1994-95*	*1995-96*	*1996-97*
NFL	BB/NW	1.7	1.5	1.4	0.6	1.3	0.8	1.2
	IB/NW	0.4	0.3	0.2	0.3	0.3	0.2	0.2
	BB&IB/NW	2.1	1.8	1.6	0.9	1.6	0.98	1.2
PPL	BB/NW	.1.3	1.7	1.1	0.7	0.6	0.4	0.4
	IB/NW	0	0	0.3	0.4	0.3	0.2	0.2
	BB&IB/NW	1.3	1.7	1.4	1.1	0.9	0.6	0.6
LFL	BB/NW	0.05	0.09	0.2	0.1	0.1	0.1	0.1
	IB/NW	0	0	0	0	0	0	0.02
	BB&IB/NW	0.05	0.09	0.2	0.1	0.1	0.1	0.10
DCL	BB/NW	1.1	0.5	0.9	1.0	1.6	0.9	0.8
	IB/NW	1.7	0.8	0.5	0.4	0.3	0.3	0.2
	BB&IB/NW	2.8	1.3	1.4	1.4	1.8	1.2	1.0
MWL	BB/NW	1.4	1.2	0.3	0.3	0.2	0.2	0.3
	IB/NW	0.7	0.4	0.1	0.01	0	0	0
	BB&IB/NW	2.1	1.6	0.4	0.3	0.2	0.2	0.3
SCFSL	BB/NW	1.9	1.2	1.1	1.1	1.4	1.7	(-4.9)
	IB/NW	0	0	0	0	0	0	0
	BB&IB/NW	1.9	1.2	1.2	1.1	1.4	1.7	(-4.9)

Source : Calculated from the Annual Reports of Select Lessor Companies.

Since SCFSL incurred huge losses in 1996-97, the borrowing ratio turned out to be negative. Consequently, the operations of leasing were stopped and diversified into other real estate activities.

The RBI later opened gates for capital movement between the providers and users through its circular dated April 15, 1997[5] pertaining to the lending by Banks to NBFCs. The RBI has removed the ceiling limit on Bank credit to NBFCs, which have complied with the Reserve Bank's requirements of registration, credit rating, and prudential norms and have been so certified by the Reserve Bank. Banks have been advised to assess and provide such NBFCs' need-based finance in accordance with the credit policy laid down by them. With respect to NBFCs, which have not complied with the requisite requirements, and Residuary Non-Banking Companies (RNBCs), the limits of Bank Finance prescribed would, however, continue to apply.

Mr. G.S. Garg, Managing Director of Lloyds Finance, was less than enthusiastic about the provision when he said, "For the big NBFCs, it does not make a difference. The removal of ceiling has no meaning, as banks have not been lending to the NBFCs even to the extent of their NOFs. If the NOF is Rs. 250 crore, nobody has been able to get Rs. 500 crore. The changes may help only to smaller NBFCs. The RBI has over the years created a picture where NBFCs are considered suspect", he said.[6]

The Government of India appointed a High Level Committee under the chairmanship of Sri M. Narasimham, to examine all aspects relating to the structure, organisation, functions and procedures of the financial system. Banking is the most important constituent of the financial system. NBFCs were officially recognised as a constituent of the Indian Financial System.

The Narasimham Committee, in its Report of November 1991, recommended, *inter alia*, the introduction of prudential norms and guidelines to govern the functioning of financial companies. These prudential guidelines, among other things, relate to capital adequacy, provisioning against doubtful debts, adherence to sound accounting and financial policies, disclosure requirements and valuation of assets.

As a follow-up of these recommendations and recognising the growing importance of financial services industry, RBI appointed a working group on financial companies in May 1992 under the Chairmanship of Dr. A.C. Shah to make an in-depth study of the role of NBFCs and suggest regulatory and control measures to ensure healthy growth of these companies.

Shah Committee

The Shah Committee after an in-depth study on financial companies, submitted its "Report", within a span of 4 months, in September 1992 and made a number of recommendations.

The important recommendations of the working group are[7]:

(i) Category-wise classification of financial companies may be abolished and uniform regulations may be applied to all financial companies.
(ii) Regulatory attention by the RBI may be confined to companies with net owned fund of Rs.50 lakhs and above.
(iii) With regard to new financial companies, entry norms should be minimum net owned fund of Rs. 50 lakhs.
(iv) The regulations may be directed to the assets side such as limit on credit concentration, prohibiting investments in undesirable activities, etc.
(v) Capital adequacy standards may be laid down based on the risk assessment of assets and credit conversion factors for off-balance sheet items.
(vi) The "exempted" category of deposits should be removed and all deposits should constitute a part of deposits.
(vii) Prudential norms for income recognition, transparency of accounts and provisions for bad and doubtful debts may be prescribed.
(viii) Setting up of Self-Regulating Organisation (SRO).

The RBI, in a circular issued in April 1993, announced its acceptance of the above major recommendations of the Shah Working Group and declared its intention to implement them in phases so as to avoid difficulties in the transition. As mentioned earlier, in April-May 1993, RBI brought inter-corporate loans/deposits (ICDs), within the definition of "deposit" allowing the acceptance of ICDs up to a limit of two times the NOF by a financial company subject to the period of such deposits not exceeding 12 months. RBI also brought the deposits accepted by private limited NBFCs from their shareholders within the purview of 'regulated' deposits. Furthermore, NBFCs which, according to the revised definition of NOF suggested by Shah Working Group, had NOF of Rs. 50 lakhs and above were asked to register themselves with RBI.

In June 1994, the second phase of the implementation of the Shah Working Group recommendations, the RBI issued guidelines on prudential norms for the registered NBFCs.

The 1994 RBI Guidelines on Prudential Norms for Registered Non-Banking Financial Companies (NBFCs)

The RBI, in June 1994, issued detailed guidelines to be followed by the registered NBFCs having net owned funds of Rs. 50 lakhs and above, on prudential norms for income recognition, transparency of accounts, provisioning for bad and doubtful debts, capital adequacy and concentration of credit/investments. The basic elements of prudential norms are mentioned below.[8]

Income Recognition, Asset Classification, and Provisioning and Accounting Norms

The income recognition, asset classification and provisioning norms are also known as "Prudential Accounting Norms". According to these norms, a finance company should not record income which is merely a book profit by resorting to a practice like crediting lease instalment or hire-purchase instalment to profit and loss account irrespective of its chance of recovery and booking the same as income or by not making provisions towards lease rental instalment/hire-purchase instalment losses because of recovery problem.

Income recognition can be done on "Accrual Basis" or on "Cash Basis". Under "accrual basis," lease rental instalment/hire-purchase instalment due is recognised as income, and the profit and loss account is credited with due instalment amount irrespective of the due amount is received or not. Under "cash basis", instalment amount is recognised as income, only when it is actually recovered from the lessee or hirer. The profit and loss account is not credited with the instalment amount until such amount is actually received.

Prior to the introduction of Income Recognition norm, finance companies followed accounting on "accrual basis" in spite of its poor record of recovery. As per the new norms, applicable from 31-3-1995, NBFCs are prohibited from recognising income on accrual basis.

Income past due but not received within a period of six months is not to be booked till such time income is actually received. Assets are to be classified as non-performing based on recovery record. Interest on non-performing assets should not be booked as income if such interest has remained outstanding for more than six months, on and from March 31, 1995.

Asset Classification

For the purpose of income recognition, NBFCs are directed by the RBI to classify their assets (i.e., loans, advances, or lease or hire-purchase asssets or any other forms of credit facilities) into four groups, viz.,

- (i) Standard Assets or Performing Assets,
- (ii) Substandard Asssets or Non-Performing Assets,
- (iii) Doubtful Assets, and
- (iv) Loss Assets.

The asset by which, no default in repayment of principal or payment of interest is perceived and which does not disclose any problem nor carry more than normal risk attached to the business is called *Performing* or *Standard Assets*. The arrears of such instalments do not exceed 180 days as at the end of a financial year. No provisioning is required for such assets.

The asset whose interest and/or instalment of principal are overdue for a period of six months on and from March 31, 1995 is called *Sub-Standard* or *Non-Performing Asset (NPA)*.

An asset classified as NPA, remains for a period not exceeding two years. In case overdues have been rescheduled, it can be classified as standard asset only after satisfactory payment for at least two years as per rescheduled terms. Until then, it will be classified as a non-performing asset as it was, before reschedulement.

A credit facility which has remained as NPA for a period

exceeding two years is to be treated as a *"Doubtful Asset"*, i.e., a term loan, or a leased asset, or a hirepurchase asset or any other asset, which remains a NPA for a period exceeding two years. An asset, which is classified as a 'Doubtful Asset' cannot be upgraded to a standard asset by just reschedule of principal and interest and thereby notional wiping out the overdue. After rescheduled, the account will continue to be classified as doubtful asset for at least two years. Only after satisfactory payment for two years as per rescheduled terms, it can be classified under Standard Asset.

An asset, which is adversely affected by a potential threat of non-recoverability due to either erosion in the value of security or non-availability of security or due to any fraudulent act or omission on the part of the borrower, is treated as Loss Asset. The identification of a loss asset can be made by the bank or by internal/ external auditors or by RBI auditors.

Provisioning Requirements against Non-Performing Assets

After considering the time lag between an account becoming doubtful of recovery, its recognition as such, the realisation of the security and the erosion over time in the value of security charged. Every NBFC shall make provision against sub-standard assets, doubtful assets and loss assets as provided hereunder w.e.f. 31-3-1995:

(a) Loans, Advances, Bills purchased and discounted and other Credit Facilities including Lease and Hire Purchase Assets

The provisioning requirement with respect to loans, advances and other credit facilities including bills purchased and discounted shall be as hereunder:

Status as	**Provision Required**			
(i) Sub-standard Assets	A general provision of 10% of total outstandings shall be made.			
(ii) Doubtful Assets		Period for which the asset has been considered as doubtful	Provision required on secured portion (as % of secured portion)	Provision on unsecured portion (as % of unsecured portion)
	(a)	Up to 1 year	20	100
	(b)	1 to 3 years	30	100
	(c)	More than 3 years	50	100
(iii) Loss Assets (i.e., an asset considered uncollectible)	Entire loss asset should be written off. If the asset is permitted to remain in the books, 100% of the total outstanding amount should be provided for.			

(b) Lease and Hire-purchase Assets

The provisions pertaining to lease and hire purchase assets are changed w.e.f. January 1998 as mentioned below (up to January 1998 the above mentioned provisions stand good)[9]:

(i) Where any amount of lease rental or hire charges are overdue up to 12 months	No provision is required.
(ii) Where any amount is overdue for more than 12 months but up to 24 months	(a) Entire amount of overdues taken to the credit of profit & loss account in earlier years shall be provided for; and (b) In addition, provision shall be made at not less than 10% of the net book value.
(iii) Where any amount is overdue for more than 24 months but up to 36 months	(a) entire amount of overdues taken to the credit of profit & loss account earlier shall be provided for; and (b) in addition, provision shall be made at not less than 50% of the net book value.
(iv) Where any amount is overdue for more than 36 months	(a) entire amount of overdues taken to the credit of profit & loss account earlier shall be provided for; and (b) in addition, provision shall be equivalent to un provided balance of net book value (i.e. 100%).

Impact

According to the reports of Association of Leasing and Finance Services (ALFS), the expenditure for 216 finance companies had increased by 52.8% in 1996-97 in comparison with the previous year due to the increase in provision for non-performing assets (NPAs) and increased operating costs.[10]

In Andhra Pradesh, the provision against NPAs, i.e. substandard/doubtful/loss assets of select lessor companies is as follows:

Table 3.6 : Provision against NPAs of Select Lessor Companies in Andhra Pradesh

(Rs.lakhs)

Year	*1990-91*	*1991-92*	*1992-93*	*1993-94*	*1994-95*	*1995-96*	*1996-97*
Provision for NPA	–	17.92	62.14	206.90	280.02	514.12	1107.06
Increase in %	–	–	246.76	232.95	35.34	83.60	115.33

Tables 3.6 and 3.7 reveal that the leasing companies have been reeling under the impact of Non-Performing Assets. The total

volume of NPAs of Select Lessor Companies increased substantially during 1995-96 and 1996-97 recording Rs. 514.12 lakhs and Rs. 1107.06 lakhs respectively. It means that almost all companies are facing recovery problems particularly from 1995-96.

As per the Annual Reports, almost 60% of total NPAs of select lessor companies are in the category of doubtful and loss assets. Of the six leasing companies two companies MWL and SCFSL — were badly affected, recording Rs. 214.08 lakhs (out of total NPAs of Rs. 230.05 lakhs) and Rs. 138.87 lakhs as loss assets (out of total NPAs of Rs. 162.69 lakhs) respectively in 1996-97 (Table 3.7). Most of NPAs of NFL are related to substandard and doubtful debts. However, the NPAs are higher in the case of NFL recording 556.39% in 1996-97, compared to other companies (Table 3.7).

Table 3.7 : Provision for Substandard/Doubtful/Loss Assets (NPAs) of Select Lessor Companies (Company-wise Analysis)

(Rs. lakhs)

Companies	*1990-91*	*1991-92*	*1992-93*	*1993-94*	*1994-95*	*1995-96*	*1996-97*
NFL	–	–	–	–	74.96	83.27	546.58
						(11.09)	(556.39)
PPL	–	–	–	–	–	11.53	28.99
							(151.43)
LFL	–	–	17.40	56.86	21.54	15.66	63.78
				(226.78)	(-62.12)	(-27.30)	(307.27)
DCL	–	7.06	13.16	10.52	44.18	32.21	74.97
			(86.40)	(–20.06)	(319.96)	(-27.09)	(132.75)
MWL	–	–	–	–	–	211.83	230.05
							(8.60)
SCFSL	–	10.86	31.58	139.52	139.52	159.62	162.69
			(190.79)	(341.79)	(0)	(14.41)	(1.92)
Total	–	17.92	62.14	206.90	280.02	514.12	1107.06
			(246.76)	(232.95)	(35.34)	(83.60)	(115.33)

Note: Figures in brackets represent percentage of increase/decrease over previous year.
Source : Annual Reports of Select Lessor Companies.

Capital Adequacy

The Basic Committee on Banking Regulations and supervisory practices appointed by the Bank of International Settlements (BIS) has prescribed certain 'capital adequacy standards' to be followed by commercial banks and these standards have been accepted by several countries for implementation. The BIS seeks to measure capital adequacy as the ratio of capital to risk weighted assets. It has prescribed weightages for different categories of assets, which include certain off-balance sheet items as well.[11]

For the purpose of calculation of capital, BIS has classified capital into two broad categories, namely Tier 1 capital consisting of share capital and disclosed reserves and Tier 2 capital consisting of undisclosed reserves, general provisions, hybrid capital and subordinated debt. Intangible assets and losses will be deducted from Tier-1 capital. It has also been indicated that Tier-2 capital should not exceed Tier-1 capital.[12]

The Reserve Bank of India has extended the same procedure to the Non-Banking Finance Companies. As per the RBI Guidelines of 1994 on prudential norms, the registered NBFCs have to maintain minimum level or more of capital to risk weighted assets. The minimum capital adequacy ratio should be of 6% by March 21, 1995 and 8% by March 31, 1996. Further, it is revised in January 1998[13] increasing a minimum capital ratio consisting of Tier-1 and Tier-2 capital which shall not be less than—

(i) 10% on or before March 31, 1998, and
(ii) 12% on or before March 31, 1999, of its aggregate risk weighted assets and of risk adjusted value of off-balance sheet items.

The degrees of credit risk expressed as percentage weightages have to be assigned to balance sheet assets and the value of each asset/item requires to be multiplied by the relevant risk weights to arrive at the risk adjusted value of assets. The aggregate shall be taken into account for reckoning the minimum capital ratio. The risk-weighted assets are to be calculated as weighted aggregate of funded items.[14] The risk adjusted value for some important assets is calculated by taking assumed figures as outstanding loan and multiplied by Risk Weight as detailed hereunder (See Table 3.8).

Here Risk Weighted Assets are Rs. 200 crores against the balance outstanding assets of Rs. 310 crores, and hence the capital adequacy requirement is 6% by March 31, 1995, and 8% by March 31, 1996, 10% by March 31, 1998 and 12% on or before March 31, 1999.

For example: Capital Adequacy requirement of 8% is Rs. 200 × 8÷100 = 16 crores

Table 3.8 : Calculation of Risk Adjusted Value of Assets (RAVA)

(Rs.crores)

Type of Asset	*Balance outstanding*	×	*Risk weight*	*RAVA*
Cash	10	×	0	0
Investment in Govt. Securities	90	×	0	0
Investment in Shares	40	×	100%	40
Stock in hire	60	×	100%	60
Inter-corporate loans	20	×	100%	20
Bills discounted	30	×	100%	30
Assets leased out	50	×	100%	50
Interest due on Govt. Securities	10	×	0	0
	Total = Rs. 310			Rs. 200

The Non-Banking Finance Companies were directed to achieve a capital adequacy (i.e., a ratio of capital to risk weighted assets and off-balance sheet items) of minimum 6% by March 1995 and 8% by March 1996, and 10% by March 1998, and this information had to be filed with RBI. With the extension of prudential norms, first to the banking system, and then to the financial institutions and finally, to NBFCs these norms now cover the entire financial sector.

According to the Annual Reports, the NFL, as per RBI norms, has maintained the capital adequacy ratio comfortably at 14% as of March 31, 1995 as against the minimum of 6%, 12.86% by March 1996 and 13.32% by March 1997 as against the minimum of 8% required as per RBI norms.

As a result of conversion of 10,35,000 cumulative convertible preference shares of Rs.100, each into equity shares of Rs.10 each at a premium of Rs. 26 per share in 1996-97, the total equity capital increased to Rs. 17.23 crores as on May 31, 1997.

With a view of infusing Tier-2 capital to meet the gearing norms and enhance capital adequacy, the NFL proposes to offer redeemable preference shares of Rs. 100 each for Rs. 20 crores. As a result, the net worth will be substantially augmented.

The PPL has been following sound accounting policies and no difficulty is envisaged in adhering to the capital adequacy ratio. The company has maintained the capital adequacy at 9% in 1994-95, 9.5% in1995-96 and 11% in 1996-97.

As LFL has traded on thick equity over the study period, constituting the capital base of more than 60% in the total capital structure, the capital adequacy ratio is higher than a minimum rate prescribed by the RBI.

The DCL company has adhered to the Prudential Norms for Income Recognition, asset classification and provisioning prescribed by the Reserve Bank of India. The company has achieved a capital adequacy of 19% against a minimum of 6% prescribed by RBI for the year March 1995. For the years 1995-96 and 1996-97, the company maintained the capital adequacy at 11% and 9% respectively which are above the minimum capital adequacy prescribed by the RBI.

According to the Annual Reports, MWL and SCFSL have also maintained capital adequacy ratios as prescribed by the RBI up to 1994-95. Later these companies incurred losses. As such the capital got eroded resulting in the fall of capital adequacy ratio and further, these two companies have not complied with the maintenance of Statutory Liquidity Ratio (SLR) of deposits.

The capital adequacy ratio for NBFCs has been significantly raised to check excessive leveraging of funds by the NBFCs. As against the existing 8%, NBFCs have had to achieve a capital adequacy ratio of 12% by March 31, 1999. A healthy capital adequacy ratio will enhance NBFCs ability to absorb risks inherent in their business.

Concentration of Credit/Investment

The main elements of concentration of credit/investment are as mentioned below,[15]

It is prudent that no NBFCs shall,

(i) lend to:
- (a) any single borrower exceeding 15% of its owned funds, and
- (b) any single group of borrowers exceeding 25% of its owned funds.

(ii) invest in:
- (a) the shares of another company exceeding 15% of its owned fund; and
- (b) the shares of single group of companies

(iii) lend and invest (loans investments taken together) exceeding

(a) 25% of its owned fund to a single party and

(b) 40% of its owned fund to a single group of parties

Any loan granted and investment made by the NBFC in excess of the ceilings specified above and existing on the date of commencement of these directions, shall be brought down by the NBFC as per the repayment schedule in due course.

Acceptance of Public Deposits by Leasing Companies

The very survival of finance companies depends upon the mobilisation of funds from various sources. Public deposits are one of the important sources of funds for leasing companies.

Acceptance of deposits by Non-Banking Financial Companies (NBFCs) is governed by Non-Banking Financial Companies (Reserve Bank) Directions, 1977, issued under Sections 45J, 45K, and 45L of Reserve Bank of India Act.

The NBFCs (Reserve Bank) Directions – 1977, amended from time to time as and when required, stipulate the maximum rate of interest NBFCs can pay on the deposits, maximum brokerage and also maintenance of a minimum percentage on liquid assets.[16]

Hire-purchase finance companies and equipment leasing companies have been allowed to accept a higher level of deposits (including borrowings from banks and financial institutions) up to 10 times their net owned funds (NOF) in view of their role in capital formation. The other NBFCs have been allowed to accept deposits (excluding borrowings from banks and financial institutions) up to 25 and 15 per cent of their NOF from public and shareholders respectively.

The Reserve Bank of India amended the earlier Non-Banking Financial Companies (Reserve Bank) Directions, 1977 effective from 28-3-1989. The main provisions are that the minimum period for acceptance of deposits by leasing companies was raised from 6 months to 24 months, while the maximum period extended from 36 months to 60 months. The payment of interest is totally prohibited if deposits are withdrawn prior to this minimum period.

During 1991-92, the Reserve Bank of India allowed 1% increase in the interest rate ceiling from 14% to 15% applicable to public deposits accepted by NBFCs. The growth in business volume through accelerated public deposits, particularly for the established companies in India as a whole and for companies in AP in particular.

Further, the reduction in Bank interest rates, helped NBFCs to mobilise higher public deposits with higher interest rates. Because of the unprecedented magnitude of the security scam, which hit the company in April-May 1992, the public lost the confidence to invest their hard-earned money in securities and diverted their funds to invest in NBFCs resulting in the increase of public deposits. It is now proposed to discuss the credit rating and its impact on acceptance of public deposits.

Credit Rating and Public Deposits

Historically, the concept of 'Credit Rating' traces its beginning to the early 1900s, when John Moody founded Moody's Investor Services to provide an opinion on the risk of the rail road bonds floated by private entrepreneurs in the United States of America. From this early focus on railroad bonds, the scope was extended to cover bonds of industrial companies, municipal entities and even Sovereign nations.[17] As such the concept of credit rating, after some decades spread to other countries and is becoming a universal phenomenon.

The concept of credit rating originated in India with the starting of the credit rating agency known as Credit Rating Information Services of India Limited (CRISIL) in 1988. In India, there are three credit rating agencies recognised by the Securities Exchange Board of India (SEBI). They are:

1. The Credit Rating and Information Services of India Limited (CRISIL): It was the first rating agency set up in Bombay, which commenced its operations in January 1988.
2. Investment Information and Credit Rating Agency of India Limited (ICRA): It was established in 1991 with its head office in Delhi.
3. Credit Analysis and Research Limited (CARE): It was set up in Bombay in 1993. In addition to the above mentioned three,

the foreign US Credit Rating Agency Duff and Phelps opened its credit rating agency in India in August 1996 with its headquarters at Calcutta.

A credit rating is an objective assessment of a borrower's credit quality in terms of business and financial risk. It is an opinion regarding the degree of certainty of timely payment of interest and principal on the debt instrument to which the rating has been assigned.

The rating is expressed in alphabetical symbols that convey in a summarised manner the rating agency's current opinion about the future risks to an investor about investing in a particular debt obligation.

Presently the debt instruments being rated are : (1) Debentures, (2) Fixed Deposits, (3) Commercial Papers. Credit rating does not apply to equity shares.

Before credit rating is introduced, investors usually determined their choice of investment largely on the basis of advice from brokers or on the basis of name recognition rather than on an analysis of credit worthiness. With the large-scale proliferation of companies in India, especially NBFCs, it is not possible for either brokers or investors to know every issuer or company. A credit rating agency would then greatly help the investor with credit rating information, which in turn will help him/her to take a proper decision to invest his/her money. The credit rating will also be helpful to the borrowing company as a marketing tool for highly rated companies, which mobilise funds at reduced interest costs. Both individual and institutional investors would be able to make investment decisions based on these ratings.

The Rating agency studies the business of NBFC in detail before rating. Various factors like diversification of income sources, risks in the various business segments and past trends in business volumes are analysed. The client base of the company and the nature of assets for which funds are advanced, etc., are examined. Only after careful analysis rating will be awarded to a company.

Thus, the capability of a company to raise/mobilise funds from the public or market depends mainly on the credit rating it gets for its debt instrument. The rating symbols of these three rating agencies are as follows:

Chart 3.2 : Rating Symbols of CRISIL, ICRA and CARE Debt

Debt Category	Debt Instrument	Rating Symbols CRISIL	ICRA	CARE	Remarks
1. Long term Instrument	Debentures, Bonds, Preference Shares	AAA	LAAA	CAREAAA	Highest Safety
		AA	LAA	CARE AA	High Safety
		A	LA	CARE A	Adequate Safety
		BBB	LBBB	CARE BBB	Moderate Safety
		BB	LBB	CARE BB	Inadequate Safety
		B	LB	CARE B	Risk Prone
		C	LC	CARE C	Substantial Risk
		D	LD	CARE D	Default
2. Medium Term Instrument	Fixed Deposits	FAAA	MAAA	CAREAAA	Highest Safety
		FAA	MAA	CARE AA	High Safety
		FA	MA	CARE A	Adequate Safety
		-	-	CARE BBB	Moderate Safety
		FB	MB	CARE BB	Inadequate Safety
		FC	MC	CARE C	Risk Prone
		FD	MD	CARE D	Default
3. Short Term Instrument	Commercial Paper	P-1	A-1	PR-1	Highest Satefy
		P-2	A-2	PR-2	High Safety
		P-3	A-3	PR-3	Adequate Safety
		P-4	A-4	PR-4	Risk Prone
		P-5	A-5	PR-5	Default

Note : The suffixes "+" (plus) or "–" (minus) signs are used with rating symbols to indicate the comparative positions of the instruments within the group covered by the symbol.

Source : Field survey.

In 1996, the Reserve Bank of India approved the name of Duff and Phelps Credit Rating India Private Limited, Calcutta (DCR India) as one of the Credit Rating Agencies for rating the non-banking financial companies. The minimum investment grade credit rating to be assigned by this company has been fixed at "Ind BBB". The registered NBFC can now approach the DCR India for rating fixed deposits and the aforesaid minimum level of credit rating will be acceptable to the Reserve Bank of India. This is the fourth rating agency approved by the RBI in this regard.[18]

A registered NBFC shall get itself rated for fixed deposits as specified below (Directions para 5A).[19]

(i) (a) Such a company having net owned funds below Rs. 2 crore, may get the rating before March 31, 1996.

(b) Such a company having net owned funds of Rs. 2 crores and above, shall get the rating before March 31, 1995.

(ii) Every such company shall obtain fresh rating at least once a year and copy of the rating should be sent to the Reserve Bank along with half-yearly return.

The minimum Credit Rating shall be as follows:

Chart 3.3 : Minimum Credit Rating

Name of the Agency	*Minimum Rating*
(a) The Credit Rating Information Services of India Ltd. (CRISIL)	FA –
(b) Investment Information and Credit Rating Agency of India Limited (ICRA)	MA –
(c) Credit Analysis and Research Ltd. (CARE)	CARE BBB (FD)
(d) Duff and Phelps Credit Rating India Private Limited (DCR India)	Ind BBB

The minimum credit rating of the above mentioned symbols indicate "adequate safety" to meet the fixed deposit debt obligations as and when they mature.

Liberalisation/Rationalisation Measures (Guidelines) for NBFCs: Announced by RBI on 24 July, 1996

The Reserve Bank of India announced wide-ranging liberalisation and rationalisation measures for Non-Banking Finance Companies (NBFCs) on 24 July, 1996. Central to these measures is the freeing of the fixation of interest rate and the removal of the ceiling on the quantum of deposits for NBFCs which fully comply with the Reserve Bank of India's directions and guidelines. The relevant and important points are mentioned below.[20]

NBFCs are segregated into two main categories, namely (i) Equipment Leasing and Hire Purchase Companies and (ii) Loan and Investment Companies.

Following the RBI announcement, registered NBFCs, which comply completely with RBI directions, credit rating requirement and prudential norms, are freed from interest rate regulations on deposits, and there would be substantial relaxation on the quantum of deposits that can be mobilised by them. The ratio of liquid assets to deposits of such companies would be brought down from 15% to 12.5%.

Before availing the concessions, the companies should get a specific certificate from RBI, which is granted for ratifying the requirements of credit rating and prudential norms.

Those companies which are registered with RBI but do not comply with credit rating requirement and/or prudential norms would continue to be subject to deposit rate regulations, and where compliance is clearly lacking, the relevant companies would face a curtailment of ceilings on the amount of deposits they can mobilise. Unregistered companies are further curtailed in their deposit mobilisation.

Earlier to these guidelines, the finance companies were offering 15% interest on public deposits plus a hefty brokerage depending on the company's need for funds. RBI prescribed prudential norms for all financial companies with owned funds of Rs. 50 lakhs and above. These companies are required to register with RBI and attain a satisfactory credit rating to enable them to raise deposits. They are required to submit half-yearly returns, giving data on the compliance with the prudential norms.

Regarding Equipment Leasing and Hire-Purchase Finance Companies which *comply with the credit rating requirement and the specified prudential norms, the overall ceiling on deposits is abolished.* The sub-limit for Inter-Corporate Deposits (ICDs), not exceeding a period of 12 months, however, remains at the existing level of two times the NOF.

For registered EL and HP companies which meet either Credit Rating requirement or the prudential norms, the overall, ceiling on deposits is retained at 10 times the NOF and the sub-limit for inter-corporate deposits, not exceeding a period of 12 months remains at the existing level of two times the NOF.

Regarding registered EL and HP companies, which meet neither credit rating requirement nor prudential norms, the overall ceiling on deposits is reduced from 10 times to 7 times the NOF. However, the sub-limit for inter-corporate deposits not exceeding a period of 12 months remains at the existing level of two times to the NOF.

The overall ceiling on deposits would stand reduced to 5 times the NOF with respect to unregistered EL and HP companies.

Further, the sub-limit for inter-corporate deposits not exceeding a period of 12 months is also brought down from the existing two times to equivalent of NOF for these companies.

Date of Effect of the Changes

The removal of the overall ceiling on deposits is effective only from the date of receipt of certificate by the eligible individual EL and HP Company from the RBI. The reduction of the limit, wherever, applicable (for those companies which could fulfil the prudential norms) was *effective from July 25, 1996.* The companies, which have accepted deposits in excess of revised limits are given time up to six months, to reduce the excess amount of deposits. They should not renew maturing deposits or take any new deposits until they comply with the new stipulations.

Liquid Assets

Liquid assets requirement of the registered hire-purchase finance, equipment leasing, loan and investment companies which comply with the credit rating requirement and the prudential norms specified by the RBI is reduced to 12.5% from the existing 15% of deposits. This relaxation is applicable from the date of receipt of the RBI certificate by the individual company. Of the reduced liquid assets to 12.5%, the stipulation is that at least 10% of the deposits be maintained in the form of Central and/or State Government Securities or Government guaranteed bonds.

All other hire-purchase finance, equipment leasing and registered loan and investment companies which have failed to comply with the credit rating requirement or prudential norms shall continue to maintain the liquid assets at 15% of the deposits and in the manner as hitherto.

During the year 1996, Madras based unregistered finance firms, Devi Gold House and GNS Nidhi managed to garner huge amounts almost overnight from depositors by offering high interest rates of 36% after taking into account various upfront incentives and commissions.[21] Later, these companies just disappeared.

Similarly, during the year 1996, the strategy adopted by the CRB group to divert funds and make everything appear hunky dory which compares well with a tale of utter corruption and deceit.[22] The CRB (Chain Roop Bansali) Mutual Fund (MF) picked up equity and debt in several unlisted and private companies of the CRB group, especially promoted by CRB capital markets through the private placement route. Since these companies did not conduct any business the money invested in them through the Mutual Fund was siphoned off by the promoters. Care was also taken by the CRB to seal the loopholes. To do away with investments in the books of CRB MF, the company sold these shares back to CRB caps and others, though in reality, there was no transactions whatsoever.

The Central Bureau of Investigation (CBI) registered a case on the night of 20-5-1997 against CR Bansali who defrauded Rs. 57 crores from the SBI. According to CBI report, of May1996, Mr. C.R. Bansali approached the SBI to grant them the facility of encashment of interest warrants and warrants of repayments of the principal amount issued by the company through different SBI branches.

Initially, CRB capital markets deposited an amount of Rs. 50 lakhs and a list of refund orders warrants and also prefunded the accounts till February 1997. Thereafter, the management stopped doing so. However, it continued issuing warrants which were encashed through various SBI branches resulting in a debit balance of Rs. 1,72,72,021.95 as on March, 1997 in the SBI accounts. The SBI officials did not issue instructions to stop CRB from encashing warrants.[23]

Thus, the unprecedented spurt in the number of NBFCs and their rates of interest much in excess of the currently prevailing rates by violating RBI regulations, giving rise to the fear that it was only a matter of time before the inevitable happens – the company folds up and the depositors are left high and dry, being taken for a ride by companies largely outside the framework of monetary regulation.

The number of NBFCs, which stood at 7,063 in 1981, increased to 25,083 in 1991 and further to 39,454 in 1995.[24] According to the RBI figures, there are around 42,000 companies in the NBFC sector by 1997.[25] Of these, 32,000 are loan and investment companies.

Most of these are holding companies of promoters of large business groups. Under the RBI amended Act, the holding companies are classified as investment companies under the NBFC umbrella. There are 1,749 Equipment Leasing and Hire Purchase Finance Companies, miscellaneous non-banking companies are 7,455 and residual non-banking companies are 540.[26]

The RBI (Amendment) Act of 1997 reduced the minimum net owned fund criterion for NBFCs from earlier proposed Rs. 50 lakhs to Rs. 25 lakhs to get them registered with RBI. NBFCs with NOF of less than Rs. 25 lakhs have been given three years time to reach that level.

Those failing to apply for registration will have to close down their businesses in terms of the amendments to the RBI Act, 1934. On January 9, 1997 the Government promulgated an ordinance, that was later ratified into a Law, giving the Central Bank sweeping powers over the NBFCs.[27]

Prohibitory orders preventing acceptance of public deposits are issued to those companies not applying to registration. These companies will have to repay all deposits they took, on the dates they mature, and dispose of their assets accordingly. The Act empowers RBI with powers to cancel registration of NBFCs on varied grounds and power to penalise for any shortfall.

The RBI regulation stipulated that all finance companies had to apply for registration by July 8, 1997 or close the business. According to the RBI directives, if an NBFC defaults, payment of public deposits, the promoters face a mandatory imprisonment for 1 to 5 years and pay an unspecified fine. The defaulter also has to pay a fixed penalty of Rs. 5 lakh and Rs. 25,000 for each day of violation.

The Reserve Bank of India plans to make its on-going registration process for non-banking finance companies as difficult and elaborate as the licensing process for banks. The idea was to ensure that only really good companies get access to public deposits.[28]

Now, any NBFC offering more than 15% interest can be considered to be a genuine one in the sense that it is complying with the prudential norms and credit rating. On the other hand when an NBFC which offers only 15% interest and continues to give higher cash incentives on the sly, can be identified as a rule-breaker.

About 15 NBFCs have received certificates from RBI, which gives them freedom to fix interest rates on deposits.[29] Nagarjuna Finance Ltd., which is selected for the study, is one among them.

Reliance capital came out with a five-year fixed deposit scheme with an interest rate of 20% on public deposits (Table 3.9). PAL credit and Capital has offered 17.5% on one years deposits, 18% on 2 years deposits, and 18.5% on three years deposits. The rates are compounded on quarterly basis and, as a result, the deposit amount gets doubled in 46 months. Mahindra and Mahindra Financial Services offered 20% interest rate on one year deposits. This is the highest rate offered on one year deposits by the NBFCs. The Sundaram Finance Ltd., which has Rs. 600 crore deposits from 5.7 lakh depositors, offered 16% interest on one year deposits. The highest deposit rates offered by some NBFCs are given in Table 3.9.

These stipulations and directives will go a long way in sending a clear message to the entire industry to shape up or to close the business.

Registration

Till the end of December 1995, the RBI received 1,555 applications from all categories of finance companies for registration, of which 745 companies with NOF of Rs. 50 lakhs were registered. As on the end of September 1995, 255 companies had filed the half-yearly prudential norms returns, and 121 had filed credit rating reports with the RBI.[30]

After the amendment of RBI Act in January 1997 reducing the NOF to Rs. 25 lakhs from Rs. 50 lakhs, massive 37,487 applications flooded the bank. Of them, 8802 were found eligible for registration on the basis of minimum NOF of Rs. 25 lakhs. Of this 7555 were granted registration, of which, only 584 have been permitted to accept public deposits. As many as 1030 applications have been rejected. Calcutta topped the list with 461 rejections followed by Delhi (229), the South was better off with the number of rejections in Chennai at 29, Bangalore 27, Hyderabad 51 and Thiruvananthapuram 12.[31]

Table 3.9 : Deposit Rates Announced by NBFCs during 1996

Name of Company	*Credit Rating Agency*	*Credit Rating Grade*	*Years*	*Interest Rate (%)*			*Grading Remarks*
				Monthly Compound	*Quarterly Compound*	*Yearly Compound*	
1. Birla			1	16.5	17.0	18.0	
Global			2	17.0	17.5	18.5	Adequate
Finance	CRISIL	FAA	3	17.5	18.0	19.0	Safety
Ltd.			4	17.5	18.0	19.0	
			5	17.5	18.0	19.0	
2. Kotak			1	16.5	17.0	18.0	
Mahindra			2	17.0	17.5	18.5	
Highest							Highest
Finance	CRISIL	FAAA	3	17.5	18.0	19.0	Safety
Ltd.			4	17.5	18.0	19.0	
			5	17.5	18.0	19.0	
3. Sunda-			1	–	16.0	–	
ram			2	–	16.5	–	Highest
Finance	CRISIL	FAAA	3	–	17.5	–	Safety
Ltd.			4	–	17.5	–	
			5	–	17.5	–	
4. Laxmi			1	–	16.0	–	
General			2	–	16.5	–	Highest
Finance	CRISIL	FAAA	3	–	16.5	–	Safety
Ltd.			4	–	17.5	–	
			5	–	17.5	–	
5. Apple			1	–	17.0	–	
Credit			2	–	17.5	–	
Corp. Ltd.	ICRA	MAAA	3	–	18.0	–	Highest
			4	–	18.0	–	Safety
			5	–	18.5	–	
6. PAL			1	–	17.5	–	
Credit &			2	–	18.0	–	Highest
Capital Ltd.	CRISIL	FAA	3	–	18.5	–	Safety
			4	–	19.0	–	
			5	–	19.5	–	
7. Reliance			1	–	15.0	–	
Capital	CARE	CARE	2	–	16.0	–	Highest
Ltd.		AAA	3	–	18.0	–	Safety
			4	–	19.0	–	
			5	–	20.0	–	
8. 20th			1	–	–	16.5	
Century	CRISIL	FAAA	2	–	–	17.5	Highest
Finance			3	–	–	18.0	Safety
Corp. Ltd.			4	–	–	19.0	
			5	–	–	19.0	
			1				
9. Lloyds	CARE	CARE	2	–	16.5	–	
Finance Ltd.		AAA	3	–	17.0	–	Highest
			4	–	18.0	–	Safety
			5	–	19.0	–	

Source : Business Line—dated September 29, 1996.

During the process of registration, the RBI found that a major problem in the effective functioning of NBFCs was the low level of NOF. As many as 28,676 companies had NOF below Rs. 25 lakhs. This low capital base reduced their ability to withstand cyclic fluctuations and provide a minimum level of service to depositors and borrowers.[32]

Even some of the larger ones had a weak bottom-line. A CMIE study of 72 NBFCs during 1997-98 indicated that though the aggregate profit after tax increased by 4.3 per cent over the previous year, it was mainly accounted for by the top quartile of 18 NBFCs. The study indicated that only small number of NBFCs with a good scale of operations, professional business approach and relatively sound balance sheet were in a position to survive the crisis.[33]

Non-Banking Financial Companies (Reserve Bank) Directions, 1998

The Reserve Bank of India having considered it necessary in the interest of public, in exercise of the powers conferred by sections 45J, 45K, 45L and 45MA of the RBI Act, 1934, and in supersession of the earlier Directions contained in Notification No. DNBC 38/ DG (H)-77 dated June 1977 issued Directions on January 1998. These Directions came to be known as the "Non-Banking Financial Companies (Reserve Bank) Directions, 1998". They come into force with effect from January 2, 1998. These guidelines prescribe to stricter prudential norms—prescribed for income recognition, provisioning for NPAs, maintenance of liquid asset ratio, and direct linking of quantum of deposit acceptance to credit rating of the finance company. The basic elements of Directions – 1998 are as follows[34]:

Definition of Public Deposits

Unsecured Debentures issued to the shareholders by a public limited company and to the general members of public, by private and public limited companies, are included in the definition of public deposit. However, unsecured debentures issued to other companies and banks/all India Financial Institutions are not public deposits. The money received in trust by NBFC is not an exempted borrowing since 2nd January, 1998 and hence forms part of the public deposit. However, other borrowings by way of ICDs, security deposits from employees (provided these are deposited in an account with a bank or a post office, jointly with the employee) and advance receipt of lease or hire-purchase instalments are exempted borrowings and hence fall outside the purview of public deposits.

Money received by a private limited NBFC from relatives and friends of Directors who are not its shareholders, is public deposit. In case of public limited companies, the deposits received from shareholders are also public deposit.

Restrictions on Acceptance of Deposits by NBFCs

On and from January 2, 1998:

1. No company registered under the Companies Act should commence or carry on business of a non-banking financial company without obtaining a Certificate of Registration from the RBI and without having minimum NOF of Rs. 25 lakhs.
2. No NBFC having net owned fund of Rs. 25 lakhs and above shall accept public deposit unless it has obtained minimum credit rating for fixed deposits from any one of the approved Credit Rating Agencies at least once a year and a copy of the rating is sent to the RBI along with return on prudential norms.
3. In the event of upgrading or downgrading of the credit rating of any NBFC to any level from the level previously held by the NBFC, it shall within 15 working days of its being so rated inform, in writing, of such upgrading/downgrading to the Reserve Bank of India.

Thus the RBI prescribed the ceiling limits for acceptance of Public deposits for NBFCs as mentioned hereunder[35]:

Chart 3.4 : Ceiling Limits

Level of Credit Rating	*Ceiling on public Deposits (As multiple of NOF)*	
	Leasing/Hire-Purchase Cos.	*Loan/Investment Companies*
A A A	3 times	2 times
A A	2 times	1 time
A	1 time	0.5 time

Regularisation of the Deposits accepted earlier and held in excess of the Ceiling

Where equipment leasing company or hire purchase finance company or a loan company or an investment company holds, at the commencement of the business on January 2, 1998, public deposits in excess of the appropriate ceiling, which it is entitled to accept under the provisions of these directions, it shall,

(i) with immediate effect stop accepting public deposits and/or renewing of such maturing deposits, as the case may be; and
(ii) reduce such excess deposits by repayment or otherwise, by December 31, 1998 or such further period as may be extended by the Reserve Bank of India.

Ceiling on the Rate of Interest

On and from January 2, 1998, no NBFC shall invite or accept or renew public deposit on a rate of interest exceeding 16%. Interest may be paid or compounded at rests which shall not be shorter than monthly rests.

Payment of Brokerage

On and from January 2, 1998 no NBFC shall pay to any broker on public deposits collected by or through him,

(i) brokerage commission, incentive or any other benefit by whatever name called, in excess of 2% of the deposit (not per annum) so collected;
(ii) expenses by way of reimbursement on the basis of relative vouchers/bills produced by him, in excess of 0.5% of the deposits so collected.

RBI modified certain Regulations for NBFCs

Detailed regulations were issued on 2nd January, 1998 to ensure orderly functioning of the NBFCs and for the protection of interests of the depositors. Since then, in response to suggestions received from various sections, RBI has held detailed consultations with leading NBFC Associations, financial experts and other professionals in order to solve any genuine problems that might arise in the implementation of the guidelines issued on January 2, 1998. In the light of these discussions, the RBI has modified some of these regulations.[36]

The ceiling on public deposits as a multiple of net owned fund (NOF) with respect to the equipment leasing and hire-purchase finance companies was enhanced. The revised limits are as mentioned below:

Chart 3.5 : Revised Limits

Level of Rating	*Existing Limits*	*Enhanced Limits*
	(As a multiple of NOF)	
AAA	3 times	4 times
AA	2 times	2.5 times
A	1 time	1.5 times
Minimum Investment Grade, i.e., A - (CRISIL & ICRA) BBB (CARE) BBB – (DCR India)	NIL	0.5 time

Note: The requirement of rating and level of public deposits for loan and investment companies remains unchanged.

Unrated and underrated (rating below the minimum investment grade) equipment leasing and hire-purchase companies with NOF of Rs. 25 lakhs and above can accept deposits up to 1.5 times of their NOF or Rs. 10 crores, whichever is less, *provided their capital reserve and adequacy ratio (CRAR) is 15% or above.*

Thus, as per the relaxed guidelines of January 2, 1998 the equipment leasing and hire-purchase finance companies carrying a minimum investment grade rating of A-, BBB, BBB- (Chart 3.5) are also allowed to access public deposits. In addition to this, the limits for these companies have also been enhanced. Equipment leasing and hire purchase finance companies which carry 'AAA' rating can raise public deposits up to 4 times their NOF as against three times earlier, while 'AA' rated companies can raise now up to 2.5 times their NOF, "A" rated firms up to 1.5 times their NOF. The minimum investment grade companies can mobilise deposits equal to 0.5 time their NOF.

Time for Regularizing the Excess Deposits

In order to take care of the mismatches in cash flows, the time limit for repayment/regularisation of excess deposits has been extended. Accordingly, NBFCs having excess public deposits as on January 1, 1998 have been allowed time to repay/regularise excess deposits till December 31, 2000 subject to the condition that 1/3rd of excess deposit is repaid by the end of December every year so that the entire excess deposit is repaid/regularised by 31st December, 2000. During this period of 3 years, the equipment leasing companies and hire-purchase finance companies which are rated investment grade or above and loan and investment companies which have rating of "A" or above are allowed to accept/renew public deposits subject to the above stipulations of reduction of the excess deposits by 1/3rd each year.

Impact of Credit Rating on Public Deposits in India

Many Non-Banking Financial Companies in the country, and many major companies have been affected by Reserve Bank regulatory regime forcing them to reduce their public deposit holding according to credit rating system. All NBFCs, which were affected have started returning deposits in excess of the tight credit rating grade system prescribed by the RBI. Since a number of companies have exceeded their deposit limit, they would find it hard to make the repayment of public deposits.

Some of the major companies which were affected are:

1. Tata Finance Limited (TFL) with current net owned funds of Rs. 234 crore and a credit rating of "AA+" is eligible to have public deposits up to Rs. 468 crores. As a result, it was to refund deposits worth Rs. 482 crores as its current deposit base is at Rs. 950 crores.[37]
2. Birla Global Finance Ltd. (BGFL), was to refund about Rs. 155 crores as it is entitled to accept deposits up to Rs. 40 crores with net owned funds of Rs. 40 crores and a rating of "AA–".[38]
3. Sundaram Finance Ltd. (rated 'AAA') which could accept public deposits more than Rs. 1200 crores is now forced to

restrict it to Rs. 776 crores.[39] It has already suspended taking fresh deposits.

4. Nargarjuna Finance Ltd. with a credit rating of AA+ and with public deposit resource base of Rs. 422 crores is forced to stop accepting deposits and reduce the deposits.[40]

According to estimates, about Rs. 5,000 crores of depositors' money and a fund base of Rs. 20,000 crores have gone down the drain. Investors' complaints are pouring into the Company Law Board (CLB) office, the RBI, at Police Stations, and Civil Courts.[41]

The Lloyds Finance Limited, the Rs. 300 crores finance arm of the Lloyds group and one of the top five NBFCs, has decided to withdraw from all fund-based activities—such as leasing, hire-purchase, finance business, etc. The company focuses various financial products—Car finance, Credit Cards, Insurance, government tax-free bonds, UTI schemes, fixed deposits of highly rated companies and public issue of equities/debt instruments. The decision follows a continuing lull in the capital markets and general tightening in fund-based businesses.[42]

Some NBFCs, instead of following RBI's stringent regulations opted to change their names to Infotech companies to exploit the boom in that sector. The Stock Exchanges have circulated the names of such listed firms, which have moved away from the financial sector to Software and other areas. Some of these companies are[43]:

	Original Name	*New Avtar*
1.	Aashley Finance	Sunstar Software Systems
2.	Arihant Housing Finance	LCC Infotec
3.	Century International Finance	Cyberspace Infotec Systems
4.	Chicaco Gutore Finance	Chicaco Software
5.	Fiduciary Capital & Finance	Omega Infotech
6.	India Lessor Ltd.	India Infotec and Software
7.	Hareshri Finance	Nexcen Softech
8.	Kolar Securities	Kolar Infotech
9.	Shalibadra Securities	Shalibadra Infotech
10.	Prashant Global Finance	Silicon Valley Infotech
11.	SRG Finance & Managing Services	Proline Software & Financial
12.	Sunrise Securities	Websity Infosystem
13.	Synergy Credit Corporation	Synergy Login

A study by Prime, a leading public issue monitor, shows that atleast 40 companies mostly NBFCs, have been rechristened to software activity.

Most of these companies' scripts are recording handsome gains in the secondary market and the possibility of several of these companies raising capital through public or rights issues is quite strong.

Prithvi Haldea of Prime says: " Unfortunately, history seems to be repeating itself. Some unscrupulous promoters are again exploiting an euphoric condition to defraud investors".[44]

Impact of Credit Rating on Public Deposits in Andhra Pradesh

The data pertaining to credit rating of select lessor companies for two years, i.e., 1996-97 and 1997-98 are presented in Chart 5.6 and data pertaining to public deposits and net worth and their ratio of select leasing companies are presented in Tables 3.10 and 3.11.

As discussed above, the freedom to raise public deposits without any limit on the quantum and interest rate made available by RBI during 1996-97 to certified NBFCs was withdrawn on 2nd January 1998. The regulatory framework reintroduced a cap on acceptance of deposits and interest rates by linking the deposit limits to a factor of NOF based on the level of credit rating.

Chart 3.6 reveals that all select lessor companies are badly exposed as far as credit rating is concerned. Out of 6 companies, the credit rating for 4 companies such as NFL, PPL, LFL and MWL were downgraded in 1997-98 from 1996-97. As far as DCL is concerned, the ICRA has retained the credit rating of MAA – indicating "high safety" for the fixed deposits schemes. One company SCFSL, has not got the credit rating assessed or revised from FA which was rated in 1995-96. This company's net worth shows a negative of Rs. 67.74 lakhs (Table 3.10) and it stopped accepting public deposits and stopped doing leasing business. Further it intends to diversify to other areas of real estate business besides intensifying recovery of existing debts.

The NFL was badly affected by the new regulatory framework of linking the public deposit limits to a level of credit rating as it is a highly geared company representing 6.5 times public deposits to its net owned fund constituting Rs. 378.15 crores of public deposits and Rs. 57.81 crores of net owned funds in 1996-97 (Table 3.10). This company, with a credit rating of "A+" is eligible to have public deposits of around Rs. 58 crores and is required to repay Rs.320 crores over the three-year period, i.e., on or before end of December, 2000 with a one-third reduction to be achieved by the end of each year.

Consequently, the company announced suspension of acceptance of public deposits from 2nd January 1998 and started repaying public deposits on maturity. Against the minimum reduction of one-third of total deposits to be achieved by 31 December, 1998, the deposit maturity claims were met by 30 June, 1998 and another Rs.125 crores, including unsecured bonds, were paid by the end of August 1998.[45] Deposits at the close of the year 1998 were Rs. 191 crores down from Rs. 378 crores in 31 March, 1997 (Table 3.10).

The company's response to the regulatory framework, is a testimony of NFL's commitment to service depositors, who have always stood by in the hour of need.

As at the close of the year 1998, the net worth stood augmented by Rs. 30 crores by conversion of cumulative convertible preference shares of Rs. 100 each into equity shares of Rs.10 each at a premium of Rs. 26 per share and increase of reserves.

The capital adequacy ratio of the NFL Company is 13.32% against the minimum of 8% required in 1996-97 and 19.40% against the stipulated minimum of 10% on 31st March, 1998.

However, the NFL is in the process of diversification for better business prospects. The company entered the crop protection business by acquiring an undertaking comprising the manufacture and sale of insecticides at Ethakota, Andhra Pradesh from Vijayalaxmi Insecticides and Pesticides Limited, an Associate company of the Nagarjuna Group, for a total consideration of Rs. 6.84 crores with effect from 1st April, 1997.

The PPL has achieved a growth of over 81% in the public deposits mobilisation. As at the end 31-3-1997, the public deposits stood at Rs. 93.18 crores as against Rs. 48.12 crores on 31-3-1996. The company has complied with the regulations framed by the RBI with regard to the capital adequacy and rating of fixed deposit schemes. In view of the recessionary conditions in the country and the general slow down in industrial growth, the operations of the company were not encouraging. The Credit Rating Agency of ICRA has downgraded the credit rating of PPL from MAA – in 1996-97 to MD in 1997-98, which indicates default in payment of deposits to deposit holders (Chart 3.6). Consequently, the company has got into liquidation process in November 1999 as some deposit holders sought legal action.

As far as LFL is concerned, the Credit Rating Agency, CRISIL, has downgraded the credit rating for the fixed deposit schemes from "FA" to "FB" on 17-2-1998 (Chart 3.6).

The new RBI regulation stipulates that no equipment leasing company or hire-purchase finance company having NOF of Rs. 25 lakhs and above but not having the minimum prescribed credit rating shall accept or renew public deposit. Here the credit rating of LFL is downgraded to "FB" (inadequate safety) on 17-2-1998 from minimum rating of "FA" in 1997 (Chart 3.6). Consequently, the company, in conformity with RBI regulations, has stopped accepting or renewing the public deposits and started making repayment of deposits. At the end of the year 1997-98, the public deposits stood at Rs.118.28 lakhs as against Rs.144.72 lakhs in 1996-97 (Table 3.10). Table 3.11 reveals that the LFL has not mobilised deposits even equal to its net owned funds from 1990-91 to 1996-97. Had the company got the minimum credit rating of "FA" in 1998, the company would have been allowed to continue to accept the public deposits.

On account of the adverse business conditions, the company has not taken up new business in the field of leasing or hire-purchase and concentrated in a limited way in the area of short term financing, viz., inter-corporate deposits, and bill discounting. Further, the company is actively pursuing recovery of outstanding amounts and has initiated legal proceedings against some lessee parties who have defaulted in payment of lease/hire-purchase instalments.

The stiff regulatory measures of January, 1998 sounded almost like a death knell to some NBFCs. The instruments rated "D" are either in default or likely to be in default soon. Such deposits are extremely speculative and the return of these deposits may be realised only on re-organisation or liquidation. The public deposits of PPL and MWL were rated "D" by credit rating agencies of ICRA and CRISIL respectively (Chart 3.6) in 1997-98.

The deposits of PPL are almost two times to its net owned funds and that of MWL are equal to its net owned funds (Table 3.11). But as the ratings of these companies were downgraded to "D" (Chart 3.6), these companies were forced to stop accepting or renewing deposits. Further, the operations of these companies are severely affected on account of recovery problems in particular and unfavourable market conditions prevailing in the NBFC sector in general. On complaint against these companies by the depositors, they are closed at present and the liquidators were appointed to settle the accounts.

Chart 3.6 : Credit rating of Fixed Deposits of Select Lessor Companies (1996-97 and 1997-98)

Lessor Cos.	*Credit Rating Agency*	*Credit Rated Years*	*Credit Rating Grades*	*Remarks*
NFL	CARE	1996-97	CARE A+	High Safety
		1997-98	CARE A	Adequate Safety
PPL	ICRA	1996-97	MAA-	High Safety
		1997-98	MD	Default
LFL	CRISIL	1996-97	FA	Adequate Safety
		1997-98	FB	Inadequate Safety
DCL	ICRA	1996-97	MAA-	High Safety
		1997-98	MAA-	High Safety
MWL	CRISIL	1996-97	FB+	Inadequate
		1997-98	FD	Safety Default
SCFSL	CRISIL	1995-96	FA	Adequate Safety
		1997-98	Not Rated	—

Note : Credit Rating for all select lessor companies is downgraded in 1997-98 as compared to 1996-97, except DCL whose credit rating remains same.
Source : Ascertained from Credit Rating Agencies.

The Reserve Bank of India has caused considerable hardship to NBFCs with its guidelines, tightening the fixed deposits and capital adequacy requirements. It may be seen from Table 3.11 that out of 6 select lessor companies, only two companies have FD/NW ratio of 5 to 9 times. NFL has recorded at 5.02 times in 1995-96 and 6.54 times in 1996-97 and DCL is registered at 6.52 times of its net worth in 1995-96 and 8.50 times in 1996-97, which

Table 3.10 : Fixed Deposits and Net worth of Select Lessor Companies

(Rs. lakhs)

Lessor Cos		*1990-91*	*1991-92*	*1992-93*	*1993-94*	*1994-95*	*1995-96*	*1996-97*	*1997-98*	*Remarks*
NFL	FD	1969.59	2733.13	3569.25	6656.41	17218.44	29191.76	37815.12	19176.57	Diversified to pesticides
	NW	1210.90	1461.92	2144.01	3577.98	4572.32	5815.73	5781.72	8786.56	
PPL	FD	23.28	71.01	70.35	404.60	2496.58	4812.17	9318.38	4090.39	It is in liquidation process
	NW	133.02	261.23	514.53	1345.55	3922.47	5344.86	5568.28	5705.65	
LFL	FD	0	3.27	13.16	59.66	125.73	181.00	144.72	118.28	Stopped doing leasing business
	NW	837.77	876.66	891.05	890.92	972.17	1018.24	1007.69	889.64	
DCL	FD	380.98	592.09	1002.36	1865.76	4505.61	8747.52	11470.06	7201.00	
	NW	280.18	582.37	648.06	1055.43	1310.59	1341.95	1350.35	1483.00	–
MWL	FD	501.78	464.74	580.59	836.82	1179.29	1179.29	1325.50	–	It is in liqui dation process
	NW	623.59	693.42	1223.96	1310.99	1955.17	1955.17	1370.13		
SCFSL	FD	29.32	35.16	36.92	73.05	81.76	81.76	68.10	–	Stopped doing leasing business
	NW	166.83	252.04	263.18	272.85	224.15	224.15	(-67.74)		

Notes :(i) Fixed Deposits = Public Deposits
(ii) Net Worth = Paid up Capital+Free Reserves (Intangible Assets + Deferred payments).

Source : Annual Reports of Select Lessor Companies.

Table 3.11 : Ratio of Fixed Deposits to Net Worth

Lessor Cos.	*1990-91*	*1991-92*	*1992-93*	*1993-94*	*1994-95*	*1995-96*	*1996-97*	*1997-98*
NFL	1.63	1.87	1.66	1.86	3.77	5.02	6.54	2.18
PPL	0.18	0.27	0.14	0.30	0.64	0.90	1.67	–
LFL	0	0.001	0.02	0.07	0.13	0.18	0.14	0.13
DCL	1.36	1.02	1.55	1.77	3.44	6.52	8.50	4.86
MWL	0.81	0.67	0.47	0.64	0.60	0.60	0.97	–
SCFSL	0.18	0.14	0.14	0.27	0.37	0.37	(-1.01)	–

Source: Calculated from Select Lessor Companies.

exceed the norm stipulated by the RBI. In terms of growth rate in mobilising deposits, DCL has occupied the first rank, followed by the NFL. But in terms of absolute figures, the NFL has mobilised Rs. 37,815.12 lakhs in 1996-97 accounting for 62.87% of total deposits (Rs. 60,141.88 lakhs) mobilised by all select lessor companies, followed by DCL representing 19.07% which constitutes deposits of Rs. 11,470.06 lakhs. PPL has occupied the third place representing 15.49%. The LFL and SCFSL share was very low, recording at 0.24% and 0.12% respectively.

To conclude, it may be inferred in connection with public deposits are concerned, the select lessor companies were adversely affected because of mandatory credit rating imposed by RBI. All lessor companies have mobilised huge amounts of public deposits and were not able to return the public deposits according to credit rating grades prescribed. As such, these companies were forced to stop accepting or renewing public deposits and the operations of these companies were severely affected. The recovery problems and unfavourable market conditions have further aggravated the problems of NBFCs in general, which led to diversify or closure of some companies.

Amendment to Sales Tax Act and Leasing

The levy of Sales Tax leasing by many States is the most irksome legislation that threatened the growth, if not the existence, of the leasing industry in our country. There was no Sales Tax on lease rentals until the Constitution Amendment Act (46th) was passed, as the lease does not fall under 'sale'. The Constitution Amendment (46th) was passed in 1982 enlarging the definition of "sale" to include, among other things, the "transfer of right to use goods for any purpose", the aim of the government was to plug the avoidance of tax through the device of leasing of films. "It is apparent from the Statement of Objects and Reasons to the Amendment Bill, was to nab anti-avoidance devices prevailing in the film industry where a sale of film will be documented as a lease instead of outright sale and thereby, sales tax would be avoided".[46]

Pursuant to this, the "transfer of right to use goods" under a lease agreement has also been brought within the definition of "sale" under the Sales Tax Act by various States. But this has unintentionally brought in lease of equipment, which has already suffered single point levy at the point of first sale in the respective States. Financial lease is only an arrangement like any other method of raising finance for acquiring goods. While the other modes of acquiring the equipment are exempt from taxation at the points of second and subsequent sales, the transaction relating to lease of equipment is, however, subject to differential treatment and is sought to be taxed over and over again.

Thus, this levy of sales tax results in multiple tax. The asset when purchased by the leasing company from the manufacturer is subjected to sales tax, being the first sale in the State and once again when it is leased out it is subjected to further levy, treating it as a sale. However, if the lessee/buyer acquires the asset by any other mode of finance, other than lease finance, say, hypothecation or hire-purchase in which case the "sale" being second in rank, is exempt from taxation. On the other hand, if the lessee/buyer chooses to acquire the asset through a lease agreement, it attracts a further levy, making leasing an expensive form of finance.

In certain advanced countries, it is acknowledged that taxing lease rentals would not lead to double taxation. For instance in the USA, all the States seek to collect tax on the purchase from the dealer/manufacturer as a tax on rentals over the period of lease. The option is given to the lessor either to pay tax on purchase of equipment or to pay tax on the rental receipts as "use tax" spread over the period of lease contract.[47]

Issue of 'C' Forms

Under Section 8(4) read with Rule 12(1) of the CST Act, one of the conditions for issuing declaration in Form 'C' is that "the goods of the class or classes specified in the certificate of registration of the registered dealer in purchasing the goods are for re-sale by him."

The consequential amendment to the Central Sales Tax Act has not been made to include lease transactions in the definition of sale. Hence, the legal position seems to be that a leasing company cannot issue a 'C' Form.

The 'C' Form is obtained by the purchasing dealer only from his State. The Sales Tax Officer issues 'C' Form on the basis that the goods purchased by the dealer on inter-State basis will be resold within the State and the first point tax will be paid under the Local Sales Tax Act on such sale.

Many States have made provisions empowering them to tax goods which are purchased by a dealer in the State on Inter-State basis and the same is sold within that State.

The purchasing dealer under the Central Sales Tax Act obtains the 'C' Form in order to facilitate movement of goods from Seller State to Purchaser State. This will be the first transaction for the seller to the buyer on Inter-State basis. The subsequent transaction, i.e., "re-sale" has to be viewed only in the context of the respective State where the re-sale is effected. When the goods are resold on Inter-State basis by the purchaser, the Central Sales Tax Act is applicable; and hence, if certain transactions are treated as sale under the local Act, then the dealer who is selling the goods within the State can issue 'C' Form in respect of such Inter-State purchases.

Taxability of Inter-State Leases

Some States have opted to treat the "Situs" of the goods as the basis for jurisdiction, while some have chosen to apply the principles of section 3/4/5 of the Central Sales Tax Act. The Bombay High Court in the case of *20th Century Finance Corporation Ltd.* 75 STC 217 approved the situs test and regarded the place of exercise of the right to use goods as the basis for taxation. The AP High Court in 1995, in the case of *ITC Classic Finance Ltd.*, STC 330, having had the benefit of Supreme Court rulings in *Gannon Dunkerly and Co.* 88 STC, rejected the situs test and applied the principle of Section 3 of the Central Sales Tax Act for determining jurisdiction.

The AP High Court in the case of *ITC Classic Finance Ltd.* differed with the view of the Bombay High Court in *20th Century Finance Corporation* and held that no State has any power to levy a tax on inter-State transactions as it is not subject to the State-tax. The ruling was rendered in 1995, i.e., 6 years after the Bombay High Court ruling, and had the benefit of the Supreme Court's ruling in *Gannon Dunkerly's case.*

Because of Bombay High Court's ruling, many State governments have been collecting tax on inter-State transactions, which is outside its ambits.

Maharashtra and Tamil Nadu have made amendments to Section 3A, retrospectively when equipment move inter-State on account of purchase by the lessor, the supplier can charge concessional duty against the issue of 'C' Form by the purchaser, i.e., the lessor. The difference between the normal rate and the concessional duty against the 'C' Form is sizable. It even goes over 8 per cent in some States. However, the lessors face practical problems when they apply to Sales Tax Departments for the issue of 'C' Form. While some States issue 'C' Forms without difficulty and others raise objections for issue of 'C' Forms or deny the same.[48] If the lessors are not allowed to issue 'C' Forms, the cost of the equipment and consequently the cost of lease will go up on account of the charging of normal duty on sale although it is an inter-State sale. Although the issue of 'C' Forms is under the Central Sales Tax Act, the reason for lessors facing difficulty is that CST Act is not modified to include lease as a deemed sale.

Consequently, the issue of 'C' forms to the lessor in the States where lease is considered a deemed sale, becomes an administrative decision of the concerned State Government. The reason for not modifying the CST Act to include lease as a sale despite lease being treated as a sale by almost all State Governments even after 18 years of relevant constitutional amendment is beyond imagination.

If the CST Act is not amended to do away with the unreasonableness of defining leasing as a deemed sale, then defining the same as deemed sale under the States Acts is equally unreasonable.

Central Sales Tax Act has not been amended as yet in pursuance of the Constitution (46th Amendment) Act. Therefore, there is no sales tax as yet on inter-State transactions of lease. Hire-purchase, however, is covered by the Central Sales Tax Act.

In spite of the clear position of law on the inapplicability of sales tax on inter-State transactions, a number of State Governments are administratively denying the benefit of inter-State sale exemption to leasing companies. Taking advantage of lack of clarity among the taxpayers and consultants, the governments are imposing tax on the leasing industry.

Pursuant to the 46th Amendment, most State Governments have exercised their power to tax leasing transactions.[49] The rates of tax, system and principles of levy are different in every jurisdiction. The overall scene is almost chaotic. Some States are treating lease transaction as any other sale and levy tax at the same rate as the rate applicable on the sale of the relevant goods (e.g., Bihar, Orissa, Haryana, Punjab, Himachal Pradesh, Tamil Nadu, etc.). While some States have a specific and separate rate of tax for leases (e.g. Karnataka, Andhra Pradesh, Gujarat, Rajasthan, U.P., West Bengal, etc.). Maharashtra has enacted a completely different law altogether for taxing leasing transactions. The rates of tax across different States vary between 2% to 12%. As such, the incremental burden of sales tax on the same lease transaction in two different States might vary in proportion of 2:12. This would definitely put fetters on the growth of the leasing industry. So much so those in several cases, a lease would become unviable option for the lessee.

Thus, the sales tax costs are imposed in two ways on the lease transaction:

(a) by denying the benefits of concessional purchase on inter-State transactions, i.e., by not issuing 'C' Forms to the lessor; and

Table 3.12 : Increased Cost of a 5-Year Lease due to Sales Tax

	Sales Tax Rates on IRRS							
Lease Rates	*3%*	*4%*	*5%*	*6%*	*7%*	*8%*	*9%*	*10%*
20	21.42	21.89	22.35	22.81	23.27	23.73	24.19	24.64
21	22.43	22.90	22.37	23.84	24.31	24.77	25.23	25.69
22	23.45	23.92	24.40	24.87	25.34	25.81	26.28	26.74
23	24.46	24.94	25.42	25.90	26.38	26.85	27.32	27.79
24	25.48	25.96	26.45	26.93	27.41	27.89	28.37	28.84
25	26.49	26.98	27.47	27.96	28.45	28.93	29.41	29.89
26	27.51	28.00	28.50	28.99	29.48	29.97	30.46	30.94
27	29.02	29.52	28.52	30.02	30.52	31.01	31.50	31.99
28	29.54	30.05	30.55	31.05	31.56	32.05	32.55	33.05

Source : Report of ALFS-1998.

(b) by imposing a tax on the lease rentals.

We shall now see how the cost of a transaction purely on account of sales tax on lease rentals increases substantially, as illustrated in the Table 3.12:[50]

Most of the State Governments have minimised extra cost due to sales tax on lease transactions. The following chart 3.7 shows the present status in major States from 1996-97.[51]

Chart 3.7 : Concessions/Exemptions and Rate of Tax

States	*Concessions/Exemptions*	*Rate of Tax*
Maharashtra	Full exemption to goods locally bought	4%
Gujarat	Specific exemption to SEBs	3% to 4%
Karnataka	Full exemption to locally bought goods	4%
Tamil Nadu	Full exemption to locally bought goods	Commodity Rate
West Bengal	Benefit of purchase @ 2% tax to lessors	Manufacturer— Lessees - 3% Others - 7 %
Uttar Pradesh	—	4%
Rajasthan	—	4%
Kerala	Full exemption to locally bought goods	4%

Source: Annual Report of Association of Leasing and Financial Services 1996 - 97.

The Association of Leasing and Financial Services Companies has done a pioneering job in this regard to reduce tax rates. Efforts are also on in other States to bring down the burden of tax.

Consequent to representation made by the ALFS, the Maharashtra State Government has exempted inter-State leases from the payment of sales tax with effect from July 4, 1997. Earlier, the State Government had exempted tax on leases of goods bought locally in that State. This, in essence means that no tax on lease transactions is payable in Maharashtra.[52]

The Maharashtra stand is most likely to be followed in other States. The reasons are: Firstly, because the circular of Maharashtra Government is an interpretation of a Supreme Court ruling which is equally applicable to all over the country.[53]

Leasing Industry is in Trouble Over Supreme Court Ruling

The leasing industry besieged by problems of sales tax since its inception. Leasing and sales tax thereon was governed by two schools of thought. First, based on the Bombay High Court ruling in the case of *20th Century Finance Corporation vs. State of Maharashtra*, where it was decided that sales tax was applicable where goods are put to use. The second based on the Andhra Pradesh High Court ruling in the matter involving ITC Classic Finance, which exempt sales tax on inter-State movement of goods.

The Supreme Court has given a new twist to the balance altogether. It has ruled that the place of signing will now determine the tax jurisdiction of a lease transaction. The leases on which tax has been paid in one State might now be taxable in another. In other words, the Supreme Court ruling has brought in a principle, which was never envisaged by the taxpayers.

The reasoning given by the Supreme Court is that the provisions of the Central Sales Tax Law (Sections 3, 4 and 5) that decide situs or inter-State character in case of normal sales, are not applicable to leases as the Central Law has not been amended to apply to leases.[54]

According to Mr.Vinod Kothari, a leading expert on lease laws, there is apparently no reason why the Central Sales Tax Law should not have been amended, 18 years after the Constitution was amended in 1982 to include several "deemed sales" into the fold of "Sales" for Sales Tax purposes.[55]

Sales Tax on Lease in Andhra Pradesh

The Andhra Pradesh State Government initially took the view that with the passage of the 46 Amendment, it had automatically derived the power to levy sales-tax on all items of transfer, the right to use any goods for any purpose including lease transactions and started imposing sales tax on lease.

A very significant notification was issued by the Andhra Pradesh Government on 23rd December, 1985 in response to the representation made by the Equipment Leasing Association (India). The Government had seen the rationale and realised the impact of a multipoint levy of sales tax on lease transactions and exempted the sales tax on lease under Section 5E. It had notified that the tax on lease of goods, which were bought subject to payment of APGST stood exempted with effect from 1st July, 1985, provided such goods have suffered tax under APGST Act.[56]

However, later in 1993, the exempting Notification was withdrawn, subjecting leases of goods even bought from within the State to incremental tax.[57] This notification came into force with effect from 7-7-1993. From this date onwards, the sales tax is applicable in the AP State on lease of all goods whether bought from within the State or outside. Further, as there is no exemption from multi-point levy, every sub-lease is also taxable.

The rate of tax in A.P. is 5%. The rates of sales taxes for different States were given in Annexure-3.1. Further the turnover tax of 1% is levied. However, no such tax was imposable if the aggregate turnover of the dealer/lessor is Rs. 2,00,000 or less. This limit of exemption has now been deleted with effect from 1-4-1995, implying thereby that any turnover is taxable under Section 5E of States Sales Tax Act. The Lease tax has been increased from 5% to 6% with effect from 1-8-1996. The turnover tax remains unchanged.[58] Further, the lease tax has increased from 6% to 8% and the turnover tax of 1% is exempted with effect from 1-1-2000.[59]

Almost all State Governments levy sales tax on lease rentals and by which it affects the cost of leasing as well as the profitability of leasing. Different States levy different rates of tax on lease. The additional tax is also different in different States. Some States link this levying of tax to the turnover of the leasing company. The details of rates of tax and additional taxes are given in Annexure 3.1.

Since different States are levying different rates of sales tax on lease lease rentals and turnover, there is an immediate need on the part of the Central Government to make a uniform legislation for all the States to levy sales tax. A separate statute may be enacted for leasing, which clearly defines all rules and procedures.

Further, Government should take steps to amend the Central Sales Tax Act so as to bring into its fold the companies, which are dealing with lease business to avail the benefit of 'C' Form. So that the severity of the levy of sales tax on lease rentals is not felt by the ultimate user of the assets.

Conclusion can be drawn from this chapter that when leasing business grew and met with initial success, there was a mushroom growth of institutions offering leasing services in India. But the absence of long-term strategy was felt strongly.

Several events led to the unexpected growth of Non-Banking Finance Companies (NBFCs). A buoyant capital market in the flush of liberalisation welcomed every public issue with huge premiums and massive over subscriptions. This was the signal for several unscrupulous promoters to set up high profile finance companies and raise money both from the capital market and through public deposits. This hectic activity in primary and secondary markets gave legitimacy to NBFCs. The Reserve Bank of India on its part, progressively relaxed its regulatory hold over the NBFC industry and made it possible for companies to raise large amounts of money from the public. Then, the Stock market scam broke in May 1992 giving the signal that some thing was malfunctioning in the stock market system. As a result, there was a shift in the flow of public money from securities market to NBFCs in the form of public deposits. Taking advantage of this major relaxation, many finance companies started accepting public deposits in a big way and the volume of public deposits held by NBFCs became quite large. Some unscrupulous NBFCs have even not followed the minimum rules prescribed by the RBI and mobilised huge deposits.

In January 1997, a prominent NBFC, CRB (Chain Roop Bansali) Capital Markets was found to be indulging in unlawful activities. CRB had accepted large sums by way of deposits and defaulted in the repayment of these deposits resulting in considerable panic among investors. Similarly, many greedy and unscrupulous promoters, who have mobilised huge deposits by offering high rates of interests and incentives, disappeared from the market.

When news about the failure of such companies are flashed in the press, some promoters were arrested but the investors never got their money back. This situation created panic among the investors and they lost the confidence and stopped investing their hard-earned money in Non-Banking Finance Companies.

With this bad experience, the RBI felt the need to bring in new regulations, as the existing norms proved to be insufficient. The euphoria of total de-regulations in July 1996, sounded death knell for NBFCs on January 2, 1998. In a complete reversal of its earlier position, the RBI introduced provisions linking limits of deposit acceptance with credit ratings and requiring finance companies to repay the excess deposits. The January 2, 1998 guidelines of RBI imposed very stringent provisioning norms for NBFCs. Almost all finance companies found it extremely difficult to comply with these norms and particularly small companies have been badly affected. Companies, which have NOF of less than Rs. 25 lakhs are simply out or diversified into other activities. Companies, which do not have a minimum credit rating are also out of the field.

However, not all is lost. The RBI has brought in relaxations wherever its stipulations hurt genuine transactions. Although RBI stipulates that any NBFC with less than Rs. 25 lakhs in NOF will not be allowed to accept public deposits, it has permitted Equipment Leasing and Hire-Purchase Finance Companies without credit ratings to tap public deposits of up to 1.5 times of their NOF or Rs.10 crores, whichever is lower, provided their capital adequacy ratio is 15% or above. With this, the NBFC sector will be rebuilt with a limited set of scrupulous players with the support of policies. If proper policies and guidelines had become sensitive to the emerging needs of the market supported the rapid growth of finance companies during the early 1980s, history would have taken a different course. Because stiff guidelines are the only way to unscrupulous investors in an age of fly-by-night operators who will exploit an euphoric condition to defraud investors.

REFERENCES

1. Siegel, Joel G. "*Dictionary of Accounting Terms*", Barron's Educational Series, inc. 250, New York, 1987, p.355.
2. Survival of Nidhis depends upon their ability to lend the resources mobilised. Nidhis specialise in granting jewel loans. Nidhis operate mainly in South India and are most popular in Tamilnadu.
3. RBI Circular IECD No.CAD 201 and 205/C 446 (LF)87-88, Dated 28, April 1988
4. RBI Notification No IECD No.14/08-12-01/94-95 dated: 28-9-1994
5. *The Economic Times*, 16-4-1997, p. 10.
6. *Ibid.*
7. S. Bandyopadhyay, *Direction of Regulation of NBFCs, India Lease Year Book, 1996*, Published by ALFS, Bombay, p.36.
8. RBI Circular No. DFC(COC) No.1707/174/93-94 dated:13-06-1994.

9. RBI Notification No. DFC.115/DG(SPT) – 98, dated: January 2, 1998.
10. *India Leasing Yearbook* published by Association of Leasing & Financial Services Companies, M.G. Road, Mumbai, 1998, p. 10.
11. Narasimham Committee Report on the Financial System, published by Nabhi Publications, New Delhi, 1993, p. 44.
12. *Ibid.*
13. Non-Banking Financial Companies Prudential Norms (Reserve Bank) Directions – 1998, RBI Notification No. DFC. 115/DG (SPT) –98 dated January 2, 1998.
14. *Ibid.*
15. *Ibid.*
16. RBI Notification No. DFC(COC) S6/DG(O)-89, dated 28-3-1989.
17. *India Lease Year Book* – Published by Association of Leasing and Financial Services, Bombay, 1994, p. 36.
18. RBI Reply – Notification No. DFC (COC) 742/02.04/96-97, dated : September 26, 1996.
19. RBI Notification No. DNBC/38/DG (H)-77 as amended up to June 18, 1997: dated: July 31, 1997.
20. Centre for Monitoring Indian Economy (CMIE), Monthly Review, July 1986.
21. Centre for Monitoring Indian Economy (CMIE), Monthly Review, September, 1996, p. 119.
22. *The Economic Times*, June 2, 1997, p.1.
23. *Ibid.*
24. Centre for Monitoring Indian Economy, Monthly Review, July 96, p. 139
25. *The Economic Times*, June 28, 1997, p. 3.
26. *Ibid.*
27. *The Economic Times,* June 28, 1997, p. 3.
28. *The Economic Times*, August 27, 1997.
29. Centre for Monitoring Indian Economy (CMIE), Monthly Review, September 1996, p. 118.
30. Centre for Monitoring Indian Economy, Monthly Review, July 1996, p. 139
31. *The Economic Times* – June 25, 1999, p. 9.
32. *Ibid.*
33. *Ibid.*
34. RBI Notification No. DFC.114/DG (SPT)-98 dated: The January 2, 1998.
35. NBFCs (Reserve Bank) Directions-1998, RBI Notification No. DFC-114/DG(SPT)-98, dated:the January 2, 1998.
36. Press Release: 1997-98/682:31-1-1998.
37. *The Economic Times*, January 6, 1998, p. 1.
38. *Ibid.*
39. *The Economic Times*, June 25, 1999, p. 9.
40. *Ibid.*
41. *The Economic Times*, December 21, 1998.
42. *The Economic Times*, June 25, 1999.
43. *Ibid.*
44. *Ibid.*
45. *Annual Report of NFL, 1998.*
46. *9th Annual Report 1996-97*, Association of Leasing and Financial Services Companies.

47. S. Raghavan, "*Problems in Leasing Industry*", paper presented at the Seminar on Leasing, organised by Can Bank Financial Services, Bangalore 29-30, December 1988.
48. Sriram Gade, Chief Manager, SBI, *Leasing – Child of Lessor God, The Economic Times,* January 9: 1997, p. 6.
49. *Asian Leasing Convention*, Published by Association of Leasing & Financial Services, Mumbai, 1997, p. 43.
50. *Op. cit.*, p. 92.
51. *Op. cit.*, p. 93.
52. *Ibid.*
53. *Ibid.*
54. *The Economic Times*, June 17, 2000, p. 10.
55. *Ibid.*
56. *A.P., Notification GO Ms. No.1388*, Revenue(s), dated, the 23rd December, 1985.
57. *A.P. Notification GO MS No. 606,* Revenue (ct-II), 3rd July 1993.
58. *APGST Amendment Ordinance - 1996.*
59. *A.P. Gazette IV-B Extraordinary*, Published by Authority – A.P. Ordinance No. 10 of 1999, dated December 31, 1999.

ANNEXURES

Annexure 3.1 : Territorial Sales Tax Position on Lease

State	*Scope of Tax*	*Rate of Tax*	*Exemptions/Concessions*	*Surcharge/Addl.Tax*	*Any other matter*
Assam	Finance Lease: General Rules Applicable to sales	4% to 25%	As applicable to general sales benefit of forms not available to lessor.	None	Lessee to deduct tax at source on rentals.
	Operating Lease: Items in Schedule VII	5%	None	None	
Andhra Pradesh	All items	5%	Exemption notification granting tax immunity to goods already having suffered tax withdrawn	Addl.Tax: @5% if total turnover >3 lakhs but < 50 lakhs @1% if total turnover >50 lakhs but <1 crore @1.5% if total turnover >1 crore	None
Bihar	All items. Most leasable items – Taxable at first point only. Items that are neither single or multi-point – taxable at last point	The rate applicable on sale of goods	Machineries sold to company intending to establish business in Bihar – 4% (Max)	Surcharge: Applicable if GT>10 lakhs. If GT>5 lakhs but <10 lakhs : 0.5% If GT >10 lakhs :0.10% of tax payable Surcharge is not recoverable. Additional tax: 0.1% of GT (excluding inter-state and outside state sales)	None
Goa	Items covered by Seventh Schedule	12%	None	Addl.Tax :10%	None

Annexure 3.1 : *(Contd.)*

State	*Scope of Tax*	*Rate of Tax*	*Exemptions/Concessions*	*Surcharge/Addl. Tax*	*Any other matter*
Gujarat	Items listed in Schedule III	2% to 5% Major items : 5%	Insignificant	Turnover tax: If TT< or =50 lakhs —Nil If TT >50 lakhs but < 2 crs.: – @ 1% of TT in excess of 50 lakhs. If TT > 2 crs but < 4 crs.: 1.5 lakhs + 1.25% of TT in excess of 2 crore If TT >4 cr. but < 8 cr.: 4 lakhs + 1.5% of TT in excess of 4 crore If TT >8 crore : 10 lakhs + 2% of TT in excess 8 crore.	None
Haryana	All items	The rate applicable on sale of goods	Some first point items: consumer electrical and electronic goods, motor vehicles, computers, generators, typewriters, etc.	Surcharge: @ 10% of the amount of tax payable	None
Himachal Pradesh	All items	The rate applicable on sale of goods	All concessions available on sales	None	None
Karnataka	Items listed in seventh schedule Provisions of Karnataka Sales Tax Act relating to leases	6% (w.e.f. 1-4-95)	Turnover of jeeps, trekkers, tractors, vans exempted from turnover tax. Lease of furniture exempt.	Turnover tax: Applicable if total turnover (TT) not less than 10 lakhs If TT > 10 lakhs but < 200	None

Annexure 3.1 : (*Contd.*)

State	*Scope of Tax*	*Rate of Tax*	*Exemptions/Concessions*	*Surcharge/Addl.Tax*	*Any other matter*
	quashed by High Court in Shetty Leasing's Case.		Sale of P & M by Karnataka Electricity Board to a leasing company in a sale and lease back transaction exempt from tax.	lakhs: @1.25% of TT. If TT >200 lakhs but <500 lakhs: @ 1.75% of TT. If TT >500 lakhs @ 2.75% of TT TOT is not passable. Surcharge: @ 15% of the amount of tax (Notification dt.30-03-95 exempts from surcharge most goods that are capable of being leased).	
Kerala	All items first schedule items: First point Fifth schedule items At two points	6%	Goods, which have already suffered tax—exempted sale of machinery @ 4% subject to declaration. Lease of cinematographic films exempt.	Surcharge: If TT > 1 lakh but < 10 lakhs @ 5% of If TT >10 lakhs @ 8% of tax payable. Not passable. Addl. Tax : 20% of tax (Recoverable)	Option to dealers TRSF. Right to use VCs to make lump sum payment.
Megha-laya	VCRs, VCPs Other items	10% 2%	All exemptions available on sale	VCRs etc.:4% Others : 5%	None
Madhya Pradesh	All items listed in notification dt.1-5-1995 w.e.f. 1-5-1995.	4%	Details not known	Details not known	None

Annexure 3.1 : (*Contd.*)

State	*Scope of Tax*	*Rate of Tax*	*Exemptions/Concessions*	*Surcharge/Addl. Tax*	*Any other matter*
Maharashtra	Goods mentioned in schedule to the Special Act	4%	Effective from 1-4-94. Lease of goods already suffered tax exempted. VAT applicable on sub-leases	None	None
New Delhi	Lease not defined as sale. Hence leases not taxable.	–	–	–	–
Orissa	All items	The rate applicable on sale of goods	Leasable items: First point tax only. Lease of goods for use in manufacture–4% on evidence of Form IV	@ 10% on tax not passable	None
Pondicherry	All items	The rate applicable on sale of goods	Lease tax exempted by notification	None	None
Punjab	All items	The rate applicable on sale of goods	First point tax goods: Motor vehicles, refrigerators, ACs; electrical appliances, office machines, wireless reception instruments, metal furniture, etc.	Additional tax: @ 10% of the tax . payable	None
Rajasthan	All items listed in Notification Dt. 27-6-1990	P&M 4% vide notification dt. 7-3-94 Tents, Kanats etc. 6%	None	None	None

Annexure 3.1 : (*Contd.*)

State	*Scope of Tax*	*Rate of Tax*	*Exemptions/Concessions*	*Surcharge/Addl.Tax*	*Any other matter*
		On other notified items – 10%			
Tamil Nadu	All items listed in first and second schedules	3% to 5%	As per amendment effective from 1-4-93. Lease of goods already suffered tax exempt.	Turnover tax: If TT > 10 lakhs but < 1 cr.: @1.5% of TT. If TT >1 cr but <5 crs.: @ 2% of TT. If TT >5crs – but < 10 cr @ 2.25% of TT If TT >10crs but < 300 cr @ 2.5% of TT If TT > 300 crs @ 3% TOT is not passable. Surcharge @ 15% of tax (recoverable).	R 48B: Intimation of every lease to be given to pre-authority in Form XXXV.
Uttar Pradesh	All items listed in Notification Dt. 27-4-1987 w.e.f. 1-5-87	4%	None	None	None
West Bengal	All items. Schedule IV goods taxable at first point only (w.e.f. 1-5-95).	7% w.e.f 1-5-95	Benefit of purchase at concessional rate of 2% available subject to issue of declaration in Form 11. Manufacturer lessee's can take on lease assets to be used in manufacture at a concessional rate of 3% on issue of declaration in Form 11.	Turnover tax abolished vide Finance Act, 1995. Surcharge @ 10% on tax payable. Applicable with effect from 1-5-1995.	None

4

PERFORMANCE OF LESSOR COMPANIES

The preceding chapter has been devoted to discuss the impact of policy framework on lease financing. This chapter aims at analysing the performance of select lessor companies in Andhra Pradesh based on relevant financial ratios and cash flow statements. Six lessor companies were selected at random for the study. The detailed methodology of sample selection is given in Chapter1 under the heading of "methodology".

Financial statement analysis is a technique of investigating the financial position, operation and progress of a business unit. By establishing certain relationships among financial statements and calculating the relevant ratios and cash flow statements, the financial performance and operating efficiency of lessor companies can be measured in terms of business investment and profitability. Analysis of financial statements gives a detailed idea of business operations, which reveal the financial performance of a company.

This chapter is divided into two sections. Section-I analyses the sources and application of funds of select lessor companies with a view of highlighting the trends in funds management. Further, operational results of lessor companies in terms of costs and revenues and their relationships with the volume of leasing business are examined. Section-II presents the cash flow analysis, which represents the sources from which the lessor companies mobilised funds, and how these funds were utilised. In its most refined form, it is a statement of changes in financial position where the flows of cash, rather than of working capital, are analysed and accounted for. This is a valuable tool in financial statement analysis to evaluate the performance of companies.

SECTION-I

Sources of Funds

The sources of funds potentially available to lessor companies are:

(i) Equity share capital including participating preference shares.
(ii) Reserves and surplus including retained earnings.
(iii) Loans :

 (a) Bank overdraft,
 (b) Bank term loans and cash credits,
 (c) Institutional loans,
 (d) Fixed deposits, and
 (e) Commercial paper.

For the purpose of convenience, the sources of funds are divided as follows:

(i) *Owned Funds* : These consist of equity share capital, participating preference shares and reserves and surplus including retained earnings.
(ii) *Borrowed Funds* : These include Bank overdraft, Bank term loans, including cash credits, institutional loans, public deposits and commercial paper. Bank overdraft is an important source of fund particularly with regard to day-to-day management of short-term liquidity problems.

The RBI guidelines provide a methodology for arriving at maximum permissible bank finance (MPBF). The details of MPBF are discussed in Chapter-3. In case borrowing concern is engaged both in leasing and in hire purchase business, banks will assess its credit requirement separately for the two categories of businesses.

The bank lending to leasing companies is linked to net owned funds (NOF) of companies. This should not exceed three times their NOF, within the prescribed overall ceiling of 10 times their NOF for their total external borrowings, including public deposits, debentures/bonds and borrowings from banks, financial institutions, etc. NOF should be calculated on the following basis

NOF = Paid up capital + free reserves (including balance in share premium account, capital and debentures redemption reserves and any other reserve not being one created for repayment of any future liability or for a depreciation in assets or bad debts or a reserve created by revaluation of the assets)

Less

Accumulated balance of loss, balance of deferred revenue expenditure, as also other intangible assets are to be deducted from NOF (further, investments in deposits with and loans/advances due from subsidiary company/affiliates are also to be deducted from NOF).

Commercial paper is an unsecured promissory note with a fixed maturity. The lessor promises to pay the investor a fixed amount on some future date but pledges no assets; only the company's liquidity status guarantees the promise.

To know the importance of public deposits as a source of finance to a leasing company, it is shown separately under the heading of Fixed Deposits.

The other sources of funds are depreciation and current liabilities.

Depreciation

Depreciation is amortisation of fixed assets. Depreciation is provided on both owned assets and leased assets so as to allocate the original cost over the estimated life of fixed assets. Depreciation reduces taxable income but does not reduce cash. As such, depreciation amount will be used during production when it is necessary according to its availability of funds in the business.

An increase in the availability of total funds is an indication of growth of leasing business in terms of owned assets, leased assets and turnover. In contrast, a decrease in the availability of total sources of funds indicates negative growth of leasing business. This growth (both positive and negative) depends upon the corresponding demand and supply of funds.

The total sources of funds such as owned funds, borrowed funds, fixed deposits, depreciation and current liabilities and application of funds such as leased assets, hire-purchase assets, owned assets and current assets of select lessor companies are calculated (as shown in Table 4.1). *The compound growth rates have been computed using semi-log trend line* (as shown in Table 4.1). Table 4.1 reveals that all types of sources of funds have

Table 4.1 : Sources and Application of Funds of Select Lessor Companies
Sources of Funds (Cumulative Figures)

(Rs.lakhs)

Composition of funds	*1990-91*	*1991-92*	*1992-93*	*1993-94*	*1994-95*	*1995-96*	*1996-97*	*C.G.R (%)*
Owned funds	3345.14	4268.74	5903.40	8606.96	13798.64	16997.96	17555.67	
	–	(27.61)	(38.29)	(45.80)	(62.32)	(23.19)	(3.28)	35.89
Borrowed	5853.00	5969.62	7565.83	10126.32	16479.68	15218.34	18297.44	
funds	–	(1.99)	(26.74)	(33.84)	(62.74)	(-7.65)	(20.23)	24.21
Fixed deposits	2904.95	3899.40	5272.63	9896.30	25607.41	44193.50	60141.88	
	–	(34.23)	(35.22)	(87.69)	(158.76)	(72.58)	(36.09)	74.11
Depreciation	1558.83	2265.91	3094.36	4195.64	5868.27	8107.12	9733.24	
	–	(45.36)	(36.56)	(35.59)	(39.79)	(38.22)	(20.06)	36.37
Current	3309.69	4308.60	4323.98	5197.55	11493.12	5214.97	7421.15	
liabilities	–	(30.18)	(0.36)	(20.20)	(121.13)	(-54.63)	(42.30)	13.96
Total	16971.61	20712.27	26160.20	38022.77	73244.12	89731.89	113149.4	
	–	(22.04)	(26.31)	(45.35)	(92.63)	(22.51)	(26.1)	41.17

Application of Funds

(Rs.lakhs)

Composition Assets	*1990-91*	*1991-92*	*1992-93*	*1993-94*	*1994-95*	*1995-96*	*1996-97*	*C.G.R (%)*
Leased assets	3952.80	5087.07	6451.29	9072.30	16748.28	22255.81	25319.56	
	–	(28.69)	(26.82)	(40.63)	(84.61)	(32.88)	(13.77)	40.28
Hire purchase	8991.85	9242.05	11017.48	15398.21	26451.60	29616.23	39303.93	
assets	–	(2.78)	(19.21)	(39.76)	(71.78)	(11.96)	(32.71)	31.32
Owned assets	374.89	424.50	619.66	676.45	1368.69	1786.78	2659.80	
	–	(13.23)	(45.97)	(9.16)	(102.33)	(30.55)	(48.86)	40.62

Composition Assets	*1990-91*	*1991-92*	*1992-93*	*1993-94*	*1994-95*	*1995-96*	*1996-97*	*C.G.R (%)*
Current assets	3652.07	5958.71	8071.77	12875.81	28675.55	36073.07	45866.09	
	–	(63.16)	(35.46)	(59.52)	(122.71)	(25.80)	(27.15)	56.05
Total	16971.61	20712.27	26160.20	38022.77	73244.12	89731.89	113149.38	
	–	(22.04)	(26.31)	(45.35)	(92.63)	(22.51)	(26.1)	41.17

Note : (i) C.G.R. = Compound Growth Rate

(ii) Compound Growth Rate $= yt = y_o\,(1+r)^t$

$= \log yt = \log y_o + t. [\log (1+r)]$

$b = \log (1+r)$

$r =$ Compound growth rate

$= (\text{antilog } b) - 1.$

Compound growth rates have been computed using semi-log trend line.

Source: Calculated from annual reports of select lessor companies.

registered an increasing trend over the study period from 1990-91 to 1994-95. After 1995, a slow growth trend has been recorded.

The Net Owned Funds (NOF) consists of equity share capital and reserves and surplus including retained earnings. Many companies, including leasing companies have successfully tapped the equity share capital during the period from 1984 to 1986 when there was a boom in the capital market.[1] Due to the securities scam, which took place in May 1992, the corporate sector was not successful in raising equity funds. It is observed from Table 4.1 that the owned funds have recorded a rising trend up to 1994-95 registering a 62.32% growth over previous year, due to the rise in reserves and surplus. Subsequently, the growth rate became very slow registering 23.19% in 1995-96 and 3.28% in 1996-97. The compound growth of owned funds was 35.89%, which was high due to two companies, viz., LFL and MWL, which have been trading on thick equity. The proportion of owned funds to total sources of LFL and MWL recorded 57.1% and 34.2% respectively and followed by PPL recording at 28.6% (Table 4.4).

Table 4.1 reveals that the public deposit is the major fund raising source for leasing companies. During1990-91 to1994-95, the accelerated effort by lessor companies in mobilising deposits yielded a record accretion of Rs. 15,711.11 lakhs to a total of Rs. 25,607.4 lakhs by 1994-95, up by 158.8% over previous year. The total deposit base increased to Rs. 60,141.9 lakhs in 1996-97, and the compound growth rate constitutes as high as 74.11%. This reflected the growing confidence of investing public. All non-banking finance companies place emphasis on raising deposits, recognising its immense potential as a major resource mobiliser. The borrowed funds have shown declining trends after 1995 due to tightening of bank lending norms by RBI. The RBI reduced the multiple times of bank lending to leasing companies from 3 times to 2 times whose income from leasing and hire-purchase is less than 75% of total income in 1995.

The analysis of Table 4.2 shows that the proportion of borrowed funds experienced a declining trend from 42.84% in 1990-91 to 17.31% in 1996-97, whereas the proportion of fixed deposits has recorded an increasing trend from 21.26% in 1990-91 to 56.88% in 1996-97. The proportion of fixed deposits to total borrowings is recorded at 53.58% (Table 4.3).

Table 4.2 : Proportion of each Component of Sources and Application of Funds of Select Lessor Companies

Sources of Funds *(Per cent)*

Sources of funds	*1990-91*	*1991-92*	*1992-93*	*1993-94*	*1994-95*	*1995-96*	*1996-97*	$\bar{X}$
Owned funds	24.49	26.02	27.03	26.22	22.35	20.11	16.60	23.26
Borrowed funds	42.84	36.39	34.65	30.85	26.69	18.01	17.31	29.53
Fixed deposits	21.26	23.77	24.15	30.15	41.47	52.29	56.88	35.71
Depreciation	11.41	13.82	14.17	12.78	9.49	9.59	9.21	11.50
Total	100	100	100	100	100	100	100	100

Application of funds *(Per cent)*

Application of funds	*1990-91*	*1991-92*	*1992-93*	*1993-94*	*1994-95*	*1995-96*	*1996-97*	$\bar{X}$
Leased Assets.	28.93	31.01	29.54	27.64	27.12	26.33	23.95	27.79
H.P.A.	65.82	56.34	50.46	46.91	42.84	35.04	37.17	47.80
Owned Assets	2.74	2.59	2.84	2.06	2.22	2.11	2.52	2.44
Other Assets	2.51	10.06	17.16	23.39	27.82	36.52	36.36	21.97
Total	100	100	100	100	100	100	100	100

Notes : i. $\bar{X}$ = Arithmetic Mean.

ii. Other assets include investments, net current assets, etc. (i.e. current assets –current liabilities).

Source: Calculated from annual reports of select lessor companies.

Table 4.3 : Component Analysis of Aggregate Borrowings of Select Lessor Companies *(Per cent)*

Borrowings	*1990-91*	*1991-92*	*1992-93*	*1993-94*	*1994-95*	*1995-96*	*1996-97*	$\bar{X}$
Bank loans	42.56	40.99	38.64	24.21	26.18	14.29	12.76	28.52
Institutional Loans	16.16	11.51	7.53	9.41	7.16	4.28	2.91	8.42
Fixed Deposits	33.17	39.51	41.07	49.43	60.84	74.39	76.68	53.58
Debentures	7.22	4.42	3.00	1.50	0.72	0.92	3.82	3.09
Other Loans	0.89	3.57	9.76	15.45	5.10	6.12	3.83	6.39
Total	100	100	100	100	100	100	100	100

Note : $\bar{X}$ = Arithmetic Mean.

Source: Calculated from Annual Reports of select lessor companies.

Depreciation is another important source of funds for leasing companies. They claim depreciation on both owned assets and leased assets; the average depreciation constitutes 12.70% of total sources of funds (Table 4.4). The compound growth rate is recorded at 36.37% (Table 4.1).

Table 4.4 : Average Proportions of Owned Funds and Borrowings of Select Lessor Companies (Companywise)

(Per cent)

Sources of Funds	*NFL*	*PPL*	*LFL*	*DCL*	*MWL*	*SCFSL*	$\bar{X}$
Owned funds	13.8	28.6	57.1	14.9	34.2	22.9	28.58
Borrowed Funds :							
Bank Loans	14.8	22.6	6.0	13.2	13.3	29.8	16.62
Institutional Loans	3.4	5.6	0.4	8.7	3.5	–	3.60
Fixed Deposits	37.0	15.0	3.9	37.5	21.8	5.2	20.06
Debentures	2.7	–	–	1.3	–	–	0.67
Other Loans	3.9	4.6	0.8	1.3	3.9	0.3	2.47
Depreciation	10.6	6.6	18.2	7.6	12.5	20.7	12.70
Current liabilities	13.8	17.0	13.6	15.5	10.8	21.1	15.30
Total	100	100	100	100	100	100	100

Note: $\bar{X}$ Arithmetic mean.
Source: Calculated from Annual Reports of select lessor companies.

Current Liabilities

Current liabilities also form a source of working capital for the leasing organisations. They finance a major portion of current assets. The current liabilities of leasing companies comprises sundry creditors for expenses, lease rentals received in advance, interest accrued but not due, unclaimed dividend, tax provision, dividend provision, etc.

The analysis of Table 4.1 shows that the aggregate liabilities of select lessor companies have registered ups and downs in their value of current liabilities. The increase of current liabilities depends upon the increase of interest accrued but not due, tax provision, dividend provision, etc. The decrease of current liabilities varies from company to company with the clearing of debts or expenses, interest, dividend, etc.

The highest current liability growth rate is recorded at 121.13% in 1994-95 over the previous year. In subsequent years these liabilities have been drastically reduced, recording negative growth rate at—54.63%, due to the payment of outstanding expenses. Though the current liabilities finance a major portion of current assets in general, these do not form significant source of funds for the leasing companies.

After discussing the trends of various sources of funds—such as owned funds, borrowed funds, fixed deposits, depreciation and current liabilities, it is pertinent to discuss the proportion of each source of funds to the total funds. This is to know which source of funds occupies prominence in the total resources of a company and why? In other words, in what proportion is the company able to mobilise resources from various sources of funds? In this connection, it is to be noted that, in order to know the companies' performance in mobilising the public deposits, the aspect of public deposit is separated from the total borrowings and shown in separate columns in Tables 4.1 and 4.2. The fixed deposits showed a faster rate of growth from 1991-92 to 1994-95 by recording 34.23% in 1991-92 and 158.76% in 1994-95. Thereafter, the growth rate is slowed down recording 72.58% in 1995-96 and 36.09% in 1996-97 (Table 4.1). Whereas, the proportion of fixed deposit to total borrowings is higher in the years 1995-96 and 1996-97 by recording 52.29% and 56.88% respectively due to lesser borrowings from banks and financial institutions (Table 4.2).

These aggregate borrowings of select lessor companies are further classified into Bank loans, Institutional loans, Fixed deposits, Debentures, and other loans as shown in Table 4.3. Further, these borrowings are analysed company-wise and presented in Table 4.4.

The analysis of data presented in Table 4.3 reveals that the sources of fixed deposits occupy the first place, recording an average proportion of 53.58% followed by bank loans recording 28.52%. Remaining sources such as institutional loans, debentures and other loans have recorded an average less than 10%. Starting from 1990-91 to 1996-97 the proportion of public deposits is above 33%. The proportion abnormally increased from 49.43% in 1993-94 to 76.68% in 1996-97 (Table 4.3).

Having burnt their fingers on the stock market, investors have started depositing money in safe and fixed income source instruments as they have lost confidence in the primary market. Almost all finance companies have offered higher deposit rates, which surpass the RBI ceiling of 15 per cent. Most finance and leasing companies have offered deposit rates of 18 to 20 per cent through innovative incentive schemes, such as upfront cash payment or precious gifts during the years 1994-95. The RBI rules permit finance companies to pay brokerage up to 1% for deposits with tenure up to 1 year. 1.5% for a period of 1-2 years and 2% for more than 2 years.

The RBI has sent its inspection teams to non-banking finance companies in the second week of November 1995 to investigate their deposit mobilisation systems. The inspection reports have pointed out that some non-banking finance companies have been offering deposit rates of 20-25 per cent through innovative incentive schemes like offering gifts, commission to deposit holders and brokers in order to mobilise more public deposits.[2] Individually, the NFL and DCL have mobilised substantial amount through public deposits recording the average proportions at 37.0% and 37.5% respectively out of total sources (Table 4.4).

These two companies (NFL and DCL) have almost maintained the same trend in mobilising public deposits, followed by bank loans which accounted for 14.8% for NFL and 13.2% for DCL (Table 4.4).

The lowest average share of fixed deposits was 3.9% for LFL, followed by 5.2% for SCFSL. These companies largely depended on owned funds, representing an average share of owned funds of 57.10% for LFL and 22.9% for SCFSL. SCFSL has largely depended on bank loans, followed by owned funds representing an average share of 29.8% and 22.9% respectively and has not availed institutional finance at all from 1990-91 to 1996-97. Out of 6 companies selected for the study, 4 companies such as PPL, LFL, MWL and SCFSL have not issued debentures at all. NFL is the only company that has raised maximum amount through debentures constituting 2.7% of total sources, followed by DCL which raised debentures representing 1.3% of total sources of funds (Table 4.4).

The Reserve Bank of India announced a major relaxation on July 24, 1996 for registered Non-banking Finance Companies (NBFCs), which have to meet the requirements on prudential norms and credit rating. The details are discussed in Chapter-3. These relaxations are freeing the interest rate ceiling on public deposits and the removal of the ceiling on the quantum of the deposits for NBFCs, which fully comply with the RBI guidelines. The companies, which do not fully comply with these guidelines, would continue to accept deposits subject to deposit rate regulation; and companies whose compliance is clearly lacking, would face a curtailment of ceilings on the amount of deposits they can raise.

However, as a punitive measure, the overall ceiling on deposits is reduced from 10 to 7 times the NOF with regard to the registered leasing and hire purchase companies which have neither met the credit rating requirement nor the prudential norms. The overall ceiling on deposits would stand reduced to 5 times the NOF with respect to the unregistered leasing and hire purchase companies.[3]

The lessor survey, pertaining to the response of the investing public towards fixed deposits, indicates that there was a good response from the public to invest their savings in leasing companies. Four lessor companies did not face any difficulty in mobilising the public deposits from 1991-92 to 1995-96, and their major source of finance was from public deposits. NFL was able to mobilise public deposits more than their expectation. Further, the company does not have the ceiling restriction for fixation of the rate of interest and quantum of deposits as the company fulfilled the prudential norms of credit rating and statutory liquidity ratio as prescribed by the RBI and got certificate from the RBI in October 1996. These relaxations helped them to mobilise excess public deposits.

The remaining two companies, i.e., LFL and SCFSL responded that they were not able to mobilise public deposits up to their expectations as the response from the public was not very encouraging. Further, their scale of business operation was limited.

Having discussed the various sources of funds, now it is proposed to discuss the uses of funds.

Uses of Funds

Most leasing companies are engaged in activities of leasing, hire purchase, bill discounting, etc. A close analysis of financial statements of leasing companies reveals that the funds of leasing companies are used for purchase of assets for ownership, leasing, hire purchase and other purposes.

Assets are created by the conversion of capital funds. In leasing industry, funds are used to finance various assets, which would have consistent demand in the lease market. Studies on various leased assets disclose the increasing trend of buying assets, which have a significant demand in the area of lease market. A phenomenal increase in the total volume of leased assets is an indication that the leasing industry is growing from strength to strength. Further, it indicates the growth of industrial production as a whole.

For sake of convenience, the total assets of select lessor companies are compiled from Annual Reports and presented in Table 4.1. The assets are broadly classified into lease assets, hire-purchase assets, owned assets and current assets in order to know the trends and volume of business done by select lessor companies.

It can be seen from Table 4.1 that the growth of all assets, such as leased assets, hire-purchase assets, owned assets and current assets have recorded a consistent growth trend registering 84.6%, 71.8%, 102.3%, 122.7% respectively in the year 1994-95 over the previous year. The leased assets stood at Rs. 16,748.3 lakhs in 1994-95 representing a growth rate of 84.6% over the previous year and further increased to Rs. 25,319.6, lakhs representing slow growth rate at 13.8% in 1996-97, as against Rs. 3,952.8 lakhs in 1990-91. The hire purchase assets stood at Rs. 26,451.6 lakhs representing 71.8% in 1994-95 and further increased to Rs. 39,303.93 lakhs representing slow growth rate of 32.7% in 1996-97. Almost the same trend is established in the case of owned assets recording at 102.3% in 1994-95 over the previous year, and current assets recording at Rs. 28,675.6 lakhs in 1994-95 over the previous year.

The trend in all the assets has witnessed a slow progress in 1996-97, due to the new regulatory framework pertaining to mandatory credit rating for finance companies and recovery problems.

The component proportion of each asset to total assets over a period of study is calculated and presented in Table 4.2. The Table reveals that the average proportion of leased assets to total assets is lower than hire-purchase assets, recording 27.79% for leased assets and 47.8% for hire-purchased assets, the average proportion of owned asset is very low, recording 2.44%. The other assets, such as investments, current assets have recorded 21.97%.

The leased assets and sub-classification of leased assets from 1990-91 to 1996-97 are discussed separately to know the types of assets leased and their demand in the lease market.

From the data presented in Table 4.2 it is clear that around 48% of the total funds are deployed to acquire hire-purchase assets and around 28% of the total funds are deployed to acquire leased assets. The remaining 24% of the funds are deployed in owned assets and other current assets. The leasing companies included the hire-purchase assets under the heading of current assets, which will be discussed in subsequent section of cash flow analysis.

Now it is pertinent to discuss the component analysis of leased assets. The data pertaining to different types of leased assets and the proportion of each component of the leased asset to total leased assets are presented in Tables 4.5 and 4.6. The company-wise analysis of the same is shown in Tables 4.7 to 4.10. The total leased assets are categorised into Plant and Machinery, Vehicles, Office Equipment and other assets. The total cumulative leased out assets stood at Rs. 25,319.56 lakhs in 1996-97 as against Rs. 3,952.8 lakhs in 1990-91, recording the compound growth rate at 40.55% (Table 4.5).

Plant and Machinery

It is seen from Table 4.5 that the growth in plant and machinery, vehicles and office equipment leasing has witnessed an upward trend from 1990-91 to 1994-95. Later, the growth rate has been very slow. The growth rates are recorded at 92.71% for plant and machinery, 100.67% for vehicles, 69.99% for office equipment and -5.67% for other assets in 1994-95 over the previous year.

Table 4.6 reveals that the average proportion of plant and machinery to total leased assets is recorded at 77.44%. The remaining proportion of 22.56% is shared by vehicles (13.11%) office equipment (4.04%) and other assets (5.41%). The lowest proportion is recorded with the office equipment at 4.04%.

It is observed from the analysis of Table 4.7 that all companies selected for the study have engaged in leasing of plant and machinery. It is evident from the table that more than half of the leasing business of plant and machinery is done by NFL recording an average proportion at 52.54%. The remaining 47.46% is shared

Table 4.5 : Types of Assets Leased Out by Select Lessor Companies

(Rs. lakhs)

Leased Assets	*1990-91*	*1991-92*	*1992-93*	*1993-94*	*1994-95*	*1995-96*	*1996-97*	*CGR %*
Plant &	3106.40	3920.86	4771.66	6690.53	12893.58	17755.23	20747.27	41.82
Machinery	–	(26.22)	(21.70)	(40.21)	(92.71)	(38.74)	(16.85)	
Vehicles	443.93	666.64	1015.65	1214.06	2436.26	2787.91	2839.71	39.42
	–	(50.17)	(52.35)	(19.54)	(100.67)	(14.43)	(1.86)	
Office	69.47	191.52	340.08	418.88	712.08	1008.39	1032.00	54.37
Equipment	–	(175.69)	(77.57)	(23.17)	(69.99)	(41.61)	(2.34)	
Other	333.00	307.99	323.90	748.83	706.36	704.28	700.58	18.13
Assets	–	(-7.51)	(5.17)	(131.12)	(-5.67)	(-0.29)	(-0.53)	
Total	3952.80	5087.01	6451.29	9072.30	16748.28	22255.81	25319.56	40.55
	–	(28.69)	(26.82)	(40.63)	(84.61)	(33.65)	(13.77)	

Note : Figures in brackets indicate growth rates.
Source : Calculated from annual reports of select lessor companies.

Table 4.6 : Share of each Component of Leased Assets of Select Lessor Companies

(Per cent)

Leased Assets	*1990-91*	*1991-92*	*1992-93*	*1993-94*	*1994-95*	*1995-96*	*1996-97*	$\bar{X}$
Plant & Machinery	78.59	77.08	73.96	73.75	76.98	79.78	81.94	77.44
Vehicles	11.23	13.10	15.75	13.38	14.55	12.53	11.22	13.11
Office Equipment	1.76	3.76	5.27	4.62	4.25	4.53	4.07	4.04
Other Assets	8.42	6.06	5.02	8.25	4.22	3.16	2.77	5.41
Total	100.00	100.00	100.00	100.00	100.00	100.00	100.00	100.00

Note : X = Arithmetic Mean.
Source : Calculated from Annual Reports of select lessor companies.

by the remaining five companies recording an average proportion of leasing business of plant and machinery at 14.41% for PPL, 12.70% for DCL, 11.06% for MWL, 5.31% for LFL and 3.98% for SCFSL.

The proportion of plant and machinery for NFL company varies from 40.96% in 1992-93 to a highest of 65.24% in 1996-97, followed by DCL company for which the proportion varies from a lowest of 5.45% in 1996-97 to 19.34% in 1990-91. The trend in the proportion of plant and machinery for DCL shows a decline due to the increasing trend of vehicle leasing (Table 4.8).

Vehicle Leasing

Leasing/hire-purchase finance essentially served as a sales aid tool for automobile manufacturers to sell their vehicles in the highly competitive environment.

In UK, many leasing companies have successfully established a major market for operating leases of company cars, which accounts for approximately 60% of the new cars sold in the country.[4]

Table 4.7 : Growth and Share of Plant and Machinery of Select Lessor Companies

(Rs. lakhs)

Lessor Cos.	*1990-91*	*1991-92*	*1992-93*	*1993-94*	*1994-95*	*1995-96*	*1996-97*	$\bar{X}$
	(51.65)	(45.16)	(40.96)	(47.74)	(54.35)	(62.69)	(65.24)	
NFL	1578.72	1770.74	1954.40	3193.79	6955.52	11130.27	13535.52	52.54
	–	(12.16)	(10.37)	(63.42)	(117.78)	(60.00)	(21.61)	
	(2.25)	(8.79)	(13.44)	(15.68)	(21.41)	(19.86)	(19.46)	
PPL	68.87	344.61	641.09	1048.77	2739.56	3526.09	4039.22	14.41
	–	(400.4)	(86.03)	(63.59)	(161.22)	(28.71)	(14.55)	
	(4.18)	(6.27)	(6.18)	(6.05)	(5.51)	(4.52)	(4.42)	
LFL	127.76	245.83	294.73	405.02	705.65	802.72	915.77	5.31
	–	(92.42)	(19.89)	(37.42)	(74.23)	(13.76)	(14.08)	
	(19.34)	(17.25)	(17.23)	(13.67)	(9.91)	(6.04)	(5.45)	
DCL	591.08	676.25	822.15	914.52	1268.26	1073.30	1130.17	12.70
	–	(14.41)	(21.57)	(11.24)	(38.68)	(-15.37)	(5.30)	
	(21.13)	(17.75)	(14.58)	(10.79)	(5.64)	(4.06)	(3.46)	
MWL	645.93	695.93	695.93	721.89	721.89	720.15	719.18	
	–	(7.74)	(0)	(3.73)	(0)	(-0.24)	(-0.14)	
	(1.45)	(4.78)	(7.61)	(6.07)	(3.18)	(2.83)	(1.97)	
SCFSL	44.03	187.50	363.36	406.54	406.54	502.70	407.41	3.98
	–	(325.85)	(93.79)	(11.88)	(0)	(23.65)	(-18.96)	
	(100)	(100)	(100)	(100)	(100)	(100)	(100)	
TOTAL	3056.39	3920.86	4771.66	6690.53	12797.42	17755.23	20747.27	100
	–	(28.28)	(21.70)	(40.21)	(91.28)	(38.74)	(16.85)	

Note : i. Figures in upper brackets indicate the share of plant and machinery of each company to total volume of plant and machinery.

ii. Figures in lower brackets indicate growth rates.

iii. $\bar{X}$ = Arithmetic Mean.

Source: Calculated from annual reports of select lessor companies.

In India, Motor Vehicles Act was enacted in 1988, which provides maximum safeguard to protect the interests of hire-purchase/leasing companies regarding their advances towards acquisition/use of vehicles. The salient features of this legislation are:

1. Noting of an endorsement about the existence of a hire-

purchase/leasing agreement in the Certificate of Registration of the Vehicle.

Table 4.8 : Growth and Share of Vehicle Leasing of Select Lessor Companies

(Rs. lakhs)

Lessor companies	*1990-91*	*1991-92*	*1992-93*	*1993-94*	*1994-95*	*1995-96*	*1996-97*	$\bar{X}$
	(52.28)	(46.58)	(53.62)	(61.64)	(73.14)	(81.05)	(81.55)	
NFL	232.08	310.50	544.64	748.39	1781.89	2259.58	2315.87	81.55
	–	(33.79)	(75.41)	(37.41)	(138.09)	(26.81)	(2.49)	
	(1.20)	(3.25)	(2.73)	(2.62)	(0.72)	(0.71)	(1.29)	
PPL	5.33	21.66	27.68	31.82	17.42	19.68	36.72	1.29
	–	(306.38)	(27.79)	(14.96)	(45.25)	(12.97)	(86.58)	
LFL	–	–	–	–	–	–	–	–
	(10.99)	(20.31)	(24.60)	(19.43)	(18.54)	(11.97)	(11.18)	
DCL	48.83	135.38	249.88	235.91	451.75	325.42	317.44	11.18
	–	(177.25)	(84.58)	(-5.59)	(91.49)	(-27.96)	(-2.45)	
	(29.91)	(22.25)	(14.88)	(12.82)	(5.87)	(5.05)	(4.49)	
MWL	132.76	148.30	151.14	155.63	142.89	140.92	127.37	4.49
	–	(11.71)	(1.92)	(2.97)	(-8.19)	(-1.38)	(-9.62)	
	(5.62)	(7.61)	(4.17)	(3.49)	(1.73)	(1.52)	(1.49)	1.49
SCFSL	24.93	50.80	42.31	42.31	42.31	42.31	42.31	
	–	(103.77)	(-16.71)	(0)	(0)	(0)	(0)	
	(100)	(100)	(100)	(100)	(100)	(100)	(100)	
TOTAL	443.93	666.64	1015.65	1214.06	2436.26	2787.91	2839.71	100
	–	(50.17)	(52.35)	(19.54)	(100.67)	(14.43)	(1.86)	

Note : i. Figures in upper brackets indicate proportion of vehicle leasing of each company to total volume of vehicle leasing.

ii. Figures in lower brackets indicate growth rates.

iii. $\bar{X}$ = Arithmetic mean.

Source: Calculated from Annual Reports of select lessor companies.

2. Retention of such endorsement makes even in the event of re-registration, sale, etc., during the pendency of such agreement.

The data pertaining to vehicles leased by select lessor companies is analysed and presented in Table 4.8. The Table reveals that the total volume of vehicles leasing has increased from Rs. 443.93 lakhs in 1990-91 to Rs. 2,839.71 lakhs in 1996-97, by registering an average growth rate of 34.2% (Table 4.8), which is moderately good. Though the vehicle leasing as a mode of financing is yet to be fully developed in Andhra Pradesh.

Out of six leasing companies, one company (LFL) never engaged in vehicle leasing. NFL occupied the first position by registering 81.55 per cent among all select leasing companies, followed by DCL registering 11.18 per cent. The remaining three companies have done very little vehicle leasing business recording below 5 per cent (Table 4.8). However, the momentum of vehicle leasing has come due to the enactment of Motor Vehicles Act, 1988, and leasing companies have played a significant role in providing the required finance to lessees for their vehicle finance.

Scope for Vehicle Leasing

The car finance business is cruising along despite the slump in the economy. Around 60 per cent of car sales worth Rs. 6,400 crores during 1994-95 was supported by loan finance of nearly 4,000 crores in India.[5] The automobile industry has boomed in terms of variety of vehicles available.

Gaining mileage from the popularity of the small car, Maruti Countrywide Auto Financial Services Limited has been floated by a powered trio of GE Capital, HDFC and Maruti Udyog.[6] Finance professionals are looking at widening the scope of the business by taking a close look at the hitherto secondary markets for utility vehicles and used cars. "Today, if an individual has to buy a second hand vehicle, he has to rely on the judgement of an informal source, to determine the price and condition of the vehicle. Presently almost every leading financing outfit is ready to fund a second hand vehicle. The only diffidence is in the assessment of the value of the vehicle. If the dealer takes on the onus, it could satisfy the need of the individual, dealer and the finance company" says Mr.Venkattu Srinivasan, Vice-President, Kotak Mahindra Finance Ltd.[7]

Hyderabad has seen a sea change in the year 1999 in the retailing automotive industry. Hyderabad today has the potential to sell 2000 cars a month.[8] During 1999, the market expansion in the city has registered a growth of 60% and is still growing when compared to the previous year of 1998.[9] The scene is unfolding gradually and more and more customers are choosing better cars and good models. Thus, the rising demand for new cars in this period saw demand for vehicle finance, i.e. increase in the financial service facilitates for the rising demand for vehicles. Financial packages are definitely one of the value additions. Almost all dealers, like Saboo (RKS Motors) Varun Motors, Mitra Agencies, etc., are now arranging well formulated financial packages through loan, hire purchase and leasing modes. A number of dealers are establishing their credibility by setting standards of excellence in quality and providing authentic sales service. All of them have one thing in common; quick, efficient service and impressive array of financial packages to their customers/clientele.

As the market for cars grow, the competition gets tougher and finance companies are forced to put more punch into their act. Some have the inherent strength of a good distribution network and a feel for the local market; others offer efficient and smart services and special incentives. But the customer will not settle for any thing piece meal. He wants it all. This gives a hint to the finance/leasing companies that offer efficient services only would survive.

Office Equipment

The growth and share of office equipment to the total volume of leased assets are presented in Table 4.9. The Table reveals that out of six select companies only two companies, namely NFL and PPL have engaged in the leasing of office equipment. The total volume of leasing office equipment is recorded at Rs. 1032.00 lakhs, of which, on an average, the NFL has done 95.32%. The remaining 4.68% was shared by PPL (Table 4.9). However, the average proportion of office equipment to total leased assets is recorded at 4.04%, which is the lowest of all leased assets (Table 4.6). The remaining four companies, viz., LFL, DCL, MWL, SCFSL have not engaged in the leasing of office equipment.

Other Assets

The assets under the heading 'others' are assets other than plant and machinery, vehicles, and office equipment. The other assets include air conditioners, lifts, xerox machines, aircoolers, consumer durables, refrigerators, etc.

In this category, most of the leased assets are consumer durables, such as TVs, refrigerators, etc. The average proportion of other assets to total leased assets constitutes only 5.41% (Table 4.6), which indicates that there is no demand for other assets (i.e.

Table 4.9 : Growth and Share of Office Equipment of Select Lessor Companies

(Rs.lakhs)

Lessor Cos.	*1990-91*	*1991-92*	*1992-93*	*1993-94*	*1994-95*	*1995-96*	*1996-97*	$\bar{X}$
	(89.88)	(95.94)	(97.78)	(96.41)	(97.93)	(95.36)	(93.96)	
NFL	62.44	183.74	332.53	403.83	697.36	961.63	969.69	95.32
	–	(194.27)	(80.98)	(21.44)	(72.69)	(37.90)	(0.84)	
	(10.12)	(4.06)	(2.22)	(3.59)	(2.07)	(4.64)	(6.04)	
PPL	7.03	7.77	7.55	15.05	14.72	46.76	62.31	4.68
	–	(10.53)	(-2.83)	(99.33)	(-2.19)	(217.66)	(33.25)	
LFL	–	–	–	–	–	–	–	–
DCL	–	–	–	–	–	–	–	–
MWL	–	–	–	–	–	–	–	–
SCFSL	–	–	–	–	–	–	–	–
	(100)	(100)	(100)	(100)	(100)	(100)	(100)	
Total	69.47	191.51	340.08	418.88	712.08	1008.39	1032.00	100
	–	(175.67)	(389.54)	(23.17)	(69.99)	(41.61)	(2.34)	

Notes : (i) Figures in upper brackets indicate proportion of office equipment of each company to total volume of office equipment; (ii) Figures in lower brackets indicate growth rates; (iii) $\bar{X}$ = Arithmetic Mean.

Source: Calculated from annual reports of select lessor companies.

Table 4.10 : Growth and Share of Assets Other than Plant & Machinery, Vehicles and Office Equipment of Select Lessor Companies

(Rs. lakhs)

Lessor Cos.	*1990-91*	*1991-92*	*1992-93*	*1993-94*	*1994-95*	*1995-96*	*1996-97*	$\bar{X}$
	(40.79)	(33.66)	(43.46)	(75.07)	(80.22)	(80.46)	(80.88)	
NFL	135.82	103.68	140.78	562.15	566.64	566.64	566.64	62.08
	–	(-23.66)	(35.78)	(299.31)	(0.80)	(0)	(0)	
PPL	–	–	–	–	–	–	–	–
	–	(1.89)	(1.80)	(0.78)	(0.82)	–	–	
LFL		5.82	5.82	5.82	5.82			0.76
		–	(0)	(0)	(0)			
DCL	–	–	–	–	–	–	–	–
	(52.96)	(57.57)	(54.74)	(24.15)	(18.96)	(19.54)	(19.12)	
MWL	176.35	177.32	177.32	180.86	133.90	137.64	133.94	35.29
	–	(0.55)	(0)	(1.99)	(-25.96)	(2.79)	(-2.69)	
	(6.25)	(6.88)	–	–	–	–	–	1.87
SCFSL	20.84	21.17						
	–	(1.58)						
	(100)	(100)	(100)	(100)	(100)	(100)	(100)	
Total	333.01	307.99	323.92	748.83	706.36	704.28	700.58	100
	–	(-7.51)	(5.17)	(131.18)	(-5.67)	(-0.29)	(-0.53)	

Note : (i) Figures in upper brackets indicate the share of other assets of each company to total volume of other assets leasing. (ii) Figures in lower brackets indicate growth rates. (iii) $\bar{X}$ = Arithmetic Mean.

Source: Calculated from Annual Reports of select lessor companies.

the assets other than plant and machinery, vehicles, and office equipment). Table 4.10 shows that out of 6 companies selected for the study, only four companies have engaged in leasing other assets. The average proportion of NFL is 62.08%, followed by MWL representing 35.29%. The other two companies namely LFL and SCFSL did very little business in leasing of other assets, recording an average proportion of 0.76% and 1.87% respectively. The remaining two companies—PPL and DCL did not lease other assets.

An in-depth interview with the Executives of Lessor Companies, on hindrance to the growth of leasing business in A.P. reveals the following.

(i) One of the main problems is the lack of demand. Interest shown by the high tax-rated companies to the leasing business is lukewarm as they lose the depreciation benefit if they opt to lease. In spite of vigorous marketing efforts by the Lessors, these companies are hesitant to opt for leasing as a dependable source.

(ii) Most of the lessee companies are perturbed more at the loss of ownership of the asset rather than the loss of depreciation benefit. In the beginning the lessee is not certain as to what will happen to the asset at the end of the lease period, although normally the lessee is assured of the right to the continued use of the asset. The lease agreements usually give lessee the right to renew the lease at nominal rental. The nominal rentals may be even one rupee for instalment.

Operating Income and Costs

Revenues are the value of outputs. They constitute gross inflow of assets. For leasing companies the major source of income is from lease and hire purchase transactions. They account for more than 87% of their total earnings. The other sources of income are interest on deposits, dividends on investments, bill discounting, merchant banking, etc. The survival of a company depends upon earning of sufficient revenues. The realization of gross income or revenue is one of the paramount criteria to decide the magnitude of sound operations of business in its efforts, to earn sufficient profits to cover the total expenses and to strengthen the liquidity position for implementing future plans.

Rental Income

Lease rentals are normally earned over a period of the lease agreement. Actual payment by the lessee to the lessor can be made on a variety of bases. Payment intervals can be fixed monthly, quarterly, half-yearly or annually, and rents can be paid in advance or in arrears. Leasing companies credit lease rentals to profit and loss account as it arises.

Under a financial lease, the primary period rental is the amount that recovers the full capital cost of the equipment (unless any residual value has been placed on the equipment). This includes related fees, interest and other expenses, which provides the lessor with the required profit during the primary lease period. The lessor is also entitled to receive renewal rentals for any secondary period, and to receive the sale proceeds or the leased equipment at the end of the lease. These additional sources of profit, which among other features distinguish leasing from lending. This may be regarded as either negligible or a factor that should be taken into account in the lessor's cash flows and financial evaluation at the time of fixation of lease rentals.

Profit is a reward for taking risk. The overall profit rewards the Lessor Company for the risks undertaken and the resources employed. It is ascertained that the main risks usually borne by lessors are: (i) non-payment of lease rentals by lessees owing to insufficient resources being available; (ii) claims from deposit holders on maturity of deposits;(iii) claims from creditors for their instalment amount of loan; (iv) increase in cost of funds over the investment period of the lease; (v) funds constraints; and (vi) corporation tax or other taxation charges, etc.

Profits are earned by lessors through the use of funds for the acquisition of capital equipment. A subsidiary factor currently available to the leasing activity is the use of tax shelter. The limit on a leasing company's ability to undertake additional profitable business is set by the availability of funds and demand for its facilities. The profit maximization for a leasing company thus involves the optimal use of its two scarce resources: funds and tax shield. The problem is one of determining the most profitable types or mix of financial leasing business, i.e., use of funds and tax benefits available to leasing companies.

Costs

The operational expenses of leasing concerns are broadly divided into four groups:

(i) *Operating and administration expenses:* consisting of rent, rates, staff salaries, fixed deposit mobilisation expenses, miscellaneous expenses etc.,
(ii) *Interest:* including interest on cash credits, fixed deposits, debentures, institutional loans etc.,
(iii) *Depreciation:* on owned assets and leased assets, etc., and
(iv) *Corporate tax:* tax levied on the flow of income as per Income Tax Act, 1961.

Almost all select lessor companies are engaged in leasing activity along with other related activities, such as hire-purchase finance, bill discounting, merchant banking, etc.The aggregate revenues and costs of select lessor companies are presented in Tables 4.11 and 4.12.

Table 4.11 reveals that, in more ways than one, the year 1991-92 has truly been a "take off" year for leasing business. The leasing business has recorded a growth rate of 99.26% in aggregate lease income of select lessor companies constituting Rs. 2,258.16 lakhs during 1991-92 as against Rs. 1133.23 lakhs in the previous year due to Government's liberalisation measures. In 1992-93, the growth rate of lease income reduced to 23.14%, from 99.26% in 1991-92, while the hire-purchase income increased to 37.06% in 1993-94 from 8.40% in 1992-93. Further, there is a significant increase in the hire-purchase income during the year 1994-95 recording a growth rate of 122.93%, while the growth rate for lease income recorded a 47.81% in 1994-95 due to Government's continued economic/financial reforms and accessibility of funds. The average proportion of lease income and hire purchase income put together constitutes 87.35% leaving 12.65% for other incomes such as bill discounting, dividends, interest on deposits, etc. However, the lease income and hire purchase income has shown a declining trend in 1995-96 and 1996-97.

Three reasons could be attributed for the decrease in lease income. First, the imposition of 5% tax on lease rentals by the A.P.

Table 4.11 : Component Analysis of Income of Select Lessor Companies

(Rs.lakhs)

Composition of Income	*1991*	*1992*	*1993*	*1994*	*1995*	*1996*	*1997*	$\bar{X}$	*C.G.R*
Lease	(38.59)	(52.34)	(55.71)	(52.01)	(42.72)	(37.55)	(30.64)		
Income	1133.23	2258.16	2780.66	3550.17	5247.33	5927.61	5726.27	44.22	30.37
	–	(99.26)	(23.14)	(27.67)	(47.81)	(12.96)	(-3.40)		
Hire	(50.86)	(37.89)	(35.50)	(35.57)	(44.07)	(49.46)	(48.74)		
Purchase	1493.30	1634.39	1771.70	2428.35	5413.49	7806.12	9109.70	43.16	41.25
Income	–	(9.45)	(8.40)	(37.06)	(122.93)	(44.20)	(16.70)		
Other	(10.55)	(9.77)	(8.79)	(12.42)	(13.21)	(12.99)	(20.62)		
Income	309.78	421.45	438.98	847.98	1621.85	2050.64	3853.58	12.62	52.58
	–	(36.05)	(4.16)	(93.17)	(91.26)	(26.44)	(87.92)		
Total	(100)	(100)	(100)	(100)	(100)	(100)	(100)		
	2936.31	4314.00	4991.34	6826.50	12282.67	15784.37	18689.55	100	38.15
	–	(46.92)	(15.70)	(36.77)	(79.93)	(28.51)	(18.41)		

Note : (i) Figures in upper brackets indicate proportion of each component of income to total income; (ii)Figures in lower brackets indicate growth rates; (iii) X = Arithmetic mean; (iv) C.G.R. = Compound Growth Rate.

Source: Calculated from annual reports of select lessor companies.

Table 4.12 : The Share of Each Component of Expenditure to Total Income of Select Lessor Companies

(Rs.lakhs)

Income & Exp.	*1991*	*1992*	*1993*	*1994*	*1995*	*1996*	*1997*	$\bar{X}$	*C.G.R*
Total	(100)	(100)	(100)	(100)	(100)	(100)	(100)		
Income	2936.31	4314.00	4991.34	6826.50	12282.67	15784.37	18689.55	100	38.14
	–	(46.92)	(15.70)	(36.77)	(79.93)	(28.51)	(18.41)		
1. Operating Exp.	(18.52)	(18.71)	(18.04)	(21.69)	(22.33)	(21.84)	(29.18)		
	543.90	807.25	900.59	1480.98	2743.17	3446.81	5453.82	21.47	47.77
	–	(48.42)	(11.56)	(64.45)	(85.23)	(25.65)	(58.23)		
2. Interest	(45.92)	(41.90)	(44.57)	(38.62)	(42.25)	(45.80)	(53.06)		
	1348.51	1807.48	2224.53	2636.53	5189.59	7229.82	9916.71	44.59	40.92
	–	(34.04)	(23.07)	(18.52)	(96.83)	(39.31)	(37.16)		
3.Depreciation	(17.77)	(16.41)	(17.66)	(18.94)	(15.24)	(19.49)	(13.70)		
	521.65	707.82	881.54	1292.75	1871.98	3077.03	2559.68	17.03	35.50
	–	(35.69)	(24.54)	(46.65)	(44.81)	(64.37)	(-16.81)		
4.Provision for tax	(1.45)	(1.29)	(0.25)	(0.16)	(0.18)	(0.01)	(1.06)		
	42.50	55.75	12.50	11.00	21.31	1.50	197.64	0.63	-7.18
	–	(31.18)	(-77.58)	(-12.00)	(93.73)	(-92.96)	(13076.0)		

Table 4.12 : (*Contd*)

5. Net	(16.34)	(21.69)	(19.48)	(20.59)	(20.00)	(12.86)	(3.00)*		
Profit	479.75	935.70	972.18	1405.24	2456.62	2029.21	561.70	16.28	11.10
	–	(95.04)	(3.90)	(44.55)	(74.82)	(-17.38)	(-72.32)		

Note : (i) Figures in upper brackets indicate proportion of each component of expenditure to total income.
(ii) Figures in lower brackets indicate growth rates.
(iii) *Loss incurred by some companies is adjusted (i.e., loss is deducted from profit).
(iv) X = Arithmetic Mean.
(v) CGR = Compound Growth Rate.

Source: Calculated from Annual Reports of Select Lessor Companies.

State Goverment as per section 5-A of General Sales Tax Act plus 1% turnover tax (the details of sales tax were discussed in Chapter 3). Next, the problems of recovery of instalments and finally, the imposition of strict RBI guidelines like provisioning for non-performing assets for income recognition, etc.

Table 4.11 shows that there is no significant difference between lease income and hire-purchase income as the average income of lease is recorded at 44.22% and hire purchase income is recorded at 43.16% over the period of study.

However, the results in 1995-96 and 1996-97 manifest clearly the strain on leasing companies' profit margins with increasing interest costs recording the proportion of interest at 45.8% in 1995-96 and 53.06% in 1996-97 (Table 4.12). The higher provision made for non-cash charges like lease equivalisation, (i.e. shortage of depreciation is now provided as per the Institute of Chartered Accountants of India), depreciation and non-performing assets, etc. On an average, depreciation constitutes 17.03% of the total expenditure, while the tax provision is less than 1% representing 0.63% (Table 4.12). It means that most of the lessor companies are reducing their tax liability under the shelter of depreciation and non-performing assets.

According to annual reports of select lessor companies, the provision for Non-Performing Assets (Provision for substandard/ doubtful/loss assets) and lease equivalisation is as follows.

As per the Annual Reports of select Lessor companies, almost 60% of the NPAs of select lessor companies is reported in the category of doubtful and loss assets. Out of 6 companies, two companies, MWL and SCFSL were badly affected due to recovery problems recording Rs. 230.05 lakhs and Rs. 162.69 lakhs respectively in 1996-97 (Table 4.13). This provisioning is required to be maintained as per RBI Guidelines on prudential norms 1994 (which were clearly discussed in Chapter 3).

The interesting fact is that there is a surge in the total income of select lessor companies, which zoomed to Rs. 12,282.67 lakhs in 1994-95 and Rs. 18,689.55 lakhs in 1996-97 from Rs. 2,936.31 lakhs in 1990-91 and a net profit of Rs. 2,456.62 lakhs in 1994-95 from Rs. 479.75 lakhs in 1990-91. Thereafter, a negative growth trend is recorded (Table 4.12).

Table 4.13 : Provision for Non-Performing Assets and Lease Equalisation

(Rs. lakhs)

	Provision for NPAs		*Provision for Lease Equalisation*	
Companies	*1995-96*	*1996-97*	*1995-96*	*1996-97*
NFL	83.27	546.58	95.71	1078.25
PPL	11.53	28.99	–	–
LFL	15.66	63.78	–	–
DCL	32.21	74.97	34.32	65.53
MWL	211.83	230.05	–	3.3
SCFSL	159.62	162.69	–	–
Total	514.62	1107.06	130.03	1147.08

Source : Annual Reports.

The proportion of interest paid when compared to other expenses is very high, recording an average interest of 44.59%. There is a marked increase in the utilisation of funds for payment of interest on loans over the years under study. The average proportion of interest costs to total operating income is recorded at 44.59% (Table 4.12). The increase in the proportion of interest payment appears to be the cause of the deployment of borrowed funds in the long-term investments.

The proportion of net profit, on an average, is recorded at 16.28% of the income of select leasing companies. The highest proportion of net profit to total income recorded in 1991-92 is 21.69% followed by 20.59% in 1993-94 and 20% in 1994-95. The lowest proportion of net profit is recorded in 1996-97 at 3.0% due to accumulated losses incurred by MWL and SCFSL.

Having discussed the net profit at macro level, it is now pertinent to discuss the return on investment, earning per share, debt-equity ratio and interest coverage ratio of select lessor companies.

Return on Capital Employed

The trends of Return on Total Capital Employed (ROCE) are calculated and presented in Table 4.14. This ratio is calculated taking the net profit plus interest divided by total capital employed. The term total capital employed includes owned funds (share capital plus reserves and surplus), borrowed funds from banks and financial institutions (both short term and long term loans) debentures and fixed deposits, i.e. public deposits. The current liabilities such as sundry creditors, tax provisions, unclaimed dividend, unmatured finance charges, etc., have been ignored. The Return on Capital Employed (ROCE) indicates how well the management has used the funds supplied by its creditors and owners. The higher the ratio of the firm, the more efficient it is, in using the funds.

Table 4.14 reveals that on an average three companies, namely: NFL, PPL and DCL have established a good performance in their earnings, recording their average returns to capital employed at 15.14%, 15.87% and 14.94% respectively. The lowest performance is recorded by SCFSL, registering an average ROI at 9.20% due to huge losses incurred in the year 1996-97 resulting in a negative ROI at -25.44%, followed by MWL recording a negative ROI at -1.31% in 1996-97.

The income of NFL has increased to Rs. 6,423.87 lakhs in 1994-95 from Rs. 3,626.52 lakhs in 1993-94 registering a growth rate of 77.14% (Annexure-4.3) but the ROI declined to 13.31% in 1994-95 from 14.22% in 1993-94. This decline is due to the expansion of its branches. The NFL has enlarged its presence geographically by opening new branches at Tirupathi, Bhimavaram and Kurnool and has expanded its business from time to time. The total branches increased to 42 locations by the financial year-ending 1997, making it well placed to utilise the business opportunities prevailing across the country. The operating expenses of the company increased from Rs. 776.09 lakhs in 1993-94 to Rs. 1,318.93 lakhs in 1994-95 recording the increase in operating expenses by 69.95% (Annexure-4.3), which resulted in the reduction of ROI for NFL to 13.31% in 1994-95 from 14.22% in 1993-94. The net profit does not match the growth in business income which recorded an increase of 51.95% at Rs. 973.59 lakhs in 1994-95 against the previous year income of Rs. 640.72 lakhs in 1993-94 (Annexure-4.3) whereas, the growth rate in income is recorded at 77.14% in 1994-95 over the previous year. The earning per share on the equity was recorded at Rs. 7.30 in the year 1994-95, which was the highest for NFL during the study period from 1990-91 to 1996-97 (Table 4.15). This witnesses the growth in business volume during 1994-95. The average earning per share for NFL recording at Rs. 5.58 is higher compared to other select lessor companies, and the performance of the company is remarkable because of its use of high debt in the capital structure and good management or rotation of funds.

Table 4.14 : Return on Capital Employed of Select Lessor Companies

(Per cent)

Companies	*1990-91*	*1991-92*	*1 992-93*	*1993-94*	*1994-95*	*1995-96*	*1996-97*	$\bar{X}$
NFL	16.51	20.00	18.33	14.22	13.31	12.27	11.32	15.14
PPL	11.90	22.58	23.26	12.08	16.84	12.23	12.23	15.87
LFL	7.67	9.11	11.60	10.67	11.31	10.68	7.04	9.73
DCL	14.06	17.15	14.95	15.80	15.00	14.11	13.52	14.94
MWL	15.98	21.53	17.03	15.52	8.47	*	(-1.31)	11.03
SCFSL	14.27	29.23	19.80	15.70	10.81	*	(-25.44)	9.20

Note : i. *These two companies have skipped the year 1995-96 and clubbed the data in 1994-95 and 1996-97 due to delay in preparation of financial statements.

ii. $\bar{X}$ = Arithmetic Mean.

Source: Calculated from Annual Reports of Select Lessor Companies.

Table 4.15 : Earning per Share of Select Lessor Companies *(Rupees)*

Cos.	*1990-91*	*1991-92*	*1992-93*	*1993-94*	*1994-95*	*1995-96*	*1996-97*	$\bar{X}$
NFL	3.45	6.04	5.52	5.49	7.30	7.05	4.20	5.58
PPL	1.57	6.19	3.61	3.17	5.08	3.78	2.25	3.66
LFL	4.28	5.59	3.96	3.49	9.42	4.24	1.81	4.68
DCL	2.00	2.31	3.08	3.55	5.98	3.72	2.06	3.24
MWL	2.58	3.11	1.70	2.19	0.85	*	(-4.80)	0.80
SCFSL	1.66	8.20	2.94	1.53	(-3.19)	*	(-12.66)	(-0.22)

Note: 1. *These two companies have skipped the year 1995-96 and clubbed the data in 1994-95 and 1996-97 due to delay in preparation of financial statements.

2. EPS = Profit After Tax— Preference Dividend ÷ No. of Equity Shares.

Source: Calculated from Annual Reports of Select Lessor Companies.

Table 4.14 reveals that the PPL has witnessed ups and downs in its return on capital employed from 1990-91 to 1996-97. The average ROI is recorded at 15.87%. The PPL has reported good results for the year 1994-95 with an all round growth in disbursements and revenues. The total income has risen from Rs. 837.38 lakhs in 1993-94 to Rs. 2,579.71 lakhs in 1994-95 (Annexure-4.3) recording an annual growth at 208.07%. The profit after tax has also registered matching growth compared to income recording at 240.14% in 1994-95 over the previous year from

Rs. 265.12 lakhs in 1993-94 to Rs. 901.79 lakhs in 1994-95 (Annexure-4.3). The earning per share for PPL is an impressive record in the years 1991-92 and 1994-95 registering at Rs. 6.19 and Rs. 5.08 respectively (Table 4.15).

The DCL Company recorded an impressive growth trend in its operations from 1990-91 to 1994-95. The ROI is recorded at 14.95% in 1993, 15.8% in 1994, 15.00% in 1995. Later in 1996 and 1997 it declined to 14.11% and 13.52% respectively. The highest EPS was recorded at Rs. 5.98 per share in the year 1994-95. Later, the EPS declined to Rs. 3.72 and Rs. 2.06 in the years 1996 and 1997 respectively as the company recorded a drop in net profit to Rs. 148.46 lakhs in 1996-97 from Rs. 265.72 lakhs in 1995-96. All select lessor companies have recorded a drop in net profit from 1995-96 to 1996-97, recording the net profit from Rs. 1025.48 lakhs in 1995-96 to Rs. 610.12 lakhs in 1996-97 for NFL, from Rs. 628.58 lakhs to Rs. 373.50 lakhs for PPL, from Rs. 95.33 lakhs to Rs. 40.76 lakhs for LFL, from Rs. 265.72 lakhs to Rs. 148.46 lakhs for DCL, from Rs. 69.20 lakhs to a loss of Rs. 392.08 lakhs for MWL and from a loss of Rs. -55.10 lakhs to a loss of Rs. – 219.06 lakhs for SCFSL (Annexure-4.3).

Consequently, the ROI has decreased from 1995-96 to 1996-97 from 12.27% to 11.32% for NFL, from 10.68% to 7.04% for LFL, from 14.11% to 13.52% for DCL, from 8.47% to a negative figure of – 1.31% for MWL and from 10.81% to a negative

Figure of – 25.44% for SCFSL (Table 4.14). The same declining trend is recorded in the earning per share (Table 4.15).

The drop in profits, ROI and EPS for the year 1996-97 is significant due to the following reasons:

1. Narrowing down of margins on account of high competition in the financial services sector.
2. Strict adherence of the prudential norms prescribed by the Reserve Bank of India for provisioning of non-performing assets, income recognition, maintenance of liquid assets ratio, direct linking of quantum of deposit acceptance to credit rating of the company, etc.

   The sudden imposition of restrictions by RBI was a shock to these leasing and finance companies. Because of these restrictions, these companies were not able to mobilise public deposits as required. With the result these companies were in financial difficulties. On the other hand the non-performing assets for these companies increased due to recovery problems. Consequently some of these companies have diverted their business lines to other activities and some more have closed their business.

3. The economy in general and financial services sector in particular experienced a rather difficult year marked by lower credit and higher risk profile.
4. The continued sluggishness in the capital market and slackness in the transport sector compounded the situation further.

Further, the sorry state of all finance and leasing companies is a compound result of many other events that took place from 1996 to 1997, ranked in order of priority. First, loss of public confidence due to CRB scam (details were discussed in chapter 3) and other unscrupulous finance companies which duped the public after taking crores of public deposits. Next, poor recoveries of lease and hire purchase instalments from lessees and hirers and accounting norms which required provisioning against non-performing assets and lease equivalisation charges, which is short of depreciation made by leasing and finance companies during primary lease period. These have culminated in the worst phase in the business cycle of finance and leasing companies so much so that many entrepreneurs have decided to quit the business altogether.

Thus with the economic slow down hurting the performance of most finance and leasing companies in tandem, and with the sluggishness in the capital markets during the years 1996 and 1997, the prospects for an early revival for the financial sector remained a distant dream. This, in turn, largely restricted business opportunities for the finance and leasing companies in general. The situation was further aggravated; through the entry of a good number of multinationals with low cost funds, vying to seize the already limited opportunities for finance companies.

Status of Leasing in 1997-98

During the year 1997-98, the MWL Ltd., closed leasing business due to recovery problems. Another company, viz., SCFSL has diversified its activities into other activities like real estate business due to recovery problems. This company incurred losses continuously for two years, i.e. 1995-96 and 1996-97 recording net loss of Rs. 55.10 lakhs and Rs. 219.06 lakhs respectively. In addition to this problem, the capital market conditions continued to be sluggish from 1995-96 to 1998-99 and also continued to be so in the year 2000. Another select company, namely, Pennar Patterson Securities Ltd. (PPL) is under liquidation process during 1998-99 due to recovery problem of lease and hire purchase instalment dues.

The high incidence of payment default by lessees to lessors pertaining to lease/hire-purchase instalments led to the higher incidence of defaults in payments by lessors to deposit holders pertaining to public deposits. This has sent the leasing companies scampering to take guard. With this, many deposit holders sought legal action against leasing companies which resulted in closing down of many companies and start liquidation process in the interest of the public. The same thing happened to MWL and PPL. As such many NBFCs have started discouraging others in their own fraternity from entering the leasing business.

In a recent development (1996-97) the hire-purchase and leasing association has brought out a list of 37 such erring companies (lessee companies) who have defaulted in paying lease and hire-purchase rentals. The list comprises as many as 11 small and large companies from Bombay and Calcutta each. The list also comprises a few companies from *New Delhi, Hyderabad, Bangalore,* and *Chennai.*[10] Large number of legal cases have been pending in various Courts of Law. Huge amounts of money, running into crores is to be recovered from these defaulter companies. The pending amount to be recovered from lessee companies by select lessor companies is Rs. 514.12 lakhs in 1995-96 and Rs. 1,107.06 lakhs in 1996-97 (Table 4.13).

The chance of recovery in most cases is poor and in certain cases, it is even zero. It is also ascertained that in a few cases arrest warrants issued against concerned persons have not proved any success. Thus, many NBFCs face a tremendous recovery problem, as they went over board funding assets without understanding or assessing the lessee's debt paying capacity.

The present status of the remaining three selected leasing companies is presented in Table 4.16. The table reveals that the amount to be recovered (otherwise called NPAs) from the lessee companies by three lessor companies, namely NFL, LFL and DCL put together comes to Rs. 685.33 lakhs in 1996-97 (Table 4.16) which constitutes 61.90% of all non-performing assets represented by six select lessor companies (Rs. 1,107.06 lakhs). The NPAs of these three (NFL, LFL and DCL) companies have increased to Rs. 1,163.33 lakhs in 1997-98 from Rs. 685.33 lakhs in 1996-97 registering an increase of 69.75% which is a negative signal for leasing companies.

It is ascertained from the lessor companies that during the year 1997-98, the finance and leasing companies have been adversely affected on account of reduced volume of business in leasing, hire-purchase and bill discounting activities in line with the unfavourable market conditions prevailing in Non-Banking Finance Companies (NBFCs) sector. The problems have been compounded on account of recent policy changes brought out by the Reserve Bank of India during January, 1998 regarding the provisioning norms for non-performing assets, income recognition and direct linking of quantum of public deposit acceptance to credit rating of NBFCs.

Pursuant to the prevailing circumstances, the NFL entered the crop protection business by acquiring an undertaking comprising the business of manufacture and sale of insecticides at Ethakota, Andhra Pradesh from Vijayalakshmi Insecticides and Pesticides Ltd., an associate company of the Nagarjuna Group, for a total consideration of Rs. 6.84 crores. This acquisition is with retrospective effect from 1st April, 1997, resulted in the combined income of both financial as well as manufacturing business.

To facilitate the process of acquisition and transfer of product registration for insecticides, the financial year of NFL was extended to 15 months. The operational performance during the 15th month period reflects the combined business of financial services and crop protection. Gross income stood at Rs. 23,715.98 lakhs in 1997-98 as against Rs. 10,840.33 lakhs in the previous year (1996-97). The

Table 4.16 : Income and Costs of Three Lessor Companies

(Rs.lakhs)

	NFL		*LFL*		*DCL*		*TOTAL*	
	1996-97	*1997-98*	*1996-97*	*1997-98*	*1996-97*	*1997-98*	*1996-97*	*1997-98*
Total Income	(100) 10840.33	(100) 23715.98	(100) 476.60	(100) 327.20	(100) 2879.47	(100) 3483.49	(100) 14196.40	(100) 27526.67
Operating Expenditure	(22.21) 2407.37	(52.97) 12562.21	(28.39) 135.31	(27.85) 91.11	(23.59) 679.20	(29.32) 1021.37	(22.70) 3221.88	(49.68) 13674.69
Interest	(52.63) 5705.76	(33.66) 7981.55	(11.31) 53.89	(11.96) 39.12	(61.29) 1764.64	(65.28) 2274.17	(53.00) 7524.29	(37.40) 10295.24
Depreciation	(13.65) 1479.50	(7.76) 1839.78	(37.10) 176.81	(54.83) 179.40	(6.60) 190.21	(5.99) 208.77	(13.00) 1846.52	(8.09) 2227.95
Prov. for NPA	(5.04) 546.58	(4.16) 986.90	(13.38) 63.78	(8.82) 28.85	(2.60) 74.97	(4.24) 147.58	(4.83) 685.33	(4.23) 1163.33
Tax Provision	(0.84) 91.00	(0.16) 37.00	(1.27) 6.05	(7.03) 23.00	(0.76) 21.99	—	(0.84) 119.04	(0.22) 60.00
Net Profit/Loss	(5.63) 610.12	(1.29) 308.14	(8.55) 40.76	(-10.49) 34.28	(5.16) 148.46	(-4.83) 168.40	(5.63) 799.34	(0.38) 105.46
Leased Assets	2497.63	140.63	113.05	60.46	97.03	87.31	2707.71	288.40

Source: Annual Reports.

net profit after providing for non performing assets as per the new norms of RBI and after tax [on account of Minimum Alternate Tax (MAT)] stood at Rs. 308.14 lakhs in 1997-98 as against Rs. 610.12 lakhs in 1996-97 (Table 4.16). The leasing activities were drastically reduced by 94.4% from Rs. 2,497.63 lakhs in 1996-97 to Rs. 140.63 lakhs in 1997-98 (Table 4.16).

In view of the unprecedented sluggishness from 1996, and given the general risk profile in this business of financial services, NFL has ceased to carry on any of the financial services activities but continued to pursue the collection of receivables which arose from the financial services activities. Effective from 10 December, 1998, the NFL has completely stopped accepting public deposits after having accepted it for a short period during August 1998. Further, NFL wrote to the RBI to treat its application for registration as a Non-Banking Financial Company in terms of Section 451A of the RBI Act, 1934 as withdrawn.

The LFL has adopted a restrained approach in the financial service activities due to prevalent adverse business environment in the NBFC sector. The company's gross income for the year 1997-98 was reduced by 31.4% from Rs. 476.6 lakhs to Rs. 327.20 lakhs. After providing for non-performing assets, the company suffered a net loss of Rs. —34.28 lakhs in 1997-98.

The volume of leased assets during 1997-98 decreased by 46.52% from Rs. 113.05 lakhs to Rs. 60.46 lakhs (Table 4.16). During 1998-99, the company did not take up new business in the field of leasing and hire-purchase and concentrated in a limited way on the area of short-term financing, viz., inter-corporate deposits and bill discounting in addition to monitoring the portfolio of investments and repayment of public deposits. Further, the company has been actively pursuing the recovery of outstanding amounts and has initiated legal proceedings against some parties who have defaulted in payment of lease/hire-purchase instalments.

The economy is passing through difficult times and the severe liquidity crisis prevailing particularly in the corporate sector has resulted in the accumulation of non-performing assets for DCL. The NPAs increased to Rs. 147.58 lakhs in 1997-98 from Rs. 74.97 lakhs in 1996-97. Though DCL is a major player in lease financing activity, a small exposure of financing to corporate sector led this company into temporary setbacks, recording a net loss of Rs. –168.40 lakhs and non-performing assets at Rs. 147.58 lakhs in 1997-98 (Table 4.16). Thus, it witnessed a sea change in the fortunes of non-banking financial companies. There is a slight decrease in the volume of leased assets from Rs. 97.03 lakhs in 1996-97 to Rs. 87.31 lakhs in 1997-98.

The period 1996-97 marked a severe and intensive competition not only from players in the industry which include banks but also from some of the foreign financial institutions, resulting in the fall of business in leased assets. The DCL company initiated appropriate steps both legal and conciliatory for recovery of the outstandings. A number of non-viable branches have been closed and staff is being reduced to the required level.

The leasing business during the year 1997-98 has come to almost a standstill.

Further, according to the information ascertained from leasing companies, the main reasons for hindrance in the growth of leasing business are: (i) sudden imposition of stringent RBI regulations or norms; and (ii) problem of recovery of dues from lessee companies. Because of RBI's prudential norms, the mobilisation of public deposits was drastically reduced as the credit rating was linked to acceptance of public deposits. As such, many leasing and finance companies have stopped accepting public deposits and were forced to return the excess public deposits to public. This in turn led to fund constraints for lessor companies and the operations of companies received a setback and eliminated the erring companies and brought the survival of the fittest in the interest of the public and steady growth of the economy.

Having discussed the revenues and costs of select lessor companies, it is now pertinent to discuss the debt-equity ratios and interest coverage ratios of select lessor companies.

Debt-Equity Ratio

The Debt-equity ratio shows the extent to which the firm is financed by debt. In other words, it is relevant to assess the extent to which the firm is using borrowed money for investment and other purposes. The debt-equity ratio is computed by dividing the total debt (excluding current liabilities) of the firm by its shareholders' equity. Equity includes preference capital plus reserves and surplus minus intangible assets and accumulated losses if any, i.e.,

D-E Ratio = Total Debt ÷ Equity

The shareholders equity is also called the net worth. Accordingly, this ratio is also called debt to net worth ratio. A high debt-equity ratio indicates a large share of financing by the creditors in relation to the owners. The performance of a company can be measured in terms of its ability to raise external funds. The more the company borrows, the more it earns for its equity shareholders. But at the same time, increased financial leverage means increased risk. Normally, for a manufacturing company, a debt-equity ratio of 2:1 is said to be the most desirable one, but this is not certainly applicable to a finance/leasing company. The RBI has fixed a debt-equity ratio at 10:1 as the upper limit of desirability for finance/leasing companies. The debt-equity ratio is calculated for all select lessor companies and presented in Table 4.17.

Table 4.17 : Debt-Equity Ratio of Select Lessor Companies

Companies	*1990-91*	*1991-92*	*1992-93*	*1993-94*	*1994-95*	*1995-96*	*1996-97*	*X*
NFL	4.20	4.06	3.77	3.34	5.55	6.54	8.65	5.16
PPL	1.45	1.90	3.69	2.03	1.88	1.60	2.35	2.13
LFL	0.05	0.11	0.20	0.16	0.31	0.28	0.33	0.21
DCL	4.46	2.50	3.56	3.14	5.31	7.80	9.48	5.18
MWL	2.95	2.25	0.93	1.15	0.86	**	1.36	1.36
SCFSL	2.11	1.31	1.27	1.39	1.82	**	*	1.13

Note : i. * Capital has eroded to the extent of Rs. —67.74 lakhs as the accumulated losses and intangible assets exceeded the capital.

ii. ** As the financial year is delayed, the respective companies clubbed the figures pertaining to the year 1995-96 in the years 1994-95 and 1996-97.

iii. $\bar{X}$ = Arithmetic Mean.

Source: Computed from annual reports of select lessor companies.

This ratio is calculated to see whether the leasing company has mobilised 10 times the debt to its net owned funds or net worth as stipulated by the RBI.

An analysis of Table 4.17 reveals the following:

No select lessor company has mobilised or borrowed from external sources—such as borrowing from banks and financial institutions and deposits from the public to the extent of 10 times to its net owned funds or net worth.

Among all companies, the NFL and DCL have been performing better in terms of mobilisation of external funds recording the mobilisation of external resources on an average, at 5.16 times and 5.18 times of debt to their net worth respectively. These companies have mobilised almost 10 times of debt to their equity/net worth in the year 1996-97 recording 8.65 times and 9.48 times respectively. This ratio has increased substantially for both the companies NFL and DCL, particularly from 1994-95 to 1996-97, recording 5.55 times in 1994-95, 6.54 times in 1995-96 and 8.65 times in 1996-97 for NFL and 5.31 times in 1994-95, 7.80 times in 1995-96 and 9.48 times in 1996-97 for DCL. PPL recording follows this on an average at 2.13 times of its debt to equity. Due to the mobilisation of more public deposits, the debt-equity ratio has increased substantially for NFL and DCL.

The remaining three companies such as LFL, MWL and SCFSL have shown poor performance in their mobilisation of external resources, recording their debtequity ratio, on an average at 0.21, 1.36 and 1.13 respectively. The lowest debt-equity ratio was recorded with the LFL, which has been trading on thick equity.

The SCFSL has recorded net worth at a negative figure of Rs. –67.74 lakhs in the year 1996-97. The capital eroded to an extent of Rs.–67.74 lakhs because of the accumulated losses, intangible assets, deferred payments, etc. However, the debt is recorded at Rs. 403.93 lakhs in the year 1996-97. As such, the debt-equity ratio is not calculated for SCFSL for 1996-97.

Three companies such, as LFL, MWL and SCFSL recorded poor performance in their mobilisation of external resources. These companies have not even mobilised the public deposits as required. These companies have been "trading on thick equity". The higher use of equity proportion in the capital structure is known as the "trading on thick equity", while a higher use of debt proportion in the capital structure is called "trading on thin equity". The NFL and DCL have been trading on thin equity as they have used higher proportion of debt in their capital structure.

Thus the financial leverage employed by a company is intended to earn on the fixed charge funds. The lessor is basically the financial intermediary collecting funds from various sources investing them on leased assets and hire-purchased assets. The company tries to raise the funds at a cost lower than the interest, which it earns from the business. Thereby, the company makes a profit, which meets its finance and operational costs, and gives a reward to the shareholders. Thus, the higher the use of debt, the higher will be the returns to the shareholders, provided the funds are managed/ rotated in a proper way.

Interest Coverage

The interest coverage ratio is calculated to relate the financial charges (interest) of a firm to its ability to cover them or pay them. This ratio is simply the ratio of earnings before interest and taxes for a particular reporting period to the amount of interest charges for the period; i.e.,

I.C. Ratio = Earnings before Interest and Taxes (EBIT) ÷ Interest Expenses

In general, the higher the ratio, the greater the likelihood that the company could cover its interest payments without difficulty. But, too high a ratio indicates that the firm is very conservative in using debt. The coverage ratios are calculated for select lessor companies by taking earnings before interest and tax (EBIT) and divided by interest amount as shown in Table 4.18. Except LFL, all companies such as NFL, PPL, DCL, MWL and SCFSL have ability to cover their annual interest less than 3.03 times with operating income. The NFL's ability to cover its annual interest payment is less than 1.41 times, which is a low margin of safety, over a period of study from 1990-91 to 1996-97. Almost the same trend was recorded with DCL, MWL registering the interest coverage at less than two times their profits to cover interest payments. The poor performance recorded by MWL and SCFSL in 1996-97 resulted in negative ratios at–0.12% for MWL and –0.64% for SCFSL. It means these companies were not able to meet their interest payments in the year 1996-97.

It may be noted that the interest and principal payment of debts are not really met out of earnings, but out of cash. Therefore it is

Table 4.18 : Interest Coverage Ratio

Cos.	*1990-91*	*1991-92*	*1992-93*	*1993-94*	*1994-95*	*1995-96*	*1996-97*
NFL	1.28	1.37	1.33	1.41	1.33	1.24	1.12
PPL	2.07	2.60	1.86	2.17	1.91	1.59	1.24
LFL	35.17	24.37	2.12	2.10	53.22	3.19	1.87
DCL	1.26	1.48	1.53	1.54	1.53	1.19	1.10
MWL	1.36	1.35	1.53	1.69	1.29	*	(-0.12)
SCFSL	1.46	3.03	1.75	1.35	0.55	*	(-0.64)

Note: *As the financial year is delayed, the respective companies clubbed the figures pertaining to the year 1995-96 in 1994-95 and 1996-97.
Source: Calculated from Annual Reports.

necessary to analyse cash-flow ability of the firms to service debt obligations by preparing cash-flow statements.

SECTION-II

Cash Flow Analysis

In the previous section, the Balance Sheets of select lessor companies presented the summary of their financial position by exhibiting different sources of funds and application of funds at a certain point of time. But these statements failed to show the nature of transactions entered into, changes in assets, liabilities and owners' equity. The statement of changes in financial position can only be known by preparing a cash flow statement.

The term "FUND" can be defined at least in three ways: It can mean (i) cash, (ii) working capital (the difference between current assets and current liabilities), or (iii) financial resources (arising from both current and non-current items).[11] The cash flow statement reveals the sources (inflows) and uses (outflows) of cash and summarises the causes for changes in the cash position between two balance sheet dates.

The success, growth and survival of every company depend on its ability to generate or obtain cash. What enables an entity to survive is the availability of tangible resource of cash, which is one of the indicators of financial performance. Thus, owners look for dividends, suppliers and lenders expect payments and repayments, employees expect wages for their services, and the tax authority look for tax revenues due.

The purpose of cash flow analysis is to present the cash inflows (sources) and outflows (uses) during a period of study from 1990-91 to 1996-97. Cash flow analysis helps in evaluating sources (inflows) and uses (outflows) of cash and the cause for changes in cash and cash equivalents by listing the activities that increase cash and those that decrease it. All activities of cash flows are segregated into three categories: *Operating, investing and financing activities.* Each activity's cash inflow or outflow is segregated according to each of the three broad categories mentioned above.

Cash Flows from Operating Activities

Cash from operations is a major source of cash to a company. The net result of various business operations during a particular period reveals the net profit or net loss. Net profit results in an inflow of cash and net loss in an outflow of cash. The cash generated from operating activities would not be equal to the net profit; or cash lost may not be equal to net loss. This is so because certain non-cash and non-operating items are charged to profit and loss account.

The funds or cash from operations is calculated by adjusting the figure of net profit before tax disclosed in the income statement for non-fund or non-cash or non-operating items and related changes in balance sheet items to determine the cash provided by operating activities. The items of depreciation on fixed assets, miscellaneous expenditure written off, loss on sale of fixed assets are added to net profit before tax. Similarly, dividend received and profit on sale of fixed asset or investment are deducted from profit to arrive at cash generated by operating activities. While preparing the cash flow statement, funds from non-operating items are worked out by comparing two items in the balance sheets of two consecutive years on the basis of the changes that occurred in the non-current items. The non-current items are issue of shares, loans, and sale and purchase of non-current assets, investments by companies to know the insight into the movement of funds to finance various investing activities.

In order to arrive at the net cash from operations after working capital changes, the current assets and current liabilities are adjusted to net profit. Increase in current assets and decrease in current liabilities reduces the cash, while decrease in current assets and increase in current liabilities increases the cash. Other sources of working capital or cash include—sale of fixed assets and long term investments, issue of share capital or debentures and borrowings. The uses of funds or cash includes acquisition of fixed assets including leased assets, or long term investments, repayment of debt or debentures and payment of cash dividend etc.

Thus, the Cash Flow Statement reveals the firm's liquidity position, movement of funds, capital expenditure incurred, dividend paid, the extent of external financing etc.

To facilitate analysis, cash flow statements for all select lessor companies are prepared to have an insight into the movement of funds and nature of activities financed and presented in Tables 4.20 to 4.25. A consolidated statement pertaining to operating activities, investing activities and financing activities of all select lessor companies is prepared and presented in Table 4.19.

The cash flow statements are prepared according to the format prescribed by listing agreement with stock exchange and the method prescribed by the Institute of Chartered Accountants of India (ICAI) which require disclosure of profits from operations. According to the Format, the increase in leased assets is considered as an investment activity while increase in stock on hire is merged with profits from operations by treating it as a current asset and considered it as operating activity.

The main sources of funds to the companies engaged in leasing and hire purchase business are borrowings and lease rentals/hire-purchase instalments. The main application of funds is disbursements by way of lease and hire purchase agreements. Whenever instalments are received towards lease rentals or hire purchase instalments, borrowing is reduced to that extent.

On the other hand, stock on hire is reduced to the extent of principal recovery in instalments received in case of hire-purchase agreements. In case of lease agreement, depreciation and lease equivalisation reserve reduce the value of leased assets to the extent of principal recovery in lease rental instalments.

The increase or decrease in current assets and current liabilities are to be adjusted to find out cash from operations because increase or decrease in current assets and current liability influence the flow of cash from operations.

While increase in debtors is deducted from net profit, decrease in debtors is added as they involve cash inflow of funds. Increase in debtors implies that collections from debtors are less than sales revenue and decrease in debtors implies that collections are more than sales revenue. Here sales revenue means lease and hire purchase assets agreement, bill discounting and other related financial services activities. If debtors decrease because of bad debts, it will have no effect on the flow of cash. Similar treatment is done in case of other current assets such as trade bills, bank deposit, inventory, loans and advances, etc. The net increase in current liabilities—such as sundry creditors, unclaimed dividends, pre-received income, interest accrued but not due and other liabilities—are added to net profit as it involves cash inflow while decrease in current liabilities are subtracted from the net profit as it involves cash outflow.

Stock on Hire

The stock on hire is merged with profits from operations and increase in the stock on hire is subtracted from net profit as it involves outflow of cash and decrease in stock on hire is added to profit as it involves inflow of cash. Table 4.19 reveals that the consolidated figure of the stock on hire shows the trend of its ups and downs. The table recorded the increasing trends (which were deducted from net profit) at Rs. 1,405.29 lakhs in 1991, Rs. 250.20 lakhs in 1992, Rs. 1,775.43 lakhs in 1993, Rs. 4,122.66 lakhs in 1994, Rs. 11,068.08 lakhs in 1995, Rs. 5,449.56 lakhs in 1996 and Rs. 9,638.03 lakhs in 1997. The highest growth rate is registered in 1992-93 and 1994-95 recording at 609.6% and 168.5% respectively. Almost the same trend percentages were recorded for NFL and DCL. The remaining 4 companies such as PPL, LFL, MWL and SCFSL did very little hire-purchase business (Tables 4.20 to 4.25). However, the consolidated figure in Table 4.2 of Section-I show that the share of hire purchase is higher than the equipment leasing business. The share of hire purchase to total application of funds is registered at 65.82% in 1991, 56.34% in

Table 4.19 : Consolidated Cash Flow Statement of Select Lessor Companies

(Rs.lakhs)

Activities	*1990-91*	*1991-92*	*1992-93*	*1993-94*	*1994-95*	*1995-96**	*1996-97*
(A) ***Cash flow from Operating Activities***							
Net Profit/(Loss) before tax	509.54	991.60	987.97	1414.77	2491.53	2016.62	884.12
Adjustments for :							
Depreciation	521.66	707.83	881.55	1292.76	1871.99	2918.57	2559.68
Misc. expenditure written off	42.61	52.77	60.38	104.26	669.67	1375.74	1659.39
Profit on sale of fixed assets/ Investments	(17.58)	(41.25)	(17.55)	(58.15)	(61.24)	(24.45)	(22.87)
Dividend received	(84.08)	(5.10)	(22.90)	(25.13)	(125.30)	(64.43)	(97.81)
Loss on sale of fixed assets	6.68	1.60	2.49	11.32	29.75	12.10	82.91
Lease equalisation charges	–	–	–	–	–	74.05	1229.60
Operating Profit before W.C. Changes	**978.83**	**1707.45**	**1891.94**	**2739.83**	**4876.40**	**6308.20**	**6295.02**
(Increase)/Decrease in stock on hire	(1405.29)	(250.20)	(1775.43)	(4122.66)	(11068.08)	(5449.56)	(9638.03)
(Increase)/Decrease in lease rental debtors	(78.56)	(107.58)	(52.19)	78.67	349.01	(538.07)	(313.57)
(Increase)/Decrease in other debtors	(114.06)	(812.11)	(350.22)	(310.78)	(3743.40)	(417.23)	317.01
(Increase)/Decrease in trade bills	(13.71)	(202.07)	(44.27)	(637.02)	(3423.84)	(4756.78)	(1382.72)
(Increase)/Decrease in bank deposits	(98.67)	(235.76)	(120.48)	(269.98)	(463.14)	(798.27)	(449.69)
(Increase)/Decrease in loans and advances	(100.80)	(12.79)	(609.74)	(871.80)	(4278.82)	(1594.55)	(819.79)
(Increase)/Decrease in other current assets	(8.32)	87.02	(579.08)	(2530.25)	355.94	356.40	(625.70)
Increase/(Decrease) in current liabilities	172.86	967.81	110.22	1115.78	6298.38	(758.28)	516.51
Cash flow before tax	(667.82)	1142.67	(1529.25)	(4808.21)	(11097.55)	(7648.14)	(6100.96)
(Direct taxes paid)/Tax refund	3.94	(48.24)	57.02	(169.61)	(169.64)	(308.56)	(1030.61)
Net cash (used in)/Generated from Operating Activities (A)	**(663.88)**	**1094.43**	**(1472.23)**	**(4977.82)**	**(11267.19)**	**(7956.70)**	**(7131.57)**

Note: (i) W.C. = Working Capital.

Table 4.19 (*Contd.*)

Activities	*1990-91*	*1991-92*	*1992-93*	*1993-94*	*1994-95*	*1995-96**	*1996-97*
(B) ***Cash flow from Investing Activities***							
Purchase of fixed assets (owned)	(83.77)	(63.62)	(167.50)	(96.48)	(304.62)	(426.50)	(795.67)
Purchase of leased assets	(727.95)	(1135.77)	(1493.31)	(2822.44)	(7905.60)	(6333.89)	(3168.61)
(Purchase)/sale of investments	(110.94)	(201.20)	(472.92)	(728.90)	(1856.49)	(3853.98)	(2524.35)
(Increase)/Decrease C.W. in progress	14.98	(90.23)	(45.67)	123.61	(64.84)	(67.11)	–
Profit on sale of fixed assets/Investments	15.40	41.25	15.84	58.15	61.24	24.45	8.82
Sale of fixed assets (owned)	2.04	3.94	3.05	3.68	5.46	3.35	47.72
Dividend received	84.08	5.10	22.90	25.13	125.30	64.43	97.81
Net cash (used in)/Generated from investing activities (B)	**(806.16)**	**(1440.53)**	**(2137.61)**	**(3437.26)**	**(9939.55)**	**(10587.25)**	**(6334.28)**
(C) ***Cash flow from financing activities***							
Proceeds from Issue of share capital	517.67	364.95	1098.75	1884.44	4641.75	2119.82	127.22
Proceeds from term loans	730.21	53.50	712.92	3680.50	2525.26	1646.71	3626.43
Proceeds from bank borrowings	584.93	458.36	1479.45	965.56	6180.28	1920.38	2772.05
Proceeds from public deposits	706.14	1204.05	2121.41	4480.00	15766.39	18660.55	15569.03
Repayment of term loans	(386.81)	(586.29)	(806.31)	(799.03)	(2352.86)	(1455.05)	(1779.26)
Repayment of bank borrowings	(279.40)	(158.84)	(547.17)	(1117.52)	(74.13)	(4313.65)	(1267.22)
Dividend paid	(213.32)	(242.80)	(383.19)	(395.70)	(683.39)	(812.19)	(903.39)
Miscellaneous expenditure	(132.61)	(159.24)	(310.13)	(410.41)	(1208.92)	(1894.18)	(2405.18)
Net cash (used in)/Generated from financing activities (C)	**1526.81**	**933.69**	**3365.73**	**8287.84**	**24794.38**	**15872.39**	**15739.68**
Net increase/(decrease) in cash and cash equivalents (A+B+C)	**56.77**	**587.59**	**(244.11)**	**(127.24)**	**3587.64**	**(2671.56)**	**2273.83**
Cash at the beginning of the year	456.66	513.43	1101.02	856.91	729.67	4317.31	1645.75
Cash at the end of the year	513.43	1101.02	856.91	729.67	4317.31	1645.75	3919.58

Note: (i) *Only 4 companies data was considered, as the two other companies—MWL and SCFSL have skipped the year 1995-96 by adjusting the months in 1994-95 and 1996-97. (ii) Sale of leased assets is not considered as total cost plus profit is included in lease rental income. (iii) Figures in brackets indicate cash outflows. (iv) C.W. = Capital Work.

Source: Annual reports of select lessor companies.

Table 4.20 : Cashflow Statement of NFL

(Rs. lakhs)

Activities	*1990-91*	*1991-92*	*1992-93*	*1993-94*	*1994-95*	*1995-96*	*1996-97*
(A) ***Cash flow from Operating Activities***							
Net Profit/(Loss) before tax	225.72	401.30	462.08	640.72	982.80	1025.48	701.12
Adjustments for :							
Depreciation	280.52	410.93	482.49	641.45	1110.81	2140.40	1479.50
Misc. expenditure written off	13.60	9.95	13.85	18.44	539.51	1081.48	1222.38
Profit on sale of fixed assets/Investments	(5.94)	–	–	–	(33.52)	(6.46)	(4.12)
Dividend received	(83.43)	(2.73)	(3.81)	(0.45)	(89.89)	(10.28)	(33.11)
Loss on sale of fixed assets	–	–	–	–	–	–	–
Lease equalisation charges	–	–	–	–	–	95.71	1078.25
Operating Profit before W.C. Changes	**430.47**	**819.45**	**954.61**	**1300.16**	**2509.71**	**4326.33**	**4444.02**
(Increase)/Decrease in stock on hire	(978.37)	(182.57)	(1398.43)	(817.20)	(5249.54)	(4635.52)	(4524.38)
(Increase)/Decrease in lease rental debtors	21.95	(6.60)	51.00	91.64	322.05	(486.57)	(322.03)
(Increase)/Decrease in other debtors	(90.81)	(597.06)	(225.47)	71.49	(3171.31)	(208.04)	505.43
(Increase)/Decrease in trade bills	(10.18)	(110.79)	106.05	(130.92)	(2153.04)	(1291.99)	(1111.18)
(Increase)/Decrease in bank deposits	(85.82)	(223.69)	(59.53)	12.37	(364.54)	(491.08)	(414.19)
(Increase)/Decrease in loans and advances	10.98	(83.17)	(734.32)	(273.25)	(3569.03)	(517.79)	(363.08)
(Increase)/Decrease in other current assets*	–	69.54	(584.90)	(1934.16)	1700.83	351.48	(700.22)
Increase/(Decrease) in current liabilities	(29.59)	875.47	(46.68)	229.61	4355.00	(314.18)	(300.02)
Cash flow before tax	(731.37)	560.58	(1937.67)	(1450.26)	(5619.87)	(3267.36)	(2785.65)
(Direct taxes paid)/Tax refund	(19.47)	(5.42)	102.63	(247.47)	(56.38)	(224.96)	(928.76)
Net cash (used in)/Generated from Operating Activities (A)	**(750.84)**	**555.16**	**(1835.04)**	**(1697.73)**	**(5676.25)**	**(3492.32)**	**(3714.41)**

Note: (i) *Other Current Assets include Stock in trade.
(ii) W.C. = Working Capital.

Table 4.20 *(Contd.)*

Activities	*1990-91*	*1991-92*	*1992-93*	*1993-94*	*1994-95*	*1995-96*	*1996-97*
(B) ***Cash flow from Investing Activities***							
Purchase of fixed assets (owned)	(32.92)	(14.24)	(42.10)	(41.27)	(75.63)	(128.09)	(459.52)
Purchase of leased assets	(402.44)	(360.13)	(671.37)	(1958.37)	(5103.54)	(4980.66)	(2497.63)
(Purchase)/sale of investments	(105.01)	(50.01)	(147.61)	(634.13)	(980.16)	(2869.99)	(1266.69)
(Increase)/Decrease in C.W. in progress	15.65	(90.23)	(45.67)	123.61	–	(29.05)	–
Profit on sale of fixed assets/ Investments	5.94	–	–	–	33.52	6.46	4.12
Sale of fixed assets (owned)	1.79	–	1.00	0.87	3.85	1.05	6.01
Dividend received	83.43	2.73	3.81	0.45	89.89	10.28	33.11
Net cash (used in)/Generated from investing activities (B)	**(433.56)**	**(511.88)**	**(901.64)**	**(2508.84)**	**(6032.47)**	**(7990.00)**	**(4180.60)**
(C) Cash flow from financing activities							
Proceeds from Issue of share capital	411.38	–	515.60	822.48	872.92	1035.00	–
Proceeds from term loans	397.11	–	429.89	2233.01	869.69	1456.71	3208.70
Proceeds from bank borrowings	235.83	116.14	917.45	–	3759.58	1865.60	2463.40
Proceeds from public deposits	550.85	931.10	1307.27	2798.84	10562.03	11973.32	8623.36
Repayment of term loans	(213.30)	(310.02)	(495.63)	(210.40)	(1763.17)	(379.47)	(1037.91)
Repayment of bank borrowings	(27.38)	(34.19)	–	(955.94)	–	(3229.91)	(1027.21)
Dividend paid	(60.93)	(93.21)	(166.80)	(216.91)	(308.57)	(395.00)	(446.49)
Miscellaneous expenditure	(108.11)	(114.54)	(223.93)	(263.93)	(879.39)	(1481.11)	(1822.37)
Net cash (used in)/Generated from financing activities (C)	**1185.45**	**495.28**	**2283.85**	**4207.15**	**13113.09**	**10845.14**	**9961.48**
Net increase/(decrease) in cash and cash equivalents (A+B+C)	1.05	538.56	(453.13)	0.58	1404.37	(637.18)	2066.47
Cash at the beginning of the year	242.39	243.44	782.00	328.87	329.45	1733.82	1096.64
Cash at the end of the year	243.44	782.00	328.87	329.45	1733.82	1096.64	3163.11

Note : (i) Sale of leased assets is not considered as total cost plus profit is included in lease rental income.
(ii) Figures in brackets indicate cash outflows.
(iii) Capital Work.

Source : Annual reports of select lessor companies.

1992, 50.46% in 1993, 46.91% in 1994, 42.84% in 1994-95, 35.04% in 1995-96 and 37.17% in 1996-97. Whereas the share of leased assets is registered at 28.93% in 1991, 31.01% in 1992, 29.54% in 1993, 27.64% in 1994, 27.12% in 1995, 26.33% in 1996 and 23.95% in 1997 (Table 4.2 of Section-I). The trend per cent for these two types of assets, leased assets and hire purchase assets, has declined. The average share of leased assets is registered at 27.79%, while the average share of hire-purchase assets was registered at 47.80% (Table 4.2). The assets such as investments, net current assets, etc., have registered an increasing trend from 2.51% in 1990-91 to 27.82% in 1994-95 and further increased to 36.52% in 1995-96 and 36.36% in 1996-97 (Table 4.2).

The distortion here is that an increase in stock on hire is merged with the profits from operations by treating it as current asset, while increase in leased assets is considered as an investment. In reality the stock on hire and leased assets are of the same nature and both should be given the same treatment in the cash flow statement. Merging the increase in stock on hire with the profits from operations distorts the figure of cash from operations as the amount involved in investment of hire purchase assets comes around to an average of 47.80% of the total investment. On the other hand, total lease rentals are treated as income while in the case of hire purchase, only hire-charges component is considered as income in the profit and loss account.

Debtors

Increase in debtors is deducted from net profit while decrease in debtors is added as it involves inflow of cash. Increase in debtors implies that the collections from debtors are less than the turnover whereas, decrease in debtors implies that the collections from debtors are more than the sales revenue/turnover. If the debtors decrease because of non-performing assets, it will have no effect on the flow of cash.

Table 4.19 shows that there is an increase in lease rental debtors in the years 1991, 1992 and 1993 recording at Rs. 78.56 lakhs, Rs. 107.58 lakhs, and Rs. 52.19 lakhs respectively, compared to their previous years which witnessed a decline in the collection of lease rentals from debtors than lease agreements. There is a decrease in lease rentals in the years 1994 and 1995, recording at Rs. 78.67 lakhs and Rs. 349.01 lakhs respectively compared to their previous years, which witnessed more collections from debtors than lease agreements. But there is again an increase in lease rental debtors in the year 1996 and 1997 recording at Rs. 538.07 lakhs and Rs. 313.57 lakhs respectively compared to previous years, mainly due to the increase of Non-Performing Assets (NPAs) and slow collection from debtors.

The provision for substandard/doubtful/loss assets (NPAs) of select lessor companies has increased from 1992 to 1997, recording Rs. 17.92 lakhs (1992), Rs. 62.14 lakhs (1993), Rs. 206.90 lakhs (1994), Rs. 280.02 lakhs (1995), Rs. 514.12 lakhs (1996) and Rs. 1,107.06 lakhs (1997). The details of NPAs were discussed in Chapter-3. The above figures prove that there is substantial increase in NPAs in 1996 and 1997 due to which lease rental debtors are increased and the recovery of overdues has become a big problem. As such, the performance of the lessor companies has been adversely affected.

The other debtors have recorded an increasing trend from 1991 to 1996 but slopped down in 1997. There is a substantial increase in other debtors, i.e. other than lease debtors in 1994-95 recording Rs. 3,743.40 lakhs. In the same year, there is a substantial decrease in lease debtors recording Rs. 349.01 lakhs. It means that there is a good collection from lease rental debtors compared to other debtors. Contrary to which, in 1997, there is an increase in lease rental debtors recording at Rs. 313.57 lakhs and decrease in other debtors (other than lease debtors) recording at Rs. 317.01 lakhs. It means that the collection from other debts is more than lease rental debtors (Table 4.19).

Almost the same trend is recorded for all select lessor companies except DCL. The debt collection is good as far as DCL is concerned recording the decrease of debtors at Rs. 3.60 lakhs in 1991, 11.79 lakhs in 1992, Rs. 3.17 lakhs in 1993, and Rs. 16.82 lakhs in 1994. However, there is a slight increase in debtors, which shows the slow pace in the collection of debts. The increase in debtors was recorded as Rs. 3.38 lakhs in 1995, Rs. 37.37 lakhs in

Table 4.21 : Cash flow Statement of PPL *(Rs.lakhs)*

	Activities	*1990-91*	*1991-92*	*1992-93*	*1993-94*	*1994-95*	*1995-96*	*1996-97*
(A)	***Cash flow from Operating Activities***							
	Net Profit/(Loss) before tax	19.99	105.45	108.20	265.12	915.30	628.58	575.64
	Adjustments for :							
	Depreciation	5.76	49.55	68.07	174.03	350.00	414.31	568.62
	Misc. expenditure written off	0.47	0.47	0.47	7.88	24.31	38.13	73.63
	Profit on sale of fixed assets/investments	–	–	–	–	–	–	–
	Dividend/income from invest. received	–	(0.93)	(3.79)	(11.22)	(15.95)	(34.39)	(58.15)
	Loss on sale of fixed assets	–	–	1.72	1.72	–	–	–
	Lease equivalisation charge	–	–	–	–	–	15.51	127.75
	Operating Profit before W.C. Changes	**26.22**	**154.54**	**174.67**	**437.53**	**1273.66**	**1062.14**	**1287.49**
	(Increase)/Decrease in stock on hire	(337.86)	12.51	(190.49)	(1830.97)	(3261.45)	1003.63	(3996.73)
	(Increase)/Decrease in lease rental debtors	(9.9)	(29.01)	18.78	(9.59)	56.54	(14.13)	–
	(Increase)/Decrease in other debtors	(2.87)	(60.33)	37.51	(81.28)	–	–	8.98
	(Increase)/Decrease in trade bills	(3.53)	1.45	(5.45)	(432.68)	(1028.04)	(2844.92)	455.33
	(Increase)/Decrease in bank deposits	(1.02)	–	0.45	(167.48)	–	–	–
	(Increase)/Decrease in loans and advances	(4.16)	(47.69)	(8.39)	(154.01)	(385.69)	(443.29)	(645.19)
	(Increase)/Decrease in other current assets*	(7.95)	5.47	15.59	(444.72)	(1281.90)	(13.58)	–
	Increase/(Decrease) in current liabilities	208.87	(72.17)	(67.05)	681.63	1310.23	(1008.30)	575.29
	Cash flow before tax	(132.20)	(35.23)	(24.38)	(2001.57)	(3316.65)	(2258.45)	(2314.83)
	(Direct taxes paid)/Tax refund	(0.49)	–	(0.63)	(0.80)	–	–	–
	Net cash (used in)/Generated from Operating Activities (A)	**(132.69)**	**(35.23)**	**(25.01)**	**(2002.37)**	**(3316.65)**	**(2258.45)**	**(2314.83)**

Note: (i) *Other Current Assets include Stock of stationery, loans against shares, policy-cum-rights issue money receivables.
(ii) W.C. = Working Capital.

Table 4.21 (*Contd.*)

Activities	*1990-91*	*1991-92*	*1992-93*	*1993-94*	*1994-95*	*1995-96*	*1996-97*
(B) *Cash flow from Investing Activities*							
Purchase of fixed assets (owned)	(8.99)	(12.16)	(64.94)	(7.38)	(111.57)	(130.98)	(171.73)
Purchase of leased assets	(77.14)	(292.81)	(302.50)	(563.25)	(1777.25)	(1097.70)	(414.57)
(Purchase)/Sale of investments	–	(53.62)	(2.76)	(32.55)	(472.86)	(468.10)	(679.34)
(Increase)/Decrease in C.W. in progress	–	–	–	–	–	–	–
Profit on sale of fixed assets/Investments	–	–	–	–	–	–	–
Sale of fixed assets (owned)	–	–	–	–	–	–	–
Dividend/Income from invest. received	–	0.93	3.79	11.22	15.95	34.39	58.15
Net cash (used in)/Generated from investing activities (B)	**(86.13)**	**(357.66)**	**(366.41)**	**(591.96)**	**(2345.73)**	**(1662.39)**	**(1207.49)**
(C) ***Cash flow from financing activities***							
Proceeds from Issue of share capital	105.48	97.00	121.73	779.45	3544.71	1008.00	103.01
Proceeds from term loans	–	–	–	1265.43	1292.87	–	191.44
Proceeds from bank borrowings	102.77	255.79	159.59	346.50	1438.39	–	207.16
Proceeds from public deposits	20.96	47.72	148.34	349.09	2125.20	2389.05	4076.91
Repayment of term loans	–	–	–	–	(215.00)	(895.34)	(427.00)
Repayment of bank borrowings	–	–	(11.75)	–	–	(319.00)	–
Dividend paid	–	(9.79)	(19.80)	(35.75)	(97.29)	(212.70)	(249.41)
Miscellaneous expenditure	–	–	(0.75)	(74.10)	(164.27)	(73.34)	(177.51)
Net cash (used in)/Generated from financing activities (C)	**229.21**	**390.72**	**397.36**	**2630.62**	**7924.61**	**1896.67**	**3724.60**
Net increase/(decrease) in cash and cash equivalents (A+B+C)	**10.39**	**(2.17)**	**5.94**	**36.29**	**2262.23**	**(2024.17)**	**202.28**
Cash at the beginning of the year	2.37	12.76	10.59	16.53	52.82	2315.05	290.88
Cash at the end of the year	12.76	10.59	16.53	52.82	2315.05	290.88	493.16

Note: (i) Share capital is adjusted of share premium and calls in arrears.
(ii) Sale of leased assets is not considered, as total cost plus profit is included in lease rental income.
(iii) Figures in brackets indicate cash outflows.

Source: Annual reports of select lessor companies.

Table 4.22 : Cash flow Statement - LFL

(Rs.lakhs)

Activities	*1990-91*	*1991-92*	*1992-93*	*1993-94*	*1994-95*	*1995-96*	*1996-97*
(A) Cash flow from Operating Activities							
Net Profit/(Loss) before tax	92.85	118.89	71.88	64.22	148.04	96.83	46.81
Adjustments for :							
Depreciation	30.58	39.85	58.42	117.75	97.97	120.14	176.81
Misc. expenditure written off	1.59	2.33	2.95	4.29	8.48	8.11	5.78
Profit on sale of fixed assets/investments	(9.34)	(33.78)	(1.71)	(26.05)	(22.17)	(15.79)	(14.05)
Dividend/received	(0.46)	(0.82)	(3.67)	(4.28)	(5.15)	(5.62)	(3.30)
Loss on sale of fixed assets	–	–	0.02	–	1.44	10.16	4.46
Lease equivalisation charge	–	–	–	–	–	(2.84)	(45.23)
Operating Profit before W.C. Changes	**115.22**	**126.47**	**127.89**	**155.93**	**228.61**	**210.99**	**171.28**
(Increase)/Decrease in stock on hire	–	(60.85)	25.56	12.11	(62.01)	33.86	(4.76)
(Increase)/Decrease in lease rental debtors	–	–	–	–	–	–	–
(Increase)/Decrease in other debtors	2.34	(4.60)	(7.84)	(37.01)	33.35	(2.02)	(90.96)
(Increase)/Decrease in trade bills	–	(92.73)	(99.71)	(2.87)	(125.57)	(1.62)	78.57
(Increase)/Decrease in bank deposits	–	–	–	–	–	–	–
(Increase)/Decrease in loans and advances	(91.82)	168.62	302.22	(0.47)	89.95	25.30	(93.89)
(Increase)/Decrease in other current assets	(29.26)	14.15	(3.03)	(102.75)	(30.61)	(76.20)	(4.14)
Increase/(Decrease) in current liabilities	6.51	33.84	13.54	4.01	129.24	(88.06)	67.66
Cash flow before tax	2.99	184.90	358.63	28.95	262.96	102.25	123.76
(Direct taxes paid)/Tax refund	31.04	(33.47)	(21.39)	89.12	7.36	5.84	(9.67)
Net cash (used in)/Generated from Operating Activities (A)	**34.03**	**151.43**	**337.24**	**118.07**	**270.32**	**108.09**	**114.09**

Note: (i) * Other Current Assets include accrued interest, prepaid expenses and inventories.

(ii) Data pertaining to lease rental debtors was not shown in financial statements by the company. However, it is ascertained that the amount of lease rental debtors is included in other debtors as it is very insignificant.

(iii) W.C. =Working Captial

Table 4.22 (*Contd.*)

Activities	*1990-91*	*1991-92*	*1992-93*	*1993-94*	*1994-95*	*1995-96*	*1996-97*
(*B*) ***Cash flow from Investing Activities***							
Purchase of fixed assets (owned)	(24.12)	(9.25)	(5.12)	(4.51)	(34.72)	(10.97)	(0.60)
Purchase of leased assets	(46.07)	(123.89)	(64.90)	(110.29)	(358.67)	(153.61)	(113.05)
(Purchase)/Sale of investments	(4.89)	(70.69)	(271.51)	82.53	(35.80)	13.67	(7.41)
(Increase)/Decrease in C.W. in progress	(0.67)	–	–	–	–	–	–
Profit on sale of fixed assets/Investments	9.34	33.78	–	26.05	22.17	15.79	–
Sale of fixed assets (owned)	–	0.06	1.71	–	–	–	15.10
Dividend received	0.46	0.82	3.67	4.28	5.15	5.62	3.30
Net cash (used in)/Generated from investing activities (B)	**(65.95)**	**(169.17)**	**(336.15)**	**(1.94)**	**(401.87)**	**(129.50)**	**(102.66)**
(*C*) ***Cash flow from financing activities***							
Proceeds from Issue of share capital	–	–	–	–	–	75.00	–
Proceeds from term loans	39.62	15.00	–	–	88.70	–	50.00
Proceeds from bank borrowings	–	81.40	101.54	74.03	16.70	54.78	44.84
Proceeds from public deposits	–	3.27	9.89	46.50	66.07	55.27	–
Repayment of term loans	–	–	(15.00)	–	–	(55.80)	(47.08)
Repayment of bank borrowings	–	(39.62)	(30.62)	(155.75)	(10.11)	(66.78)	–
Dividend paid	(35.00)	(37.50)	(45.00)	(45.00)	(52.50)	(60.00)	(63.00)
Miscellaneous expenditure	–	–	(2.89)	–	(6.78)	–	–
Net cash (used in)/Generated from financing activities (C)	**4.62**	**22.55**	**17.92**	**(80.22)**	**102.08**	**2.47**	**(15.24)**
Net increase/(decrease) in cash and cash equivalents (A+B+C)	**(27.30)**	**4.81**	**19.01**	**35.91**	**(29.47)**	**(18.94)**	**(3.81)**
Cash at the beginning of the year	38.86	11.56	16.37	35.38	71.29	41.82	22.88
Cash at the end of the year	11.56	16.37	35.38	71.29	41.82	22.88	19.07

Notes: (i) Sale of leased assets is not considered as total cost plus profit is included in lease rental income; (ii) Figures in brackets indicate cash outflows; (iii) C.W. = Capital Work.

Source: Annual reports of select lessor companies.

1996 and Rs. 86.69 lakhs in 1997 (Table 4.23) indicating the slow collection from debtors. Further, the increase of Non-performing assets has adversely affected the performance of the company.

Trade Bills

The consolidated cash flow statement (Table 4.19) reveals that the use of cash towards discounting the Trade Bills has (though had ups and downs in some years) registered an increasing trend and deducted from net profit as it involved cash outflow. The recording was Rs. 13.71 lakhs in 1990-91, Rs. 202.07 lakhs in 1991-92, Rs. 637.02 lakhs in 1993-94, Rs. 3,423.84 lakhs in 1994-95, Rs. 4,756.78 lakhs in 1995-96 and Rs. 1382.72 lakhs in 1996-97. The highest growth rate is recorded at 215.24% in 1993-94 and at 437.5% in 1994-95 due to availability of more funds particularly public deposits. In 1996-97, the growth rate is very slow which could have been due to the impact of RBI guidelines. Almost the same trend is maintained by NFL, PPL and LFL (Tables 4.20 to 4.25). DCL has recorded a constant increasing trend from 1992-93 to 1996-97 recording at Rs. 45.16 lakhs in 1992-93, Rs. 70.55 lakhs in 1993-94, Rs. 117.19 lakhs in 1994-95, Rs. 618.25 lakhs in 1995-96 and Rs. 805.44 lakhs in 1996-97 registering growth rates at 56.2%, 66.12%, 427.56%, and 30.27% in 1993-94, 1994-95, 1995-96 and 1996-97 respectively. The highest growth rate is recorded in the year 1995-96 due to the availability or accessibility of funds. However, the slow growth rate recorded in 1996-97 could be due to the non-availability of sufficient funds and the effect of RBI guidelines.

According to RBI Notification,[12] certain NBFCs received money by way of rediscounting the Bills of Exchange with other corporate bodies, societies, trusts, educational institutions, individuals, etc. In many cases, the bills discounted do not arise out of genuine business transactions and are merely in the nature of accommodation bills. In this connection, all NBFCs were advised that they should discount only *bona fide* Trade Bills. The companies were cautioned that, any money received by the way of re-discounting of Bills, which are not supported by genuine trade transactions, would be treated as regulated deposits. The regulated deposits are attracted by all the provisions of the directions relating to ceiling on total amount of deposits, rate of interest, period of deposit, maintenance of liquid assets, etc., as issued by the Reserve Bank of India. It is further clarified that, while the RBI has no objection to discounting and re-discounting of genuine bills by the companies, any transactions related to the handling of accommodation bills would attract the penal provisions as prescribed in the Reserve Bank of India Act, 1934.

Bank Deposits and Loans and Advances

Bank deposits consist only of term deposits with Banks but not deposits in current accounts. Deposits in current accounts are treated as cash in hand. Loans and Advances consist of: Loans against public deposits, advances to employees, prepaid expenses, interest accrued on investments, interest accrued on advances, etc. Income Tax payments and Tax deducted at source (TDS) though come under the heading of loans and advances these two are treated separately and are shown under the heading of Direct Tax Paid/ Refund.

These two items of Bank deposits and loans and advances have shown an increasing trend (Table 4.19) indicating the use of cash. In the case of bank deposit, using/reducing cash balances accumulate the term deposits. In the case of loans and advances, cash is used towards sanction of loans/advances to employees or others. There is an increasing trend in bank deposits upto 1995-96 recording an increase of Rs. 463.14 lakhs in 1994-95 and Rs. 798.27 lakhs registering the growth rate of 72.36% in 1995-96 over the previous year. Later, this increasing trend has slowed down to 43.67%, whereas in the case of loans and advances, the substantial increasing trend retained up to 1994-95 from 1990-91, recording Rs. 871.80 lakhs in 1993-94 and Rs. 4,278.82 lakhs in 1994-95. The growth was registered at 390.80% in 1994-95 over the previous year due to the availability of funds. Further, this increase in loans and advances has slowed down to 62.73% in 1995-96 and 48.59% in 1996-97 (Table 4.19) due to non-availability of funds.

The slow growth in 1996-97 was a general phenomenon due to the capital market conditions and RBI guidelines. Almost the

Table 4.23 : Cash Flow statement of DCL

(Rs.lakhs)

Activities	*1990-91*	*1991-92*	*1992-93*	*1993-94*	*1994-95*	*1995-96*	*1996-97*
(A) ***Cash flow from Operating Activities***							
Net Profit/(Loss) before tax	44.96	113.95	152.90	241.85	428.39	265.73	170.44
Adjustments for :							
Depreciation	65.63	82.02	109.70	139.03	154.75	243.72	190.21
Misc. expenditure written off	14.35	22.41	28.14	62.41	89.43	248.02	352.30
Profit on sale of fixed assets/Investments	(2.18)	(2.58)	(2.44)	(13.73)	(2.54)	(2.20)	(3.73)
Dividend received	(0.19)	(0.62)	(11.63)	(9.18)	(14.31)	(14.14)	(3.25)
Loss on sale of fixed assets	5.89	0.08	0.53	8.91	0.04	1.94	2.28
Lease equalisation charge	–	–	–	–	–	(34.33)	65.53
Operating Profit before W.C. Changes	**128.46**	**215.26**	**277.20**	**429.29**	**655.76**	**708.74**	**773.78**
(Increase)/Decrease in stock on hire	(262.06)	(506.27)	(492.74)	(1232.22)	(2781.73)	(1851.53)	(1403.24)
(Increase)/Decrease in lease rental debtors	3.60	11.79	3.17	16.82	(3.38)	(37.37)	(86.69)
(Increase)/Decrease in other debtors	1.28	–	–	(7.08)	1.04	(207.17)	14.29
(Increase)/Decrease in trade bills	–	–	(45.16)	(70.55)	(117.19)	(618.25)	(805.44)
(Increase)/Decrease in bank deposits	(11.83)	(7.93)	(58.57)	(64.83)	(106.97)	(307.19)	(36.76)
(Increase)/Decrease in loans and advances	(17.20)	(25.17)	(47.00)	(512.00)	(367.99)	(658.77)	237.25
(Increase)/Decrease in other current assets*	29.66	–	–	–	(86.69)	94.70	3.36
Increase/(Decrease) in current liabilities	64.53	110.70	177.11	433.30	431.55	652.26	294.78
Cash flow before tax	(63.56)	(201.62)	(185.99)	(1007.27)	(2375.60)	(2224.58)	(1008.67)
(Direct taxes paid)/Tax refund	–	(1.22)	(2.32)	(5.09)	(37.29)	(89.44)	(72.33)
Net cash (used in)/Generated from Operating Activities (A)	**(63.56)**	**(202.84)**	**(188.31)**	**(1012.36)**	**(2412.89)**	**(2314.02)**	**(1081.00)**

Note: (i) *Other Current Assets include — stock of plots (real estate), prepaid expenses, income tax refund receivable, etc.
(ii) W.C. =Working Captial

Table 4.23 (*Contd.*)

Activities	*1990-91*	*1991-92*	*1992-93*	*1993-94*	*1994-95*	*1995-96*	*1996-97*
(B) Cash flow from Investing Activities							
Purchase of fixed assets (owned)	(6.80)	(16.85)	(50.31)	(18.93)	(65.83)	(156.46)	(158.68)
Purchase of leased assets	(120.24)	(171.72)	(277.45)	(109.16)	(569.58)	(101.92)	(97.03)
(Purchase)/sale of investments	0.39	(28.13)	(39.19)	(137.98)	(301.80)	(529.56)	(381.04)
(Increase)/Decrease in C.W. in progress	–	–	–	–	(64.84)	(38.06)	–
Profit on sale of fixed assets/Investments	–	2.58	2.44	13.73	2.54	2.20	3.73
Sale of fixed assets (owned)	0.25	0.33	0.19	2.81	1.35	4.30	15.19
Dividend received	0.19	0.62	11.63	9.18	14.31	14.14	3.25
Net cash (used in)/Generated from investing activities (B)	**(126.21)**	**(213.17)**	**(352.69)**	**(240.35)**	**(983.85)**	**(805.36)**	**(614.58)**
(C) Cash flow from financing activities							
Proceeds from Issue of share capital	0.81	267.95	3.11	281.51	42.81	1.82	8.31
Proceeds from term loans	293.48	38.50	283.03	170.80	204.00	190.00	–
Proceeds from bank borrowings	–	5.03	297.30	470.00	950.40	–	–
Proceeds from public deposits	121.93	211.11	410.27	863.40	2638.85	4242.91	2722.54
Repayment of term loans	(53.50)	(45.51)	(141.75)	(494.12)	(171.03)	(124.44)	(153.80)
Repayment of bank borrowings	(130.81)	–	–	(5.83)	–	(697.96)	(235.46)
Dividend paid	(45.18)	(36.14)	(68.24)	(79.51)	(106.35)	(144.49)	(144.49)
Miscellaneous expenditure	(15.65)	(33.88)	(39.10)	(71.33)	(158.48)	(339.73)	(405.30)
Net cash (used in)/Generated from financing activities (C)	**171.08**	**407.06**	**744.62**	**1134.92**	**3400.20**	**3128.11**	**1791.80**
Net increase/(decrease) in cash and cash equivalents (A+B+C)	**(18.69)**	**(8.95)**	**203.62**	**(117.79)**	**3.46**	**8.73**	**96.22**
Cash at the beginning of the year	48.72	30.03	21.08	224.70	106.70	110.36	119.09
Cash at the end of the year	30.03	21.08	224.70	106.90	110.36	119.09	215.31

Note : (i) Sale of leased assets is not taken into consideration as total cost plus profit is included in lease rental income; (ii) Figures in brackets indicate cash outflows; (iii) C.W. = Capital Work.

Source: Calculated from annual reports of select lessor companies.

Table 4.24 : Cash Flow Statement of MWL

(Rs. lakhs)

Activities	*1990-91*	*1991-92*	*1992-93*	*1993-94*	*1994-95**	*1995-97*
(A) ***Cash flow from Operating Activities***						
Net Profit/(Loss) before tax	102.05	124.60	142.04	176.34	72.10	(390.83)
Adjustments for :						
Depreciation	125.87	76.68	78.15	88.01	74.14	78.76
Misc. expenditure written off	11.25	16.26	11.22	7.33	1.54	1.54
Profit on sale of fixed assets/Investments	–	–	–	–	–	–
Dividend received	–	–	–	–	–	–
Loss on sale of fixed assets	0.78	0.47	0.18	0.09	28.27	4.31
Lease equivalisation charges	–	–	–	–	–	3.30
Operating Profit before W.C. Changes	**239.95**	**218.01**	**231.59**	**271.77**	**176.05**	**(302.92)**
(Increase)/Decrease in stock on hire	189.38	413.59	129.14	(293.78)	285.43	242.74
(Increase)/Decrease in lease rental debtors	(93.52)	(73.73)	(104.43)	87.74	(10.70)	2.86
(Increase)/Decrease in other debtors	(24.00)	(150.12)	(154.42)	(256.90)	(606.48)	(120.73)
(Increase)/Decrease in trade bills	–	–	–	–	–	–
(Increase)/Decrease in bank deposits	–	(4.14)	(2.83)	(50.04)	8.37	0.63
(Increase)/Decrease in loans and advances	0.07	(7.31)	(31.75)	23.38	(73.32)	30.84
(Increase)/Decrease in other current assets	(0.77)	–	–	–	–	89.27
Increase/(Decrease) in current liabilities	(64.19)	19.88	(24.52)	(132.11)	56.18	(110.15)
Cash flow before tax	246.92	416.18	42.78	(349.94)	(164.47)	(167.46)
(Direct taxes paid)/Tax refund	(2.09)	(5.63)	0.60)	(5.26)	(71.61)	(70.07)
Net cash (used in)/Generated from Operating Activities (A)	**244.83**	**410.55**	**43.38**	**(355.20)**	**(236.08)**	**(237.53)**

Note: (i) The accounts for 1994-95 and 1995-97 are prepared for 18 months each and hence the year 1995-96 is skipped by the company; (ii) W.C. =Working Captial

Table 4.24 (*Contd.*)

Activities	*1990-91*	*1991-92*	*1992-93*	*1993-94*	*1994-95**	*1995-97*
(B) Cash flow from Investing Activities;						
Purchase of fixed assets (owned)	(7.30)	(0.36)	(0.91)	(15.43)	(15.15)	(4.95)
Purchase of leased assets	(30.07)	(17.56)	(22.40)	(38.14)	–	(18.22)
(Purchase)/sale of investments	–	–	–	–	(48.05)	(103.05)
(Increase)/Decrease in C.W. in progress	–	–	–	–	–	–
Profit on sale of fixed assets/Investments	–	–	–	–	–	–
Sale of fixed assets (owned)	–	–	–	–	0.26	–
Dividend received	–	–	–	–	–	–
Net cash (used in)/Generated from investing activities (B)	**(37.37)**	**(17.92)**	**(23.31)**	**(53.57)**	**(62.94)**	**(126.22)**
(C) Cash flow from financing activities						
Proceeds from Issue of share capital	–	–	416.00	–	181.31	15.90
Proceeds from term loans	–	–	–	11.26	70.00	176.29
Proceeds from bank borrowings	188.78	–	–	62.35	–	41.67
Proceeds from public deposits	–	–	243.88	391.04	359.63	146.22
Repayment of term loans	(120.01)	(230.76)	(153.93)	(94.51)	(203.66)	(93.91)
Repayment of bank borrowings	(121.21)	(52.13)	(504.80)	–	(64.02)	(4.55)
Dividend paid	(56.00)	(48.00)	(60.00)	–	(97.92)	–
Miscellaneous expenditure	(8.85)	(10.82)	(19.46)	(1.05)	–	–
Net cash (used in)/Generated from financing activities (C)	**(117.29)**	**(341.71)**	**(78.31)**	**369.09**	**245.34**	**281.62**
Net increase/(decrease) in cash and cash equivalents (A+B+C)	**90.17**	**50.92**	**(58.24)**	**(39.68)**	**(53.68)**	**(82.13)**
Cash at the beginning of the year	119.46	209.63	260.55	202.31	162.63	108.95
Cash at the end of the year	209.63	260.55	202.31	162.63	108.95	26.82

Note : (i) Sale of leased assets is not taken into consideration as total cost plus profit is included in lease rental income.
(ii) Figures in brackets indicate cash outflows.
(iii) * The accounts for 1994-95 and 1995-97 are prepared for 18 months each and hence, the company skips 1995-96.
(iv) C.W. = Capital Work.

Source : Calculated from annual reports of select lessor companies.

same trend is recorded in the individual companywise as presented in Tables 4.20 to 4.25 except the LFL and SCFSL companies which do not have the bank term deposits over a period of study.

The other current assets include— investment in Chits, Income Tax Refund Receivable, Deposits recoverable, and inventory or stock in trade. Table 4.19 reveals that there is substantial increase in other current assets in 1992-93, 1993-94 and in 1996-97, registering Rs. 579.08 lakhs in 1992-93 and Rs. 2,530.25 lakhs in 1993-94 which are outflows to the company, registering the growth rate at 336.94% in 1993-94 over the previous year. The decrease in other current assets recorded at Rs. 355.94 lakhs in 1994-95 and Rs. 356.40 lakhs in 1995-96, which are inflows to the companies and are added to the profit. The individual companies record almost the same trend. NFL recorded the highest inflow in 1994-95 registering Rs. 1,700.83 lakhs (Table 4.20).

Current Liabilities

Current liabilities include sundry creditors, unclaimed dividends, pre-received income, interest accrued but not due, advances from customers share application money refundable, bills payable and other liabilities.

Increase in current liabilities shows the inflow of funds and decrease in current liabilities shows the outflow of funds. Table 4.19 presents that except in 1995-96, the inflow of funds has increased over a period of study. There is a substantial increase in the inflow of funds during the period from 1992-93 to 1994-95 recording Rs. 110.22 lakhs in 1993, Rs. 1,115.78 lakhs in 1994, and Rs. 6,298.38 lakhs in 1994-95 registering the growth rate at 912.32% in 1993, 464.48% in 1994 (Table 4.19). This is due to the increase in pre-received income, unclaimed dividends, interest accrued but not due.

Depreciation

Table 4.19 reveals that on an average, 43.4% of the operating profit before working capital changes goes to replace depreciating assets. Here, the lessor claims the depreciation on leased assets against his earnings, which is not available to any other financier. The leasing companies have been claiming depreciation on leased assets during primary as well as secondary lease period whereas, the cost plus profit on leased assets were being recovered during primary lease period only, resulting in higher profits and recorded in profit and loss account. Based on the guidelines issued by the Institute of Chartered Accountants of India (ICAI), the companies are now claiming depreciation only during primary lease period as per the matching concept. The shortage of depreciation was shown under the heading of lease equalisation charge from 1995-96. As such, the lease equalisation amount is recorded at Rs. 74.05 lakhs in 1995-96 and Rs. 1229.60 lakhs in 1996-97 (Table 4.19).

The net cash from operations is negative, i.e., the cash spent is more than the cash generated for all the years except in 1991-92. Because of fewer amounts spent on hire-purchase business in 1991-92 (i.e. Rs. 250.20 lakhs), the cash from operations is positive and the net cash generated is recorded at Rs. 1,094.43 lakhs. The hire-purchase business (or the amount spent on purchase of hired assets) is higher from 1992-93 to 1996-97, recording Rs. 1,775.43 lakhs in 1992-93, Rs. 4122.66 lakhs in 1993-94, Rs. 11,068.08 lakhs in 1994-95, Rs. 5,449.56 lakhs in 1995-96 and Rs. 9,638.03 lakhs in 1996-97. As such, the net cash generated from operations is negative (Table 4.19).

Cash Flow from Financing Activities

The consolidated cash flow statement (Table 4.19) shows that the lessor companies have been mainly dependent upon borrowed funds especially on the fixed deposits followed by Bank loans.

The amount of share capital raised in the primary market through issue of shares registered ups and downs from 1991-92 to 1996-97 and there is a decreasing trend in capital raised after 1994-95, as there was no response from the public (Table 4.19). It shows that investors have lost the confidence in the primary market. The high premium issues and the experience of the share market scam in 1992 drove the investors to the fixed deposit market. However, the increase in share capital during the year 1994-95 is somewhat better, recording the mobilisation of capital at Rs. 4,641.75 lakhs.

Term loans consist of loans from financial institutions,

Table 4.25 : Cash Flow statement of SCFSL

(Rs.lakhs)

Activities	*1990-91*	*1991-92*	*1992-93*	*1993-94*	*1994-95**	*1995-97*
(A) Cash flow from Operating Activities						
Net Profit/(Loss) before tax	23.97	127.41	50.87	26.52	(55.10)	(219.06)
Adjustments for :						
Depreciation	13.30	48.80	84.72	132.49	84.32	65.78
Misc. expenditure written off	1.35	1.35	3.75	3.91	6.40	3.76
Profit on sale of fixed assets/Investments	(0.12)	(4.89)	(13.40)	(18.37)	(3.01)	(0.97)
Dividend received	–	–	–	–	–	–
Loss on sale of fixed assets	0.01	1.05	0.04	0.60	–	71.86
Lease equivalisation charge	–	–	–	–	–	–
Operating Profit before W.C. Changes	**38.51**	**173.72**	**125.98**	**145.15**	**32.61**	**(78.63)**
(Increase)/Decrease in stock on hire	(16.38)	73.39	151.53	39.40	1.22	48.34
(Increase)/Decrease in lease rental debtors	(0.69)	(10.03)	(20.71)	(107.94)	(15.50)	92.29
(Increase)/Decrease in other debtors	–	–	–	–	–	–
(Increase)/Decrease in trade bills	–	–	–	–	–	–
(Increase)/Decrease in bank deposits	–	–	–	–	–	–
(Increase)/Decrease in loans and advances	1.33	(18.07)	(90.50)	44.55	27.26	14.28
(Increase)/Decrease in other current assets	–	(1.24)	(6.74)	(48.62)	54.31	(13.34)
Increase/(Decrease) in current liabilities	(13.37)	0.09	57.82	(100.66)	16.18	(11.05)
Cash flow before tax	9.40	217.86	217.38	(28.12)	116.08	51.89
(Direct taxes paid)/Tax refund	(5.05)	(2.50)	(21.87)	(0.11)	(11.72)	50.22
Net cash (used in)/Generated from Operating Activities (A)	**4.35**	**215.36**	**195.51**	**(28.23)**	**104.36**	**102.11**

Note: (i) The accounts for 1994-95 and 1995-97 are prepared for 18 months each and hence the company skipped the year 1995-96.
(ii) W.C. =Working Captial

Table 4.25 (*Contd.*)

Activities	*1990-91*	*1991-92*	*1992-93*	*1993-94*	*1994-95**	*1995-97*
(B) *Cash flow from Investing Activities*						
Purchase of fixed assets (owned)	(3.64)	(10.76)	(4.12)	(8.96)	(1.72)	(0.19)
Purchase of leased assets	(51.99)	(169.66)	(154.69)	(43.23)	(96.16)	(28.11)
(Purchase)/sale of investments	(1.43)	1.25	(11.85)	(6.77)	(17.82)	(86.82)
(Increase)/Decrease in C.W. in progress	–	–	–	–	–	–
Profit on sale cf fixed assets/Investments	0.12	4.89	13.40	18.37	3.01	0.97
Sale of fixed assets (owned)	–	3.55	0.15	–	–	11.42
Dividend received	–	–	–	–	–	–
Net cash (used in)/Generated from investing activities (B)	**(56.94)**	**(170.73)**	**(157.11)**	**(40.59)**	**(112.69)**	**(102.73)**
(C) *Cash flow from financing activities*						
Proceeds from Issue of share capital	–	–	42.31	1.00	–	–
Proceeds from term loans	–	–	–	–	–	–
Proceeds from bank borrowings	57.55	–	3.57	12.68	15.21	14.98
Proceeds from public deposits	12.40	10.85	1.76	31.13	14.61	–
Repayment of term loans	–	–	–	–	–	(19.56)
Repayment of bank borrowings	–	(32.90)	–	–	–	–
Dividend paid	(16.21)	(18.16)	(23.35)	(18.53)	(20.76)	–
Miscellaneous expenditure	–	–	(24.00)	–	–	–
Net cash (used in)/Generated from financing activities (C)	**53.74**	**(40.21)**	**0.29**	**26.28**	**9.06**	**(4.58)**
Net increase/(decrease) in cash and cash equivalents (A+B+C)	**1.15**	**4.42**	**38.69**	**(42.54)**	**0.73**	**(5.20)**
Cash at the beginning of the year	4.86	6.01	10.43	49.12	6.58	7.31
Cash at the end of the year	6.01	10.43	49.12	6.58	7.31	2.11

Note : (i) Sale of leased assets is not taken into consideration as total cost plus profit is included in lease rental income.
(ii) Figures in brackets indicate cash outflows.
(iii) * The accounts for 1994-95 and 1995-97 are prepared for 18 months each and hence the company skips year 1995-96.
(iv) C.W. = Capital Work.

Source: Calculated from annual reports of select lessor companies.

debentures, inter-corporate deposits, etc. The trend of term loans shows ups and downs recording the growth rate at 1232.6% in 1992-93, 416.0% in 1993-94.

The growth rate decreased to 32.0% in 1994-95 and 35.0% in 1995-96 over the previous years. However, again it increased to 120.0% in 1996-97.

The growth rate for Bank borrowings recorded 222.0% in 1992-93, 540.0% in 1994-95, and 44.0% in 1996-97. The growth rate decreased to 21.63% in 1991-92, 35.0% in 1993-94 and 69.0% in 1995-96 over the previous years. The trend of bank borrowings is almost similar to term loan borrowings except in 1993-94 and 1994-95. In 1993-94 the term loans have registered increasing growth rate at 416% whereas bank borrowings have decreased by 35%. In 1994-95, the bank borrowings have increased by 540% while the term loans decreased by 32% due to their respective credit policies. During 1994, banks were allowed to enter the leasing field, hire-purchase, factoring and other related activities on their own. Earlier these banks could engage the leasing business only through leasing division/subsidiaries. Banks on the one hand have access to vast funds at low rates of interest and on the other hand are reluctant to continue with the cash credit facilities they have granted to NBFCs in the past. Further, the Reserve Bank of India has tightened lending norms to extend loans to Non-Banking Financial Companies. As such the Bank borrowing is marked by a reduction necessitating a shift of resource mix to fixed deposits, term loans, and other debt instruments like debentures and securitised notes, etc., during the year 1993-94. In the year 1994-95 bank borrowings have increased by 540%, term loans decreased by 32% may be due to liberalised policy followed by Banks.

Later during 1995-96 the bank borrowings have showed a decline of 69% over the previous year (Table 4.19). For the NBFCs, the tightening of bank credit coupled with reduction in the lending norms by the banking sector accentuated the dearer money conditions further. The continued slump in the capital market brought no cheer during the year 1995-96 and 1996-97. The year on the whole reviews their regressive plans, as resource options were largely restricted to fixed deposits and debt securities.

As seen in the cash flow statement, the total borrowings are broadly classified into term loans (institutional loans, debentures, and intercorporate deposits), bank borrowings, and fixed deposits. The fixed deposits as an average percentage of total borrowings of select lessor companies are registered at 60.38%. Term loans and bank borrowings (Table 4.27) share the remaining 39.92%. It may be seen from Table 4.27 that almost all select lessor companies are largely dependent upon public deposits as a source of finance.

Out of six companies, the NFL has maintained consistency in the mobilization of public deposits starting from 1990-91 to 1996-97. On an average, the NFL has maintained the public deposits at 64% of its total borrowings. The remaining 36% was shared by bank loans, institutional loan, debentures and inter corporate deposits (Table 4.27). Further, the NFL has recorded the highest growth rate in mobilisation of public deposits during 1994-95 recording 277.4% constituting Rs. 10,562.03 lakhs. (Table 4.20).

The DCL Company relied on public deposits to the extent of an average 68% of total borrowings (Table 4.27). The four companies PPL, DCL, MWL and SCFSL have depended on public deposits to the maximum extent of 100% during 1995-96, 1996-97, 1992-93 and 1991-92 respectively (Table 4.27). This indicates that the companies were able to mobilise public deposits without any difficulty.

Table 4.26 shows that there is a remarkable growth rate for fixed deposits mobilised by all select lessor companies over a period of study recording the growth rate at 70.5% in 1991-92, 76.2% in 1992-93, 111.2% in 1993-94, and 251.9% in 1994-95. However, the average growth rate is very slow in 1995-96 recording 18.36% and negative growth rate is recorded at –16.57% in 1996-97, mainly due to the mandatory credit rating and its linking to the acceptance of public deposits. On an average the fixed deposit growth rate is recorded at 73.1% per annum. The highest growth rate is recorded at 251.9% in 1994-95 compared to that of the previous year constituting a total deposit of Rs. 15,766.39 lakhs. The continued increase in mobilisation of fixed deposits from the public reflects the inherent goodwill that leasing and finance companies enjoyed from 1991 to 1996.

The 251.9% increase in deposit mobilisation reflects the growing confidence of the investing public in leasing and finance companies, testifying the credibility, commitment and care underlying their operations. Companies continued to place emphasis on raising deposits, recognising its immense potential as a major resource mobilizer and as fixed deposit schemes continue to enjoy a good response from the investing public, despite the continued turbulence in the financial markets. Almost the same trend is recorded as far as public deposits are concerned by the individual companies. Out of six companies the highest growth rate is recorded by the NFL registering 69.02% in 1991-92, 40.4% in 1992-93, 114.1% in 1993-94, 277.4% in 1994-95, 13.4% in 1995-96 and—27.98% in 1996-97 (Table 4.26). The share of NFL among all select lessor companies is recorded at 78.0% in 1991, 77.3% in 1992, 61.6% in 1993, 62.5% in 1994, 67.0% in 1995, 64.2% in 1996 and 55.04% in 1997. It means that the share of NFL in raising public deposits is varied between 55.04% (1997) and 78.0% in 1991 (Table 4.26). The remaining five select lessor companies PPL, LFL, DCL, MWL and SCFSL shared the remaining percentage over a period of study. One of the reasons for the remarkable mobilisation of public deposits, is the removal of the overall ceiling on public deposits and freedom to choose interest rates: provided, the company has to meet the prudential norms and credit rating requirements as stipulated by the RBI.

As per the notification issued by the RBI in July 1996 in connection with the prudential norms and credit rating, the NFL is the only leasing company which obtained the requisite certificate from the RBI permitting acceptance of deposits without any limit and freedom to choose interest rates. Having met the prudential norms and credit rating requirements (The details of prudential norms and credit rating were discussed in Chapter 3), it raised public deposits substantially recording Rs. 11,973.32 lakhs during the year 1996 which is 64.2% of the total deposits raised by all six lessor companies (Table 4.26).

According to the Annual Reports of NFL, the company has raised its cumulative public deposits to Rs. 378.15 crores at the close of the financial year 1996-97. However, the freedom to raise deposits without any limit on the quantum and interest rate made available by RBI was withdrawn on 2nd January, 1998. The NFL was affected by the RBI guidelines issued on 2nd January 1998. The new Regulatory Framework reintroduced a cap on acceptance of deposits interest rates by linking the limits to a factor of Net Owned Funds (NOF) based on the level of credit rating. As such, the company was affected and was required to repay the excess deposits by December 2000. The calculations based on the current credit rating (CARE - A) required Rs. 200 crores of excess deposits to be repaid over a period of three years, with one-third reduction to be achieved by the end of each year, till December 2000. Consequently, the NFL has announced suspension of acceptance of public deposits from 2nd January, 1998 and started repaying deposits on maturity.

As per the Annual Report of 1996-97, the cumulative public deposits of the PPL stand at Rs. 9,318.38 lakhs as on 31-3-1997. It is evident from Table 4.26 that the PPL has mobilised more public deposits in the year 1994-95 recording the growth rate at 508.78% constituting Rs. 2125.20 lakhs. The average proportion of the public deposits to the total borrowings is 47.64% (Table 4.27). This company is mainly dependent on public deposits and bank borrowings.

The fixed deposits portfolio of LFL presents that on an average, the proportion of fixed deposits to total borrowings is very meagre representing only 19.93% (Table 4.27). This company depends mainly on its owned funds and bank borrowings. According to the Annual Reports of 1996-97, the LFL has raised public deposits from Rs. 59.67 lakhs in 1993-94 to Rs. 125.7 lakhs (cumulative figure) in 1994-95 registering a growth rate of 110.6%. Table 4.26 reveals the year-wise mobilisation of deposits. The highest growth-rate is recorded at 370.17% in 1993-94 constituting mobilization of deposits up to Rs. 46.50 lakhs. According to the Annual Reports of the LFL, during 1997-98, in conformity with RBI regulations, it has not accepted or renewed public deposits. As such the company has reduced its deposits to Rs. 118.28 lakhs in 1997-98 from Rs. 144.7 lakhs in 1996-97 and further reduced to Rs. 5.89 lakhs in 1998-99 from Rs. 118.28 lakhs as against 1997-98.

Table 4.26 : Share of Fixed Deposits by Each Select Company (Year-wise Figures) *(Rs. lakhs)*

Lessor Companies	*1990-91*	*1991-92*	*1992-93*	*1993-94*	*1994-95*	*1995-96*	*1996-97*	$\bar{X}$
	(78.01)	(77.33)	(61.62)	(62.47)	(66.99)	(64.16)	(55.39)	66.57
NFL	550.85	931.10	1307.27	2798.84	10562.03	11973.32	8623.36	
		(69.02)	(40.40)	(114.10)	(277.40)	(13.36)	(-27.98)	
	(2.97)	(3.96)	(6.99)	(7.79)	(13.48)	(12.80)	(26.19)	
PPL	20.96	47.72	148.34	349.09	2125.20	2389.05	4076.91	10.60
	–	(127.67)	(210.85)	(135.33)	(508.78)	(12.42)	(70.65)	
		(0.27)	(0.47)	(1.04)	(0.42)	(0.30)		0.35
LFL	–	3.27	9.89	46.50	66.07	55.27	–	
		–	(202.45)	(370.17)	(42.09)	(-16.35)		
	(17.27)	(17.53)	(19.34)	(19.27)	(16.74)	(22.74)	(17.49)	18.63
DCL	121.93	211.11	410.27	863.40	2638.85	4242.91	2722.54	
		(73.14)	(94.34)	(110.45)	(205.63)	(60.79)	(-35.83)	
	–	–	(11.50)	(8.73)	(2.28)	–	(0.93)	3.35
MWL			243.88	391.04	359.63		146.22	
			–	(60.34)	(-8.00)		(-59.34)	
	(1.75)	(0.91)	(0.08)	(0.70)	(0.09)	–	–	0.50
SCFSL	12.40	10.85	1.76	31.13	14.61			
	–	(-12.5)	(-83.78)	(1668.75)	(-53.07)			

Table 4.26 (*Contd.*)

TOTAL	(100) 706.14 –	(100) 1204.05 (70.51)	(100) 2121.41 (76.19)	(100) 4480.00 (111.18)	(100) 15766.39 (251.93)	(100) 18660.55 (18.36)	(100) 15569.03 (-16.57)	100

Note : (i) Figures in upper brackets represent the share of each company.
(ii) Figures in lower brackets represent growth rates.
(iii) $\bar{X}$ = Arithmetic Mean.

Source: Calculated from annual reports of select lessor companies.

Table 4.27 : Fixed Deposits as a Percentage of Total Borrowings of Select Lessor Companies

(Per cent)

Lessor companies	*1990-91*	*1991-92*	*1992-93*	*1993-94*	*1994-95*	*1995-96*	*1996-97*	$\bar{X}$
NFL	46.53	88.91	49.25	55.62	69.53	78.28	60.32	64.06
PPL	16.94	15.72	48.17	17.80	43.76	100	91.09	47.64
LFL	0	3.28	8.88	38.58	38.53	50.22	0	19.93
DCL	29.35	82.91	41.42	57.40	69.57	95.71	100	68.05
MWL	0	0	100	84.16	83.71	–	40.15	44.00
SCFSL	17.73	100	33.02	71.06	48.99	–	0	38.69
TOTAL	34.94	70.17	49.18	49.09	64.43	83.95	70.87	60.38

Note: $\bar{X}$ = Arithmetic Mean.

Source: Calculated from Annual Reports of select lessor companies.

The DCL Company has achieved growth of 205.63% in 1994-95 over the previous year representing the mobilisation of deposits in that particular year as Rs. 2,638.85 lakhs. However, negative growth of deposits is registered at –35.83% in 1996-97.

The remaining two companies, MWL and SCFSL, were not able to mobilise deposits in 1995-96. The MWL recorded decreased growth rate in 1996-97 registering at 59.34%. MWL was in the process of liquidation during 1997-98. The SCFSL has diverted its activities to real estate business.

Almost all companies except PPL witnessed a decline in mobilisation of public deposits during the year 1996-97 recording at –27.98% by NFL, –35.83% by DCL and –59.34% by MWL. The two companies, LFL and SCFSL, have not mobilised deposits at all during 1996-97 (Table 4.26).

The declining trend during the year 1996-97 was recorded due to the effect of RBI regulatory framework which re-introduced a cap on accepting of public deposits and fixation of interest rates by linking the limits to a factor of Net Owned Funds (NOF) based on the level of credit rating.

The resultant impact was regressive, as highly geared companies were required to repay the excess desposits. Another reason for decline in fixed deposits was due to the failure of some unscrupulous NBFCs, which deceived the public in paying their fixed deposits as, and when they matured (The details of credit rating and its linking to NOF were discussed in Chapter 3).

Thus, the lessor companies have increasingly relied upon borrowings mainly on public deposits as a source of finance from 1990-91 to 1995-96. The year 1996-97 has witnessed decrease in the growth rate due to the RBI regulations explained above. On an average more than 60% of the companies' requirements have been financed through the source of public deposits.

In order to mobilise more fixed deposits from the public, the lessor companies spent huge amount towards fixed deposit mobilisation expenses. Around 97% of the miscellaneous expenses are pertaining to fixed deposit mobilisation expenses. The fixed deposit mobilisation expenses are on high side recording at Rs. 132.61 lakhs in 1990-91, Rs. 159.24 lakhs in 1991-92,

Rs. 310.13 lakhs in 1992-93, Rs. 410.41 lakhs in 1993-94, Rs. 1,208.92 lakhs in 1994-95, Rs. 1,894.18 lakhs in 1995-96, and Rs. 2,405.18 lakhs in 1996-97 (Table 4.19). The growth rate is recorded at 20.1%, 94.8%, 32.3%, 194.60%, 56.7%, and 26.9% respectively.

The increasing trend in the trend of miscellaneous expenditure shows that the companies spent more amount of funds towards fixed deposit mobilisation expenses by offering gifts, commission to brokers, etc., in order to mobilise more funds by way of fixed deposits from the public to finance various activities. However, these companies have consistently used a small proportion of borrowed funds towards the re-payment of loans and public deposits.

The second largest source of funds has been funds from operations, which have contributed around one-third of total resources. Table 4.19 reveals that over the period from 1991 to 1996, the contribution of this source of funds has increased, thereby indicating a rise in the level of business activities.

Cash Flow from Investing Activities

As regards the aggregate uses of funds, a large chunk of funds have been utilised in acquiring the hire-purchased assets (varies between 65.82% and 35.04%) followed by leased assets (varies between 31.01% and 23.95%) during the period of study. On an average the leased assets expenditure constitutes 27.8% and hire-purchased assets expenditure constitutes 47.8%, both put together constitutes 75.6% of total assets (Table 4.2 of Section-I).

Analysis of individual companies reveals that the NFL has done substantial amount of lease business to the total lease business done by all select lessor companies. It has recorded its share at 55.3% in 1991, 31.7% in 1992, 44.9% in 1993, 69.4% in 1994, 64.6% in 1995, 78.6% in 1996, 78.8% in 1997 (calculated from Tables 4.20 and 4.19). On an average, the amount spent on leased assets by NFL constitutes 60.46% of total leased assets of all select lessor companies. The remaining proportion of 39.54% is shared by the remaining five companies such as PPL, LFL, DCL, MWL, SCFSL.

All companies have deployed funds in the purchase of

investments (shares). There is a remarkable increase in investments in the year 1994-95 recording 154.70% over the previous year and 107.65% in 1995-96. However, the decline that set in, during 1996-97 recording –34.5%, is due to the deceleration in the Capital Market (Table 4.19).

On the whole, the leasing companies tried to promote leasing business by investing in leased assets. They found external financing mainly through fixed deposits to be the most prudent way of raising funds over the years. Because of some unscrupulous finance companies, which seemed to have been quite reluctant in repaying the public deposits, the public lost confidence in finance companies to deposit their money. Further, because of linking of credit rating to a factor of Net Owned Funds, some well established companies, who have accepted excess deposits stopped accepting public deposits and started repayment of excess public deposits to the public as per RBI directions. As such, the total business activities declined during 1996-97, as the leasing and finance companies were mainly dependent on public deposits.

A close analysis of the cash flow statements of select lessor companies reveal that almost all lessor companies followed a suicidal policy of borrowing short term loans (1 year to 3 years) and deploying them in the long term (5 years to 8 years) commitments. For leasing companies the major source of finance is public deposits and short terms loans. As such, these companies were not able to meet short-term obligations as and when they matured, which led to legal problems. The MWL underwent liquidation process in 1998, as the deposit holders resort for legal solution when the MWL failed to pay back the public deposits on time. Similarly, PPL also started the liquidation process from November 1999. The general finding is that almost all select lessor companies have gained the maximum by way of tax benefits through claiming depreciation on leased assets and by way of borrowing huge amounts of money through public deposits by paying high rate of interest.

All leasing companies have declared handsome dividends over a period of study from 1990-91 to 1996-97, recording a growth rate of 13.8% in 1991-92, 57.8% in 1992-93, 3.3% in 1993-94, 72.7% in 1994-95, 18.8% in 1995-96 and 11.2% in 1996-97.

Usually the interest is the profit for finance companies. But the lease rentals include profit plus principal repayment, which is inherent in the lease rentals. Since the whole of the lease rentals is treated as business income these companies are showing higher income and paying higher dividend to the shareholders. This is only to build up their goodwill in the capital market. But this tantamount to payment of dividend out of capital. However, two companies such as MWL and SCFSL have not declared dividend in the year 1996-97 as they have incurred losses during that period.

The proportion of dividend paid to total operating profit before working capital changes is recorded at 21.8% in 1991, 14.2% in 1992, 20.3% in 1993, 14.4% in 1994, 14.01% in 1995, 12.9% in 1996 and 14.4% in 1997. On an average, these companies are paying dividend at 16% of operating profit before working capital changes. The remaining operating profit before working capital changes is spent on current assets—such as hired assets, trade bills, bank deposits, loans and advances and other current assets.

With the above analysis, it is clear that the companies have to build up their image first and then gain confidence of the investors by adopting a uniform policy of raising and deploying the funds and repaying the debts as and when they mature. This is possible only by separate mandatory regulations and accounting procedures, which can be imposed by the appropriate governing bodies.

To conclude the chapter the inference may be drawn that the total borrowings are broadly classified into term loans, bank borrowings, and fixed deposits. Among all the sources, public deposit is the major fund raising source for leasing companies due to impressive deposit interest rates.

The fixed deposits as an average percentage of total borrowings of select lessor companies are registered at 60.38%. Term loans and bank borrowings share the remaining 39.92%. This proves that there was a remarkable growth rate for fixed deposits mobilised by all select lessor companies over the study period.

Regarding the aggregate uses of funds, a large chunk of funds have been utilised in acquiring the hire-purchased assets (varies between 65.82% and 35.04%) followed by leased assets (varies between 31.01% and 23.95%). On an average, the leased assets expenditure constitutes 27.8% and hire-purchased assets expenditure constitutes 47.8%. Both put together constitutes 75.6% of total assets. Owned assets and other assets shared the remaining percentage of 24.4.

Analysis of individual companies reveals that NFL has done substantial amount of lease business. On an average, the amount spent on leased assets by NFL constitutes 60.46% of total leased assets of all select lessor companies. The remaining 5 companies of PPL, LFL, DCL, MWL and SCFSL shared the remaining proportion of 39.54%.

On the whole, the leasing companies tried to promote leasing business by investing in leased assets. They found fixed deposits to be the most prudent way of raising funds over the years. Because of some unscrupulous finance companies, which seemed to have been quite reluctant in repaying the public deposits as and when they matured, the public lost the confidence in finance companies to deposit their money. Further, because of sudden imposition of restrictions like linking of credit rating to a factor of net owned funds, some well-established companies, who have accepted excess deposits, stopped accepting public deposits as per RBI directions. As such the total leasing business activities declined during 1996-97, as the leasing and finance companies were mainly dependent on public deposits.

REFERENCES

1. Naresh Kumar Gupta, *Lease Finance, Concept, Practice*, Deep and Deep Publications, New Delhi, pp. 41 and 42.
2. *The Economic Times*, November 24, 1995, p. 1.
3. *The Economic Times*, July 24th and 25th, 1996.
4. S. Raghavan, *Development of Vehicle Leasing in Indian Market*, Paper presented at the seminar on Leasing, organized by Canbank Financial Services Ltd., at Bangalore, 29-30 December, 1988.
5. *The Economic Times*, April 4, 1997, p. 8.
6. *Ibid.*
7. *Ibid.*
8. *The Economic Times*, February 25, 2000.
9. *Ibid.*
10. *The Economic Times*, May 2, 1997.
11. I.M. Pandey, *Financial Management*, Vikas Publishing House Pvt. Ltd., New Delhi, 1994, p. 67.
12. RBI Notification No. NBC-FCD, 1/19.02.001/96-97.

ANNEXURES

Annexure 4. 1 : Sources of Funds of Select Lessor Companies

(Rs. lakhs)

	1990-91						1991-92					
Cos.	*O.F*	*B.F*	*F.D*	*Depn.*	*C.L.*	*Total*	*O.F.*	*B.F.*	*F.D.*	*Depn.*	*C.L.*	*Total*
NFL	1255.33	3113.49	1969.59	915.88	1832.8	9087.1	1495.99	3195.04	2733.31	1326.49	2693.0	11443.65
PPL	141.47	168.96	23.28	5.81	261.3	600.9	323.61	425.47	71.01	55.37	200.05	1075.51
LFL	837.77	39.62	0	117.20	229.6	1224.2	876.66	96.41	3.27	157.01	229.57	1362.92
DCL	297.85	869.68	380.98	212.36	319.96	2080.9	611.51	865.22	592.09	294.34	462.76	2825.92
MWL	638.90	1338.96	501.78	280.31	479.25	3239.2	703.29	1093.1	464.74	356.64	511.13	3128.89
SCFSL	173.82	322.29	29.32	27.27	186.78	739.48	257.68	294.39	35.16	76.06	212.09	875.38
Total	3345.14	5853.00	2904.95	1558.83	3309.7	16971.7	4268.74	5969.62	3899.40	2265.91	4308.6	20712.27

	1992-93						1993-94					
Cos.	*O.F*	*B.F*	*F.D*	*Depn.*	*C.L.*	*Total*	*O.F.*	*B.F.*	*F.D.*	*Depn.*	*C.L.*	*Total*
NFL	2275.20	4517.02	3569.25	1777.02	2560.97	14699.46	3578.86	5294.48	6656.41	2400.56	2423.01	20353.32
PPL	517.81	722.31	70.35	123.44	149.70	1583.61	1415.05	2324.61	404.60	153.55	892.25	5190.06
LFL	891.05	162.30	13.16	215.40	228.53	1510.44	890.92	80.59	59.66	333.15	165.38	1529.70
DCL	688.19	1303.85	1002.36	387.28	654.14	4035.82	1104.47	1444.71	1865.76	503.67	1111.28	6029.89
MWL	1242.06	562.39	580.59	434.67	426.61	3242.32	1322.81	676.29	836.82	521.73	392.42	3750.07
SCFSL	289.09	297.96	36.92	156.55	304.03	1084.55	294.85	305.64	73.05	282.98	213.21	1169.73
Total	5903.40	7565.83	5272.63	3094.36	4323.98	26160.20	8606.96	10126.32	9896.30	4195.64	5497.55	38022.77

Annexure 4.1 (*Contd.*)

	1994-95						1995-96					
Cos.	O.F	B.F	F.D	Depn.	C.L.	Total	O.F.	B.F.	F.D.	Depn.	C.L.	Total
NFL	5025.44	8159.71	17218.5	3508.31	6873.65	40785.55	6668.46	8834.80	29191.76	5583.44	1245.26	51523.72
PPL	4167.15	4875.11	2496.58	402.35	2235.09	14176.28	5554.33	3733.23	4812.17	555.31	1275.93	15930.97
LFL	972.18	175.87	125.73	375.53	253.12	1902.43	1018.24	108.08	181.00	437.88	170.63	1915.83
DCL	1428.68	2447.61	4505.61	642.60	1571.96	10596.46	1551.74	1720.85	8747.52	594.01	1963.85	14577.97
MWL	1965.44	494.63	1179.29	569.18	350.67	4559.21	1965.44	494.63	1179.29	569.18	350.67	4559.21
SCFSL	239.75	326.75	81.76	367.30	208.63	1224.19	239.75	326.75	81.76	367.30	208.63	1224.19
Total	13798.6	16479.7	25607.4	5865.27	11493.12	73244.12	16997.96	15218.34	44193.50	8107.12	5214.97	89731.89

	1996-97					
Cos.	*O.F*	*B.F*	*F.D*	*Depn.*	*C.L.*	*Total*
NFL	7233.90	12191.44	37815.12	6166.16	2555.60	65962.22
PPL	5916.83	3765.76	9318.38	1123.93	1781.85	21906.75
LFL	1007.69	192.12	144.72	614.39	264.88	2223.80
DCL	1613.13	1331.59	11470.06	763.16	2347.47	17525.41
MWL	1581.26	480.70	1325.50	640.31	243.82	4271.59
SCFSL	202.86	335.83	68.10	425.29	227.53	1259.61
Total	17555.67	18297.44	60141.88	9733.24	7421.15	113149.38

Source: Annual Reports
Note : O.F. = Owned Funds B.F. = Borrowed Funds
F.D. = Fixed Deposits C.L. = Current Liabilities

Annexure 4.2 : Application of Funds of Select Lessor Companies *(Rs.lakhs)*

Cos.	1990-91 L.A	H.P.A	O.A	Inv.	Other C.A	Total	1991-92 L.A.	H.P.A.	O.A.	Inv.	Other C.A.	Total
NFL	2009.06	5110.60	141.29	120.26	1705.88	9087.09	2368.66	5293.17	154.58	317.88	3309.36	11443.65
PPL	81.23	461.71	11.01	0	46.90	600.85	374.04	449.20	23.18	53.62	175.47	1075.51
LFL	127.76	0	144.51	139.78	812.11	1224.16	251.65	60.85	147.19	210.47	692.76	1362.92
DCL	639.91	1188.10	39.66	52.69	160.47	2080.83	811.63	1694.37	53.57	80.82	185.53	2825.92
MWL	1005.04	1635.56	33.38	0.10	565.12	3239.20	1021.56	1221.97	33.75	0.10	851.51	3128.89
SCFSL	89.80	595.88	5.04	7.36	41.40	739.48	259.47	522.49	12.23	6.11	75.08	875.38
Total	3952.80	8991.85	374.89	320.19	3331.88	16971.61	5087.01	9242.05	424.50	669.00	5289.71	20712.27

Cos.	1992-93 L.A	H.P.A	O.A	Inv.	Other C.A	Total	1993-94 L.A.	H.P.A.	O.A.	Inv.	Other C.A.	Total
NFL	2972.35	6691.60	226.91	170.27	4638.33	14699.46	4908.16	7309.47	232.80	952.01	6950.88	20353.32
PPL	676.32	639.69	88.11	56.38	123.11	1583.61	1095.64	2470.07	95.50	88.93	1439.91	5190.05
LFL	300.55	35.29	150.20	481.98	542.42	1510.44	410.84	23.18	154.72	399.44	541.52	1529.70
DCL	1072.03	2187.11	103.66	120.01	553.01	4035.82	1150.43	3877.32	118.28	257.99	625.87	6029.89
MWL	1024.37	1092.83	34.67	0.10	1094.35	3246.32	1058.38	1386.61	50.08	55.10	1199.90	3750.07
SCFSL	405.67	370.96	16.11	17.96	273.85	1084.55	448.85	331.56	25.07	24.73	339.52	1169.73
Total	6451.29	11017.48	619.66	846.70	7225.07	26160.20	9072.30	15398.21	676.45	1778.20	11097.60	38022.76

Annexure 4.2 (*Contd.*)

Cos.	1994-95 L.A	H.P.A	O.A	Inv.	Other C.A	Total	1995-96 L.A.	H.P.A.	O.A.	Inv.	Other C.A.	Total
NFL	10001.41	12559.01	303.17	1932.17	15989.48	40785.55	14918.15	15006.12	429.17	4802.16	16368.2	51523.72
PPL	2771.70	5716.83	207.07	562.79	4917.89	14176.28	3592.53	4713.20	338.04	1029.89	6257.31	15930.97
LFL	711.47	85.20	189.44	435.25	481.07	1902.43	802.72	51.34	200.41	421.58	439.78	1915.83
DCL	1720.01	6659.04	184.11	559.79	1473.51	10596.46	1398.72	8414.05	334.57	1089.35	3341.28	14577.97
MWL	998.68	1101.18	457.80	103.15	1898.40	4559.21	998.68	1101.18	457.80	103.15	1898.40	4559.21
SCFSL	448.85	330.34	26.79	42.55	279.50	1224.19	545.01	330.34	26.79	42.55	279.50	1224.19
Total	16652.12	26451.60	1368.69	3635.70	25039.85	73244.12	22255.81	29616.23	1786.78	7488.68	28584.39	89731.89

Cos.	1996-97 L.A.	H.P.A	O.A.	Inv.	Other C.A.	Total
NFL	17387.75	19530.49	879.87	6068.85	22095.26	65962.22
PPL	4138.25	8709.93	469.08	1684.23	6905.26	21906.75
LFL	915.77	56.10	200.41	428.99	622.53	2223.80
DCL	1447.61	9812.53	636.31	1470.39	4158.57	17525.41
MWL	980.46	858.44	461.16	0.10	1971.43	4271.59
SCFSL	449.72	336.44	12.97	129.37	331.11	1259.61
Total	25319.56	39303.93	2659.80	9781.98	36084.16	113149.38

Source: Annual Reports.
Note : L.A. = Leased Assets H.P.A. = Hire Purchase Rates
O.A. = Owned Assets Other C.A. = Other Current Assets

Annexure 4.3 : Component Analysis of Income and Expenditure of Select Lessor Companies (from 1990-91 to 1996-97) *(Rs.lakhs)*

Cos.	1990-91						1991-92					
	Interest	*Depn.*	*Tax Prov.*	*Op. Exp.*	*Net Profit*	*Total Income*	*Interest*	*Depn.*	*Tax Prov.*	*Op. Exp.*	*Net Profit*	*Total Income*
NFL	813.58	280.52	—	317.72	225.72	1637.54	1077. 48	410.93	—	453.46	401.30	2343.17
PPL	18.73	5.76	—	20.26	19.98	64.73	66.11	49.55	0.50	56.46	104.95	277.57
LFL	3.05	30.58	40.00	38.49	64.23	176.35	5.09	39.85	35.06	71.38	83.89	235.27
DCL	170.24	65.62	—	63.93	44.96	344.75	235.81	82.02	—	90.82	113.95	522.60
MWL	290.39	125.87	—	90.07	103.39	609.72	360.21	76.67	—	112.80	124.39	674.07
SCFSL	52.52	13.30	2.50	13.43	21.47	103.22	62.78	48.80	20.19	22.33	107.22	261.32
Total	1348.51	521.65	42.50	543.90	479.75	2936.31	1807.48	707.82	55.75	807.25	935.70	4314.00

Cos.	1992-93						1993-94					
	Interest	*Depn.*	*Tax Prov.*	*Op. Exp.*	*Net Profit*	*Total Income*	*Interest*	*Depn.*	*Tax Prov.*	*Op. Exp.*	*Net Profit*	*Total Income*
NFL	1413.41	482.49	—	527.28	462.07	2885.25	1568.26	641.45	—	776.09	640.72	3626.52
PPL	126.04	68.07	—	69.15	108.19	371.45	227.06	174.03	—	171.17	265.12	837.38
LFL	64.37	58.42	12.50	26.27	59.38	220.94	57.61	117.75	11.00	108.34	52.37	347.07
DCL	288.75	109.70	—	138.34	152.90	689.69	448.12	139.03	—	199.99	241.84	1028.98
MWL	264.39	78.14	—	104.22	138.77	585.52	259.71	88.00	—	182.46	178.67	708.84
SCFSL	67.57	84.72	—	35.33	50.87	238.49	75.77	132.49	—	42.93	26.52	277.71
Total	2224.53	881.54	12.50	900.59	972.18	4991.34	2636.53	1292.75	11.00	1480.98	1405.24	6826.50

Annexure 4.3 (*Contd.*)

Cos.	1994-95						1995-96					
	Interest	*Depn.*	*Tax Prov.*	*Op. Exp.*	*Net Profit*	*Total Income*	*Interest*	*Depn.*	*Tax Prov.*	*Op. Exp.*	*Net*	*Total Income*
NFL	3011.33	1110.81	9.21	1318.93	973.59	6423.87	4353.00	2140.40	—	1990.45	1025.48	9509.34
PPL	1000.34	349.99	3.60	323.99	901.79	2579.71	1069.88	414.31	—	406.34	628.58	2519.22
LFL	2.82	97.97	6.00	180.89	141.25	428.93	44.25	120.14	1.50	185.52	95.33	446.74
DCL	813.43	154.75	2.50	415.87	425.89	1812.44	1401.02	243.72	—	361.01	265.72	2271.47
MWL	238.21	74.14	—	418.31	69.20	799.86	238.21	74.14	—	418.31	69.20	799.86
SCFSL	123.46	84.32	—	85.18	(55.10)	237.86	123.46	84.32	—	85.18	(55.10)	237.86
Total	5189.59	1871.98	21.31	2743.17	2456.62	12282.67	7229.82	3077.03	1.50	3446.81	2029.21	15784.37

Cos.	1996-97					
	Interest	*Depn.*	*Tax Prov.*	*Op.Exp.*	*Net Profit*	*Total Income*
NFL	5705.76	1479.50	91.00	2953.96	610.12	10840.33
PPL	1908.55	568.62	78.60	675.71	373.50	3604.98
LFL	53.89	176.81	6.05	199.09	40.76	476.60
DCL	1764.64	190.21	21.99	827.11	148.46	2952.41
MWL	350.34	78.76	—	510.25	(392.08)	547.28
SCFSL	133.53	65.78	—	287.70	(219.06)	267.95
Total	9916.71	2559.68	197.64	5453.82	561.70	18689.55

Source: Annual Reports.
Note : Op.Exp. = Operating Expenditure.

5

EVALUATION OF LESSEE COMPANIES

The preceding chapter provided an insight into leasing activity and the role of leasing in the investment pattern of selected lessor companies.

This chapter is devoted to analyse the use of leasing and its effectiveness as an alternative source of finance for lessee companies. The effectiveness of lease financing is assessed in terms of types of assets taken on lease by lessee companies, cost of leasing and the reasons for the lessees' preference of leasing. Nine lessee companies were selected at random for the study. The detailed methodology of selection of sample companies is given in Chapter 1 under the heading of 'Methodology'.

The term "investment" connotes the capital expenditure incurred to acquire property equipment and other capital assets that generate revenue.[1]

Acquisition of capital equipment, in the ordinary course of heavy capital investment, sometimes beyond the financial capacity of the actual user of the asset. In this context leasing becomes an important source of acquiring a capital asset without incurring any capital expenditure.

All businesses require capital equipment such as plant and machinery, office equipment including computers, vehicles, etc. The acquisition of such assets through leasing is known as the use of leasing to finance capital investment and is undertaken for the following reasons:

(i) to replace equipment,
(ii) to expand productive capacity to meet the demands,
(iii) to reduce production costs,
(iv) to provide new facilities in order to produce new products.

The finance managers analyse the determinants in terms of the micro-economic and macro-economic factors, which affect the business decisions.

The major factors are:

1. Government policy with respect to
   (a) interest rates,
   (b) taxation (e.g. rates of taxation and rules on depreciation),
2. The cost and availability of finance,
3. The liquidity position of the firm,
4. The rate of change of demand for goods produced with the machinery and the degree of confidence in the future,
5. The amount of technological change.

The above factors affect the financing decision because of their impact on either the expected yield (or benefit) or on the cost to the firm.

One of the important functions of a Finance Manager is to determine the sources from which the required funds for capital investment are to be raised. Such funds may be raised either through internal financing or external financing. Once an asset is purchased, it confers certain ownership rights to the purchaser but at the same time such investment bestows on the purchaser the responsibility of all-consequential risks/rewards or losses/gains if such assets are to be disposed of.

An alternative to this is to get the assets on lease and use them as per the terms and conditions of lease agreement.

Thus, there are several ways by which the firm can acquire the right to use the asset. The asset may be acquired out of owned funds or borrowed funds or through lease financing mode or through hire-purchase financing mode.

The decision to lease or borrow to buy an asset can be made only after a specific financial analysis that weighs the merits of each choice. In financial evaluation, the alternatives available are:

(i) to buy the equipment outright with owned funds,
(ii) to borrow funds first and then buy the equipment,
(iii) to acquire the capital equipment facilities through lease financing mode, and
(iv) to acquire the required asset through hire purchase financing.

After the decision is made to acquire the required capital asset, method of acquisition will be evaluated for its impact on industrial investment.

The scope of this chapter is confined only to the analysis of use of leasing to finance capital asset, reasons for leasing, and its impact on lessees capital investment.

To investigate the effect of leasing on lessee's investment pattern, the survey of lessee companies has been conducted through questionnaires and interviews. The investigation includes the mode of operation, use of leasing to finance capital asset, reasons for leasing decision and tax benefits to assessee and analysis of significance of each of these factors on the investment behaviour of the lessee companies.

The structured questionnaire/interviews conducted for the executives of lessee companies provide considerable insight into leasing pattern in the lessee companies in Andhra Pradesh.

Broadly, the questionnaire administered to the lessee companies covers the following:

(i) types of assets and volume of assets taken on lease;
(ii) types of lease agreements entered and the effect of tri-partite agreement;
(iii) effect of leasing on quantity and timing of investment;
(iv) effect of depreciation rates and cost of leasing;
(v) effect of lease rentals, depreciation and interest on tax liability;
(vi) reasons for the lessee companies to prefer leasing.

Based on the survey, the above aspects are analysed hereunder.

Types of Assets taken on Lease

The assets taken on lease by select lessee companies are given in Tables 5.1 to 5.7. Table 5.1 presents the total types of assets taken on lease by lessees during the period of study. The total leased assets of company-wise and year-wise of selected companies is given in Tables 5.2 and 5.3. The leased assets of plant and machinery company-wise and year-wise are given in Table 5.4, while the leased assets pertaining to vehicle leasing are shown in Tables 5.5 and 5.6. The leased assets of office equipment are shown in Table 5.7.

The lessee survey indicated that lessee companies have taken a wide range of assets on lease. The main types of assets that are taken by the select lessee companies on lease fall under the following categories :

(i) *Plant and machinery*—includes pollution control equipment, electrical equipment, turbines, boilers, transformers, work rolls, back up rolls, energy saving equipment, textile machinery, diesel generators, shovel, industrial machinery, etc.
(ii) *Vehicles* — include busses, Ambassador cars, Maruti-800 cars, jeeps, trucks/lorries, vans etc.
(iii) *Office equipment* —includes computers, office furniture, photocopiers, communication equipment etc.
(iv) *Other assets*— include consumer durables such as television sets, refrigerators, air coolers, air conditioners, vacuum cleaners, micro woven, etc.

The types of lessees selected for the study involved in this sector of lease market are varied in their nature. They fall into the following categories:

(i) Power generation company
(ii) Paper manufacturing companies
(iii) Road transport corporation
(iv) Fertilizer company
(v) Aluminium and steel companies
(vi) Textile manufacturing companies
(vii) Cigarettes manufacturing company

Table 5.1 presents the data pertaining to the types of assets taken on lease by select lessee companies. Table 5.1 shows the lease of plant and machinery has posted the highest growth rate among all types of assets, registering the highest growth rate at 218.36% in 1993-94 over the previous year and the compound growth rate is registered at 83.50%, followed by vehicles (41.31%) and office equipment (13.33%). The proportion of plant and machinery to the total leased assets varies between 89.85% in 1990-91 and 99.03% in 1996-97. The average proportion of plant and machinery to the total leased assets is recorded highest at 94.71%

followed by office equipment recording at 3.95%, vehicles 1.33% and other assets at 0.01%.

The same data about types of leased assets is presented company-wise in Table 5.2. An analysis of the table reveals that out of 9 lessee companies selected for the study, only one company, viz., VST could engage in the lease of all the four types of assets listed out in the table. Two companies such as APR and ITC have dealt with three types of assets such as plant and machinery, vehicles, and office equipment. One Unit, i.e. APSRTC could engage only two types of assets such as plant and machinery and vehicles (buses). The other company, CML, could deal with only plant and machinery and office equipment. The remaining 4 companies – such as APSEB, PAL, PSL and PSM have taken only the plant and machinery on lease as per their requirement. The interesting point to be noted here is that only APSEB has taken assets of plant and machinery such as electrical equipment, turbines, transformers, etc. to the extent of Rs. 1,10,500.00 lakhs constituting 92.73% of total leased assets. The remaining companies shared the rest 7.27%, which is insignificant.

Table 5.3 presents year-wise data pertaining to total assets leased by the select lessee companies during the period 1990-91 to 1996.97. The data reveals the following:

(i) Regarding the total volume of assets taken on lease by lessee companies, the highest amount was recorded by APSEB constituting Rs. 1,10,500.00 lakhs and the highest compound growth rate is also recorded by the APSEB registering at 96.20%.

(ii) The total volume of assets taken on lease has increased from Rs. 4,175.38 lakhs to Rs. 1,19,165.72 lakhs over a period of study recording the compound growth rate at 80.16%.

(iii) In terms of absolute figures, APSEB occupied the first rank recording its share of total volume of leased assets to total assets leased by all select lessee companies. It has recorded Rs. 1,10,500.00 lakhs accounting for 92.73% followed by APR recording Rs. 3,860.52 lakhs accounting for 3.24%, which is insignificant and the others have much more insignificant ITC recording at Rs. 1,270.06 lakhs representing

1.06%, VST recording Rs. 1,218.61 lakhs representing 1.02% and APSRTC at Rs. 1,186.00 lakhs representing 1.00%. The remaining four companies such as CML, PAL, PSL and PSM, have recorded the volume of leased assets below Rs. 500 lakhs recording at Rs. 451.78 lakhs (0.38%), Rs. 91.71 lakhs (0.08%), Rs. 190.00 lakhs (0.16%), and Rs. 397.00 lakhs (0.33%) respectively.

Having discussed the magnitude of the total volume of leased assets taken by the lessee companies, now it is proposed to analyse the extent of growth in each type of asset. The data pertaining to plant and machinery (year-wise), taken on lease by lessee companies is given in Table 5.4.

During the study period, the total volume of plant and machinery taken on lease by all lessee companies has increased from Rs. 3,751.58 lakhs in 1990-91 to Rs. 1,18,011.68 lakhs in 1996-97, indicating the compound growth rate of 83.5%. Table 5.4 reveals that all select lessee companies have engaged in taking the plant and machinery on lease. Further, Table 5.4 reveals the following:

1. The highest volume of assets of plant and machinery has been taken by the APSEB recording at Rs. 1,10,500 lakhs, recording the highest compound growth rate at 96.20% (Table 5.3). The APSEB has taken the plant and machinery of electric meters, turbines, boilers, transformers, pre-stressed concrete poles, etc. on lease. It has taken from the following lessor companies.
2. ITC Classic Ltd., Calcutta, (ii) Apple Finance Limited, Bombay, (iii) Shaw & Wallace Finance Limited, Calcutta, (iv) Nagarjuna Finance Limited, Hyderabad, (v) DCL Finance Limited, Hyderabad, and (vi) ITC Bhadrachalam Paper Boards Limited, Hyderabad, this company acted as both the lessor and the lessee. All leased assets are 100% depreciable assets.

It is interesting to note that APSEB is the first power unit to take the assets on lease in India. Later, the power units of Gujarat, Tamil Nadu, Madhya Pradesh, Maharashtra and West Bengal

Table 5.1 : Types of Assets taken on Lease by Lessee Companies (Cumulative Figures)

(Rs. lakhs)

Types of Assets	*1990-91*	*1991-92*	*1992-93*	*1993-94*	*1994-95*	*1995-96*	*1996-97*	*C.G.R*	$\bar{X}$
Plant & Machinery	(89.85) 3751.58	(91.06) 6652.61 (77.33)	(91.42) 7035.78 (5.76)	(95.48) 22399.11 (218.36)	(97.68) 44828.61 (100.14)	(98.45) 73306.68 (63.53)	(99.03) 118011.68 (60.98)	83.50	94.71
Vehicles	(0.42) 17.45	(2.94) 214.55 (1129.51)	(2.88) 221.48 (3.23)	(1.50) 353.03 (59.40)	(0.78) 355.79 (0.78)	(0.48) 355.79 (0)	(0.30) 355.79 (0)	41.31	1.33
Office Equipment	(9.73) 406.35	(6.00) 438.91 (8.01)	(5.70) 438.91 (0)	(3.02) 706.68 (61.01)	(1.54) 706.68 (0)	(1.02) 761.37 (7.74)	(0.64) 761.37 (0)	13.33	3.95
Other Assets	–	–	–	–	–	(0.05) 36.88 (100)	(0.03) 36.88 (0)	–	0.01
Total	(100) 4175.38	(100) 7306.07 (74.98)	(100) 7696.17 (5.34)	(100) 23458.82 (204.81)	(100) 45891.08 (95.62)	(100) 74460.72 (62.26)	(100) 119165.72 (60.04)	80.16	1.00

Note: (i) Figures in upper brackets indicate proportion of each component of asset to total assets leased. (ii) Figures in lower brackets indicate growth rates. (iii) C.G.R. = Compound Growth Rate. (iv) $\bar{X}$ = Arithmetic Mean.

Source: Field survey.

Table 5.2 : Types of Total Assets taken on Lease by lessee companies (From 1990-91 to 1996-97) *(Rs. lakhs)*

Lessee Cos.	*Plant & Machinery*	*Vehicles*	*Office Equipment*	*Other Assets*	*Total*
	(93.63)				(92.73)
APSEB	110500.00	–	–	–	110500.00
	(100)				(100)
	(3.25)	(1.98)	(2.17)		(3.24)
APR	3836.98	7.04	16.50	–	3860.52
	(99.39)	(0.18)	(0.43)		(100)
	(0.84)	(54.25)			(100)
APSRTC	993.00	193.00			1186.00
	(83.73)	(16.27)	–	–	(100)
	(0.38)	–	(0.54)		(0.38)
CML	447.64	–	4.14	–	451.78
	(99.08)	–	(0.92)		(100)
	(0.82)	(9.41)	(35.17)		(1.06)
ITC	968.86	33.47	267.77	–	1270.10
	(76.28)	(2.63)	(21.09)		(100)
	(0.08)				(0.08)
PAL	91.71				91.71
	(100)	–	–	–	(100)
	(0.16)				(0.16)
PSL	190.00	–	–	–	190.00
	(100)				(100)
	(0.34)				(0.33)
PSM	397.00	–	–	–	(397.00)
	(100)				(100)
	(0.50)	(34.36)	(62.12)	(100)	(1.02)
VST	586.49	122.28	472.96	36.88	1218.61
	(48.13)	(10.03)	(38.81)	(3.03)	(100)
TOTAL	(100)	(100)	(100)	(100)	(100)
	118011.68	355.79	761.37	36.88	119165.72
	(99.03)	(0.30)	(0.64)	(0.03)	(100)

Note: (i) Figures in upper brackets represent the share (percent) of each company.
(ii) Figures in lower brackets represent per cent of each component of asset to total leased assets.

Source: Field Survey.

Table 5.3 : Total Leased Assets taken on Lease by Lessee Companies (Cumulative Figures)

(Rs. lakhs)

Lessee *Cos.*	*1990-91*	*1991-92*	*1992-93*	*1993-94*	*1994-95*	*1995-96*	*1996-97*	*CGR (%)*
APSEB	2390.00	5000.00	5000.00	20000.00	41300.00	69300.00	110500.00	96.20
	–	(109.21)	(0)	(300.00)	(106.50)	(67.80)	(59.45)	
APR	350.48	500.52	500.52	500.52	500.52	500.52	3860.52	
	–	(42.81)	(0)	(0)	(0)	(0)	(671.30)	29.31
APSRTC	0	193.00	193.00	193.00	1186.00	1186.00	1186.00	*
		(100)	(0)	(0)	(514.51)	(0)	(0)	
CML	40.87	40.87	91.72	383.25	383.25	451.78	451.78	61.63
	–	(0)	(124.72)	(317.85)	(0)	(17.88)	(0)	
ITC	887.98	892.08	899.01	1176.05	1178.81	1270.10	1270.10	6.83
	–	(0.34)	(0.75)	(26.84)	(0)	(7.81)	(0)	
PAL	0	25.06	50.06	66.33	91.71	91.71	91.71	*
		(100)	(99.76)	(32.50)	(38.26)	(0)	(0)	
PSL	50.00	100.00	125.00	150.00	190.00	190.00	190.00	4.20
	–	(100.00)	(25.00)	(20.00)	(26.67)	(0)	(0)	
PSM	46.00	69.00	299.00	313.00	338.00	367.00	397.00	42.57
	–	(50.00)	(333.00)	(4.68)	(7.99)	(8.58)	(8.17)	
VST	410.05	485.54	537.86	676.67	722.79	1103.61	1218.61	19.57
	–	(18.41)	(10.78)	(25.81)	(6.82)	(52.69)	(10.42)	
TOTAL	4175.38	7306.07	7696.17	23458.82	45891.08	74460.72	119165.72	
	–	(74.98)	(5.34)	(204.81)	(95.62)	(62.26)	(60.04)	80.16

Note :(i) * Compound Growth Rate is not calculated since zeros in those years are indicated by asterisks.

(ii) Figures in brackets indicate growth rates.

Source: Field survey.

Table 5.4 : Plant and Machinery taken on Lease by Lessee Companies (Cumulative figures)

(Rs. lakhs)

Lessee Cos.	1990-91	1991-92	1992-93	1993-94	1994-95	1995-96	1996-97	CGR (%)
APSEB	2390.00	5000.00	5000.00	20000.00	41300.00	69300.00	110500.00	96.20
	–	(109.21)	(0)	(300.00)	(106.50)	(67.80)	(59.45)	
APR	326.94	476.98	476.98	476.98	476.98	476.98	3836.98	30.19
		(45.89)	(0)	(0)	(0)	(0)	(704.43)	
APSRTC	–	–	–	–	993.00	993.00	993.00	*
						(0)	(0)	
CML	36.73	36.73	87.58	379.11	379.11	447.64	447.64	64.68
		(0)	(138.44)	(332.87)	(0)	(18.08)	(0)	
ITC	877.57	877.57	877.57	877.57	877.57	968.86	968.86	1.78
		(0)	(0)	(0)	(0)	(10.40)	(0)	
PAL	0	25.06	50.06	66.33	91.71	91.71	91.71	*
			(99.76)	(32.50)	(38.26)	(0)	(0)	
PSL	50.00	100.00	125.00	150.00	190.00	190.00	190.00	22.61
		(100)	(25.00)	(20.00)	(26.67)	(0)	(0)	
PSM	46.00	69.00	299.00	313.00	338.00	367.00	397.00	42.57
		(50.00)	(333.00)	(4.68)	(7.99)	(8.58)	(8.17)	
VST	24.34	67.27	119.59	136.12	182.24	471.49	586.49	71.01
		(176.38)	(77.78)	(13.82)	(33.88)	(158.72)	(24.39)	
TOTAL	3751.58	6652.61	7035.78	22399.11	44828.61	73306.68	118011.68	83.50
		(77.33)	(5.76)	(218.36)	(100.14)	(63.53)	(60.98)	

Note : i. Figures in brackets indicate compound growth rates.

ii. * Compound growth rate is not calculated since zeros in those years are indicated by asterisks.

Source: Field Survey.

Governments have started taking assets on lease following the example of APSEB. Further the lessee survey, pertaining to the main reasons for leasing, revealed the following:

1. 99% of the total leased assets is under "sale and lease back arrangement". The APSEB has taken assets on lease already owned by it. It is an alternative mode of using its assets as a rentier, instead of as an owner. It is a mode of unlocking the investment already made in an asset and releasing the capital invested therein. This can be used for an alternative purpose like working capital.
2. The APSEB is eligible to take loans from (i) Power Finance Corporation and (ii) Rural Electricity Corporation, who need government's guarantee to sanction loans. The interest rate is 16.5% per annum. But no restrictions exist in lease financing arrangement. Moreover, it is an instant finance and easy mode of financing.
3. Leasing is a cheaper source of finance since double depreciation is claimed by both the lessee before selling the asset to the lessor or financier and by the lessor after the asset is purchased from the lessee under the sale and lease back arrangement. The cost of leasing varies from 11% to 12% depending upon the term of the agreement and the depreciation claim. The primary lease period usually varies between 5 years and 7 years. In addition, the management fee of 1% and lease tax of 5% will be added to the cost of leasing. With this the total cost of leasing varies between 17% and 18%. This cost of leasing varies every year depending on the imposition and variation of lease tax from time to time, since the imposition of sales tax and turnover tax is a prerogative of State Government. Further the lessee respondent said that leasing was not 100% financing, and APSEB was required to put 10% margin money in the lease deal.

The APR has taken Plant and Machinery worth Rs. 3836.98 lakhs. The highest amount of Plant and Machinery that was taken on lease by APR was Rs. 3360 lakhs in 1996-97. With this the cumulative figure of the plant and machinery recorded Rs. 3836.98 lakhs in 1996-97 (Table 5.4).

Pollution control equipment, Turbo generator, ClO_2 plant which produces Chlorine Dioxide, Boilers, ESP System, Job Front, End Loader are some types of equipment/plant and machinery that are taken by APR on lease from DCL Finance Ltd., Hyderabad, Cholamand-alam Investment and Finance Limited, Madras, Credit Capital Finance Corporation Ltd., Bombay and ICDS Limited, Manipal. All assets of plant and machinery are 100% depreciable assets.

The lessee respondent revealed that the following factors were influential in deciding to prefer leasing:

1. Easy way to access funds particularly when the company is facing funds crunch as leasing is a less restrictive source of finance.
2. The company policy to borrow funds is based on Debt-Equity ratio. Since Lease financing is off-balance sheet method, it does not affect the Debt-Equity Ratio and hence the companies prefer lease-financing mode.
3. It facilitates free flow of cash, as the lease financing does not block the company's money in fixed assets.
4. Another important point here is that, since APR was a sick company and was referred to BIFR (Board of Industrial Financial Reconstruction), no financial institution or bank came forward to lend money for the company except the lease financing mode and hence, leasing was the only alternative left. The lease financing arrangement helped to revive the company from 1989-90 and started paying tax from 1994-95.
5. The lessee company responded that the company preferred 100% depreciable assets of plant and machinery since the lessor passes on the depreciation benefit to the lessee and fixes the leasing at low lease rates. The interest rate varies from 11% to 13% per annum. By including a management fee of 1% and 5% lease tax on lease rentals, the final cost of leasing for 5 years, varies between 17% and 19%. Further, 1% turnover tax levied by State Government was lifted from 1-4-1995.

The APSRTC has taken plant and machinery of Wind Electric Generators (windmills costing Rs. 993 lakhs in the year 1994-95 from Sundaram Finance Ltd, Madras. Its Branch office is located in Hyderabad. After 1995, it could not take any asset on lease arrangement, as the internal generated sources are available.

The lessee responding to a question as to why leasing is preferred to borrowing said that to the extent of funds constraint, leasing was resorted to instead of borrowing. Since leasing is an easy way of acquiring the required capital assets, the cost of leasing varies between 17% and 18.0% including all other taxes. Since the APSRTC is considered a charitable institution, it is subject to concessional sales tax. The lessee further said that the other capital assets required were built up through internal resources, as the internal generated funds were available to meet the requirement.

As per the lease agreement between APSRTC and Sundaram Finance Ltd., the primary lease tenure is 7 years. Lease rent is fixed at Rs. 15.75 per month per thousand. Residual value is Rs. 1000 per lakh. The asset is 100% depreciable item. Pattern of payment is monthly advance instalment. The cost of funds to the lessor is 16% p.a., which was then the prime bank-lending rate.

The above lease rate translates into an effective rate of 9.11% p.a. only. If the lease management fee is at 1% of the cost of the asset, the lease tax of 6% (varies from time to time) and turnover tax of 1% are added. The total cost of lease varies between 17% and 18%. Since the interest rates are floating as per RBI guidelines, the lease rentals are subject to revision.

A lease management fee at 1% of the cost of the asset is payable by the lessee at the time of signing the lease agreement or is built up in the lease rentals depending upon the agreement. Sales tax on lease rentals, if applicable, shall be payable by the lessee at the applicable rate along with monthly rentals. The bus lease transactions are exempt from sales tax in so far as APSRTC is concerned. However, the acquisition of Windmills plant and machinery is subject to sales tax @ 6% in 1995. Naturally, the cost of leasing increases to the extent of sales tax.

Further, the agreement says that on the expiry of the lease period, the lessee may pay the residual value in case the sale is not concluded immediately. Consequent to the payment towards residual value, the lessee can continue the usage of the Windmills until such time as the sale is concluded. It is ascertained that the APSRTC has not taken any asset on lease during 1997-98.

The ITC Bhadrachalam Paper Boards Limited has taken plant and machinery items such as Chemical Recovery Boiler; Turbine, Rewinder Machinery; Lifts; Pollution Control Equipment from SBI Capital Markets; ITC Badrachalam Finance and Investments Limited (its subsidiary company) Mumbai; ITC Classic Finance Limited, Calcutta; Shetty Leasing (India) Limited, Bangalore, Cholamandalam Investment and Finance Company Limited, Chennai; Can Bank Financial Services Ltd., Bangalore. This company stands fourth in order of rank recording the total volume of the leased plant and machinery at Rs. 968.86 lakhs. But it recorded the least compound growth rate at 1.78% (Table 5.4). However, it concentrated on the lease of office furnitures and vehicles (Table 5.2). This company acted both as a lessor and a lessee. It has given electrical equipment to APSEB worth Rs. 499.00 lakhs in the year 1993-94 at Rs. 19.50 per month per Rs. 1,000 for five years lease. The effective rate of interest comes to 10.96%. By adding the lease tax and management fee and lease turnover tax, this interest rate goes up to around 18% p.a. Thus, this company acted as a lessor to take full benefits of depreciation for tax purpose. Similarly, the company has taken assets from its group company and from its subsidiary company to give depreciation benefits to those companies from whom it has taken the assets on lease.

The CML company is ranked sixth in terms of the volume of lease of plant and machinery recording Rs. 447.64 lakhs which is very insignificant compared to total. The compound growth rate is recorded as high as 64.68% (Table 5.4).

According to survey, the CML company has taken the following assets on lease: Komatsu Dozer Shovel (moving machine) from SBI Capital Markets, SO_2 Gas Cooler from SBI Capital Markets, air pollution control equipment from Cholamandalam Investment and Finance Ltd., Madras, etc.

As per the information ascertained from the lessee company the lease rates (lease rentals) vary from Rs. 22 to 24 per month per Rs. 1,000, for 5-year lease. The effective rate of interest (annual percentage rate) would be 10.49% and 14.42% respectively. The actual cost of leasing varies between 19% and 23% after adding the management fee lease tax and turnover tax, etc. Further, the lessee responded that the outright purchase through borrowing is cheaper than the leasing mode of finance: as this company being a high tax paying company and can avail the full depreciation facility and interest part of borrowed money as tax exempted. He said that the opportunity loss (depreciation benefit) might not be favourably compared with the leasing alternative. However, when funds are not available for outright purchase, leasing was preferred and it proved useful. During 1997-98, no leasing was done by CML.

The PAL belongs to Pennar group. The company was promoted in 1989 and production was started during 1990-91. This company has taken the plant and machinery of Rolling Mill Rolls. The cumulative figure of lease of plant and machinery represents Rs. 91.7 lakhs only. After 1995-96 the company has not taken any asset on lease. This company was declared sick by December 1993 and at the instance of Financial Institutions, the company management was taken over by the Pennar group. The sale volume of this company was improved during 1995-96 recording Rs. 17,288 lakhs from Rs. 9,953 lakhs in 1994-95 and the company was turned from loss making unit to a profit making company in just two years after it was taken over by the Pennar group. However, volume of leased assets is very less. The compound growth rate is not calculated, as there is a zero of leased assets in 1990-91. But, the average growth rate is recorded as 24.36% (Table 5.4). During the year 1997-98 the company has not taken any asset on lease.

The PSL also belongs to Pennar group. The total volume of plant and machinery, which were leased by PSL, recorded Rs. 190 lakhs. The compound growth rate was posted at 22.61% (Table 5.4.). The PSL has taken the plant and machinery of Work Rolls and Back-up Rolls, Crane and Transformer, etc., from Canbank Financial Services, Bangalore, ITC Classic Finance Ltd., Calcutta, Pennar Paterson Securities Limited, Hyderabad, Kotak Mahindra Finance Limited, Mumbai.

The PSL acted both as the lessee and lessor. The PSL has given plant and machinery on lease costing Rs. 111.96 lakhs in 1993-94 and leased out electrical meters to APSEB costing Rs. 300 lakhs in 1994-95. The second lease deal is a tripartite agreement involving three parties (i) The APSEB (the original owner) that sold assets to ITC Classic Finance Ltd., and got immediate finance, which was used for other important purposes. The ITC Classic has sold the same asset to Pennar Steels Ltd., on hire-purchase basis. In turn the Pennar Steels Ltd., has given the same asset to APSEB on lease under sale and lease back arrangement by fixing the lease rentals equal to hire-purchase instalments and directed the APSEB to pay lease rentals to ITC Classic Finance Ltd. Thus, Pennar Steels acted both as the lessor and the lessee and avoided or reduced the payment of corporation tax liability over the study period from 1990-91 to 1996-97.

For a question, in an interview, the lessee company responded that leasing is helpful to each other mainly for tax planning purposes.

Further, the PSL Company has leased out the plant and machinery of Rs. 1,192.68 lakhs during the year 1997-98, in order to reduce the tax liability by claiming depreciation, and hence the lessee opined that the tax benefits of leasing influenced to lease out plant and machinery.

The PSM is a textile company. This company has taken plant and machinery of Diesel Generators and Textile machines to replace the existing machines on lease from ICICI, IDBI, Sundaram Finance Ltd., Madras and DCL Finance Limited, Hyderabad. The total volume of leased plant and machinery is Rs. 397 lakhs. The compound growth rate is posted at 42.57%.

The lessee survey indicates that no margin money was paid and no advance rentals were paid for all lease agreements. To the question of whether leasing is useful for a tax paying company or zero tax paying company? The lessee responded that the lease rentals would be fixed according to the convenience of both the lessor and the lessee to reduce the tax liability. The cost of leasing varies between 18% and 23% p.a. depending upon the term of the agreement and the nature of asset the details are discussed under the heading of 'cost of leasing' in this Chapter. Here the Diesel Generator comes under 100% depreciable assets category whereas the Textile machinery comes under 25% depreciable assets category, (the details are discussed under the subsequent heading of 'depreciation rates') and hence the cost of leasing here is higher compared to other lessee companies.

VST is ranked fifth in terms of volume of plant and machinery leased, recording a cumulative figure of Rs. 586.49 lakhs by 1996-97 (Table 5.4). The compound growth rate is registered at 71.01%, which is an impressive growth rate (Table 5.4).

The plant and machinery of PMD machines (tobacco processing machines), SMD machines (cigarette manufacturing and packing machine), Energy Saving Equipment, etc., were leased by the VST from Sundaram Finance Ltd., ICICI Ltd., Ind Bank, Merchant Banking Ltd., etc.

The lessee responded that the cost of leasing varies from 18% to 23% p.a. depending upon the lease agreement and the nature of asset. Here, the industrial machinery comes under 25% of depreciable items, while the Energy Saving Equipment comes under 100% depreciable items. The leasing rates vary from Rs. 22 to 26.90 per month per Rs. 1,000 over a period of study for plant and machinery. This company has taken the PMD machine on lease at Rs. 26.90 per month per Rs. 1,000 for four years primary lease period in the year 1993-94. The effective rate of interest comes to 14.26% p.a. After adding lease tax, management fee, turnover tax, etc., the rate of interest goes up to 22% p.a. Since plant and machinery is not under 100% depreciable items, the lease rentals are fixed at high rate, i.e. the cost of leasing is at higher level compared to other lessee companies.

Further, this company has taken computers at Rs. 29 per month per Rs. 1,000 for four years lease agreement. The cost of the lease is at 19.20%.

Having discussed the lease of plant and machinery, it is now proposed to discuss other leased assets – such as vehicle leasing and leasing of office equipment, which includes computers.

Vehicle Leasing

Vehicle leasing as a concept is yet to be fully accepted in AP and in the country as a whole, while the system of hire-purchase finance for acquiring automobiles has been firmly established in this country. About 70% of the population still live in rural areas and the Railways, with heavy capital investments involved, have serious limitations in meeting the rising demands. Hence the Road

Transport Industry provides the basic infrastructure for the economic growth in all parts of the country. Development of vehicle leasing in all parts of the country is correlated to the development of basic infrastructure facilities in the country. The hire purchase and leasing companies in AP and in the country have been playing a significant role in the development of the Road Transport Industry.

The sub-classification of vehicle leasing by select lessee companies is given in Table 5.5 and company-wise vehicles, which were taken on lease by leasing of select lessee companies is given in Table 5.6.

Table 5.5 reveals that the leasing of cars and buses has a moderate growth recording the compound growth rate at 41.31%. The table presents that, out of total worth of vehicles which were taken on lease constituting Rs. 355.79 lakhs, the buses represent 54.25% (i.e. Rs. 193 lakhs) followed by cars 43.78% constituting Rs. 155.75 lakhs and trucks and vans recorded a lower proportion of 1.79% representing Rs. 7.04 lakhs. The proportion of leasing of trucks and vans is very insignificant due to low demand for the same.

The survey of lessee companies indicates that out of total cars worth Rs. 155.75 lakhs, the ITC has taken cars worth Rs. 33.47 lakhs on operating method of leasing representing 21.5% of total volume of cars. VST Ltd. shares the remaining 78.5%. It means that only two companies have taken cars on lease. Five companies, namely APSEB, CML, PAL, PSL and PSM, have not taken any kind of vehicles on lease but have taken only plant and machinery on lease except CML, which has also taken the office equipment for Rs. 4.14 lakhs in addition to plant and machinery. The remaining two companies, APR and APSRTC, have taken vehicles of trucks (1990-91) and buses (1991-92) on lease respectively.

Among all select lessee companies, APSRTC has taken 34 buses on lease in 1991-92, and stands the first representing 54.25% followed by VST representing 34.36%, ITC representing a low proportion of 9.41% and APR representing 1.98% (Table 5.6).

The ITC is the only company, which has taken cars under operating lease (Table 5.8), the amount represented being Rs. 33.47 lakhs.

The overall picture indicates that vehicle leasing in AP from

Table 5.5 : Sub-Classification of Vehicle taken on Lease by Lessee Companies (Cumulative Figures)

(Rs. lakhs)

Vehicles	*1990-91*	*1991-92*	*1992-93*	*1993-94*	*1994-95*	*1995-96*	*1996-97*	*C.G.R. (%)*
	(59.66)	(6.76)	(9.68)	(43.34)	(43.78)	(43.78)	(43.78)	
Cars	10.41	14.51	21.44	152.99	155.75	155.75	155.75	62.15
	–	(39.39)	(47.76)	(613.57)	(1.80)	(0)	(0)	
	–	(89.96)	(87.14)	(54.67)	(54.25)	(54.25)	(54.25)	
Buses		193.00	193.00	193.00	193.00	193.00	193.00	*
		(100)	(0)	(0)	(0)	(0)	(0)	
Trucks	(40.34)	(3.28)	(3.18)	(1.99)	(1.97)	(1.97)	(1.97)	
&	7.04	7.04	7.04	7.04	7.04	7.04	7.04	0
Vans	–	(0)	(0)	(0)	(0)	(0)	(0)	
Others	–	–	–	–	–	–	–	*
	(100)	(100)	(100)	(100)	(100)	(100)	(100)	
Total	17.45	214.55	221.48	353.03	355.79	355.79	355.79	41.31
	–	(826.38)	(3.23)	(59.40)	(0.78)	(0)	(0)	

Note : (i) C G R is not calculated since there are zeros in those years indicated by asterisks.
(ii) Figures in upper brackets indicate proportion of each component of vehicle to total volume of vehicles.
(iii) A figure in lower brackets indicate growth rates.

Source: Field survey.

Table 5.6 : Company-wise Analysis of Vehicles taken on Lease by Lessee Companies (Cumulative Figures)

(Rs. lakhs)

Lessee Cos.	*1990-91*	*1991-92*	*1992-93*	*1993-94*	*1994-95*	*1995-96*	*1996-97*
APSEB	–	–	–	–	–	–	–
							(1.98)
APR	7.04	7.04	7.04	7.04	7.04	7.04	7.04
		(0)	(0)	(0)	(0)	(0)	(0)
							(54.25)
APSRTC	–	193.00	193.00	193.00	193.00	193.00	193.00
		(100)	(0)	(0)	(0)	(0)	(0)
CML	–	–	–	–	–	–	–
							(9.41)
ITC	10.41	14.51	21.44	30.71	33.47	33.47	33.47
		(39.39)	(47.76)	(43.24)	(8.99)	(0)	(0)
PAL	–	–	–	–	–	–	–
PSL	–	–	–	–	–	–	–
PSM	–	–	–	–	–	–	–
							(34.36)
VST	–	–	–	122.28	122.28	122.28	122.28
				–	(0)	(0)	(0)
							(100)
Total	17.45	214.55	221.48	353.03	355.79	355.79	355.79
		(826.38)	(3.23)	(59.40)	(0.78)	(0)	(0)

Note : (i) Figures in upper brackets indicate proportion of vehicle leasing of each company to total vehicle leasing.

(ii) Figures in lower brackets indicate growth rates.

Source : Annual reports of select lessee companies.

the point of view of lessee companies has not been encouraging. This may be due to the high cost of leasing compared to that of plant and machinery, as the maintenance will be borne by the lessor and included in lease rentals. However, from the point of view of lessor companies, the momentum of vehicle leasing has been slowly increasing because individuals are also taking interest in car leasing.

The operating leasing has not gained wide popularity though it enables the user to shift the responsibility of maintenance to the lessor. To express as a percentage of the original cost of the car, a typical residual value would be 40% after two years or 30% after three years depending on the use and make or model concerned. The size of the residual value anticipated by the contract will have a cash flow effect as well as the pricing of the lease.

The financial leasing of a car/fleet leaves the user with the management of responsibilities. The lessee arranges and pays for insurance, licence, maintenance, repairs and other running costs.

Both operating leasing and financial leasing facilities are widely available for all vehicles. Light vans are often treated as if they are cars for finance lease or for operating lease. The maximum period usually allowed is three to five years. Heavier commercial vehicles are more commonly leased for longer primary periods of up to seven or eight years, usually on a full payment basis, i.e. financial lease basis. Financial lease for a heavy truck is therefore no different from the lease of any other item of plant and machinery.

Office Equipment

The office equipment was taken on lease by only four companies namely APR, CML, ITC and VST. Table 5.7 reveals that the APR and CML have taken computers on lease only in 1990-91 for Rs.16.50 lakhs and Rs. 4.14 lakhs respectively. ITC has taken the office equipment of wireless communication system EPABX (Telephone operation system) on lease for Rs. 267.77 lakhs in the year 1993-94 only and later no office equipment was taken on lease by ITC. VST has taken office equipment of computers and Tata Telecom equipment for intercom arrangement in the company. The cumulative figure comes to Rs. 472.96 lakhs.

In addition to the office equipment, VST has taken other assets like Air Coolers, Air-conditioners, Refrigerators, Vacuum Cleaners, etc. in 1996-97. The total volume of other assets comes to Rs. 36.88 lakhs.

The leasing of office equipment is not very encouraging. This may be due to the high cost of leasing of these assets, which get obsolete in a short period. The VST has taken computers for Rs. 29.50 per month per Rs. 1000 for 4 years in the year 1991-92. The effective rate of interest comes to Rs. 20.38%. After adding other taxes, the cost of leasing goes up to the extent of extra taxes.

Similarly, the CML has taken computers in 1990-91 for 5 years. The lease rentals are fixed at Rs. 24 per month per Rs. 1000. The effective rate of interest comes to 17.31% (The details of lease costs are discussed under the heading of 'cost of leasing' in this Chapter).

The total picture of total leased assets and their share is drawn in a pie-diagram. The pie-diagram indicates the average proportion of each asset leased by lessee companies over a period of study from 1990-91 to 1996-97. The order of each asset is mentioned below (Table 5.1).

Asset	*Per cent*
1. Plant & Machinery	94.71
2. Office Equipment	3.95
3. Vehicles	1.33
4. Other Assets	0.01
Total	100.00

Table 5.7: Computers and Office Equipments taken by Lessee Companies on Lease (Cumulative Figures)

(Rs. lakhs)

Lessee Cos.	*1990-91*	*1991-92*	*1992-93*	*1993-94*	*1994-95*	*1995-96*	*1996-97*
APSEB	–	–	–	–	–	–	–
							(2.17)
APR	16.50	16.50	16.50	16.50	16.50	16.50	16.50
		(0)	(0)	(0)	(0)	(0)	(0)
APSRTC	–	–	–	–	–	–	–
							(0.54)
CML	4.14	4.14	4.14	4.14	4.14	4.14	4.14
		(0)	(0)	(0)	(0)	(0)	(0)
							(35.17)
ITC	–	–	–	267.77	267.77	267.77	267.77
				(100)	(0)	(0)	(0)
PAL	–	–	–	–	–	–	–
PSL	–	–	–	–	–	–	–
PSM	–	–	–	–	–	–	–
							(62.12)
VST	385.71	418.27	418.27	418.27	418.27	472.96	472.96
		(10.07)	(0)	(0)	(0)	(13.08)	(0)
							(100)
TOTAL	406.35	438.91	438.91	706.68	706.68	761.37	761.37
		(9.55)	(61.01)	(0)	(0)	(7.74)	(0)

Note : i. Figures in upper brackets indicate the proportion of each company to the total leasing of computers and office equipment.

ii. Figures in lower brackets indicate growth rates.

Source: Field Survey.

Now it is clear that the asset-wise analysis reveals that, plant and machinery occupied the first position among all assets leased by lessee companies. This indicates that among all assets taken on lease, the demand is more for plant and machinery in the lease market. There has been a scarce demand for vehicles and other assets such as T.V. sets, Refrigerators and other consumer durables or domestic appliances.

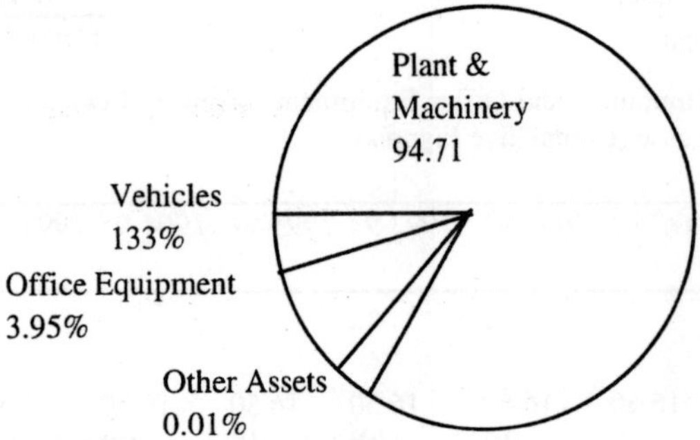

Fig. 5.1 : The Proportion of each Asset to Total Assets taken on Lease

Further, it is observed that in terms of company-wise analysis, APSEB occupied first position recording its leased assets at 92.73% of all assets leased by select lessee companies. This is followed by APR recording a less proportion 3.24%. The remaining 4.03% is shared by remaining seven lessee companies (Table 5.2).

It is clearly seen that the demand for lease finance has emanated primarily from the APSEB. And strongly enough, the demand from APSEB has been for 100% depreciation assets that too under the sale and lease back arrangement. This has led to a crash in lease rentals. Another reason for why APSEB preferred sale and lease back arrangement is that leasing provides them with immediate liquidity or funds without any restrictions. Usually the main source for the Electricity Board for liquidity is from the Power Finance Corporation and Rural Electricity Corporation. But these institutions have strict procedure/rules to sanction loans. They provide only 50% of the book value of the assets. APSEB is the first Electricity Board, which raised funds through leasing route in India, followed by Gujarat Electricity Board, Tamil Nadu Electricity

Board, Madhya Pradesh Electricity Board, West Bengal Electricity Board and Maharashtra State Electricity Board.

It is ascertained that most State Electricity Boards have raised more funds through leasing route under sale and lease back arrangement, which constitute bulk of leasing market in India. The effective rate of interest on 100% depreciable items varies between 10% and 12%. However, the rate of interest obviously goes up if other taxes like lease tax on lease rentals, turnover tax, lease management fee, insurance etc., are added. But these taxes vary in different states; whereas, some State Governments have exempted the tax on lease rentals. For instance, the Maharashtra State Government has exempted the lease tax on lease rentals. The AP Government, realising the effect of multi-point levy of sales tax on lease transactions, had notified in 1985 that the tax on lease of goods, which were subject to payment of APGST, stood exempted. But in 1993 the exemption notification was withdrawn. Hence, at present, sales tax is applicable in AP on lease of all goods. However, the provision imposing turnover tax on certain transactions, including leases has been deleted with effect from 1-4-1995 by the APGST (Third Amendment) Act, 1995. (The details of Sales Tax are discussed in Chapter 3). Thus, the cost of leasing varies from State to State depending upon the State Governments' taxes and also varies within the State from year to year; depending upon the Amendment of General Sales Tax Act from time to time.

In fact, the method of lease arrangement may be useful in general and suitable for public sector undertakings in particular provided, a uniform method of tax is followed by all State Governments as far as lease taxes are concerned.

Now, it is pertinent to analyse the leased assets falling under different types of lease agreements.

Leasing by Type of Agreement

The term of leases, called "lease period", is the period for which the agreement of lease shall be in operation.

Lessee companies have broadly entered into three types of lease agreements with the lessor companies, such as "finance lease", "operating lease" and "sale and lease back".

In a *financial lease*, the period of leasing is fixed almost equal to the economic life of the asset, so that the lessee enjoys the use of the asset for almost its entire useful period as the owner enjoys. But the lessor may not be prepared to keep his investment at stake for the whole life of the lease period. The lessor company prefers to recover its investment and interest by way of lease rentals within a reasonable period. The lease agreement will be divided into two periods: primary lease period during which the lessor company desires to recover its investment along with interest and the secondary lease period for the balance of the life of the asset. During the secondary lease period only nominal rentals are charged to keep the lease agreement operative. The length of the primary lease period is an important factor in evaluating a lease proposal. A lessee's choice of the most suitable available period depends on a number of factors, including the anticipated period of use of the asset and the possible need to match cash inflows (earning capacity of the assets) with outflows (lease rentals).

For larger items of assets such as aircraft, ships etc., longer periods are appropriate and lease of 10 years and more are common. However, there is no recognised maximum primary lease period as such.

The *operating lease* is a short-term lease and viable with respect to assets like vehicles, computers, electronic equipment, etc. The maturity of the lease agreement is considerably lower than the useful economic life of the asset. The lessor, unlike in finance lease, may not seek to recover the full cost of the equipment leased. The remaining cost of the equipment and interest or profit is recovered either by renewing the lease to the same party or leasing it to other parties or by disposing of the asset. In operating lease, the maintenance and other expenses are borne by the lessor; and further, the lessor bears the risk of obsolescence. Thus, with the operating lease, there is a commercial rationale as well as a possible fiscal reason, for the lessee not to acquire ownership. The asset may be required for a shorter period, based on the need, than its expected useful life.

Under sale and lease back arrangement, the owner of an asset sells the owned assets to a finance company and immediately reacquires the right to use the asset by entering into a lease agreement with the finance company (purchaser). Here the seller becomes the lessee and the purchaser (finance company) becomes the lessor. Thus, a sale and lease back arrangement entails funding by a finance company based on a piece of asset which is usually revalued to provide the maximum gain. For instance, the company seeking funds revalues a particular asset sought to be sold and leased back. The finance /leasing company would ostensibly buy the asset and provides the required cash immediately and leases it back to the seller company concerned. For the user, it is an alternative mode of using his assets as a rentier instead of as an owner. In financial sense, it is a mode of unlocking the investment already made in an asset to be used for an alternative purpose.

The sale and lease back agreement is arranged in such a way that the actual funds flowing into the company would be lower than the revalued figure of the asset, though on paper the fund flow would be equal to the figure of revalued asset. To the lessee company it does not matter much since it is able to get intended amount. Secondly, it would be showing a higher lease rental in terms of pay out, which reduces its taxable income. The lessor company in such cases would get a higher depreciation cover at revalued higher amount.

Eventually, the Lessee Company may even default on the lease rental after a certain period of time. But that may not bother the lessor much as it already receives the cost plus profit based on the actual hidden cost. As such, the lessor company may have to show a lower rental income or make some provision against defaults in the name of the Non-Performing Assets, which in turn reduces its taxable income. As such, the practitioners of this sale and lease back arrangement are avoiding their legitimate dues of taxes.

Thus, the sale and lease back transactions can be treated (i) as a "Sham", as the transaction is a circulating transaction and has no economic essence; and (ii) as a finance transaction as there is no real acquisition of an asset by the lessor or no real lease back thereof.

After an analysis of different types of lease financing arrangements and their associated procedures, it is now proposed to make a critical analysis of the data relating to the volume of leased assets *vis-a-vis* lease agreements of select lessee companies over the study period from 1990-91 to 1996-97. The relevant data is given in Table 5.8. The Table reveals that the sample units have been obtaining their required leased assets under different lease financing arrangements or methods. There are only three methods in practice among these. They are (i) financial lease, (ii) operating lease and (iii) sale and lease back method.

The volume of assets taken on lease by each lessee company over a span of period is shown under four categories of lease agreement in Table 5.8, viz., (i) financial lease, (ii) operating lease, (iii) sale and lease back, and (iv) others.

Table 5.8 reveals the total volume of assets taken on lease by select lessee companies from 1990-91 to 1996-97 is recorded at Rs. 1,19,165.72 lakhs. The proportion of financial lease, operating lease, and sale and lease back arrangement is recorded at Rs. 7,699.25 lakhs (6.46%), Rs. 33.43 lakhs (0.03%), and Rs. 1,11,433.00 lakhs (93.51%) respectively. The data reveals that lessee companies have dealt only with three types of lease arrangements as mentioned above. The most commonly used method of lease is financial lease, which we find in the case of every company. However, in terms of volume of assets taken on this kind of lease accounts only for 6.46% of total assets taken on lease under all the three types put together. In terms of volume of assets taken on lease under sale and lease back method of lease accounts for the largest share 93.5%, which is essentially in fact only because of one concern, i.e., APSEB, which accounts for Rs. 1,10,350 lakhs. In fact there is only two more concerns, viz., ITC and PSL, which have taken assets on lease under this method, but their shares being negligible. The operating method of lease is the least important in terms of the volume as well as number of concerns going in for this kind of lease.

It is interesting to note that the APSEB stood first in the State in obtaining the leased assets under the sale and lease back arrangement recording at 92.60% of the total volume of assets of select lessee companies obtained under the three lease arrangements of financial lease, operating lease and sale and lease back put together. Further most of the transactions of sale and lease back arrangements took place from 1991-92 to 1995-96.

Out of 9 units selected for the study, six units, viz., APR, APSRTC, CML, PAL, PSM and VST have dealt with 100% lease transactions only under financial lease arrangement and not in operating lease or sale and lease back arrangements (Table 5.8). ITC is the only company to take assets on lease under all the three lease agreements of financial lease, operating lease and sale and lease back arrangements recording at Rs. 278.63 lakhs (21.94%), Rs. 33.43 lakhs (2.63%), and Rs. 958.00 lakhs (75.43%) respectively. The company has taken vehicles, such as Cars (Ambassadors, Contessa etc.,) and Mahindra Jeeps under operating lease during the period 1991-92 to 1995-96 from ITC Classic Ltd., its group company. The main advantage of operating lease is that the operating expenses are borne by the lessor company (ITC Classic Ltd.,). The other advantage of operating lease is that since these two companies belong to same group, the lease rentals could be fixed according to their convenience keeping their tax liability in view.

The reasons for preferring sale and lease back arrangement are:

1. By entering into sale and lease back arrangements, the lessee could unlock the investment already made in an asset and release the capital for other alternative purposes or working capital purposes in order to strengthen or improve the business activities.
2. The second advantage is the double depreciation facility. A relatively run down asset is revalued phenomenally and sold to a cash rich finance company or other corporate entity, which needs depreciation as a tax shelter. The same asset is then leased back to the original seller. Such deals, which in reality are mere book entries, are entered mainly for 100% depreciation items or assets (on which the seller could already claim the depreciation) as tax laws allow the lessor (buyer) of such equipment to claim depreciation.

If we observe the Indian Scenario, the Income Tax Authorities made the probe, during the middle of 1996, into dubious sale and lease back transactions. The best example in this regard is the Industrial Development Bank of India (IDBI). In case of a sale and lease back deal entered by IDBI with the Gujarat State Electricity

Board, the Financial Institution is alleged to have wrongly claimed Rs. 10 crore as depreciation for the assessment year 1993-94 which has been disallowed.[2] Further, the tax authorities are more surprised to learn that the IDBI has reportedly entered into several sale and lease back deals with private parties as well. The tax authorities have fully investigated deals entered into by IDBI with Western Paques India Ltd. IDBI reportedly purchased four-biogas pilot plant equipment's (depreciable at 100%) for a revalued price of Rs. 50 lakhs each. The same equipment was believed to have been subsequently leased back to Klestern Paques. IDBI reflected a depreciation of Rs. 2 crore, whereas the lessee, Western Paques, was richer by Rs. 2 crore (sale price).[3] This deal was also pertaining to the assessment year 1993-94. Other sale and lease back transactions entered into by IDBI for the assessment year 1994-95 are with 20th Century Finance, and ALPIC Finance, to name a few.[4]

However the death-knell has been sounded for the phenomenon of sale and lease back of public sector assets. The Union Finance Ministry has issued instructions to all government enterprises and Public Sector Undertakings not to raise resources against their assets through sale and lease back arrangements with finance companies.[5] The Government's step is expected to strain the finances of the Public Sector Undertakings further.

Among the first on the hit list would be the State Electricity Boards, which have raised sizeable working capital through sale and lease back transactions. A number of public and private sector banks in India, apart from the financial institutions are affected since these banks were big lessors of such assets.

The budget 1995-96 has plugged this loophole in the sale and lease back system by stating that in case of a sale and lease back deal, depreciation will be available to the lessor only against the written down value of the asset standing in the books of the original seller (Lessee).[6]

The impact of the application of this rule is as follows: For instance, the lessee buys and instals a thermally efficient boiler and claims 100% depreciation thereon, allowable under the Income Tax Rules. Next year, the lessee decides to unlock his investment and take the asset on lease. The asset is sold for its determined value, say, Rs. 1 crore. Under Section 50 of the Income Tax Act, the lessee will be charged to a capital gains tax on Rs. 1 crore. At the same time, the lessor's purchase price will be ignored, and the lessee's Written Down Value (WDV) being NIL, no depreciation is allowed to the lessor. Further, the Lessors entire lease rentals earning, based on an investment of Rs. 1 crore is charged to tax. It means a tax on lease rentals without any depreciation allowance certainly cannot be said to be tax on income, as the lease rental consists of principal amount and interest (profit).

Anticipating the changing mood of the authorities towards such deals mentioned above, some financial companies have stopped undertaking the sale and lease back transactions as a matter of policy, despite these proving to be too lucrative to resist in terms of tax saving advantages. For example, no sale and lease back deals figured in the Rs. 80 crore depreciation claimed by Lloyds Finance in the first half of 1995-96.[7]

Finally, it is observed that only three types of lease arrangements – such as financial lease, operating lease, and sale and lease back- have been followed by select lessee companies. The financial lease arrangement for lease deals, followed by select lessee companies, constituted Rs. 7,699.25 lakhs representing 6.46% of total lease deals arranged under all lease agreements. The sale and lease back deal has recorded 93.51% constituting Rs. 1,11,433.00 lakhs of total assets (Rs. 1,19,165.72 lakhs) taken on lease by select lessee companies. Thus the sale and lease back method became popular within a short period as it releases the capital already invested in the asset and the released capital would be useful for alternative purposes, or for working capital requirements. And later in 1996 the Government discouraged it, as there was a loophole in the system.

Sale and Lease Back and Tripartite Agreement

It is a new type of lease agreement in which three parties are involved, viz., the lessor (finance company), the manufacturer (or any other company) and the lessee. The usual practice under leasing agreement is that the lessor purchases the equipment from the supplier and gives it on lease to the lessee company for an agreed period of time for its use. But here, the asset is purchased by a finance company (first party) from a supplier, who may or may not be the manufacturer as usual and then gives the same to another

Table 5.8 : Volume of Leased Assets by Type of Lease Agreement 1990-91 to 1996-97

(Rs. in lakhs)

Name of company	*Financial lease*	*Operating leases*	*Sale and lease back*	*Others*	*Total*
APSEB	150.00 (0.14)	–	110350.00 (99.86)	–	110500.00 (100)
APR	3860.52 (100.00)	–	–	–	3860.52 (100)
APSRTC	1186.00 (100.00)	–	–	–	1186.00 (100)
CML	451.78 (100.00)	–	–	–	451.78 (100)
ITC	278.63 (21.94)	33.43 (2.63)	958.00 (75.43)	–	1270.10 (100)
PAL	91.71 (100.00)	–	–	–	91.71 (100)
PSL	65.00 (34.21)	–	125.00 (65.79)	–	190.00 (100)
PSM	397.00 (100.00)	–	–	–	397.00 (100)
VST	1218.61 (100.00)	–	–	–	1218.61 (100)
TOTAL	7699.25 (6.46)	33.43 (0.03)	111433.00 (93.51)	–	119165.72 (100)

Note: Figures in brackets indicate percentages.
Source: Field Survey.

company (second party) on hire-purchase basis. The second party, i.e., the company that has taken an asset on hire-purchase basis, gives the same asset on lease to the lessee (third party). Here the lease rental instalments are fixed equal to hire purchase instalments.

The data pertaining to sale and lease back and Tripartite Agreement is shown in Fig. 5.2. According to the Chart, the APSEB (original owner) has sold the Meters and Transformers to ITC Classic worth Rs. 300 lakhs in the month of March 1994 and the ITC Classic has sold the same asset to M/s. Pennar Steels Limited under the hire-purchase agreement. In turn, the PSL has given the same assets on lease to the APSEB. The lease rentals are fixed equal to the hire-purchase instalments.

Here APSEB is required to pay lease rentals to M/s PSL as it has become the lessee for taking the same assets (which it has sold to ITC Classic Ltd.) on lease from M/s. PSL. The PSL is required to pay hire purchase instalments (though it has become legal owner of the asset) to ITC Classic as it has entered into hire-purchase agreement with the ITC Classic Ltd. But the final result is that the APSEB was directed to pay lease rentals directly to ITC Classic Ltd., since the hire purchase instalments and lease rentals are same.

Out of 9 Select Lessee Companies, only one company, viz., APSEB has entered this type of tripartite lease agreement.

Out of six Select Lessor Companies, only one company viz., SCFSL has entered into this similar type of tripartite agreement

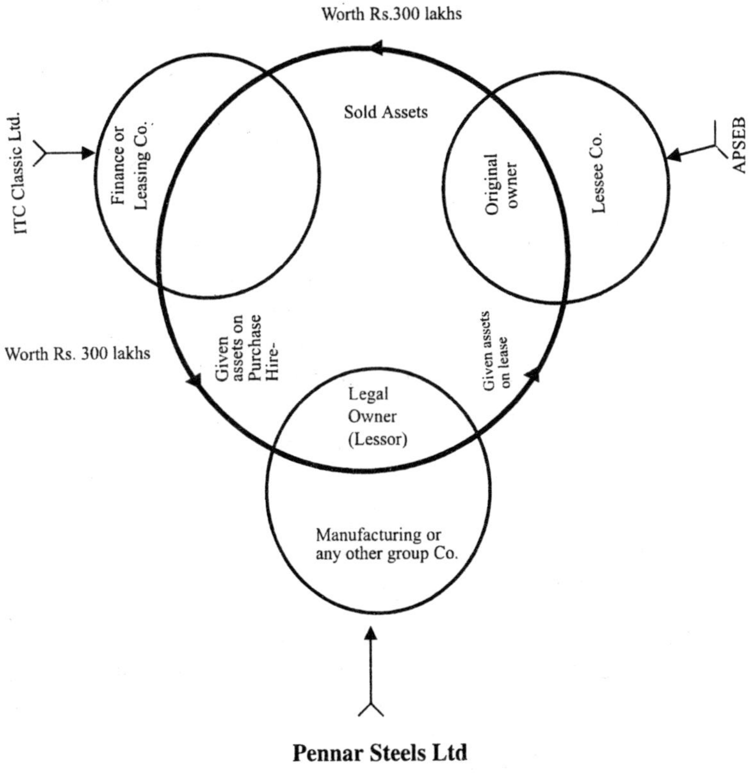

Fig. 5.2 : Tripartite Agreement under Sale and Lease back method

involving S&S Switch Company (lessee company) which has sold the assets to SCFSL worth Rs. 18 lakhs during the year 1994 and GSH Cements Limited (Lessor Company), which has taken assets from SCFSL on hire purchase basis and given the same assets on lease to S&S Switch Company. The lessee company is not under selected company for the study.

Impact of Tripartite Agreement

1. *Lessee (original owner of the asset):* The APSEB (lessee company) has raised additional funds to an extent of Rs. 300 lakhs by selling its owned assets of Electrical Meters and Transformers to ITC Classic Limited. Further, the lease rentals are tax exempted and the leased assets are not required to be shown in the balance sheet.
2. *Finance Company:* The ITC has just played the role of finance company. It has purchased the asset from APSEB and sold the same under hire-purchase scheme to the PSL. at 14% flat rate. Since it has sold or arranged the asset under the Hire-Purchase Scheme, this company is not entitled for claiming depreciation. The interest is the profit to this company.
3. *Lessor (Legal owner) :* The PSL has become the legal owner of the asset as the company has given the assets on lease to APSEB, which earlier sold the same assets to ITC Classic Ltd. The lease rentals are fixed in such a way that they are equal to the hire-purchase instalments, which the company is required to pay to ITC Classic, and directed the APSEB to pay to ITC Classic. The benefit here for this company is claiming of depreciation on the leased assets as it is the legal owner, so that this company has avoided or reduced the payment of corporate tax to the extent of the eligibility of depreciation on leased assets.

Thus, the lease transaction has brought benefits to three parties and the Government. For, the lessor it is a "tax saver" that produces "sudden highs". For the lessee, it is a convenient off-balance-sheet fund raiser. For financier, it is the profit on investment, and for sales tax man, it is a sales transaction.

All the above transactions are only paper transactions and not real transactions. The main reason behind these transactions is allowing 100% depreciation on those assets. It would be better if such types of paper transactions were discouraged.

Effect of Leasing on Quantity of Investment

Investment is a dynamic process and the company's investment decision depends on both internal and external factors, which tend to vary according to the type of asset.

The data pertaining to year-wise investment pattern including leasing undertaken by select lessee companies is presented in Table 5.9. From the table, it is observed that the average proportion of leasing to year-wise total investment varies from 0.5% (in PAL) to 29.2% (in APR). Out of 9 select lessee companies, only three companies—such as APR, APSEB and VST have used leasing on an average of above 16% of their year-wise investment to finance the capital assets, recording an average proportion of 29.3%, 26.2% and 16.8% respectively. The lease financing proportion for APSTRC and PAL is negligible the average proportion being 1.6% and 0.5% respectively. The two companies, viz., CML and PSL have maintained the average proportion of leased assets at 3% and 3.4% respectively. The remaining two companies, ITC and PSM have used leasing on an average of 8.6% and 5.7% respectively.

Individual company-wise and year-wise analysis reveals that the proportion of lease financing to total investment made ranged from 0% to 76% during the years 1990-91 to 1996-97. The proportion of lease financing is 49.5% for APSEB and 76% for APR in 1996-97. In terms of volume of leased assets, it ranged from Rs. zero to Rs. 41,200 lakhs over the period of study.

Among all Select Lessee Companies, the APSEB has taken the highest volume of leased assets. The cumulative figure constituting Rs. 1,10,500 lakhs, accounted for 92.73% of all assets taken on lease by Select Lessee Companies.

Twenty-two per cent of Select Lessee companies, when interviewed responded that leasing had moderate effect in increasing the level of capital investment and on saving of time. This is mainly for two reasons: (i) the capital investment was

Table 5.9 : Year-wise Leased Assets and Investments in other than Leased Assets of Lessee Companies *(Rs.lakhs)*

	1990-91		*1991-92*		*1992-93*		*1993-94*		*1994-95*		*1995-96*		*1996-97*		$\bar{X}$	$\bar{X}$
	IOA	*LA*	*IOA*	*LA*	*IOA*	*LA*	*IOA*	*LA*	*IOA*	*LA*	*IOA*	*LA*	*IOA*	*LA*	*IOA*	*LA*
APSEB	43600.00	2390.0	10500.0	2610.0	20147.0	–	23775	15000	105030.0	21300	65503.0	28000	42038.0	41200.0	44370	15786
	(94.8)	(5.2)	(80.1)	(19.9)	(100.0)	(0)	(61.3)	(38.7)	(83.1)	(16.9)	(70.1)	(29.9)	(50.5)	(49.5)	(73.8)	(26.2)
APR	341.0	351.0	195.0	150.0	644.0	–	875.0	–	884.0	–	5350.0	–	1059.0	3360.0	1335.0	552.0
	(49.3)	(50.7)	(56.5)	(43.5)	(100.0)	(0)	(100.0)	(0)	(100.0)	(0)	(100.0)	(0)	(24.0)	(76.0)	(70.7)	(29.3)
APSRTC	16002.0	–	13519.0	193.0	9664.0	–	18578.0	–	113.0	993.0	816.0	–	14207.0	–	10414.0	169.0
	(100.0)	(0)	(98.6)	(1.40)	(100.0)	(0)	(100.0)	(0)	(10.2)	(89.8)	(100.0)	(0)	(100.0)	(0)	(98.4)	(1.6)
CML	1543.0	41.0	1642.0	–	515.0	50.0	734.0	292.0	3860.0	–	2973.0	69.0	3390.0	–	2068.0	65.0
	(97.4)	(2.6)	(100.0)	(0)	(91.2)	(8.8)	(71.5)	(28.5)	(100.0)	(0)	(97.6)	(2.4)	(100.0)	(0)	(97.0)	(3.0)
ITC	1905.0	919.0	1536.0	3.0	1456.0	7.0	5139.0	249.0	2340.0	–	1057.0	92.0	33.0	–	1924.0	181.0
	(67.5)	(32.5)	(99.8)	(0.2)	(99.5)	(0.5)	(95.4)	(4.6)	(100.0)	(0)	(92.0)	(8.0)	(100.0)	(0)	(91.4)	(8.6)
PAL	31.0	–	28.0	25.0	39.0	25.0	861.0	16.0	15968.0	25.0	110.0	–	2192.0	–	2747.0	13.0
	(100.0)	(0)	(52.8)	(47.2)	(60.9)	(39.1)	(98.2)	(1.8)	(99.8)	(0.2)	(100.0)	(0)	(100.0)	(0)	(99.5)	(0.5)
PSL	86.0	50.0	108.0	50.0	187.0	25.0	384.0	25.0	866.0	40.0	958.0	–	2851.0	–	772.0	27.0
	(63.2)	(36.8)	(68.4)	(31.6)	(88.2)	(11.8)	(93.9)	(6.1)	(95.6)	(4.4)	(100.0)	(0)	(100.0)	(0)	(96.6)	(3.4)
PSM	370.0	46.0	873.0	23.0	540.0	230.0	785.0	14.0	1415.0	25.0	1799.0	29.0	850.0	30.0	948.0	57.0
	(88.9)	(11.1)	(97.4)	(2.6)	(70.1)	(29.9)	(98.2)	(1.8)	(98.3)	(1.7)	(98.4)	(1.6)	(96.6)	(3.4)	(94.3)	(5.7)
VST	325.0	374.0	637.0	136.0	403.0	52.0	1110.0	139.0	1273.0	47.0	1797.0	356.0	499.0	115.0	863.0	174.0
	(46.5)	(53.5)	(82.4)	(17.6)	(88.6)	(11.4)	(88.9)	(11.1)	(96.4)	(3.60)	(83.5)	(16.5)	(81.3)	(18.7)	(83.2)	(16.8)

Notes: (i) IOA =Investment on Other Assets (i.e., other than Leased Assets); (ii) LA = Leased Assets; (iii) Figures in brackets represent percentages to total; (iv) $\bar{X}$ = Arithmetic Mean.

Source: (i) For IOA: Annual Reports, (ii) For LA: Field Survey.

determined by operational requirements and formed a part of corporate planning structure, which made leasing more accessible; and (ii) capital investment is required as per time schedule which leasing provides instant finance without complex procedure. 45% (4) of respondents indicated that the leasing had a little effect in increasing their level of investment due to flexible procedure and lack of availability of other alternative funds. 33% (3) of Select Lessee Companies felt that leasing had no effect on quantity of investment because its use was very limited and it would have taken place whether leasing was available or not. Further they said that the assets, which were taken on lease, were peripheral to the main business activity such as pollution control equipment, wind electric generators, shovels, computers, etc.

It can be concluded that the average effect of leasing in increasing level of investment ranged from 0.5% to 29.3% and the proportion of assets taken on lease to total investment varies from company to company and from year to year. However, the average proportion of assets taken on lease to total investment of all Select Lessee Companies over the study period of 1990-91 to 1996-97 registered Rs. 17,024.0 lakhs per annum representing 10.6% per annum.

Now it is relevant to examine the consistency or deviation of investment involved in assets acquired through lease financing and assets other than leased ones by applying a statistical tool of Standard Deviation.

"Standard Deviation is the most usual measure of DISPERSION. It represents the square root of the VARIANCE of a group of numbers, i.e., the square root of the sum of the squared differences between a group of numbers and their ARITHMETIC MEAN. It takes into account not only of the spread between the lowest and the highest numbers but also the intermediate values."[8] The higher the standard deviation or dispersion, the higher the discrepancy or inconsistency.

The average proportions of the amount of assets taken on lease and investment involved in assets other than leased assets were calculated and the mean values are obtained for each company by considering 7 years data. Further, to have an idea of the deviation among the companies the statistical tool of Standard Deviation is also calculated for both leased assets and investment involved in other than leased assets.

Investment Involved in Other than Leased Assets

With the help of standard deviation the variations in investment involved in assets other than leased assets are calculated as mentioned hereunder.

Investment Involved in Other than Leased Assets

No. of Observations	$\overline{X}$	*d = X–89*	d^2
1.	73.8	–15.2	231
2.	70.7	–18.3	335
3.	98.4	9.4	88.4
4.	97.0	8	64
5.	91.4	2.4	5.8
6.	99.5	10.5	110.3
7.	96.6	7.6	57.8
8.	94.3	5.3	28.1
9.	83.2	5.8	33.6
9	805	$\Sigma d = 3.9$	$\Sigma d^2 = 954$

$$\bar{X} = \frac{\Sigma x}{N} = \frac{805}{9} = 89.4$$

$$\sigma = \sqrt{\frac{\Sigma d^2}{N} - \left(\frac{\Sigma d}{N}\right)^2}$$

Where: N = Number of observations

$\overline{X}$ = Arithmetic Mean

Σd = Sum of deviations of all values of variables taken from arithmetic mean

Σd^2 = Sum of the products of squared deviations taken from the mean,

$$\sigma = \sqrt{\frac{954}{9} - \left(\frac{3.9}{9}\right)^2}$$

$$\sigma = \sqrt{\frac{954}{9} - \frac{15.21}{81}}$$

$$\sigma = \sqrt{106 - 0.19} = \sqrt{105.81} = \sigma = 10.28$$

The investment on an average is 89.4%. The standard deviation or variability about its investment involved in other than leased assets is ±10.28.

With the application of statistical tools of arithmetic mean and standard deviation, the following conclusions emerged.

The amount of average investment involved in other than leased assets is 89.4% of total investment.

The value of standard deviation is 10.28. It can be interpreted that the amount of investment involved in the selected companies in other than leased assets does not vary much. This is evident, based on the standard deviation value, which is 10.28. The variation in the investment in the selected companies in other than leased assets cannot be greater than ± 10.28 to the mean value. Hence, it can be concluded that the magnitude of investment involved in other than leased assets is almost the same and the investment made from year to year over a period of study is consistent.

Leased Assets

On making comparison between mean value and standard deviation value, the deviations or variations are observed in the amount of assets acquired through leasing.

Leased Assets

No. of Observations	$\overline{X}$	*d = X–10*	*d^2*
1.	26.2	16.2	262.4
2.	29.3	19.3	372.5
3.	1.6	–8.4	70.6
4.	3.0	–7.0	49.0
5.	8.6	–1.4	1.9
6.	0.5	–9.5	90.3
7.	3.4	–6.6	43.6
8.	5.7	4.3	18.5
9.	16.8	6.8	46.2
9	95.1	$\Sigma d = 5.1$	$\Sigma d^2 = 954$

$$\bar{X} = \frac{\Sigma X}{N} = \frac{95.1}{9} = 10.6$$

$$\sigma = \sqrt{\frac{\Sigma d^2}{N} - \left(\frac{\Sigma d}{N}\right)}$$

Where, N = Number of observations

$\bar{X}$ = Arithmetic Mean

Σd = Sum of deviations of all values of variables taken from arithmetic mean

Σd^2 = Sum of the products of squared deviations taken from the mean

$$\sigma = \sqrt{\frac{954}{9} - \left(\frac{5.1}{9}\right)^2}$$

$$\sigma = \sqrt{\frac{954}{9} - \frac{26.01}{81}}$$

$$\sigma = \sqrt{106 - 0.32} = \sqrt{105.68}$$

$$\sigma = 10.28$$

The volume of leased assets on an average is 10.6%. The standard deviation or variability regarding its volume is ± 10.28.

With the application of statistical tool arithmetic mean and standard deviation the following conclusions are emerged.

The average amount of assets acquired through leasing is 10.6% of total investment.

The value of standard deviation is ±10.28. It can be interpreted that the amount of assets acquired through leasing varies much wider. This is evident, based on the standard deviation value, which is ±10.28. This is a unique situation where the value of mean and the value of standard deviation are almost the same and variation is almost 98%. It implies that the amount of assets acquired through leasing vary abnormally from company to company and the amount of leasing made from year to year over a period of study is inconsistent. It means a company like APSEB is giving top priority to leasing activity when compared to other companies.

The comparison between two mean values and standard deviations shows that there is uniformity in the investment with regard to the amount of assets involved in other than leased assets. Whereas, wide variations are observed in the volume of assets acquired through leasing.

Rates of Depreciation

The assets taken on lease are Plant and Machinery, Vehicles, Office Equipment, and others. The assets either cost less than Rs. 5000, each which are eligible for 100% depreciation or those assets, which are entitled to depreciation as per Income Tax Rules.

Depreciation is allowed on the "actual cost" of the Assets, falling within a block, as per rates given in the Income Tax Rules.

The depreciation is completely as per books of account. Tax depreciation is:

- granted on declining balances on all assets;
- at rates stipulated in the schedule to the Income Tax rules;
- granted on the basis of Blocks of Assets;
- granted irrespective of the period of use;
- completely disallowed in the year of sale.

Three conditions are to be fulfilled for claiming depreciation.

(i) Asset should be naturally depreciable;
(ii) Assessee should own the asset
(iii) Assessee should use the asset wholly and exclusively for the purposes of his business.

Assessee, the lessor, uses the asset for the purpose of his business of leasing the asset. Hence, what is relevant is the use by the lessor. In certain cases, keeping the asset in usable condition would also amount to use, such as in the case of hiring of buses, taxies, etc.

For assets installed during the year, and used for less than 180 days, only half year's depreciation is allowable.

All assets under a particular classification are eligible for the same rate of depreciation, form a Block. This new method of computing depreciation has been brought w.e.f. the assessment year 1988-89, where an asset forming part of a Block is sold, the sale proceeds are deducted there from, without considering any profit or loss on sale of the asset. Any asset acquired during the year forms part of the Block.

The broad structure of rates at which depreciation is admissible as a percentage of written value is as follows[9]:

1. *Buildings*
   5% office Buildings
   10% other Buildings
   20% Hotel Buildings
   100% Temporary Structures

2. *Furniture and Fixtures*
   10% General Furniture
   15% Furniture in case of Cinema Halls, Restaurants, etc.

3. *Plant and Machinery*
   20% Cars
   25% General Plant
   40% Taxies, Lorries and Buses plying on Hire, etc.
   40% Machinery & Plant uses in semi-conductor industry
   100% Pollution Control Devices
   100% Energy Saving Devices, Gas Cylinders, Rollers
   100% Books for professional purposes

4. *Ships*
   20% Ocean going ships
   20% Speed Boats
   10% Vessels plying in Inland Waters

There are four rates of Depreciation for Plant and Machinery under the simplified depreciation schedule. The normal rate of 25% is applicable to all cases where the special rates do not apply. The depreciation is 20% in the case of cars and 40% in the case of taxies and vehicles used in the business of running them on hire. Pollution control devices are allowed 100% depreciation, as energy saving devices like gas cylinders, rollers, and studio lights in the case of film makers, etc. Another new entry in the depreciation schedule with 40% depreciation is machinery and plant used in the semi-conductor industry.

Leasing has been increasingly used as a tax-planning device by a large number of high profit companies to reduce the tax liability. The lessor companies leased assets, which are entitled for high rate of depreciation preferably 100%, 40% and 25% depreciable assets. In case the manufacturing with high profits company identifies a suitable lessee, the same company may act as a lessor company and finance an asset required by the lessee and thus, the lessor is entitled to claim the depreciation as per the Income Tax rules.

Table 5.10 reveals 99% of assets, which were taken on lease by lessee companies, was high depreciation assets. Of the total volume of leased assets (i.e., Rs. 1,19,165.72 lakhs), 99% constituting Rs. 1,17,976.99 lakhs of leased assets come under 100% depreciation rate. The 100% depreciation items are: electrical equipments, turbines, boilers, transformers, pollution control equipment, air conditioners, computers, wind electric generators, work rolls, etc. Only 0.70 per cent of the leased assets like general plant and machinery comes under 25% and 0.30 per cent of leased assets such as vehicles fall under 40% depreciation items and whose proportion to total volume of leased assets is only 1% and hence insignificant. The leased assets, which fall under 5%, 10%, 15%, 20% are nil and hence the lessor companies do not prefer to lease low depreciable assets.

The high depreciation assets are suitable for lease as lessors are using the high rate of depreciation benefit as a tax planning measure. The lessors claim 100% depreciation and pass a part of the depreciation benefit to the lessee in the form of low lease rentals or low lease rates. The lessee does not get the depreciation allowance on leased assets but claims lease rentals as tax-deductible expense by debiting the same to the profit and loss account.

Cost of Funds

Cost of funds is an important factor associated with source of finance. In the case of equity, the cost is the dividend and capital

Table 5.10 : Volume of Leased Assets falling under Different Rates of Depreciation

(Rs. lakhs)

	Less than 20% Nil	*25%*	*40%*	*100%*	*Total*
1. *APSEB:* (a) Electrical Equipment Turbines, Boilers, Transformers etc.	–	–	–	110500.00	110500.00
2 *APR :*					
(a) Turbine Generators Pollution Control Equipment, Computers, . Boilers, etc				3853.48	3860.62
(b) Vehicles	–	–	7. 04		
3. *APSRTC*:					
(a) Wind Electric Generators	–	–	–	993.00	1186.00
(b) Vehicles (Buses)	–	–	193.00		
4. *CML*:					
(a) Pollution Control Equipment,Computers, SO_2 Gas, etc.	–	–	–	440.60	451.78
(b) Shovel (moving machine)	–	11.8	–	–	
5. *ITC:*					
(a) Air Conditioners, Back pressure Turbines, Computers, Boilers, etc.,	–	–	–	1236.63	1270.10
(b) Vehicles	–	–	33.47		
6. *PAL:*					
(a) Rolling Mill Rolls	–	–	–	91.71	91.71
7. *PSL:*					
(a) Work Rolls, Back up Rolls, Transformers, etc.	–	–	–	190.00	190.00
8. *PSM:*					
(a) Diesel Generators	–	–	–	100.00	397.00
Textile Machines	–	297.00	–		
9. *VST:*					
(a) Energy Saving Equip., Telecom Equip., Computers, Air Conditioners, Refrigerators, etc.	–			571.57	– 1218.61
(b) Vehicles	–	–	122.28	–	
(c) Industrial Machinery	–	524.76			
		(0.70)	(0.30)	(99.00)	(100.00)
Total	–	832.94	355.79	117976. 99	119165.72

gain that shareholders expect to receive. According to the Annual Reports of select lessee companies, the dividend rate varies from 12% to 25% for all lessee companies.

A common feature of debt instruments is the explicit statement of the rate of interest. The cost of debt in India is an administered function under the purview of the Reserve Bank of India. The corporate debentures/bonds carry interest rate of 14% to 15% and varies from time to time and from secured debenture to unsecured debentures. Fixed Deposits raised by the corporate sector from the public bear interest of 14% to 16% depending on the period of the deposit. The credit from commercial banks is available at interest rate, which varies from 15% to 19% depending upon the term of the loan. The institutional loans have interest cost ranging from 11.5% to 14% depending on the term of the loan agreement.

The premium on redemption of a debt instrument and the issue and documentation charges constitute costs additional to the interest costs.

The lease rentals are quoted based on the type of asset, rate of depreciation, residual value and period of lease agreement. In lease agreement, the lease rental is fixed on the basis of a specified rate. For example, if the lease rentals were Rs. 22 per thousand per month (PTPM), this would mean that lease rental of Rs. 22 would be payable monthly for every Rs. 1,000 of the amount financed. Invariably it is the cost of the asset leased. Normally the lessor also collects service charges, known as lease management fee (LMF) from the lessees at the rate of 1% of the amount financed. This amount is payable at the time of lease agreement. The residual value of the leased asset usually varies from 1% to 5%.

The data pertaining to leasing rates that are charged by lessor companies and lease agreements are shown in Tables 5.11 and 5.12.

Table 5.11 shows that leasing rates for 7-year lease agreement vary from a low rate of Rs. 15.75 per month per thousand, in the case of APSRTC, to the highest of Rs. 18 PMPT in the case of PSM. The corresponding interest cost varies from 9.11% to 14.46%. The real cost of lease after factoring add-ons, such as tax on lease rentals (usually varies from 4% to 6% in AP from 1990-91 to 1996-97 and further exempted in 1985 and reimposed from 1993) turnover tax of 1% over and above the turnover of Rs. 10,00,000 (the same is lifted w.e.f. 1-4-1995) management fee of 1% of the cost of the asset and insurance, etc., goes up from 16% to 22%. As the lease tax was not there in the year 1991-92, the cost of lease was further reduced from 16% to 12%. 20 lease agreements are there in 7 years lease arrangement. The companies, which have entered in 7 years lease agreement, are APSEB, APR, APSRTC and ITC (Table 5.12).

Table 5.11 : Leasing Rates [Leasing rates per month per thousand (pmpt)]

For 7 years Lease Agreement							
Lease Rates			Rs. 15.75	Rs. 16	Rs. 17	and	Rs. 18
Interest Rates (%)			9.11	9.71	12.08	and	14.46
For 6 years Lease Agreement							
Lease Rates			Rs. 18	Rs. 19	Rs. 20	and	Rs. 21
Interest Rates (%)			9.73	12.10	14.47	and	16.83
For 5 years Lease Agreement							
Lease Rates	Rs. 21	Rs. 22	Rs. 23	Rs. 24	Rs. 25	and	Rs. 26
Interest Rates (%)	10.23	12.59	14.95	17.31	9.67	and	22.03
For 4 years Lease Agreement							
Lease Rates		Rs. 26	Rs. 27	Rs. 28	Rs. 29	and	Rs. 30
Interest Rates (%)		12.15	14.50	16.85	19.20	and	21.55
For 3 years Lease Agreement							
Lease Rates				Rs. 33	Rs. 34	and	Rs. 35
Interest Rates				12.19	14.53	and	16.86

Flat Rate = Leasing Rate × No of months – Rs. 1000 ÷ No of years
Effective Rate = (Flat Rate × No of months) × 2 ÷ (No of months +1)

Table 5.12 : Lease Agreements of Lessee Companies from 1990-91 to 1996-97

Name of the Company	*Number of Lease Agreements Primary Lease Period*					*Secondary Lease Period*
	3 Yrs	4 Yrs	5 Yrs	6 Yrs	7 Yrs	
1. APSEB	–	–	9	–	14	4 to 7 years
2. APR	–	–	4	6	2	3 to 4 years
3. APSRTC	–	–	1	–	1	2 to 10 years
4. CML	–	2	5	–	–	4 to 5 years
5. ITC	4	6	12	6	3	4 to 6 years
6. PAL	–	–	4	–	–	3 to 5 years
7. PSL	–	–	5	2	–	3 to 5 years
8. PSM	–	–	5	–	–	3 to 5 years
9. VST	–	2	4	2	–	4 to 5 years
Total	4	10	49	16	20	

Source: Field Survey.

The main reason for low interest rate is that the leased assets of APSEB, which were arranged under sale and lease back agreement, are 100% depreciation assets. Further, both parties, i.e., the lessee and the lessor have claimed the depreciation and the lessor has reduced lease rates to the extent of depreciation benefits.

The rate of interest under 6 years agreement and 5 years agreement, more or less the same, varies from 9.73% to 22.03% (Table 5.11). After adding other taxes it varies from around 16.5% to 24%. 4 companies such as APR, ITC, VST, and PSL have entered into 6 years lease agreement, while all companies have entered into 5 years lease agreement. 90% (90) of total agreements under 5 years, 6 years and 7 years are pertaining to plant and machinery, the rest (9) are pertaining to office equipment. The agreements under 4 years, 3 years belong to computers and vehicles. Only three companies such as CML, ITC and VST have entered into this short period lease agreement (Table 5.12). Generally the interest rates are higher in short-term lease period. The VST has taken computers at lease rates of Rs. 29 per month per thousand for 4 years lease agreement. The effective cost of lease comes to 19.20%. It goes further up if other taxes are added up.

The ITC has taken cars under 3 years lease agreement fixing the lease rates at Rs. 33 pmpt. The effective cost of leasing comes to 12.19%. Further the interest increases up to 19% if other taxes are added. Since the vehicles come under 40% depreciation items, the interest rates for vehicles are high. Though the computers are 100% depreciable items, as these electronic goods get obsolete in very short period, the lease rates are fixed on high side.

Thus, the lease rentals quoted by the lessors; taking into consideration the type of asset, rate of depreciation, residual value and period of lease agreement, vary:

(i) from 9.11% to 14.46% for 7 years lease agreement,
(ii) from, 9.73% to 16.83% for 6 years lease agreement,
(iii) from 10.23% to 22.03% for 5 years lease agreement
(iv) from 12.15% to 21.55% for 4 years lease agreement
(v) from 12.19% to 16.86 % for 3 years lease agreement

For 1990-91 to 1996-97, these percentages are calculated by applying the following formula:

Flat Rate = Leasing Rate × No. of months – Rs. 1000 ÷ No. of years

Effective Rate of Interest = Flat Rate × No of months × 2 ÷ (No of months +1)

These calculated percentages do not include lease management fee, lease tax, etc. If these are added, the real cost of leasing would go up. Besides, these calculations ignore the depreciation opportunity foregone by the lessees.

Leasing Rates and Equivalent Interest Rates for 5 Years Lease Agreement

The leasing rates and their equivalent interest rates and bank weighted lending rates and how these rates vary from year to year over a study period from 1990-91 to 1996-97 are given in Table 5.13.

Table 5.13 : Leasing Rates and Equivalent Interest Rates for 5 Years Lease Agreement

Years	*Leasing Rates PTPM*	*Equivalent Interest Rates*	*Commercial Bank Weighted Lending*	*SBI Advance Rate*
1990-91	21-24	10.23-17.31	16.38	16.5
1991-92	22-25	12.59-19.67	16.70	16.5
1992-93	23-26	14.95-22.03	16.00	19.0
1993-94	23-26	14.95-22.03	16.40	19.0
1994-95	22-25	12.59-19.67	15.00	15.0
1995-96	22-25	12.59-19.67	16.50	16.5
1996-97	22-24	12.59-17.31	14.00-15.5	14.5

Source : i. For Leasing Rates: Field Survey
ii. For Bank Rates: *The Economic Times*, March 31, 2000.

Table 5.13 reveals that the range of lease interest rates vary from 10.23% (in 1990-91) to 22.03% (in 1993-94) for a 5-year lease agreement from 1990-91 to 1996-97. Some lessor companies have quoted lower leasing rates to the extent of their depreciation benefits. Some lessor companies have quoted higher leasing rates, sometimes even higher than bank interest rates depending upon their tax incentives. Even then the lessee companies have preferred leasing because of the lack of availability of other alternative sources. Further, the public deposits are not easily accessible except for good companies. Bank funds are available at rates not less than 16% to 19% over a period from 1990-91 to 1993-94. The bank interest rates increased until 1993-94 and later they have followed a decreasing trend (Table 5.13). Similarly, there was a swing in leasing rates from 1990-91 to 1993-94, which later fell down (Table 5.13).

The big push to financial liberalisation in 1991 led to large swings in interest rates in general until 1993-94 and later the interest rates have declined in response to liberalisation. The level of interest rates is affected by several factors – such as inflation, the cyclical state of the economy, money market operations of the RBI, etc.[10]

On the whole, the respondents of lessee companies felt that the effective rate of interest for leasing on an average ranges from 10% to 13% for 100% depreciation assets and 16% to 19% for 25% depreciation assets (excluding other taxes). If other taxes like sales tax on lease rentals, lease turnover tax, etc., are added to the cost of leasing would increase to the extent of other taxes. Normally, the other taxes vary from 6% to 8% and vary from time to time and from State to State.

Having discussed the investment pattern of lessee companies, it is more relevant to evaluate the alternative means of financing the acquisition of the capital asset to choose between mutually exclusive investments by analysing the costs in the lease or borrows to buy appraisal.

Evaluation of Alternative Means of Financing

The financing decisions of the firm involved are:

1. determining the proper amount of funds to acquire the required capital asset, i.e., to take investment decision;
2. selection of projects and capital expenditure analysis; and
3. raising required funds on the most favourable possible terms, i.e., to take financing decision.

Once the mix of financing is decided, the finance manager is still required to determine as to how best to acquire the required funds from the capital market to meet the company's requirement for financing the projects – such as expansion, diversification, promotion of new projects, etc.

The lessee's decision to enter into leasing agreement is primarily a financing decision as it is a source of finance. Managers are required to make the investment decision first – i.e., to determine what specific investment projects the company should undertake within a planned capital budget and then select the methods by which the investments are to be financed.

The method of finance is to be decided by identifying and weighing the financial and non-financial factors and then comparing the costs of various alternative methods. Sometimes, the non-financial factors are of critical importance for decision making, eliminating the need for any cost comparison. In some circumstances, the additional debt may not be obtainable or company may not wish to increase its overall borrowing to what might be regarded as an excessive level. Where a firm's debt capacity limit has been reached or exceeded the budgetary level, the leasing arrangement may be preferred, but where a company's debt capacity limit has not been reached, the leasing and borrowing alternatives are to be examined by taking tax implications. The decision to lease or buy (or borrow to buy) an asset can be made only after specific financial analysis that weighs the merits of each choice. There are various evaluative models in use developed by financial experts over a period of time, and there is a considerable amount of controversy about which particular model is more appropriate. Here we confine our analysis to leasing decision to a simple Net Present Value (NPV) model, which is used in practice.

The NPV is one of the Discounted Cash Flow (DCF) techniques, which explicitly recognises the time value of money. The steps involved in the present value method are:

1. An appropriate rate of interest is selected to discount cash outflows (The rate of interest is firm's opportunity cost of capital, which is equal to the minimum rate of return by investors).
2. Find out the present values of cash outflows of leasing as well as borrowing to buy.

3. Choose the lowest cost alternative between leasing and borrowing to buy on the basis of comparison of present values obtained in step-2.

When we examine alternative methods of financing the acquisition of an asset, we again choose between mutually exclusive investments. The basic rule we normally follow in this kind of situation is to choose the investment with the highest NPV surplus. However, as we will ignore all the benefits from the use of the asset on the grounds that they are common to both methods of financing and it is relevant to examine costs only in the lease or borrow to buy appraisal. The more attractive option, therefore, is the one with the least NPV cost. This is the decision rule to follow.

An attempt has been made here to develop a simple model, which evaluates a lease proposal against a term loan proposal to finance the capital asset. In this model, the Net Present Value (NPV) method has been used to compare a lease *vis-a-vis* a term loan. The NPV is arrived at by discounting the entire after tax rental flows at a pre-determined rate of discount.

In the case of leasing, the lease rentals provide tax savings to the extent of lease rent (1–tax rate), as it is tax-deductible expense. The tax savings are deducted from lease payments to ascertain the actual cash outflows.

Symbolically, the actual cash outflows under leasing are calculated as mentioned hereunder:

$$\text{Tax Saving} = T(Lr)$$

$$\text{Cash outflows} = Lr - T\,(Lr)$$

or

$$= Lr\,(1-t)$$

Where: Lr = Annual Lease rentals

T = Corporation Tax Rate

This calculation of actual lease rental outflows is extended for the period of lease; say 'n' years, for which lease rentals are paid.

In case of loan alternative, the interest portion and depreciation provide tax savings to the extent of interest and depreciation (1–tax rate). The tax savings are deducted from loan instalments to ascertain the actual cash outflows.

Symbolically the actual cash outflows under loan arrangement are calculated as mentioned below:

Tax saving = T (I+D)
Cash outflows = Ai – T (I+D)
or
= Ai (1–t)

Where, Ai = Loan instalment
I = Interest amount
D = Depreciation
T = Corporation Tax Rate

The calculation shown above is extended for a period for which loan instalments are paid.

Here one example is set on the lines of lease agreement entered between APSRTC (Lessee) and the Sundaram Finance Ltd. (Lessor) and analysed to decide as to whether leasing alternative is viable compared to borrowing to buy alternative.

Example

A Modern Limited has decided to acquire capital asset at a cost of Rs. 1,00,000. The leasing company has offered leasing terms as an alternative to borrowing to buy. The leasing agreement stipulates 5 yearly low lease rental payments of Rs. 30,000 payable at the end of each year. The Modern Limited's cost of capital is 16%.

For the same asset, the banker is willing to lend the firm Rs. 1,00,000 at an interest rate of 16%. The bank informs that it is required to make annual payments at Rs. 30,541 for 5 years. The company is maintaining depreciation at 20% on Written Down Value method. The residual value of the asset is Rs. 13,000. The Corporate Tax Rate is 46%. The annual payment is calculated by taking the loan amount of Rs. 1,00,000 divided by 5 years Annuity Factor at 16% interest as mentioned hereunder.

Annual instalment = Rs. 1,00,000 ÷ 3.2743 = Rs. 30,541.
3.2743 is present value factor of 5 years at 16% rate of interest.

Here the example is worked out and shown in Exhibits I, II and III. The cash outflows of two alternatives – leasing and borrowing – are discounted at a pre-determined rate of 16% over the period and calculated present values. The alternative that has lower present value of cash outflows is preferred.

The company, being the owner of the asset under borrowing option is entitled to have the tax benefit of interest and depreciation. The interest and depreciation are calculated for 5 years and shown in columns 3 and 6 of Exhibit-I. The tax saving that result to the company is 46% of interest and depreciation, both being tax-deductible expenses. The same is shown in column 8. The cash outflows are calculated for each year by deducting the tax savings from loan instalment payments and shown in column 9. These net cash outflows over a period of 5 years are discounted to arrive at their present values. The discounted values (present values) are given in column 11. Thus, the total present value comes to Rs. 58,416 under borrowing option (Exhibit-I).

Similarly, Exhibit-II shows lease rentals, which are fully tax-deductible expenses. These lease rentals, therefore, result in tax savings equal to 46% and the same is calculated in column 3. The net cash outflows, after deducting the tax savings from lease rentals, are shown in column 4. These cash outflows are discounted by 16% present value factors, which are shown in column 5. The present values are calculated and shown in column 6 and the aggregate present value comes to Rs. 53,044 under lease option.

The above analysis reveals that the net effective cost to the buyer (Lessee) under the borrowing option is Rs. 58,416, and under leasing option, it is Rs. 53,044. Since the cost under the leasing option is lower by Rs. 5,372, the leasing option is preferred.

This analysis is made under the following assumptions: (a) tax rate 46%, (b) discounting rate 16%, (c) depreciation rate 20% and (d) the residual value of the asset is Rs. 13,000.

The question whether leasing decision is advantageous or not depends on these assumptions. A change in any of these assumptions may affect calculations and may even upturn our decision.

Suppose the asset is eligible for depreciation at the rate of 33.33% assuming all other variables as constant, the effect is shown

Exhibit- I : Borrowing to Buy Option with 20% Depreciation

(Rupees)

Year	*Instl. payment*	*Interest at 16%*	*Principal repayment*	*Loan out-standing*	*Depn. at 20%*	*Interest + Depn.*	*Tax saving at 46%*	*Net cash outflow*	*P.V. factor at 16%*	*P. values of cash outflow*
(1)	*(2)*	*(3)*	*(4)*	*(5)*	*(6)*	*(7)* (3+6)	*(8)*	*(9)* (2-8)	*(10)*	*(11)*
1.	30541	16,000	14,541	85,459	20,000	36,000	16,560	13,981	0.86207	12,053
2.	30541	13,673	16,868	68,591	16,000	29,673	13,650	16,891	0.74316	12,553
3.	30541	10,975	19,566	49,025	12,800	23,775	10,937	19,604	0.64066	12,560
4.	30541	7,844	22,697	26,328	10,240	18,084	8,319	22,222	0.55229	12,273
5.	30541	4,213	26,328	–	8,192	12,405	5,706	24,835	0.47611	11,824
Residual Value, i.e., Cash inflow after tax								(5980)	0.47611	(2847)
	1,52,705	52,705	1,00,000	–	67,232	1,19,937	55,172	91,553	–	58,416

Note: i. Instalments = $\frac{\text{Loan Amount}}{\text{Annuity Factor at 16\% of } 5^{th} \text{ Year}}$ = 1,00,000 ÷ 3.2743 = 30,541

ii. Residual Value = 13,000, Tax Saving = 13000 x 0.46 = Rs.5,980

Exhibit-II : Leasing Option *(Rupees)*

Year	*Lease Rentals*	*Tax Saving at 46%*	*Net Cash outflow*	*Present Value Factor at 16%*	*Present Values of cash outflows*
(1)	*(2)*	*(3)*	*(4)*	*(5)*	*(6)*
1	30,000	13,800	16,200	0.86207	13,966
2.	30,000	13,800	16,200	0.74316	12,039
3.	30,000	13,800	16,200	0.64066	10,379
4.	30,000	13,800	16,200	0.55229	8,947
5.	30,000	13,800	16,200	0.47611	7,713
	1,50,000	69,000	81,000		53,044

as in Exhibit-III. With the introduction of higher rate of depreciation at 33.33%, there has been a substantial effect on discounted cash flows. The aggregate of Rs. 58,416 under borrowing option at 20% depreciation (Exhibit-I) is reduced to Rs. 50,853 (Exhibit-III) at 33.33% depreciation. This is lesser than the effective cost under leasing option calculated at Rs. 53,044 (Exhibit-II).

Therefore, while leasing turns out to be cheaper than the borrowing option with a depreciation rate of 20%, the borrowing option becomes cheaper by Rs. 2191 (Rs. 53,044–50,853) than the leasing option at a depreciation rate of 33.33%.

Let us now see the effect on decision making without considering the tax incentives. Assume that it is a zero tax company and remove the tax effects altogether. If the tax incentives are removed in both borrowing option and leasing option, then the instalment amounts of Rs. 30,541 per annum in the case borrowing and Rs. 30,000 per annum in the case of leasing are actual cash outflows.

The present values are as follows :

	Instalment payment Or cash outflow	*Annuity Factor at 16% for 5 years*	*Present Values*
Borrowing option	30,541	3.2743	1,00,000
Leasing option	30,000	3.2743	98,229

From the above analysis, it is apparent that in reality there is no cash flow advantage of leasing, if leasing simply replaces loan

Exhibit–III : Borrowing to Buy Option with 33.33% Depreciation

(Rupees)

Year (1)	*Instalment Payment* (2)	*Interest at 16%* (3)	*Principal repayment* (4)	*Loan out-standing* (5)	*Depn. at 33.33%* (6)	*Interest + Depn.* (7) (3+6)	*Tax saving at 46%* (8)	*Net cash outflow* (9) (2–8)	*P.V. factor at 16%* (10)	*P. Values of Cash outflow* (11)
1.	30541	16,000	14,541	85,459	33,330	49,330	22,692	7,849	0.86207	6,766
2.	30541	13,673	16,868	68,591	22,221	35,894	16,511	14,030	0.74316	10,427
3.	30541	10,975	19,566	49,025	14,815	25,790	11,863	18,678	0.64066	11,966
4.	30541	7,844	22,697	26,328	9,877	17,721	8,152	22,389	0.55229	12,365
5.	30541	4,213	26,328	—	6,585	10,798	4,967	25,574	0.47611	12,176
Residual Value, i.e., Cash inflow after tax								(5,980)	0.47611	(2,847)
	1,52,705	52,705	1,00,000		86,828	1,39,533	64,185	82,540	50,853	

Note: (i) Instalment = $\frac{\text{Loan Amount}}{\text{Annuity Factor at 16\% of 5}^{th}\text{ year}}$ = Rs. 1,00,000 ÷ 3.2743 = 30541

(ii) Residual Value = Rs. 13,000; Tax Saving = Rs. 13,000 × 0.46 = Rs. 5,980.

financing on a rupee for rupee basis and if the lease rental instalments are fixed at Rs. 30,541 (Rs. 1,00,000 ÷ 3.2743).

However, one of the reasons attributed to the growth of leasing is the tax benefit passed on to the lessee by the lessor on the asset leased by way of fixing low lease rentals to the extent of tax incentives. Since the lessor (owner of leased out asset) enjoys the depreciation benefit and the residual value of the asset, he can lease the asset at low lease rentals to the extent of tax benefits and this is possible only when the leasing company is a tax paying company.

If the lessee company were a zero tax company, it would not benefit from tax incentives if the asset were purchased. But the lessee can still receive the tax benefits by way of reduced lease rentals if the asset is leased. Thus, it may be concluded that the leasing option is more viable between a high tax paying lessor company, as the high tax incentives of depreciation and residual value are available, and a low tax paying lessee company, as the lease rentals are tax-deductible.

Further, the lease rentals may be fixed to the lowest possible level as the lessor passes on tax incentives to the lessee.

Here a non-parametric statistical tool χ^2 is applied to a hypothetical example, which is framed on the lines of lease agreement entered by APSRTC (Lessee) with the Sundaram Finance Ltd. (Lessor) to find out the preference of buying and leasing options among different companies.

It proceeds with a null hypothesis stating that "there is no significant difference between the buying option and leasing option. Both options are going to give the same benefit to the companies".

To test this hypothesis, the χ^2 statistical tool is used and calculated χ^2 value is 4.227.

Now it can be interpreted that, since the calculated value is less than the table value (14.9) the null hypothesis is accepted. It means that there is no significant difference between the buying and leasing option. Both decisions are going to give almost the same benefits.

It can be inferred from the table that the values of cash outflows are lower at the beginning and they increase year after year to the maximum. With respect to the buying option as the tax benefits of depreciation and interest are higher at the beginning and decrease year after year. Whereas, in leasing option, the values of cash outflows are higher in the beginning and gradually they decrease from year to year to a minimum, because the tax benefits of lease rentals are constant and present value factors decrease every year.

On the whole, the total value of cash outflows in case of leasing option and buying option is almost the same with a little variation. The only difference in the buying option is in ascending order and leasing option is in descending order. But altogether it makes no significant difference in terms of benefits accrued to the company. The same is proved with the help of the statistical tool.

Buying and Leasing Options

No of Years	*Present values of Buying Options* (A_1)	*Present values of Leasing Options* (A_2)	*Total*
(B_1) 1	6.7	13.9	20.6
(B_2) 2	10.4	12.0	22.4
(B_3) 3	11.9	10.3	22.2
(B_4) 4	12.3	8.9	21.2
(B_5) 5	12.1	7.7	19.8
	53.4	52.8	106.2

	O	*E*	*(0–E)²*	*(0–E)²/E*
A_1B_1	6.7	10.36	13.39	1.29
A_2B_1	13.9	10.24	13.39	1.30
A_1B_2	10.4	11.26	0.74	0.065
A_2B_2	12.0	11.14	0.74	0.066
A_1B_3	11.9	11.16	0.54	0.048
A_2B_3	10.3	11.03	0.53	0.048
A_1B_4	12.3	10.7	2.56	0.239
A_2B_4	8.9	10.5	2.56	0.243
A_1B_5	12.1	9.95	4.62	0.464
A_2B_5	7.7	9.84	4.57	0.464

Observed Values (O) = P.V. of Leasing and borrowing (at 33.33%) option.

Expected Values (E) = Average of P.V. of Leasing and borrowing (at 33.33%) option.

$\Sigma(O\text{–}E)^2 = 43.64$

$\Sigma(O\text{–}E)^{2/E} = 4.227$

$$x^2 = \frac{\Sigma(O\text{–}E)^2}{E} = 4.227 \text{ (Calculated Value)}$$

Table Value = V= (r–1) (c–1) = 4×1 = 4

For V (Degrees of freedom) = 4 $\chi^2 0.05 = 14.9$ (Table Value). Since the calculated value of χ^2 is lesser than the table value, the hypothesis is accepted. Hence, there is no significant difference between the buying option and leasing option.

Thus, it may be inferred that unless the lessor passes on his tax incentives of 100% depreciable assets to the lessee at reduced lease rentals, there is no significant difference between buying option and leasing option.

The insignificant variations, which are found in the borrowing to buy option and leasing option, can be attributed to the following reasons:

(i) the effect of variation in cost of the asset may be to the extent of passing on the depreciation benefit and residual value benefit by the lessor to the lessee which we have analysed in Exhibits -I, II and III.

(ii) the effect of direct tax advantage may be to the extent of the magnitude of lease rentals being paid by the lessee companies, which are tax, exempted.

Now it is proposed to analyse the component analysis of expenses of select lessee companies to find out the effect of lease rental expenses on tax liability.

Component Analysis of Expenses

The expenses of select lessee companies are broadly classified as (i) operating expenses – which include manufacturing, administration, selling and other expenses, (ii) interest – such as interest on term loans, debentures, bank loans, etc., (iii) depreciation on fixed assets and (iv) lease rentals.

Tables 5.14 and 5.15 provide the data pertaining to component analysis of expenses of select lessee companies.

From Table 5.14, it is observed that there is a steady increase in the depreciation and lease rental expenses from 1990-91 to 1996-97. With respect to operating expenses, a marginal decrease was noticed from 82.9% in 1993-94 to 77.5% in 1996-97. The company-wise analysis also shows almost the same trend with APSEB, APR and PAL, PSL and PAL (Table 5.15).

Similarly, the interest expenditure is reduced from 13.4% in 1995-96 to 12.5% in 1996-97. The company-wise analysis (Table 5.15) shows that a similar trend of decrease in interest expenditure is registered with only three companies – APSEB from 21.9% to 20.1%, CML from 5.7% to 4.7% and VST from 2.8% to 2.5% from 1995-96 to 1996-97. This decrease was mainly due to the clearance of a major chunk of bank loans and very little fresh bank borrowings during the year 1995-96. Instead of bank borrowings, the lessee companies concentrated on leased assets. Consequently, the payment of lease rental proportion increased from a mere 0.3% in 1994-95 to 2.0% in 1996-97 (Table 5.14). A major portion of leased assets was taken by APSEB worth Rs. 28,000 lakhs during the year 1995-96 and worth Rs. 41,200 lakhs during the year 1996-97 (Table 5.4). Consequently, the proportion of payment of lease rentals increased from Rs. 800 lakhs in 1994-95 to Rs. 10,392.40 lakhs in 1995-96 and further increased to Rs. 15,224.50 lakhs in 1996-97. With this result, the proportion of lease rentals of APSEB increased from mere 0.3% in 1994-95 to 2.7% in 1995-96 and further to 3.5% in 1996-97 (Table 5.15).

Table 5.14 : Component Analysis of Expenses (Aggregate) of Select Lessee Companies

(Per cent)

Expenses	*1990-91*	*1991-92*	*1992-93*	*1993-94*	*1994-95*	*1995-96*	*1996-97*	*Average*
Operating Expenses	81.5	82.9	81.9	82.9	79.4	77.2	77.5	80.5
Interest	10.8	9.9	11.0	10.2	12.6	13.4	12.5	11.5
Depreciation	7.3	6.8	6.8	6.5	7.7	7.7	8.0	7.3
Lease Rentals	0.4	0.4	0.3	0.4	0.3	1.7	2.0	0.7
Total	100	100	100	100	100	100	100	100

Source: Calculated from Annual Reports of Select Lessee Companies.

Table 5.15 : Component Analysis of Expenses (Company-wise) of Select Lessee Companies *(Per cent)*

Lessee Cos.	*Expenses*	*1991*	*1992*	*1993*	*1994*	*1995*	*1996*	*1997*	*Average*
	Op. Exp	67.6	72.0	71.4	74.0	68.7	66.1	66.8	69.5
	Interest	24.0	20.0	20.6	18.1	21.6	21.9	20.1	20.9
APSEB	Depn.	8.2	7.6	7.7	7.6	9.4	9.3	9.6	8.5
	L. Rental	0.2	0.4	0.3	0.3	0.3	2.7	3.5	1.1
	Total	**100**	**100**	**100**	**100**	**100**	**100**	**100**	**100**
	Op. Exp	84.4	84.4	89.1	93.4	92.4	93.5	90.7	89.7
APR	Interest	5.4	7.1	6.8	1.8	3.4	3.6	5.1	4.7
	Depn.	8.0	6.5	1.7	2.5	2.5	2.3	3.5	3.9
	L. Rental	2.2	2.0	2.4	2.3	1.7	0.6	0.7	1.7
	Total	**100**	**100**	**100**	**100**	**100**	**100**	**100**	**100**
	Op. Exp	88.0	87.8	88.2	89.3	89.2	89.6	89.5	88.8
	Interest	1.3	1.5	1.6	1.1	0.7	0.5	0.7	1.1
APSRTC	Depn	10.6	10.6	10.1	9.5	10.0	9.8	9.7	10.0
	L. Rental	0.1	0.1	0.1	0.1	0.1	0.1	0.1	0.1
	Total	**100**	**100**	**100**	**100**	**100**	**100**	**100**	**100**
	Op. Exp	93.0	93.2	89.9	91.9	92.1	92.0	92.6	92.1
	Interest	4.2	5.1	7.9	6.1	5.6	5.7	4.7	5.6
CML	Depn	2.7	1.6	2.1	1.4	1.7	1.9	2.3	2.0
	L. Rental	0.1	0.1	0.1	0.6	0.6	0.4	0.4	0.3
	Total	**100**	**100**	**100**	**100**	**100**	**100**	**100**	**100**
	Op. Exp	83.9	83.5	84.2	85.2	84.6	84.4	84.3	84.3
	Interest	8.0	8.5	8.5	9.1	9.3	10.1	10.8	9.2
ITC	Depn	5.2	5.4	5.4	3.9	4.5	4.5	4.5	4.8

Table 5.15 *(Contd.)*

Lessee Cos.	*Expenses*	*1991*	*1992*	*1993*	*1994*	*1995*	*1996*	*1997*	*Average*
	L. Rental	2.9	2.6	1.9	1.8	1.6	1.0	0.4	1.7
	Total	**100**	**100**	**100**	**100**	**100**	**100**	**100**	**100**
	Op. Exp	—	84.6	40.1	28.5	84.3	76.2	77.6	65.2
	Interest	—	10.5	57.7	69.6	10.6	18.0	19.0	30.9
PAL	Depn.	—	2.5	1.1	1.2	4.9	5.7	3.3	3.1
	L. Rental	—	2.4	1.1	0.7	0.2	0.1	0.1	0.8
	Total		**100**	**100**	**100**	**100**	**100**	**100**	**100**
	Op. Exp	88.5	87.3	89.9	91.8	92.4	92.1	89.9	90.3
	Interest	8.9	9.8	7.5	5.8	5.5	5.4	7.5	7.2
PSL	Depn	2.2	2.3	2.0	1.8	1.6	1.9	2.0	1.9
	L. Rental	0.4	0.6	0.6	0.6	0.5	0.6	0.6	0.6
	Total	**100**	**100**	**100**	**100**	**100**	**100**	**100**	**100**
	Op. Exp	87.9	89.2	89.7	91.6	91.2	91.9	89.5	90.1
	Interest	5.5	5.8	6.7	5.0	5.7	5.2	6.0	5.8
PSM	Depn.	5.2	4.1	2.9	2.2	2.2	2.3	2.8	3.1
	L. Rental	1.4	0.9	0.7	1.2	0.9	0.6	0.3	1.0
	Total	**100**	**100**	**100**	**100**	**100**	**100**	**100**	**100**
	Op. Exp	98.5	98.3	98.0	97.2	96.8	95.8	96.0	97.3
	Interest	0.6	0.8	1.2	1.8	2.1	2.8	2.5	1.7
VST	Depn	0.5	0.5	0.5	0.7	0.7	1.0	0.0	0.6
	L. Rental	0.4	0.4	0.3	0.3	0.4	0.4	0.5	0.4
	Total	**100**	**100**	**100**	**100**	**100**	**100**	**100**	**100**

Source: Calculated from Annual Reports of Select Lessee Companies.

The company-wise analysis (Table 5.15) shows that the average proportion of lease rental expenses for 5 companies such as APSRTC, CML, PAL, PSL and VST accounted for less than 1%, whereas, for the remaining 4 companies, viz., APSEB, APR, ITC and PSM, it ranged between 1% and 2%.

However, Table 5.14 shows that the average proportion of lease rental expenses, which are 100% tax deductible, accounted for only 0.7% of all expenses of select lessee companies. Since the average proportion of lease rental expenses was 0.7%, the impact of tax advantage due to magnitude of lease rental was negligible for lessee companies. The major expenditure proportion was shared by operating expenses, accounting for an average proportion of 80.5% of all expenses followed by interest expenditure representing 11.5%, and depreciation expenditure constituting 7.3%.

Unless the lessor passes on some of his tax benefits to the lessee companies by fixing low lease rentals, the direct tax incentive of lease rental payments to the lessee companies is very little or negligible.

Having discussed the tax incentives and their effect on leasing decision, it will be relevant now to examine the qualitative analysis of reasons for leasing.

Reasons for Leasing

The bottom line reason for why equipment leasing has grown dramatically especially during the years from 1991 to 1996 is that leasing has met the needs of so many types and sizes of companies. Some companies may lease equipment to keep bank credit lines open for other purposes. New companies may take assets on lease to conserve cash for utilisation in other important investment purposes or for working capital purposes. The conserved working capital may be utilised in acquiring inventories needed for an increase in production or for hiring additional labour, etc. Thus, the profitability of the enterprise can be increased through the leverage of additional debt of leasing.

The reasons for leasing may differ from company to company depending on the type and nature of the company. To ascertain the important and marginal reasons for leasing decision, a field investigation was made by means of questionnaires and interviews to 16 lessee companies. The executives of these companies were asked to identify the relevant reasons for leasing and to give them ranking in order of preference.

Paired comparison method is used to convert the rank order data of the preferences into the matrices of preferences to indicate the relative importance of each response. The data pertaining to reasons for leasing (opinions of the Executives of 16 lessee companies on 7 reasons for leasing) are shown in Tables 5.16 and 5.17.

Table 5.16 shows that out of 16 lessee companies, 13 companies (81%) considered the factor of convenience and instant finance as "very relevant" and 3 companies considered it "relevant" to their leasing decision. There was a feeling amongst the companies that no other sources of finance were as convenient in providing instant loan finance as leasing. It is evident from the matrix Table 5.17 that convenience and instant finance, which was ranked first in the order of preference, has been preferred as effective reason over others when the lessees decide to lease the assets.

Almost all lessee companies responded that taking an asset on lease is more convenient for the following reasons:

Leasing is free from restrictive covenants, which are often attached to loan financing. Additional convenience and cost saving are obtained with operating lease where maintenance and other costs are borne by the lessor. The form of lease agreement can be very flexible in fixing lease rentals and easy documentation with fewer formalities. The pattern and size of lease payment can be better tailored to the specific needs of the lessee as follows:

(i) *Step Leases*: Lease agreement that allows the lessee's payment to either increase (step-up lease) or decrease (step-down lease) over the term of the lease to meet the lessee's cash flow constraints (Fig. 5.3) in a better way.

(ii) *Skipped Payment Lease:* A lease agreement requiring the lessee to make payment only during certain months or periods each year is called skipped payment lease. Skipped payment leases are structured to meet the seasonal or other cash flow constraints of a specific lessee.

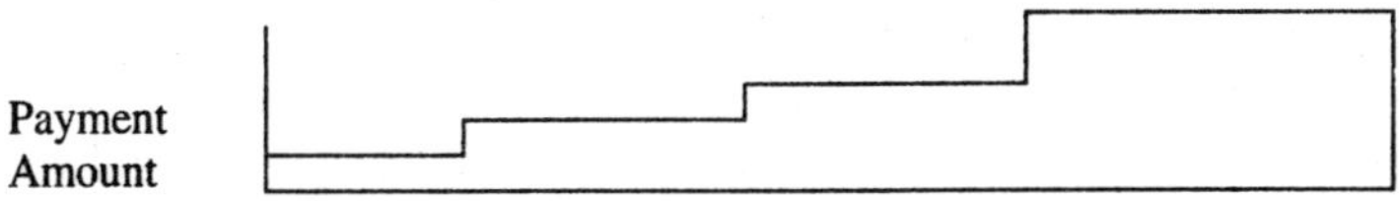

(i) (a) Step-up Lease

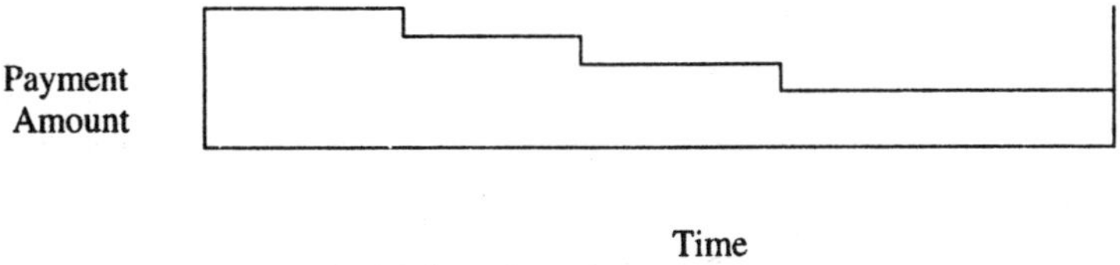

(i) (b) Step-down Lease

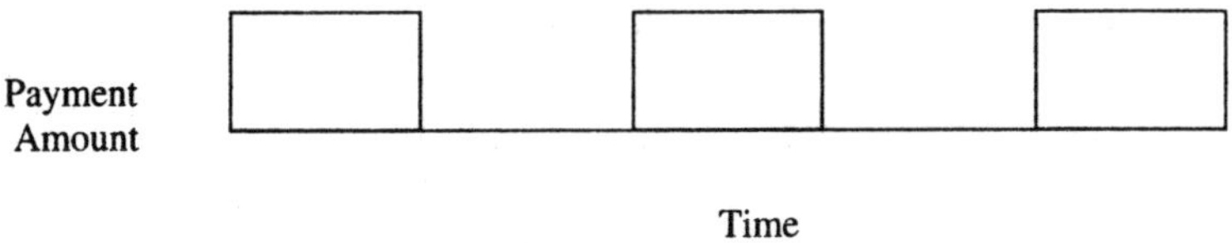

(ii) Skipped Payment Lease

Fig. 5.3 : Step Leases

Thus, leasing is easier to arrange compared to other sources of finance, and payment of lease rentals can be structured to meet the revenue pattern of the lessee.

Further, for lessor ownership of the asset gives a strong form of security and hence the lessor would arrange finance facility through lease agreement immediately.

The Matrix Table 5.17 reveals that the factor "leasing provides liquidity facility and avoids large capital outlay" has been ranked II over other factors. Table 5.16 shows that 12 (75%) out of 16 companies agree that leasing avoids large capital outlay and there was no other easy source available to finance capital asset. Observations by most of the respondents reveal that the general importance given by lessees is to the cash flow effects of leasing rather than to the tax and cost considerations.

A company may enter into a sale and lease back device to set free some funds that are tied up in fixed assets so that they can be used elsewhere in the business. Under this method, the owned asset is sold to the leasing company and leased back for use in business. This provides liquidity or additional working capital facility for the firm. Thus sale and lease back transactions have become more and more popular source of working capital in India in general and in AP in particular.

Table 5.16 : Reasons cited for Leasing by 16 Lessee Companies

S.No.	*Reasons for Leasing*	*Very Relevant*	*Relevant*	*Irrelevant*
1.	Cheaper Source of Finance	1	10	5
2.	Provides100% financing	3	6	7
3.	Convenient and Instant finance	13	3	0
4.	Provides tax advantages	1	9	6
5.	Offers protection against the risk of obsolescence	1	6	9
6.	Provides liquidity and avoids large capital outlay	12	4	0
7.	Overcomes borrowing restrictions as leasing is off-balance sheet financing	11	3	2

Source : Field survey.

Table 5.17 : Matrix of Preferences of Executives of 16 Lessee Companies for Reasons for Leasing

Preferred	*Over*							*Total*	
	A	B	C	D	E	F	G	*Scoring*	*Ranks*
A	**X**	12	0	13	12	0	2	39	IV
B	5	**X**	0	3	7	1	3	19	VI
C	16	16	**X**	16	16	16	15	79	I
D	4	13	0	**X**	13	0	2	32	V
E	4	9	0	3	**X**	1	1	18	VII
F	16	15	0	16	15	**X**	15	77	II
G	14	13	1	14	15	1	**X**	58	III

Source: Field Survey.

Note: In the above table:

'A' represents: Cheaper source of finance
'B' represents: Providing 100% financing
'C' represents: Convenience and Instant finance
'D' represents: Providing tax advantages
'E' represents: Offers protection against the risk of obsolescence
'F' represents: Provides liquidity facility and avoids large capital outlay
'G' represents: Overcomes borrowing restrictions as the leasing is off-balance sheet financing

Nine (9) select lessee companies have taken assets on lease worth Rs. 1,19,165.72 lakhs over the period of study from 1990-91 to 1996-97 under different lease arrangements – such as financial lease, operating lease and sale and lease back. Out of this, the assets worth Rs. 1,11,433.00 lakhs were taken on lease under sale and lease back arrangement due to the liquidity or working capital facility. This constitutes 93.51% of total leased assets. Respondent companies felt that this is the easiest way to get funds particularly when companies are facing funds crunch.

The sale and lease back arrangements were mostly paper transactions from where both parties in the deal were profiting significantly.

Thus, the two factors convenience and liquidity facilities, though appear to be minor, their cumulative effects on the leasing business is very significant.

However, the sale and lease back arrangements, which provide instant liquidity facility, were objected by the RBI and stopped claiming depreciation on sale and lease back transactions from 1995-96. This is one of the reasons to the decrease of leasing business particularly after 1996.

The factor preferred III in rank over other factors as shown in matrix of preferences (Table 5.17) is that "Leasing overcomes borrowing restrictions as it is off-balance sheet financing". Table 5.16 shows that 11 companies (69%) out of 16 companies indicated the above said reason as very relevant for taking the leasing decision.

When lending to a company, a banker typically builds restrictive loan covenants into the loan agreement. Restrictive covenants typically include current ratio and debt-equity ratio limits and certain other minimum measures of profitability. In the case of public sector undertakings, the budgetary limits are fixed to borrow amounts. The leasing covenants do not contain any restrictive form of financing.

Many large companies and public sector undertakings choose to lease for one very real reason – to circumvent various capital budget constraints. To acquire the required capital asset beyond the capital budget is a difficult task and time consuming too.

Because of this reason, the APSEB has taken assets on lease worth Rs. 1,10,500.00 lakhs as on 31-3-1997, which constitutes 92.73% of total leased assets (Rs. 1,19,165.72 lakhs) of 9 select lessee companies in AP. Similarly, APR has taken assets worth Rs. 3,860.52 lakhs, as on 31-3-1997 as leasing is off-balance sheet financing. Since APR became a sick company in 1990, the leasing became best alternative source of finance for it, as other alternatives were not available.

Thus, off-balance sheet financing, which does not affect the firm's debt-equity ratio, is one of the important factors for leasing decision and contributed to the growth of leasing during the initial stages.

One of the reasons for leasing is "the cheaper source of finance" and is ranked IV in the order of preference (Table 5.17). Similarly the factor "tax advantages" is given V rank in the order of preference (Table 5.17). Table 5.16 reveals that 10 lessee companies and 9 lessee companies indicated the factors of "cheaper source of finance" and tax advantages are "relevant" for leasing decision. These two factors are interrelated and interdependent. Not only leasing provides many advantages discussed above, it can also be a less expensive method of acquiring the use of equipment provided the lessor passes on the "tax benefits" to the lessee in the form of low lease rentals. Typically, financial alternatives such as a lease versus a loan are compared on a present value after tax basis in earlier pages of this chapter. The alternative with lower cost, adjusted for the impact of taxes and the time value of money, is selected.

The total lease rentals paid by the lessee are treated as operating expenses and are fully deductible for corporation tax purposes. Similarly, the lessors can claim the tax related benefits such as depreciation, investment allowance (if available) against profits. Further, the lessor enjoys the residual value of leased assets. Since the lessor enjoys the depreciation allowance and residual value of the asset; he can lease the asset at low lease rentals.

The remaining two factors such as "100% financing" and "protection against the risk of obsolescence" is given last ranks of VI and VII respectively (Table 5.17). Table 5.16 reveals that 7

(44%) companies responded to the factor of 100% financing is irrelevant and not that important a reason for leasing as majority of lessor companies were not providing 100% financing without requiring any immediate down payment. Margins in case of term loans vary from 20% to 30%. However, under the lease agreement, majority-leasing companies insist some rentals in advance or 5% to 10% margin money.

With respect to the other factor of "protection against the risk of obsolescence", 9 respondents (56%) indicated that it is an irrelevant reason to decide to lease. Obsolescence means the decline in value of a fixed asset through external causes such as technological change or changes in demand. The respondents felt that the lessor anticipates the obsolescence and compensates for this risk by changing higher lease rentals and hence is non-important factor for leasing decision.

Thus, the main reasons why lessee companies prefer to lease in the order of preference are convenience and liquidity. And off-balance sheet financing comes as the third order of preference. From comments made by the respondents, it may be inferred that the convenience, liquidity and off-balance sheet financing are the three important reasons for leasing and eliminating the need for any cost comparison other reasons are marginal considerations.

The findings of foreign studies on reasons for leasing in the US, the UK and other countries reveal that reasons for leasing differed from company to company and from country to country depending on the tax and accounting policies.

Evidence is available from a very few UK studies on why lessees lease. Fawthrop and Terry (1975) investigated the use of debt and lease finance by 54 major corporations located in the UK. Their most important findings reveal that almost half of the companies in the survey considered the "tax considerations of leasing" as irrelevant to their leasing decision. The most popular reason for leasing is its use as another source of finance in balanced financial package.

Sykes (1976) undertook a postal questionnaire survey of leasing and produced evidence on the advantages perceived in favour of leasing by lessees. According to him, there are three important findings. First, companies appear to lease for a wide variety of reasons. Second, as with the Fawthrop and Terry study, companies do not seem to consider taxation factors as important. Third, a large percentage of companies look at the effects of leasing on cash flows, i.e. liquidity facilities.

The results of a third study are reported in Tomkins, Lowe Morgan (1979) Survey. They found, as with other studies, that there was little tendency to lease for tax reasons, and that a very good reason for the popularity of leasing was that "no other sources of finance were available."

From the above evidence we may conclude that there are many varied reasons for lessees to use leasing. Some of them may lease only for one reason and others may lease for a variety of reasons.

Some findings of foreign studies on reasons for leasing are in direct contrast and some are similar to our findings. On the whole for one reason or the other, the leasing seems to fill a gap in the financial market for some companies.

To conclude, it may be inferred that this chapter analysed the use of leasing to finance the capital asset and its effectiveness as an alternative source of finance for lessee companies. The effectiveness of leasing to finance capital asset is assessed in terms of types of assets leased, investment pattern, cost of leasing and reasons for why the lessee companies prefer leasing.

The main types of assets that are taken on lease by the select lessee companies are – plant and machinery, vehicles, office equipment and other assets which include air conditioners, refrigerators, etc.

The total volume of leased assets taken on lease has increased from Rs. 4,175.38 lakhs to Rs. 1,19,165.72 lakhs, over a period of study from 1990-91 to 1996-97, recording the compound growth rate at 80.16%. The total volume of plant and machinery leased by all lessee companies has increased from Rs. 3,751.58 lakhs in 1990-91 to Rs. 1,18,011.68 lakhs in 1996-97 registering the compound growth rate at 83.50%. The average share of plant and machinery of all assets leased by lessee companies is recorded at 94.71%.

Among all select lessee companies, APSEB has taken the highest volume of leased assets. The cumulative figure constituting

Rs. 1,10,500.00 lakhs, accounts for 92.73% of all assets leased by select lessee companies. It means that APSEB has been giving top priority to leasing activity when compared to other companies.

It is found that the average proportion of leased assets in increasing the level of year-wise total investment varies from 0.5% to 29.2% over period of study. Out of 9 select lessee companies, only three companies – such as APR, APSEB and VST have used leased assets above 16% of their year-wise investment to finance the capital assets recording the average proportion at 29.3%, 26.2% and 16.8% respectively. The leased assets proportion for other select companies varies from 1.6% to 8.6%.

According to the result of standard deviation, it is observed that there is uniformity in the investment with regard to acquiring assets other than leased assets. Whereas, wide variations are observed in acquiring the assets through lease financing mode.

The 100% or high depreciation assets are suitable for leasing as the lessor passes on the tax benefit to the extent of depreciation benefit in the form of reduced lease rentals.

The cost of leasing on an average ranges from 10% to 13% for 100% depreciation assets and 16% to 19% for 25% depreciation assets (excluding other taxes). Normally the other taxes, like leasing tax, turnover tax, etc., varying from 6% to 8% and varying from time to time and from State to State.

The field survey reveals why lessee companies prefer leasing, in the following order of preference:

(i) convenience and instant finance,
(ii) provides liquidity facility and avoids large capital outlay,
(iii) overcomes borrowing restrictions as the leasing is the off-balance sheet financing,
(iv) cheaper source of finance,
(v) provides tax advantages,
(vi) provides 100% financing,
(vii) offers protection against the risk of obsolescence.

Further, the lessee survey indicates that there are varied reasons for lessees to use leasing. Some of them may lease only for one reason and others may lease for a variety of reasons.

REFERENCES

1. *Dictionary of Finance and Investment Terms*. Baron's Educational Series, Inc. New York (1985).
2. *The Economic Times*, January 4, 1997, p.1.
3. *Ibid.*
4. *Ibid.*
5. *The Economic Times*, October 4, 1995, p.1.
6. *The Economic Times*, January 4, 1997, p.1.
7. *The Economic Times*, October 4, 1995, p.1.
8. R.H. Parker, *MacMillan Dictionary of Accounting*, The MacMillan Press Ltd., London, 1985. p. 163.
9. Girish Ahuja and Ravi Gupta, *Direct Taxes – Law and Practice including Tax Planning*, Taxman Publications (P) Ltd., New Delhi.
10. *The Economic Times*, March 31, 2000, p. 8.

6

CONCLUSIONS AND SUGGESTIONS

SECTION -A

Conclusions

This chapter is divided into two sections. In Section-A, the summary of important findings and conclusions, which emerged from this study are presented. Section-B is devoted to make suggestions. Based on the findings of the study, appropriate suggestions are made for a sustainable and steady development of the leasing/financial services industry.

Chapter -1 : Introduction

This chapter explains the need and importance of the study and also the conceptual analysis of leasing. It also explains the objectives and methodology of the study. Further, it covers the profile of select companies and limitations of the study.

The objectives of the study are:

(i) to examine the leasing business in India and its contribution to industrial finance;

(ii) to evaluate the impact of policy framework on lease financing;

(iii) to analyse the financial performance of select lessor companies by using cash flow technique;

(iv) to evaluate the select lessee companies in terms of assets taken on lease, cost of leasing, the extent of reliance of lease financing and its impact on lessees' investment and reasons for leasing.

Chapter - 2: Leasing Business in India

This chapter dealt with the concept of lease financing in India and abroad. Further the contribution of lease financing in Andhra

Pradesh and in India were analyzed. The following are the broad conclusions of this chapter :

1. Equipment Leasing is a source of business finance and the concept of equipment leasing emerged for the first time in Madras in 1973. When leasing business grew and met initial success, there was a mushroom growth of leasing and finance companies offering leasing services in India. By 1982, the leasing business picked up momentum.

   There has been a remarkable growth of financial institutions of leasing companies, merchant banks, venture capital funds, etc. All these come under the Non-Banking Financial Companies (NBFCs). The mushroom growth of NBFCs witnessed during 1991-92 and the number increased from 7,063 in 1981 to 41,361 in 1994. This figure includes leasing companies numbering 1,722. Such proliferation of NBFCs is no indication of the health of the industry. By 1997, around 700 of these were active in the financial market. The rest were an essentially front outfit of corporate or small private limited companies with negligible net owned funds.
2. Normally, the assets of plant and machinery earth moving equipment, energy saving equipment, pollution control equipment, ships, industrial equipment, aircraft, vehicles, etc., are leased.
3. The global penetration of leased assets as a percentage of total industrial assets is at around 21% of all assets bought by industrial undertakings.
4. On an average, leasing accounts for around 30% of all US investment in capital equipment, whereas it accounts for around 19% of all UK capital investment. In India, average leasing accounts for around 4% of capital investment, while in AP it accounts for around 0.60% of capital investment.
5. The sources and application of funds of member-companies of Association of Leasing and Financial Services at all India level reveal that the average proportion of fixed deposits is higher registering at 35.79%, followed by bank borrowings (22.51%), institutional borrowings (17.69%), and other

borrowings (17.08%). Debentures registered at lower of 6.93%.

6. Out of total the sources of funds, on an average, around 31.47% of funds are deployed for leasing business and around 38.18% of funds are deployed for hire purchase business. Among leased assets, plant and machinery has more demand in the lease market. The average proportion of plant and machinery is registered at 70.60% and others at 29.40% (Table 2.7). The data also revealed that leasing business and hire purchase business showed a declining trend during 1996-97 due to lack of demand and general market conditions.
7. The Return on Capital Employed has increased from 5.03% in 1991-92 to 6.02% in 1994-95. But it has dropped from 4% in 1995-96 to 1.29% in 1996-97, which indicates the poor performance of the companies. General market conditions and an increase in non-performing assets could have been a significant reason to this 2.71% fall.
8. The ICICI is the first all India level financial institution to enter leasing business in 1983. Later, other financial institutions entered the leasing field. Among all financial institutions, the ICICI has a better record in sanctions registering the compound growth rate at 55.48% followed by IDBI registering the compound growth rate at 41.88% per annum.
9. The present industrial scenario in Andhra Pradesh is very vibrant and is poised to be success. AP comes under moderate industrially developed State and is yet to be fully developed. Analysis reveals that there is a constant increase with respect to the AP industrial investment in the years 1994-95 and 1995-96 indicating 9.62% and 9.93% growth respectively. With respect to the lease financing contribution to industrial finance in AP, it is observed that there is a decreasing trend from 1990-91 to 1992-93 representing the proportion of leased assets to AP industrial investment at 0.24% in 1990-91, 0.16% in 1991-92 and 0.02% in 1992-93. Thereafter, it has increased its representation 0.62% in 1993-94, 0.81% in

1994-95, 0.94% in 1995-96 and 1.20% in 1996-97. The contribution of leasing to State Electricity Board is notable, representing 92.73% of all assets leased by select lessee companies in AP As such there is a need on the part of the Government of AP to encourage non-banking finance companies in all respects as they have been promoting industrialisation by helping lessee companies in financing capital assets.

10. It will be a greater challenge for NBFCs to survive. Unless the Government regulators and lenders come out with favourable policies and accounting standards, NBFCs (which already finding difficult) will find the going much more difficult.

In the present day context, it would be wrong to assume that leasing business is a momentum of its own by itself. Growth and success in leasing business call for well-planned marketing efforts in identifying the appropriate lease proposal and clinch the deal.

Faced with lower volumes and declining margins, the key strategy for lessor companies to improve from the bottom line is to substantially increase productivity by significantly lowering transaction cost. This is coupled with an extremely vigilant debt recovery collection mechanism, which would help companies to survive in these difficult times.

Chapter - 3: Impact of Policy Framework on Lease Financing

The main findings in this chapter are as follows:

Banks Lending to Leasing and Finance Companies

Banks extend finance facilities to leasing and finance companies by way of cash credit and term loans within the purview of RBI guidelines. According to RBI guidelines, the loan facility should be three times the company's net owned funds (NOF) and within the overall ceiling of 10 times to its NOF.

The ratio of bank borrowing to net worth at all India level and AP level is examined by taking bank borrowings separately and further the ratio is examined by taking bank borrowings plus institutional borrowings combinedly.

In both the cases, the average ratio is as follows:

		Bank Borrowing to Net Worth	*Bank Borrowing plus Institutional Borrowing to Net Worth*
(i)	All India Level	0.53	0.97
(ii)	AP Level	0.72	0.93

It is observed from the above figures that the trend of bank borrowings and institutional borrowings of leasing and finance companies at all India level and AP level (during the study period from 1990-91 to 1996-97) is more or less similar and recorded an average proportion of bank borrowing to NOF and bank borrowings plus institutional borrowings to NOF at less than one time to their NOF.

As such, it is found that leasing and finance companies at all India level and AP level were not even able to mobilise the bank borrowings equal to their NOF and this shows that the RBI restrictions pertaining to banks lending to leasing and finance companies had no impact at all.

Non-Performing Assets (NPAs)

The new RBI guidelines issued in June 1994 stipulate that the registered NBFCs have to follow prudential norms for income recognition, transparency of accounts, provisioning for bad and doubtful debts for Non-Performing Assets.

Prior to the introduction of income recognition norms, leasing and finance companies used to follow accounting on accrual basis even if there was a poor record of recovery. In the absence of proper accounting, the instalment amount of principal repayment and interest were taken as revenue and profits were overstated and dividends were declared out of illusory profits. Thus the borrowing power increased based on fictitious addition to reserves. As per the new norms applicable from 31-3-1995, NBFCs were prohibited from recognising income on accrual basis. Further, the NBFCs were directed to follow cash basis of accounting pertaining to

Non-Performing Assets (NPA). The asset, with respect to which interest and/or instalments of principal are overdue for a period of 6 months on and from March 31, 1995, is called substandard asset or Non-Performing Asset (NPA). The NBFCs are required to make a provision against the NPAs as stipulated by the RBI.

In AP, provision against NPA of Select Lessor Companies is as follows:

Year	*1990-91*	*1991-92*	*1992-93*	*1993-94*	*1994-95*	*1995-96*	*1996-97*
Prov. for NPAs (Rs. lakhs)	17.92	62.14	206.90	280.82	514.12	1107.06	

It is observed from the above figures that leasing companies have been reeling under the impact of Non-Performing Assets.

The total volume of NPAs of Select Lessor Companies has increased substantially in the years 1995-96 and 1996-97. Further, according to the reports of Association of Leasing and Financial Services (ALFS), the expenditure for 216 finance companies has increased by 52.8% in 1996-97 over the previous year due to the increase in provision for NPAs.

Leasing operations received a major setback recording a drop in income by more than 50% for the year 1996-97, which was mainly due to the non-performing assets. Receivables for the year 1996-97 had gone up around 70-90 per cent for some large companies. On the other hand, in spite of having funds, banks refused to extend finance facilities to finance companies on account of damaged balance sheets. Thus, the non-availability of funds and the increase of overdues led to a peculiar situation for finance companies.

Credit Rating and Public Deposits

RBI stipulated that a registered NBFC should get itself rated for fixed deposits and every company should obtain fresh rating at least once in a year. Credit rating indicates the borrower's credit quality in terms of financial risk.

The minimum credit rating shall be as follows:

Name of the Credit Rating Agency	*Minimum Rating*
(i) CRISIL	FA
(ii) ICRA	MA
(iii) CARE	CARE BB (FD)
(iv) DCR India	Ind BBB

The minimum credit rating of the above mentioned symbols indicate "Adequate Safety" to meet the fixed deposit obligations as and when they mature.

RBI announced wide-ranging liberalisation and rationalisation measures on July 24, 1996 for NBFCs. The central theme to these measures is freeing the interest rate ceiling on public deposits and removal of the ceiling on the quantum (i.e., removal of ceiling of 10 times the NOF) of deposits for NBFCs which fully comply with credit rate requirement and prudential norms.

According to a CMIE Report, about 15 NBFCs have received certificates from RBI (during September 1996) which give them the freedom to fix interest rates on public deposits. Nagarjuna Finance Limited (one of the Select Companies for the study) is one among them.

Under the shelter of liberalisation measures, most finance companies have mobilised public deposits by offering high rates of interests and gifts to deposit holders. After some time, some unscrupulous companies, which mobilised huge amount of public deposits disappeared from the market and some companies could not pay back deposit amount to deposit holders on the maturity.

The RBI, having considered it necessary in the public interest and in supersession of the earlier Directions, issued new Guidelines on 2nd January, 1998.

The RBI guidelines of 1998 prescribed ceiling limits on acceptance of public deposits for NBFCs as mentioned hereunder:

Level of Credit Rating	*Ceiling on Public Deposits (As multiple of NOF)*
AAA	4 times
AA	2.5 times
A	1.5 times

Now the freedom to raise public deposits without any limit on the quantum and interest rate made available by RBI during the year 1996 and 1997 to certified NBFCs was withdrawn on 2nd January, 1998. The regulatory framework reintroduced a cap on acceptance of deposits and interest rates by linking the deposit limits to a factor of NOF based on the level of credit rating.

The credit rating grades awarded by Credit Rating Agencies for select lessor companies are as follows:

Companies	*Year*	*Credit Rating Grade*	*Remarks*
NFL	1996-97	CARE A+	High Safety
	1997-98	CARE A	Adequate Safety
PPL	1996-97	MAA-	High Safety
	1997-98	MD	Default
LFL	1996-97	FA	Adequate Safety
	1997-98	FB	Inadequate Safety
DCL	1996-97	MAA-	High Safety
	1997-98	MAA-	High Safety
MWL	1996-97	FB+	Inadequate Safety
	1997-98	FD	Default
SCFSL	1996-97	FA	Adequate Safety
	1997-98	Not Rated	-

Ratio of Fixed Deposits to Net Worth of Select Lessor companies is as follows:

Cos.	*1990-91*	*1991-92*	*1992-93*	*1993-94*	*1994-95*	*1995-96*	*1996-97*	*1997-98*
NFL	1.63	1.87	1.66	1.86	3.77	5.02	6.54	2.18
PPL	0.18	0.27	0.14	0.30	0.64	0.90	1.67	—
LFL	0	0.01	0.02	0.07	0.13	0.18	0.14	0.13
DCL	1.36	1.02	1.55	1.77	3.44	6.52	8.50	4.86
MWL	0.81	0.67	0.47	0.64	0.60	0.6C	0.97	—
SCFSL	0.18	0.14	0.14	0.27	0.37	0.37	(—1.01)	—

It is observed from the above credit rating analysis that all select lessor companies are badly exposed as far as credit rating is concerned.

As per the new RBI Guidelines 1998, excess public deposits, which are likely to arise on account of downgrading of credit rating of non-banking finance companies, have to be regularised by making repayment at the time of maturity of such deposits. However, during the interregnum, these companies have been barred from accepting fresh public deposits until the quantum of such deposits held by them is brought within the permissible ceiling.

The above analysis pertaining to credit rating shows that out of 6 companies, only two companies, NFL and DCL, had Fixed Deposits to Net Worth ratio of 5 to 9 times recording the NFL at 5.02 times in 1995-96 and 6.54 times in 1996-97. DCL registered 6.52 times its net worth in 1995-96 and 8.50 times of its net worth in 1996-97. Both companies have exceeded the norm prescribed by the RBI and hence were aggressively affected by the new regulatory framework of linking the public deposit limits to a level of credit rating and stopped accepting or renewing fresh public deposits and started making repayment of public deposits.

The credit rating for another two companies, PPL and MWL, was drastically downgraded to 'D', which indicated default in making payment of public deposits. These two companies were under liquidation process at the instance of public legal complaints.

The LFL, in conformity with RBI regulations, has stopped accepting or renewing public deposits and started making repayment of deposits. On account of adverse business conditions, the company has not taken up new business in the field of leasing and hire-purchase and concentrated in a limited way in the area of short term financing, viz., inter-corporate deposits and bill discounting.

The remaining company SCFSL has not got the credit rating assessed or revised from FA, which was rated in 1995-96. According to its Annual Report, the SCFSL's Net Worth shows a negative of Rs. –67.74 lakhs and it has stopped accepting public deposits and stopped doing leasing business.

However, RBI has brought in relaxation in December 1998 wherever necessary. Although the RBI stipulates that any NBFC with less than Rs. 25 lakhs in net owned funds (NOF) will not be allowed to accept public deposits, it has permitted equipment and hire purchase companies without credit rating to tap public deposits of up to 1.5 times of their NOF or Rs. 10 crores, whichever is lower.

Sales Tax

Pursuant to the 46th Amendment, most States have exercised their power to tax leasing transactions. The rates of tax system and principles of levy are different in every jurisdiction. The overall scene is almost chaotic. Some States are treating a lease transaction as any other sale and levy tax at the same rate as the rate applicable on the sale of the relevant goods. (e.g., Bihar, Orissa, Haryana, Punjab, Himachal Pradesh, Tamil Nadu, etc.). While some States have a specific and separate rate of tax for leases (e.g., Karnataka, Andhra Pradesh, Gujarat, Rajasthan, U.P., West Bengal, etc., Maharashtra has enacted a completely different law altogether for taking leasing transactions. The rates of tax across different States vary between 2% to 12% . As such the incremental burden of sales tax on the same lease transaction into two different States might vary in proportion of 2:12. The rate of lease tax in Andhra Pradesh is 5%. Further, the turnover tax of 1% is levied. However, no such tax was there if the aggregate turnover of the lessor is Rs. 2,00,000 or less this limit of exemption has been deleted w.e.f. 1-4-1995, implying thereby that any turnover is taxable under section 5-E of States Sales Tax Act. The lease tax has increased from 5% to 6% w.e.f. 1-8-1996. The turnover tax remains unchanged. Further, the lease tax has increased from 6% to 8% and the turnover tax of 1% is exempted w.e.f. 1-1-2000.

Thus, almost all State Governments levy sales tax on lease rentals and by which it increases the cost of leasing and affects the profitability of leasing.

Chapter-4: Performance of Lessor Companies

This chapter attempts to present the sources and uses of funds including the analysis of cash flow statement. Further, the analysis of operating income and costs makes us know the performance of leasing companies. The following are the broad findings and conclusions :

1. The sources of funds that are potentially available to lessor companies are: Equity share capital, Reserves and surplus, Bank loans, Institutional loans, Public deposits and Commercial paper. The other sources of funds are depreciation and current liabilities.
2. It is observed that all types of sources of funds have registered

an increasing trend over the period of study from 1990-91 to 1994-95. After 1995, a slow growth trend has recorded.

3. Among all the sources, public deposit is the major fund raising source for leasing companies. During 1990-91 to 1994-95, the deposit mobilization increased to Rs. 25,607.4 lakhs. In 1994-95, the deposit mobilisation was up by 158.8% over previous year. The compound growth rate of public deposits recorded 74.11%, while others have recorded 35.89% for owned funds, 24.21% for borrowed funds, 36.37% for depreciation and 13.96% for current liabilities. Two reasons could be attributed to this remarkable growth of public deposits. Firstly, having had a bad experience in the stock market during 1992, investors invested their money in safe and fixed income source of fixed deposits. Secondly, almost all leasing and financial companies offered impressive deposit interest rates ranging between 14% and 20% through various incentive schemes such as brokerage commission, gifts for investors, etc., specially during the years from 1990-91 to 1995-96. After 1996, there is a slow progress in public deposits and other sources of funds, due to RBI's stringent regulations like making credit rating mandatory and linking the deposit limits to a factor of NOF based on the level of credit rating.

4. (a) The analysis of data pertaining to sources of funds of select lessor companies reveals that the fixed deposits occupied first rank, recording an average proportion at 53.58% followed by bank loans recording 28.52%. The remaining sources such as institutional loans debentures and other loans have recorded an average proportion of less than 10%.

   (b) The major sources of income for leasing companies are from lease and hire purchase transactions. The average income of lease is recorded at 44.22% and hire-purchase income is recorded at 43.16% over the period of study. The other sources of income are interest on deposits, dividends on investments, bill discounting, merchant banking, etc.

   However, lease and hire purchase income has shown a declining trend in 1995-96 and 1996-97 mainly due to recovery problems of instalments and provisioning for non-performing assets.

(c) As far as the uses of funds are concerned, the funds are deployed to finance various assets, which could contain consistent demand in the lease market.

5. It is observed from Table 4.1 that the growth of all assets—such as leased assets, hire-purchase assets, owned assets and current assets—have recorded a consistent growth trend registering at 84.6%, 71.8%, 102.3%, 122.7% respectively in the year 1994-95 over previous year. However, the growth trend declined recording 32.88% for leased assets, 11.96% for hire purchase assets, 30.55% for owned assets and 25.80% for current assets in 1995-96, mainly due to the limited sources of funds as the acquisition of assets depends upon the availability of funds.

6. It is observed from Table 4.2 that the proportion of leased assets and hire-purchased assets have gradually decreased at a slow pace with the passage of time from 1990-91 to 1996-97.

   The following reasons could be attributed for this gradual decrease.

   (i) Due to the prevailing competition and other growing activities–such as venture capital, mutual fund, merchant banking, hire purchase, bill discounting, etc., the leased assets composition could have been reduced, and

   (ii) Due to availability of limited funds.

   In addition to the specific causes mentioned above, the general factor of not owning the ownership of an asset has been a disincentive for leasing. As people psychologically prefer to have the ownership of an asset where the asset owner or purchaser would enjoy the benefits of depreciation, residual value, etc. But in lease transactions these benefits are not available to the lessee and hence the demand for leasing has not been that encouraging.

7. All select lessor companies have engaged in lease of plant and machinery throughout the period of study. It is observed from Table 4.6 that the average proportion of plant and machinery to the total leased assets is recorded at 77.44%,

followed by vehicles recording 13.11% and the office equipment and other assets have recorded 4.04% and 5.41% respectively. It may be concluded that relatively there has been a high demand for plant and machinery, which could be due to the primary requirements of various sectors of manufacturing and other business activities.

8. In terms of the proportion of lease business done by each select company to the total, NFL occupied the first position recording 52.54% for plant and machinery (Table 4.7), 81.55% for vehicles (Table 4.8), 95.32% for office equipment (Table 4.9), and 62.08% for other assets (Table 4.10).

Section-II of the chapter dealt with cash flow analysis of select lessor companies and it reveals the following:

9. The cash flow statements are prepared according to the form prescribed by listing agreement with Stock Exchange and the method prescribed by the Institute of Chartered Accountants of India (ICAI).
10. Increase in the leased assets is considered as an investment activity, while increase in stock on hire is merged with profits from operations by treating it as a current asset. Table 4.19 reveals that the consolidated figure of stock on hire shows a trend of both ups and downs. The highest growth rate is registered in 1992-93 recording 609.6%, followed by 168.5% in 1994-95. Almost the same trend was recorded for NFL and DCL. The remaining four companies PPL, LFL, MWL, SCFSL did very little hire-purchase business.
11. There is a decrease in lease rentals in the years 1993-94 and 1994-95 recording Rs. 78.67 lakhs and Rs. 349.01 lakhs respectively which means more collections than lease agreements. But there is an increase in lease rental debtors in the years 1996 and 1997 recording Rs. 538 lakhs and Rs. 313.37 lakhs respectively, which is mainly due to the increase in non-performing assets (NPAs) of select lessor companies and slow collection from debtors.
12. The consolidated cash flow statement (4.19) reveals that the use of cash towards discounting the trade bills has increased up to 1995-96, and decreased in 1996-97, registering a growth

rate of 215.24% in 1993-94, 437.50% in 1994-95 and 38.93% in 1995-96, due to the availability of more funds. In 1996-97, the growth rate decreased registering —70.93%, due to the impact of RBI guidelines and non-availability of funds.

13. Increase in current liabilities show inflow of funds and decrease in current liabilities shows the outflow of funds. There is substantial increase in the inflow of funds registering the growth rate at 912.32% in 1993, 464.48% in 1994 due to an increase in pre-received income, unclaimed dividend, interest accrued but not due, etc.
14. The amount of share capital raised in the primary market through issue of shares has registered ups and downs from 1990-91 to 1996-97, which shows that the investors have lost confidence on the primary market. The high premium issues and the experience of share market scam in 1992 drove the investors towards the fixed deposit market.
15. The growth rate for bank borrowings and term loans is almost similar and has registered ups and downs except in 1993-94 and 1994-95. In 1993-94, the term loans registered increase in growth rate at 416% whereas, bank borrowings decreased by 35%.

    In 1994-95, bank borrowings increased by 540%, while term loans decreased by 32% due to their respective credit policies. Further, RBI has tightened the lending norms to extend loans to NBFCs. As such, bank borrowing is marked by a reduction necessitating a shift of the resource mix to fixed deposits, term loans, debentures, etc.
16. Regarding the deployment of funds, a large chunk of funds have been utilised in acquiring the hire-purchased assets (varies between 65.82% and 35.04%) followed by leased assets (varying between 31.01% and 23.95%). On an average, the leased assets expenditure constitutes 27.8% and hire-purchased assets expenditure constitutes 47.8%, and both put together constitutes 75.6% of the total funds or assets (Table 4.2 of Section-I)
17. Company-wise analysis reveals that the NFL has done substantial amount of lease business to total lease business

done by all other select lessor companies recording its share at 55.3% in 1991, 31.7% in 1992, 44.9% in 1993, 69.4% in 1994, 64.6% in 1995, 78.6% in 1996, 78.8% in 1997. On an average, the amount spent on lease assets by NFL constitutes 60.46% of total leased assets of all select lessor companies. The remaining companies such as PPL, LFL, DCL, MWL and SCFSL share the remaining per cent of 39.54%.

A close analysis of the cash flow statements of select lessor companies reveal that almost all select lessor companies followed a suicidal policy of borrowing short term loans (1 year to 3 years) and deploying them in long term (5 years to 8 years) commitments. For lessor companies, the major sources of funds are public deposits and short term loans. As such these companies were not able to meet the short term obligations as and when they matured; which in turn, led to legal problems and further led to the liquidation of some unmanageable companies.

The legal problems are pertaining to depreciation claim, sales tax and income tax. The main controversy between leasing companies and Income Tax Department was regarding claim for depreciation as some companies were found to have made exaggerated the claim of depreciation. Almost all companies as well as the Income Tax Department were in appeal and the appeals were in various stages of disposal.

Chapter-5: Evaluation of Lessee Companies

This chapter dealt with the use of leasing to finance capital assets and impact on lessee's investment and reasons for leasing. The main findings and conclusions of the study are as follows :

1. In general, the acquisition of capital equipment involves heavy capital investment sometimes beyond the financial capacity of the actual user of the asset. As such leasing becomes an important source of acquiring a capital asset without incurring any capital expenditure.
2. The decision to lease or borrow to buy an asset can be made only after a specific financial analysis that weighs the merits of each choice. After the decision is made to acquire the

required capital asset, the method of acquisition will be evaluated for its impact on industrial investment. This chapter presents an analysis of the impact of use of leasing to finance capital asset and its impact on lessee's capital investment, and reasons for the lessee companies to prefer leasing.

3. The lessee survey indicated that companies acquired a wide range of assets on lease. The main types of assets that are leased by select lessee companies fall under the following categories :
   (i) Plant and machinery—includes pollution control equipment, electrical equipment, turbines, boilers, transformers, work rolls, back up rolls, energy saving equipment, textile machinery, diesel generators, shovel, industrial machinery, etc.
   (ii) Vehicles—include Buses, Ambassador Cars, Maruti Cars, Jeeps, Trucks/Lorries, Vans, etc.
   (iii) Office equipment—- includes computers, office furnitures, photocopiers, communication equipments, etc.
   (iv) Other assets include consumer durables such as television sets, refrigerators, air coolers, air conditioners, vacuum cleaners, microwoven, etc.
4. The types of lessees selected for the study involved in this sector of lease market are varied in their nature. They fall into the following categories :
   (i) Power Generation Company
   (ii) Paper Manufacturing Companies
   (iii) Road Transport Corporation
   (iv) Fertilizer Company
   (v) Aluminium and Steel Companies
   (vi) Textile Manufacturing Companies
   (vii) Cigarettes Manufacturing Company
5. The analysis of data pertaining to the types of assets acquired on lease by the select lessee companies reveals that the lease of plant and machinery is posted highest compound growth rate registering at 83.50% among all assets followed by vehicles (41.31%) and office equipment (13.33%).

   The proportion of plant and machinery to the total leased

assets varied between 89.85% in 1990-91 and 99.03% in 1996-97. The average proportion of plant and machinery to the total leased assets is recorded highest at 94.71% followed by office equipment recording at 3.95% vehicles 1.33%, and other assets at 0.01%.

6. Company-wise analysis reveals that the APSEB unit occupied the first place recording its share of total volume of leased assets to total assets. The APSEB has taken assets on lease worth Rs. 1,10,500.00 lakhs accounting for 92.73% followed by APR recording at Rs. 3,860.52 lakhs accounting for 3.24%, ITC recording at Rs. 1,270.06 lakhs representing 1.06%, VST recording at Rs. 1,218.61 lakhs representing 1.02%, and APSRTC at Rs. 1,186.00 lakhs representing 1.00%. The remaining 4 companies CML, PAL, PSL and PSM have recorded the volume of leased assets below Rs. 500.00 lakhs recording Rs. 451.78 lakhs (0.38%), Rs. 91.71 lakhs (0.08%), Rs. 190.00 (0.16%) and Rs. 397.00 lakhs (0.33%) respectively.
7. The total volume of assets taken on lease by all select lessee companies has increased from Rs. 4,175.38 lakhs to Rs. 1,19,165.72 lakhs over a study period recording the compound growth rate at 80.16%.
8. During the study period, the total volume of plant and machinery taken on lease by all lessee companies increased from Rs. 3,751.58 lakhs in 1990-91 to Rs. 1,18,011.68 lakhs in 1996-97 which constitutes 99.03% (Table 5.2) of total volume (Rs. 1,19,165.72 lakhs) of assets acquired on lease by select lessee companies.
   The highest volume of assets of plant and machinery has been taken by the APSEB recording Rs. 1,10,500.00 lakhs which constitutes 93.63% of total volume (Rs. 1,18,011.68 lakhs) of plant and machinery taken on lease by all select lessee companies (Table 5.2). The APSEB has taken only plant and machinery on lease and no other type of assets during the study period.
9. The lessee survey indicates that leasing is a cheaper source of finance since double depreciation is claimed by both the

lessee before selling the asset and by the lessor after the asset is sold to the lessor by the lessee under the "sale and lease back arrangement". The analysis revealed that 93.51% of total leased assets are under sale and lease back arrangement. Further, the lessee companies responded that the 100% depreciable assets are preferred since the Lessor Company passes on the depreciation benefit to the lessee company and fixes the lease agreement at low lease rates.

The cost of leasing varies from 11% to 12% depending upon the term of the agreement and the depreciation claim. In addition, a management fee of 1% and lease tax of 5% will be added to the cost of leasing. With this, the total cost of leasing varies between 17% and 18%. This cost of leasing varies from year to year depending upon the imposition and variation of lease tax from time to time since the imposition of sales tax and turnover tax is a prerogative of State Government.

10. The analysis of vehicle leasing reveals that the leasing of cars and buses has its own moderate growth recording the compound growth rate at 41.31%. Further, it presents that out of total worth of vehicles constituting Rs. 355.79 lakhs, the buses represent 54.25% (i.e. Rs. 193 lakhs) followed by cars 43.78% constituting Rs. 155.75 lakhs and trucks and vans recorded at a lower proportion of 1.79% representing Rs. 7.04 lakhs which were taken on lease by the lessee companies. The proportion of leasing of trucks and vans is very insignificant due to low demand for the same.

The lessee companies survey indicates that out of total cars worth Rs. 155.75 lakhs, the ITC has taken cars worth Rs. 33.47 lakhs on operating method of leasing representing 21.5% of total volume of cars. VST Ltd shares the remaining 78.5%. It means only two companies have taken cars on lease. Five companies APSEB, CML, PAL, PSL and PSM did not take any kind of vehicles on lease but they took on lease only plant and machinery except CML, which acquired office equipment on lease for Rs. 4.14 lakhs in addition to plant and machinery. The remaining two companies APR and

APSRTC took the vehicles of trucks (1990-91) and buses (1991-92) respectively on lease.

The overall picture indicates that vehicle leasing (in operating method) in AP from the point of view of lessee companies has not been encouraging. This may be due to the high cost of leasing compared to plant and machinery as the maintenance will be borne by the lessor (in operating lease) and included in lease rentals.

11. The office equipment was leased by only four companies, namely APR, CML, ITC and VST. Analysis reveals that the APR and CML have taken computers on lease in 1990-91 for Rs. 16.50 lakhs and Rs. 4.14 lakhs respectively. The ITC has taken the office equipment of wireless communication system EPABX (Telephone operation system) system on lease for Rs. 267.77 lakhs in the year 1993-94 only and later no office equipment was taken on lease. The VST has taken office equipment of computers and Tata Telecom equipment for intercom arrangement in the company. The cumulative figure of office equipment comes to Rs. 472.96 lakhs.

12. (a) The total picture of the total leased assets that were taken by lessee companies and their average share is shown as hereunder:

	Asset	*Per cent*
1.	Plant & Machinery	94.71
2.	Office equipment	3.94
3.	Vehicles	1.33
4.	Other assets	0.01
	Total	100.00

It is observed, from the asset-wise analysis, that the plant and machinery occupies the first position among all assets taken on lease by lessee companies. This indicates that among all assets leased, demand is more for plant and machinery in the lease market. There has been scarce demand for vehicles and other assets (Table 5.2).

(b) Further, it is observed that in terms of the company-wise analysis, APSEB occupied first position recording the leased assets at 92.73% of all assets taken on lease by select lessee companies followed by APR recording a less proportion of its leased assets at 3.24%. The remaining 4.03% is shared by remaining seven lessee companies (Table 5.2).

13. It is clearly evident that the demand for lease finance has emanated primarily from APSEB. And strangely enough, the demand from APSEB has been for 100% depreciation assets and that too under the sale and lease back arrangement. This has led to a crash in lease rentals. Another reason for why the APSEB preferred sale and lease back arrangement is that leasing provides them immediate liquidity or funds without any restrictions.

14. The volume of leased assets done by each lessee company over a span of study period is shown under four categories of lease, agreement, viz., (i) financial lease, (ii) operating lease, (iii) sale and lease back, and (iv) others.

    The analysis reveals that the total volume of assets taken on lease by select lessee companies from 1990-91 to 1996-97 is recorded at Rs. 1,19,165.72 lakhs. The proportion of financial lease, operating lease and sale and lease back arrangement is recorded at Rs. 7,699.25 lakhs (6.46%), Rs. 33.43 lakhs (0.03%) and Rs. 1,11,433.00 lakhs (93.51%) respectively (Table 5.8).

    Further, the data significantly discloses that 93.51% of the total volume of leased assets is under sale and lease back arrangement involving only three companies, viz., APSEB, ITC and PSL. The proportion of these three companies done under sale and lease back arrangement to total assets taken by all lessee companies under all the three lease arrangements is recorded at Rs. 1,10,350.00 lakhs (92.60%), Rs. 958.99 lakhs (0.80%) and Rs. 125.00 lakhs (0.12%) respectively. These three companies of APSEB, ITC and PSL have also obtained the leased assets under financial lease but their proportion is very insignificant compared to sale and lease back arrangement.

15. The reasons for preferring sale and lease back arrangement for taking assets on lease are: (i) the lessee could unlock the investment already made in an asset and release the capital for other alternative purposes or working purposes to

strengthen or improve the business activities; (ii) double depreciation facility. The owned asset is sold to a finance company, which needs depreciation as a tax shelter. Such deals, which in reality are mere book entries, are entered into mainly for 100% depreciation items or assets (on which the seller could already claim the depreciation) as tax laws allow the lessor (buyer) of such equipment to claim depreciation.

Recognising the sale and lease back transaction as paper transaction, the Budget 1995-96 has plugged the loophole in the system by stating that depreciation will be available to the lessor only against the written down value of the asset standing in the books of the original seller (lessee). Paper transactions of this type are better if not encouraged.

16. The data pertaining to year-wise average investment pattern including leasing undertaken by select lessee companies revealed that the average proportion of leasing to year-wise total investment varies from 0.5% (in case of PAL) to 29.2% (in case of APR). Out of 9 select lessee companies, only three companies—APR, APSEB, and VST—have used leasing on an average above 16% of their year-wise investment to finance the capital assets recording an average proportion of 29.3%, 26.2% and 16.8% respectively. The lease financing proportion for APSRTC and PAL is negligible recording an average proportion of 1.6% and 0.5% respectively. The two companies—CML and PSL—have maintained an average proportion of leased assets at 3.0% and 3.4% respectively. The remaining two companies—ITC and PSM—have used the leasing on an average at 8.6% and 5.7% respectively.

Individual company-wise and year-wise analysis over a study period reveals that the proportion of use of leasing to total investment made ranged from 0% to 76% during the years from 1990-91 to 1996-97. The proportion of lease financing is 49.5% for APSEB and 76% for APR in 1996-97. In terms of volume of leased assets, it ranged from Rs. 0 to Rs. 41,200 lakhs over a study period.

Among all select lessee companies, the APSEB has taken

highest volume of assets on lease. The cumulative figure of leased assets constituting Rs. 1,10,500.00 lakhs which, accounts for 92.73% of all assets taken on lease by select lessee companies.

17. Comparison between two mean values and standard deviation values revealed that there is uniformity in the investment with regard to the amount of assets other than leased assets. Whereas, wide variations are observed in the amount of asset acquired through leasing.

18. (a) Leasing has been increasingly used as a tax-planning device by a large number of high profit companies to reduce the tax liability. The lessor companies used to lease such assets, which are entitled for high rate of depreciation preferably 100% depreciable assets. In case the high profit manufacturing company identifies a suitable lessee, the same company acts as a lessor company and finance the asset required by the lessee and thus, the manufacturing company becomes the lessor and the lessor entitles to claim the depreciation as per the Income Tax rules.

    (b) The analysis reveals that 99% of the assets, which were taken on lease by the lessee companies, were high depreciation assets. Out of the total volume of leased assets (i.e.Rs. 1,19,165.72 lakhs), 99% constituting Rs. 1,17,976.99 lakhs of leased assets come under 100% depreciation rate (Table 5.10).

    (c) The 100% depreciation assets are Electrical equipments, Turbines, Boilers, Transformers, Pollution control equipments, Air conditioners, Computers, Wind electric generators, Work rolls, etc.

    (d) Thus, high depreciable assets are leased to claim the benefit of depreciation for tax planning purpose. The lessor normally passes on the tax benefit to the extent of depreciation, more in the case of 100% depreciable assets in the form of reduced lease rentals. The lessee does not get the depreciation allowance on leased assets but can claim lease rentals as tax deductible expense by debiting the same to the profit and loss account.

19. The effective rate of interest on 100% depreciable assets varies between 10% to 12%. The rate of interest goes up if other taxes like lease tax on lease rentals (usually varies between 4% to 8%) turnover tax (usually of 1%) lease management fee (usually of 1%), insurance, etc., are added. But these taxes vary from State Government to State Government. Some State Governments exempted the tax on lease rentals. For instance, the Maharashtra State Government has exempted the lease tax on lease rentals. The A.P. Government, realising the effect of multi-point levy of Sales Tax on lease transactions, had notified in 1985 that the tax on lease of goods, which were subject to payment of APGST stood exempted. But in 1993, the exempting notification was withdrawn. Hence, at present sales tax is applicable to lease of all goods in A.P. However, the provision of imposing turnover tax on certain transactions, including leases has been deleted with effect from 1-4-1995 by the A.P.G.S.T. (Third Amendment) Act, 1995. Further, the cost of leasing varies from agreement to agreement depending upon the term of the agreement.

20. (a) The expenses of select lessee companies are broadly classified as (i) operating expenses, (ii) interest, (iii) depreciation on fixed assets and (iv) lease rentals.

    (b) Analysis shows that the average proportion of lease rental expenses, which are 100% deductible expenses, is accounted for only 0.70% of all expenses of select lessee companies. Since the average proportion of lease rental expenses is 0.70%, the impact of tax advantage due to magnitude of lease rentals is very little or negligible for lessee companies. The major expenditure proportion is shared by operating expenses accounting for average proportion of 80.5% of all expenses followed by interest expenditure representing 11.5% and depreciation expenditure constituting 7.3%.

    (c) Unless the lessor passes on some of his tax benefits to lessee companies by fixing low lease rentals, the direct tax incentive of lease rental payments to the lessee companies is very little or negligible.

21. The χ^2 (Chi square) test reveals that there is no significant difference between the borrowing to buy option and the leasing option.

    The significant variations are:

    (a) to the extent of passing on the depreciation benefit by the lessor to the lessee; and

    (b) to the extent of magnitude of lease rentals being paid by the lessee companies as these are tax exempted.

22. The field survey reveals reasons for why lessee companies prefer leasing. The order of preference is mentioned hereunder:

    (i) Convenient and instant finance;

    (ii) Provides liquidity facility and avoids large capital outlay;

    (iii) Overcomes borrowing restrictions as the leasing is the off-balance sheet financing;

    (iv) Cheaper source of finance;

    (v) Provides tax advantages;

    (vi) Provides 100% financing;

    (vii) Offers protection against the risk of obsolescence.

Further, the lessee survey indicates that there are so many reasons for lessees to use leasing. Some of them may take assets on lease only for one reason and others may take assets on lease for more than one reason.

SECTION-B

Suggestions

Based on the study following suggestions are made to rejuvenate leasing industry and also for its steady growth.

Lease Financing and Public Sector Undertakings

The Government of India has drastically cut the budgetary allocation for public sector undertakings (PUCs). For instance, against Rs. 8,204.99 crore actually provided by the Government as budgetary support in the form of equity and loans to 207 PSUs during 1994-95, the Government has budgeted only Rs. 7,013.20

crores during 1995-96. A clear drop of about 15% is seen and these PSUs had to resort to leasing to meet part of their asset build up plans.

Another instance pertaining to Railways is that the Railways are faced with a shortage of over 30,000 coaches. The Railways have also been denied access to external borrowings. Given the tight liquidity position in the economy, lease financing seems to be the only answer.

Thus, the demand for the use of leasing as a source of funds can be mainly seen from the three sectors—the State Electricity Board (SEBs), Railways and Telecommunications. The demand for leasing is also expected to be generated by public sector Steel Companies, Heavy Engineering Units, Oil and Gas Companies, Shipping and Petro Chemicals, etc.

Some important lease deals done by some public sector undertakings during 1994-95 are mentioned hereunder :

- The Industrial Development Bank of India (IDBI) did a Rs. 50 crores deal for Shipping Corporation of India for financing the acquisition of a single ship.
- SBI Capital Markets (SBI Caps) the 100% merchant banking subsidiary of SBI syndicated a Rs. 240 crores lease deal for Mangalore Refinery and Petro Chemicals Ltd.
- Infrastructure Leasing and financial Services Ltd. (IL&FL) has syndicated a Rs. 200 crores lease deal for Maharashtra State Electricity Board (MSEB).
- Kotak Mahindra Finance Ltd (KML) has structured another Rs. 300 crores transmission and distribution equipment lease deal for Maharashtra State Electricity Board.
- A syndicate of Leasing Companies provided Rs. 250 crores lease finance to the Rajasthan State Electricity Board.
- Andhra Pradesh State Electrictiy Board has taken assets worth Rs. 1,105 crores on lease from various leasing companies from 1990-91 to 1996-97.

It is evident that public sector undertakings have definitely emerged as a strong demand base for lease financing.

Thus, keeping the above analysis in view and the present drain of financial resources on the part of Government, it is suggested that there is a need on the part of both Central and State Governments to encourage leasing and finance companies which will be able to explore new avenues to mobilise resources and public deposits to meet the corporate demand: so that the Government's financial commitment towards PSUs may be reduced and the revenue may be increased by collecting corporate tax both from lessee companies and lessor companies. Further, employment may be created by supporting lessor companies.

Policy Measures should not be too Liberal and too Rigid

Considerable deregulation of financial markets has taken place in India since 1991. Reforms undertaken have increased competitiveness within the financial sector by means of freeing interest rates, allowing new financial institutions and instruments and lifting controls on the entry of new domestic and foreign banks. As such, the scope and activities of banks and non-banking finance companies were expanded since 1991 due to the liberalisation drive.

In tune with the liberalisation policy of the Government, RBI announced in July 1996 that it would issue certificates to NBFCs which were (i) registered with RBI, (ii) credit rated and (iii) comply with the prudential norms. Those companies which were issued certificates by the RBI were allowed to accept public deposits without any upper limit and were given freedom to pay interest (freedom to fix interest rate) on the public deposits without a ceiling on interest rate. This relaxation is effective from July 25, 1996. The certificate was valid till June 1997 and was renewed for a further period of three months till September 1997.

Taking advantage of these major relaxations many leasing and finance companies accepted huge amounts of public deposits without following the norms stipulated by the RBI.

In January 1997, a prominent NBFC, CRB Capital Markets and many other NBFCs who had accepted large sums by way of deposits and defaulted in repayment of these deposits resulting in considerable panic among investors. The RBI, therefore, announced a set of new guidelines, on January 2, 1998. The new framework prescribed stringent norms such as ceiling on quantum deposits linked solely to Credit Rating, enhancement in Capital Adequacy

Ratio, increase in SLR, provisioning for NPAs, etc. These new guidelines have had adverse impact on the business prospects of NBFCs. The suddenness and harshness of the new regulations were responsible for drastic decline of leasing business and many companies have posted much reduced profits or even losses.

Thus the new regulatory/policy measures imposed to control the leasing industry has been far from effective. Because these measures encouraged leasing industry at the beginning, later on tightened, which virtually choked the leasing industry.

If only these regulations had been brought about over a period in a phased manner, the situation would have been different. Further, there should be consistency in the regulatory or policy measures being imposed from time to time. Frequent changes in norms or regulatory measures pertaining to bank finance, rate of interest on public deposits, liquidity requirements, etc., upset the operations and affect the sources and applications of funds.

Therefore, the future growth of leasing business depends on the clear cut rules or guidelines and policy regulations. On the other hand, if leasing and finance companies build up professional standards with good customer service orientation, there is good scope for them to grow.

Credit Rating and Public Deposits

As per the new regulations of 1998, only an NBFC with a credit rating could accept deposits. A triple "A" rated company could accept public deposit upto 4 times of its net owned funds (NOF). A double "A" rated company upto 2.5 times and a single "A" rated company upto 1.5 times of its NOF. The maximum rate of interest was also fixed at 16% per annum. It means the new regulatory framework reintroduced a cap on acceptance of public deposits and interest rates by linking the deposit limits to a factor of NOF based on the level of credit rating. Further, the deposits accepted in excess of the permitted limits were required to be repaid as per the dates stipulated by the RBI.

This created a major panic not only among the companies but also among the investors. The demand for repayment of public deposits increased by manifold and nobody was willing to renew the deposit.

Some NBFCs began to default in repayment of matured deposits and this created further panic among investors. Since the NBFCs are doing business only with public money, RBI should relax linking of credit rating to acceptance of public deposits. Further, RBI should ensure that the amount borrowed from the public is properly deployed in income earning assets and not in speculative activities and other unrelated ventures. What is required is a continuous vigil or supervision by RBI to monitor the working of NBFC and not linking of credit rating to acceptance of public deposits. Further, it should be ensured that every NBFC is inspected thoroughly once a year and action should be resorted immediately in case of any irregularity. And those NBFCs who comply with the RBI directions/guidelines should be encouraged.

In this connection, it is pertinent to point out that why a fraud committed by a single company should affect the entire industry. Fraud can take place in any organisation and the financial sector is no exception. Experience of developed countries teach two things. Firstly, remove the bad egg instantly lest it should immediately spoils others. The cancerous growth has to be cut out straightaway, so that it does not come in the way of normal functioning of the overall healthy body. Secondly, every such crisis is both a challenge as well as an opportunity. It helps to draw valuable lessons, so that the same mistakes are not repeated in the future. Thus, RBI should ensure that the NBFCs should grow in an orderly and healthy manner.

Leasing and Transport Sector

The hire purchase finance companies and leasing companies have been playing an important role in the finance of the Road Transport Sector. One estimate puts this around 25-30 per cent of all commercial vehicles are leased/ hire purchased.

In the Fifties, Railways handled 80% of the passenger and goods traffic, whereas today Road Transport handles 80% of the passenger and goods traffic. This has been possible mainly due to liberal financial assistance extended by the NBFCs to small transport operators. Though the rate of interest charged by them is slightly higher compared to banks, a transport operator prefers to deal with an NBFC as there are no cumbersome procedures to get the loan.

The Government may realise the important role played by the NBFCs in the development of the transport industry in particular and the national economy in general and encourage NBFCs by issuing a directive to banks and financial institutions to extend liberal financial support to NBFCs for on-lending to small transport operators and others who require finance.

Sales Tax

The levy of sales tax on lease rentals by many State Governments is the most irksome legislation that threatened the growth, if not the existence of the leasing industry in our country. Different States levy different rates of tax on lease. Since different States are levying different rates of Sales Tax on lease transaction, there is an immediate need on the part of the Central Government to make a uniform legislation for all the States to levy sales tax. A separate statute may be enacted for leasing clearly defining all the rules and procedures. The Central Government should take steps to amend the Central Sales Tax Act so as to bring into its fold the companies, which are dealing with leasing business to avail the benefit of "C" Form so that the severity of the levy of Sales Tax on lease rentals is not felt by the ultimate user of the assets.

Further, the Government of Andhra Pradesh may consider reducing the levy of Sales Tax to a nominal rate from the existing 8%. This encourages leasing and finance companies to restart or regain the position and help to contribute the industrial growth.

Mismatch of Funds

More than 80% of the public deposits accepted by the leasing and finance companies ranged between one year and three years. But these companies lent even upto 8 years.

Further, many small finance companies or unincorporated (with RBI) finance companies accepted huge public deposits by offering high interest rates and incentives and diverted these funds either to purchase personal properties or invested in speculative ventures. As such, leasing and finance companies became default in making payment of interest as well as principal to the deposit holders as and when they matured.

Therefore, it is imperative on the part of companies to avoid mismatch of funds. So long as the long-term sources of funds are invested for long term investments and short-term sources of funds are invested for short-term investments, the mismatch problem would not arise. Hence the RBI has to look into these aspects and ensure proper utilisation of resources. And action may be resorted on erring companies.

Setting up of Debt Recovery Tribunal (DRT) and Asset Reconstruction Company (ARC)

NBFCs have been an integral and important part of the Indian Economy and are playing a vital role. With appropriate and uniform regulations, these companies could play a useful complementary role to that of banks.

The Association of Leasing and Financial Services Companies made a representation that the Government and RBI should urgently consider setting up of a Debt Recovery Tribunal (DRT) for leasing and hire-purchase companies to recover the instalment due amounts. Unless NBFCs recover instalment amounts, they cannot meet their debt obligations to the banks, depositors and other creditors on due dates. This is relevant particularly in the context of wilful defaulters/unscrupulous lessees who run their companies to the ground and take shelter under the BIFR. Further, delays in the court proceedings encourage borrowers to default. Constitution of a Debt Recovery Tribunal is therefore essential in order to avoid inordinate delay in recovering the legitimate dues of NBFCs on the same lines of banks.

Further, it is imperative on the part of the Government to amend Negotiable Instruments Act to hasten prosecution of issuers of cheques that bounce. So that aggrieved creditors (like lessors) can proceed against defaulters without detailed witness examination. Thus, the amendment will facilitate online paperless transactions to penalise cheque bouncers. So that the delay that bothers creditors may be avoided.

The Government can also think of constituting an Asset Reconstruction Company (ARC) for NBFCs like factoring financial services. The non-performing assets can be sold to the ARC at a discounted price and the proceeds can be utilised for repayment of debt obligations. The ARC can in turn collect the amounts from the borrowers/lessee companies.

Mergers and Acquisitions

The business environment of financial services industry is not very encouraging today. The sources of funds have considerably dried up as the capital markets are down and there is a general downward trend in the economy. There is a general apathy on the part of banks and financial institutions in lending to NBFCs. The sources of public deposits have suddenly slowed down as the public has lost confidence due to some frauds committed by a few NBFCs. Further, the problems of recovery of due instalments and repossession of leased/hired assets have increased. All these have resulted in the reduction of turnover and a marginal increase in NPAs and NBFCs. To add fuel to the fire banks, financial institutions and multinational companies have started competing with NBFCs. In this context it is therefore suggested that only through a merger, amalgamation or acquisition NBFCs can overcome problems to some extent, which will bring them economies of scale by bringing down their cost of borrowing and other costs.

However, there is a positive hope for professionally managed companies, which are able to mobilise, required funds in a cost-effective manner. The process of rebuilding confidence of the public, commercial banks, and financial institutions is essential to rejuvenate the financial services industry.

Computer Leasing

Information technology has achieved a remarkable widespread use in a very short period. Software industry in Andhra Pradesh took a quantum jump particularly form 1996-97 with the personal initiative of the present Chief Minister, N.Chandrababu Naidu. In order to make Hyderabad the centre of Information Technology and off-shore financial centre, there is a need on the part of the Government to encourage leasing and financial services industry in all respects.

Micro Leasing

Poverty alleviation is rightly emerging as the main objective in the social agenda of all countries in the world. Micro credit has been identified as one of the important tools to achieve the same. Micro leasing (which forms an important aspect of micro credit) refers to leasing, income-generating assets to the poor. Micro leasing would include providing micro enterprise items on lease such as solar pump sets for open wells, solar cookers, etc.

With active encouragement from the Government in the form of subsidies or other fiscal incentives like income tax benefits, income generating assets can be leased. Thus, vulnerable sections of the society can acquire the required items on cheap credit terms. Mr.V. Sitaram Rao Management Consultant, Hyderabad, is developing a viable project on micro leasing.

If this is done, micro leasing would emerge as a very important tool in alleviating poverty in developing countries like India.

Marketing and Monitoring of Leases

On an average the total volume of leasing business in AP is less than 1% (All India level it is around 4%) of the capital formation compared to around 10% of Japan, about 19% of UK and around 30% of US. This itself gives an idea of the vast untapped potential for leasing in India. However, in the present day context, it would be wrong to assume that leasing business has a momentum of its own and will traverse heights by itself. Growth and success in leasing business call for well-planned marketing efforts in identifying right clients, educating them on the pros and cons and the modalities eventually clinching the deal.

Subsequently, proper evaluation of lease business pertaining to collection of lease rentals, periodical physical verification of the leased equipment, etc., should be undertaken.

To conclude, the evaluation of the lessor and lessee companies has confirmed that the mode of lease financing as a source of business finance supplement the activities of banks in the fields of deposit mobilisation and lending. Leasing and finance companies are capable of playing a dynamic role in the development of the economy provided, there is a constant support and proper regulation from the Government.

The Government, on its part, will have to stipulate a regulatory framework to safeguard the savings of the public. At the same time, it has to provide a supportive policy framework for leasing/financial services industry to grow on healthy lines. On the other hand, leasing/financial services industry will have to perform in such a manner that the safety of depositor's money is ensured and strengthening of the supportive policy framework is also ensured.

BIBLIOGRAPHY

Books

Ahuja, Girish & Ravi Gupta, *Direct Taxes – Law & Practices Including Tax Planning,* Taxmann Publications (P) Ltd., New Delhi.

Amembal, Sudhir P. *et al., Equipment Leasing*, McGraw-Hill, Inc. New York, 1992.

Beera Jr., Henri S. *Computer Leasing,* Lifetime Learning Publications, California, London, 1983.

Bhole, L.M., *Financial Institutions and Markets – Structure, Growth and Innovations,* Tata McGraw-Hill Publishing Company Limited, New Delhi, 1996.

Bierman, H. Jr., and Seymone Smidt, *The Capital Budgeting Decision–Economic Analysis of Investment Projects,* MacMillan Publishing Company, New York, 1984.

Bierman, Harold Jr., *Financial Management and Inflation,* Collier MacMillan Publishers, London, 1981.

Biswasroy, P.K. and Mishra D.P. *Lease Financing in India*, Kanishka Publishers – Distributors, New Delhi, 1992.

Brahmaiah, B., *Lease Financing*: *Theory and Practice,* Himalaya Publishing House, Mumbai, 1998.

Chandra, Prasanna, *Financial Management – Theory and Practice*, Tata McGraw-Hill Publishing Company Ltd., New Delhi, 1994.

Clark, T.M., *Leasing,* Tata McGraw-Hill, London, 1978.

Clark, Tom. (Ed.) *Leasing Finance*, Euromoney Publications Ltd., Nestor House, London, 1985.

Dayal, Sharmila, *Lease Financial in India*, Sarup & Sons, New Delhi, 1994.

David G. Mayes and G. Mayes and Clive S. Nicholas, *The Economic Impact of Leasing,* The MacMillan Press Ltd., London, 1988.

Dictionary of Finance and Investment Terms, Baron's Educational Series, Inc. New York, 1985.

Faronk Irani *Inside Leasing,* Tata McGraw-Hill Publishing Company Limited, New Delhi, 1995.

Ferrare, W.L., Thied, J.B. and Dirsmith, M.W., *The Lease Purchase Decision*, National Association of Accountant, USA, 1980.

Finnerty, John. D., *Corporate Financial Analysis*, McGraw-Hill Book Company, New York. 1986.

Gosh, P.K. and Gupta, G.S., *Fundamentals of Leasing and Lease Financing,* Vision Books, New Delhi, 1985.

Gupta, Naresh Kumar, *Lease Financing – Concepts and Practice,* Deep & Deep Publications, New Delhi, 1993.

Gupta, N.C. Kaura and Sharma, G.I., *Corporate Financing – Emerging Options,* Anmol Publications, New Delhi, 1991.

Halay, C. and Schall, L., *The Theory of Financial Decision*, New York, McGraw Hill, 1973.

Hampton, John, J., *Financial Decision Making*, Prentice-Hall of India Private Limited, New Delhi, 1994.

Hanumantha Rao, V. *et al.,* (Ed), *Andhra Pradesh at 50 Years,* Data News Features, Banjara Hills, Hyderabad.

Hoshi, Premlal, *Leasing Comes of Age: Indian Scene,* M/s. Prakash Kanna, Bombay, 1986.

India Leasing Year Book 1994, Association of Leasing and Financial Services Companies, 121, M.G. Road, Bombay, 1995.

India Leasing Year Books, 1994, 1996 and 1998, Leasing and Financial Services Companies, Bombay, 1994,1996 and 1998.

Industrial Dictionary of Andhra Pradesh, 1996. Government of Andhra Pradesh, 1996.

Jain, Nabhi Kumar. *How to do Lease Financing and Hire-Purchase Business*, Nabhi's Publications, New Delhi 1995.

Jur. Alfred W. Fink, *A Practical Guide* to Leasing, McGraw Hill Book Company, England, 1994.

Kamath, K.V.; Kerkar, S.A.; and Viswanath, T., *The Principles and Practice of Leasing*, Lease Asia, Surrey, London, 1990.

Karuppiah, *Lease Finance*, Sterling Publishers Pvt. Limited, New Delhi, 1988.

Khan, M.Y., *Indian Financial System – Theory and Practice,* Vikas Publishing House Pvt. Limited, New Delhi, 1999.

Kothari, Vinod. *Lease Financing and Hire-Purchase*, Wadhwa & Company Pvt. Ltd., Law Publishers, Nagpur, 1996.

Kucchal, S.C., *Financial Management,* Chaitanya Publishing House, Allahabad, 1994.

Lease Finance, Select Readings, Equipment Leasing Association, 1990.

Mathur, B.L. (Edited), *Readings in Lease Financing,* Arihant Publishers, Jaipur, 1990.

Nagaraja Naidu, V., *et al.*, (Ed), *Lease Financing in India,* Delta Publishing House, Hyderabad, 1995.

Narayanaswamy, R., *Accounting for Leases by Lessors: A Research Study*, Indian Institute of Management, Bangalore, 1990 (This study was sponsored by SBI Capital Markets Limited).

Pandey, I.M., *Financial Management*, Vikas Publishing House Pvt. Limited, New Delhi, 1994.

Parker, R.H., *MacMillan Dictionary of Accounting*, The MacMillan Press Ltd., London, 1985.

Penguin Dictionary of Commerce, 2nd Ed.

Purchure, Rajas, and Ashok Kumar, N., *Introduction to Lease Financing*, Times Research Foundation, Pune, 1985.

Purchure, Rajas, *Lease Financing,* The Times Research Foundation, Pune, 1983.

Ritchard, Robert E. and Thomas J. Hindelan. *Making the Lease/Buy Decision,* American Management Association, New York, 1984.

Satyanarayana, J., Ramakrishna, K. and Rama Murthy, S. *Lease Financing*, Himalaya Publishing House, New Delhi, 1995.

Satyanarayana Murthy, P., *Leasing Industry in India: A Study of Selected Equipment Lease Contracts,* Unpublished thesis submitted to Osmania University for the award of the Degree of Doctor of Philosophy in Business Management, 1992.

Shankariah, K., *Organising for Higher Productivity Systems and Practices in Coal Industry,* University Publications and Press, Osmania University, Hyderabad, 1997.

Siegel Joel, G., *Dictionary of Accounting Terms*, Barron's Educational Series, Inc., New York, 1987.

Sriram, K., *Hand Book of Lease Financing, Hire Purchase and Factoring*. The Institute of Chartered Financial Analysts of India, 1992.

Srinivasa Murthy, S., *Lease Purchase Decisions in the Indian Corporate Sector*, Unpublished thesis submitted to University of Madras for the award of the Degree of Doctor of Philosophy in Commerce, 1994.

Srivastava, R.M., *Financial Decision Making,* Sterling Publishers Pvt., New Delhi, 1984.

Terry, A., Isom and Sudhir P.Amembal, *The Hand Book of Leasing: Techniques and Analysis,* PBI a Pertrocelli Book, Princeton, New York, 1982.

Van Horne JC., *Financial Management and Policy*, Prentice Hall of India, New Delhi, 1994.

Vancil, Richard, *Leasing of Industrial Equipment*, Tata McGraw-Hill Book Company, New York, 1963.

Venkaiah, V *et al.*, (Ed.), *Financial Services – Emerging Trends*, Delta Publishing House, Hyderabad, 1997.

Verma, J.C., *Lease Financing Concept, Laws and Procedure*, Bharat Law House, New Delhi, 1994.

Williamson, *Leasing and Finance Companies*, The Institute of Chartered Accountants in England and Wales, Moorgata Place, London, 1991.

World Leasing Year Book, Euromoney Publications, Nestor House, London, 1989 and 1996.

Articles

Anantha Ramakrishna, R., "Publishing Leasing Companies" *Business Line*, March 12, 1994.

Balasubramaniam, P.S., "Market Review", *World Leasing Year Book*, Euromoney Publications Plc., Nestor House, London, 1996.

Balasubramania, S., "Leasing: Accounting and Presentation", *Chartered Secretary,* August 1985.

Bandyopadhyay, S. "Direction of Regulation of NBFCs", *India Lease Year Book*, Association of Leasing and Financial Services, Bombay, 1996.

Bhalla, G.S., and Sandu, H.S., "Lease Financing An Evaluation", *The Indian Journal of Commerce,* April—June, 1988.

Bhansali, Jayesh D., "The Leasing Industry Paper Profits", *The Economic Times*, June 13, 1991.

Bhattacharya, N., "Cost of Capital for a Finance Company", *Chartered Financial Analyst*, July–August 1990.

Brahmaiah, B., "Leasing - A Growing Industry," *The Indian Management*, January,1990.

———,"Leasing Industry in India: Problems and Prospects," *ASCI Journal of Management,* June, 1991.

———,"Profitability Analysis of Leasing Companies in India", *Decision*, 1991.

Bower, R.S. *et al*., "Lease Evaluation," *The Accounting Review*, April, 1966.

Bowman, R.G., "The Debt Equivalence of Leases: An Empirical Investigation", *The Accounting Review*, April 1980.

Clark, T.M., "The Dawn of International Leasing", *The Banker*, April,1982.

Clifford, W., *et al*., "Determinants of Corporate Leasing Policy", *The Journal of Finance,* July 1985.

Das Gupta, Arindam. "Taxation, Non-Tax Policy and Capital Equipment Leasing", *Economic and Political Weekly*, May 26, 1990.

Dass, Basu Dev, "Leasing Companies Skating on thin Ice", *Business India,* June 29—July 12, 1987.

Farouk Irani, "Financial Services—A look into the Future", *Business India*, November 27 - December 10, 1989.

———,"The Leasing Industry - Revisited", *Business India*, November 14 - 27, 1988.

Fawthrop, R.A., and Terry, B., "Debt Management and the use of Leasing in U.K., Corporate Financing Strategies", *Journal of Business Finance and Accounting*, Autumn, 1975.

Hari Bhakti, S.V., "Accounting for Lease Transactions", *The Chartered Accountant,* December, 1985.

Harwood Gordon, B., and Hermanson, "The Lease or Buy Decision", *The Journal of Accountancy,* September,1976.

Hull, J.C., and Hubbard, G.L., "Lease Evaluation in the U.K., Current Theory and Practice", *Journal of Business Finance and Accounting,* Winter, 1980.

Julian R. Franks, *et al*., " Lease Valuation when Taxable Earnings are a Scarce Resource" The *Journal of Finance,* September,1987.

Kajaria, U.N., "Tax Planning through Leasing", *The Chartered Accountant*, June 1989.

Kothari, Vinod, "Leasing: Hit by Unjustified Sales Tax", *Business Standard*, April 30, 1987.

———, "An overview", *The Economic Times*, March 23, 1994.

Kumara, Sundaram S., "Equipment Leasing - Complementary Role in Financing of Industry", *Economic and Political Weekly*, August, 1982.

Lubna Kably, "Leasing Companies seek Time to meet new norms", *The Economic Times*, June 23, 1994.

Ojha, P.D., "Some Aspects of Lease Financing", *Reserve Bank of India Bulletin*, March 1988.

Osamu Nagano, "The Basic Leasing Concept", *World Leasing Year Book,* Euromoney Publications plc., Nestor House, London, 1989.

Pandey, I.M., and Raghunathan, V., "Issues in Lease Evaluation", *Vikalpa,* July-September, 1987.

Miller, M.H., and Upton, C.W., "Leasing, Buying and the Cost of Capital of Service", *The Journal of Finance*, June 1976.

Nadkarni, V.K., "Equipment Leasing", *The Economic Times*, June 18, 1983.

Narayana Swamy, R. "Off-balance Sheet Finance: A threat to Financial Reporting", *The Chartered Accountant*, August1988.

Raghavan, S., "Problems in Leasing Industry", Paper presented at the Seminar on *Leasing*, organised by Canbank Financial Services, Bangalore, 29 - 30 December, 1988.

Raghunathan, V., "Leasing—An Investment or a Financing Decision, *The Chartered Accountant,* May 1986.

Ramamoorthy, V.E., "Lease does not sell by itself: You have to Market it", *Lease Financing,* (Ed.) J. Satyanarayana, *et al.*, Himalaya Publishing House, Bombay, 1995.

Rao, K.V., "Leasing Industry: Financial and Accounting Jugglery", *Deccan Chronicle,* August 10, 1993.

Rick Elam., "The Effect of Lease Data on Productive Ability of Financial Ratios", *The Accounting Review*, January 1975.

Samkara Subramanian, K., "Disclosures and Debtors in Finance Companies—Accountant Proposes, Auditor Endorses", *Business Line,* July 14, 1994.

Sanghvi, A.R., "Accounting Policies and Standards", *The Economic Times*, November 8, 1986.

Shah, V.C., "Fundamentals of Leasing Part - I, Comparative Evaluation", *The Economic Times,* August 19, 1986.

———, "Fundamentals of Leasing Part – II, Comparative Evaluation", *The Economic Times*, August 19, 1986.

Srikanth, A., "Dividend out of Profits", – *Business Line*, April 17, 1994.

———, "R.B.I. Seeks Legal Power to close down Erring NBFCs", *The Economic Times*, June 27, 1994.

Srinivasan, N.P. and Srinivasa Murthy, S., "Factors Influencing the Decision to Lease : An Indian Perspective", *Vikalpa – The Journal for Decision Makers,* July – September 1994.

Sriram Gade, "Leasing – Child of Lesser God", *The Economic Times,* January 9, 1997.

Sykes, A., "The Lease – Buy Decision: A Survey of Current Practices in 202 companies", *Management Survey Report No. 29*, British Institute of Management, 1976.

Tirumalai, S., and Ravi, K., "Lease Financing Accounting and Taxation Aspects", U.G.C Seminar on *Lease Financing and Accounting,* Department of Commerce, Osmania University, March 25, 1990.

Vancil Richard F., "Lease or Borrow – New Method of Analysis", *Harward Business Review,* September 1961.

Vaidya Nathan, S., "Finance Companies Imminent Shake Out", *Business Line,* April 17, 1994.

Vijayaraghavan, R., "Curbs on Leasing Companies", *The Economic Times*, May 9, 1990.

Reports

Annual Reports of Equipment Leasing Association India, (ELAI), Chennai, 1990-91 to 1997-98.

Annual Reports of Association of Leasing and Financial Services, Mumbai, 1996-97.

APGST Amendment Ordinance – 1996.

A.P. Gazette iv – B, Extra-ordinary, A.P. Ordinance No. 10 of 1999, December 31,1999.

A.P. Notification G O M S No. 1388, Revenue(s), December 23, 1985.

A.P. Notification G O M S No. 606 Revenue July 3, 1993.

Assam Leasing Convention, Association of Leasing & Financial Services, Mumbai, 1997.

Centre for Monitoring Indian Economy(CMIE), *Monthly Reserves,* 1990-91 to 1997-98.

IDBI Report on Development Banking in India, IDBI Tower, Mumbai, 1990-91 to 1997-98.

Narasimham Committee 1991, *Report on Financial System,* 1991.

NBFCs (Reserve Bank) Directions – 1998, RBI Notification No. DFC-114/DG(SPT)-98, dated 02-01-1998.

New series on State Domestic Product, *Andhra Pradesh*, Directorate of Economics and Statistics, Hyderabad, Govt. of A.P., 1993-94 to 1998-99.

Non-Banking Financial Companies Prudential Norms (Reserve Bank) Directions–1998, RBI Notification No. DFC.115/ DG(SPT) – 98, dated : 02-01-1998.

Report on the Financial System, Nabhi Publications, New Delhi, 1993.

RBI *Report and Trend an Progress of Banking in India* 1985-86.

RBI *Cirular IECD No. CAD 201 and 205/c 446(LF) 87-88*, April 28,1988.

RBI *Notification No.DFC(COC) S6/DG(O)-89*, dated : 28-03-1989.

Reserve Bank of India Bulletins 1990 to 1999.

Reserve Bank of India Annual Report 1990-91 to 1997-98.

Reserve Bank of India Report on Trend and Progress of Banking in India, 1990-91 to 1997-98.

RBI *Notification No. IECD No. 14/08-12-01/94-95,* dated : 28-09-1994.

RBI *Notifcation No. DFC(COC) 742/02.04/96-97,* dated : September 26,1996.

RBI *Notification No. DNBC/38/DG(H) – 77 as amended upto June18, 1997, dated July 31,* 1997.

Reports on Currency and Finance, Economic Review, Reserve Bank of India – 1990 – 91 to 1997 – 98.

Report on Annual Survey of Industries, Central Statistical

Organisation, Dept. of Statistics, Ministry of Planning and Programme Implementation, Government of India, New Delhi.

Report on Leasing in Emerging Markets, the World Bank, Washington DC, USA, 1996.

Reports on the Annual Survey of Industries in A.P. Directorate of Economics & Statistics, Government of A.P., Hyderabad 1990-91 to 1996 – 97.

Report on Pre-Budget Memorandum : 1997-98, Association of Leasing and Financial Services Companies, Mumbai.

Reports of Economic Times, 1997 to 2000.

Stock Exchange Official Directory, Stock Exchange, Hyderabad, 1990-91 to 1997-98.

Tandon Committee – 1975, *Study Group to Review the System of Cash Credit*, RBI Mumbai, 1975.

The Economic Times – 1990–91 to 1999-2001, Cholamandalam Investments and Finance Company : Leasing Literature, 1990.

The Economic Survey : 1999-2000, Finance and Planning (PLG Wing) Department, Andhra Pradesh, Hyderabad.

The Hindu Survey of Indian Industry, 1994-95 to 1998-99.

INDEX

Acquisitions, 323
Additional convenience, 284
All India Development Banks, 65
All India Financial Institutions, 65-70
Andhra Pradesh, Contribution of Leasing, 75-77
  credit rating on public deposits in, 120-24
  industrial development in, 71-72
  industrial investment, 295
  sales tax on lease in, 131-34
APGST Act, 131
APP Company, 23, 249
APSEB Company, 21
APSED, 226, 227
APSRTC, 25, 249
Asian Leasing Association (Asia Leased), 46
Assets, 159-61
  categories, 11
  classification, 95-96
  growth of, 304
  types of, 224-25
Asset Reconstruction Company (ARC), 332
Association of Leasing and Financial Services (ALFS), 61, 98, 298, 332
  member companies funds for, 53-54
  application of funds, 294
  leased assets, 59-60

Banking Borrowing, 89-92, 206
  growth rate of, 205
Bank deposits, 196
Bank facility, nature of, 85
Bank lending, maximum limit for, 83-84
Bank liberalised policy, 205
Bank loans, 280
Beera, Henry S., 10
Birla Global Finance Ltd. (BGFL), 118
Board for Industrial and Financial Reconstruction (BIFR), 29, 232
Borrowed funds, 143
Borrowings arrangements, 88
  option, 273-74
Brahmaiah, B., 12
British Institute of Management (BIM), 14
Brokerage Commission, 303
Budget 1995-96, 250, 313

'C' Form, 126-28, 132
  benefit of, 132
  issues of, 126-28
Capital adequacy ratio, 318
Capital budget constraints, 287
Capital employed, return on, 168
Capital expenditure, 222
Cash flow analysis, 5, 181-84
  from financing activities, 202
  from operating activities, 182-84
Cash outflows, total value of, 278
Ceiling Limits, 45
Central Bureau of Investigation (CBI), 110
Central Sales Tax Act, 126, 128
Centre for Monitoring Indian Economy (CMIE), 4
Chain Roop Bansali (CRB), 110
Chandra, Prasanna, 9
Chi square test, 5, 316
Cholamandalam Investment and Finance Company Limited, Madras, 34
CMC Company, 26, 249
  assets on lease, 235
Commercial Banks, 26
  subsidiaries of, 50
Computers, 257
Computer Leasing, 323
Consolidated cash flow statement, 202, 305
Consumer financing, 16
Controversy, 307
Corporate tax, 163
Corruption, 110
Cost of funds, 263-69
Credit/investment, concentration of, 102-03
Credit rating, 104-07, 298-99, 318-20
Cross Border Lease, 41
Current Liabilities, 149-52] 201

Dahotre Committee, 83
Data analysis, 4-5
DCL company, 19, 207, 211, 215
  cash flow statement of, 197-98

Debt instruments, common feature of, 265
Debt Recovery Tribunal (DRT), 322
Debtors, 189-91
Depreciations, 144-47, 201-02, 273-74
 assets, 247, 314
 items, 263
 opportunity, 268
 rates of, 261-63
Discounted Cash Flow (DCF) techniques, 270
Doubtful asset, 97
Down value method, 12

Equipment Leasing, 10, 294-95

Fawthrop, R.A., 14, 259
Ferrara, W.L., 15
Finance companies, registration for, 112-13
Finance and investment companies, 47-48
Financial evaluation, 223, 269-70
Financial institutions, 50-65
Financial lease arrangement, leasing rates, 245, 257, 268, 287-88
Fink, Jur, Alfred W., 16
5–Years lease agreement, equivalent interest rates for, 268-69
Fixed assets, amortisation of, 144
Fixed deposits, 205-06
Fund, 181
 mismatch of, 321-22
 sources of, 142-44
 uses of, 152-44
Funds and application, sources of, 62

Garg, G.S., 93
Ghosh, P.K., 10
Gross Domestic Product (GDP), 3
Gross State Domestic Product (GSDP), 72, 73
Gupta, G.S., 10
Gupta, N.C., 9

Hampton, John J., 9
High costs equipments, 38
Hire Purchase agreement, 58, 252
Hire Purchase Business, 88
Hire Risk Weighted Assets, 100
Housing Finance Companies (HFCs), 80
Hubbard, G.L., 14
Hull, J.C., 14

Income Tax Act, 163
Income Tax Authorities, 249
Income Tax Payments, 196
Income Tax Rules, 314
Independent Leasing Companies, 48
Indian Pattidari system, 43
Industrial Development Bank of India (IDBI), 26, 65, 66, 249, 295
Industrial Credit and Investment Corporation of India Ltd. (ICICI), 65, 66, 295
Industrial Finance Corporation of India Ltd. (IFCI), 65, 70
Industrial Investment Bank of India Ltd. (IIBI), 65
Industrial Reconstruction Bank of India (IRBI), 70
Institute of Chartered Accountents of India (ICAI), 202
Institutional Accounting Standards Committee (IASC), 35, 37
Institutional Borrowings, 91-92
Inter-State Leases, taxability of, 127

Japanese Leasing Company, 43
Joshi, Premlal, 10

Kamath, K.V., 10
Kotak Mahindra Finance Ltd., 158
Kuchhal, S.C., 9

Lease agreement, 223, 233, 237, 245-50, 249, 265, 267, 315
 categories, 248, 312
 types of, 36-39, 245-50, 251-52
Lease assets, 258-62
 composition of, 58
 modern development, 42-43
Lease financing, 3-7, 312, 316-18
 concept of, 34-36
 domestic appliances taken of lease, 244
 office equipment taken of lease, 242-44
 policy framework on, 79-132, 296-302
Lease Management Fee (LMF), 265
Lease Markets categories, 225-26
Lease and Hire Purchase Assets, 97
Leasing areas, 16
 evolution of, 41-47
 options, 275, 278-79
 rates, 266
Leasing world over, 44-47
Leasing Business, 47-48, 293-96
 composition of income, 61-64
 special features of, 87-88

Leasing Companies, acceptance of public deposits by, 103-104
bank lending to, 296-97
current liabilities of, 149-50
norm for lending to, 83-93
questionnaire/interviews, 229
shareholders of, 12
sources of funds, 302
sub-classification of vehicle taken of lease, 240
Leasing on quality of investment, 255-57
Lessee Companies, 21-30
assets types of, 224-27
categories of, 308-309
evaluation of, 222-270, 307-10
expansis, components analysis of, 279-83
investment pattern of, 269-70
lease agreements, 245-48
lease arrangements, 265-66
net profit and leased assets of, 24, 227, 256-57
plant and machinery taken on lease, 231
reasons for leasing, 283-86
types of assets taken on lease, 228-30
Lessor Companies, 6-7, 16-21, 161-62
application of funds, 148, 218
cash flow analysis, 212-15, 305-307
consolidated cash flow statement, 185-86
debt equity ratio, 177
fixed deposits, 123-24, 210
income and cost of, 175
income and expenditure, 220
interest coverage, 180-81
performance of, 142-180, 302-307
profit of, 16-21
public deposits, 211
sources of funds, 216
trade bills, 195
types of, 48-50
Leveraged lease, 39
LFL company, 18, 179, 207, 211, 215, 305
cash flow statement, 193-94
Liquid assets, 109-10
LIC, 26
Liberalisation, 19
measures, 299
process, 301
Lloyds Finances 93
Loan Companies, 81
Loans and advances, 196
London Financial Group (LFG), 44

Machkund Hydro Electric (Joint) Scheme, 21
Manufacturing companies, leasing subsidiaries of, 49-50
Marketing leasing, 324-25
Maruti Udyog, 158
Mathur, B.L., 10
Maximum Permissible Bank Finance (MPBF), computations of, 85-87
Mayes, D.G., 13
Mean values, 259
Micro leasing, 324
Moody, John, 104
Monitoring leasing, 324-25
Murthy, Satyanarayana, 10
Mutual benefit financial company, 81
Mutual funds, 16, 110
MWL company, 20, 179, 207, 305
cash flow statement of, 199-200

Nagarjuna Finance Ltd., 112, 119
Nagarjuna, Naidu V., 10
Narasimhan Committee, 93
Narayana Swamy, R., 11
NFL Company, 16, 211, 305
annual reports of, 207-208
cash flow statement of, 187-88
National Housing Bank (NHB), 80
National Institute of Economic and Social Research (NIESR), 13
Net Present Value (NPV) model, 270
Net Owned Funds (NOF), 84, 87, 117, 143, 147, 296, 303, 319
Nevitt, Peter K, 45
New Industrial Policy, 62
Nicholas, C.S., 13
Non-Banking Financial Companies (NBFC), 1, 79, 93, 114-16, 205, 294, 320, 322
classification of, 80-81
deposits rates announced by, 213
liberalisation/rationalisation measures, 107-109
unexpected growth of, 133-34
Non-Performing Assets (NPA), 20, 96, 97, 98, 167-68, 247, 297-98, 305
NSICL, 66, 70

Off balance sheet financing, 288
Office equipment leasing of, 159
Operating lease, 246, 251
Owned funds, 143

Panday, I.M., 9
Pattidari, 43
Per capita income, 71-75
Plant and Machinery, leasing of, 154-55
Pollution control equipment, 257
Promoting Industrial investment, 52-55
Prudential Accounting Norms, 95
PAL company, 17, 28, 211, 215, 226, 249
 cash flow statement of, 191-92
PSL, 29, 226
PSM company, 30, 226, 241
Public deposits, 104-107, 118-20, 298-300, 319-20
 definition of, 114-15
 mobilization of, 206
Public legel complaints, 301
Public sector undertaking, 316-18
Purchure, Rajas, 10

Rate of interest, 267
Regularizing excess deposits, 118
Rental income, 162
Reserve Bank of India (RBI), 84, 87, 93, 106
 Amendment Act, 111
 guidelines, 79, 100, 208
 liberalisation policy, 318
 restrictions, 89
 stringent regulations, 119-20
Residuary Non-Banking Company (RNBCs), 81-83-93
Restrictions, 244
Restrictive Convenants, 286, 287
Return on Total Capital Employed (ROCE), 168

Sales Tax, 201-302, 321
Sales tax Act and Leasing, amendment to, 125-126
Sale and Lease Back, 39, 246, 251-52, 287
 agreements, reasons for, 249-50
Sample companies, selection of, 5-7
SCFSL Company, 21, 93, 179, 207, 211, 215, 305
 cash flow statement of, 203-204
Securities Exchange Board of India (SEBI), 79
Shah Committee, recommendations, 94-95
Skipped payment lease, 284
Small Industries Development Bank of India (SIDBI), 65
South-West Economic Planning Region (SWEPR), 13
Sreenivasa, Murthy S., 11
Srivastava, R.M., 9
Standard deviation, 257-60
Statutory Liquidity Ratio (SLR), 102
State Domestic Product, 71-75
Step Leases, 284
Straight-Line Method (SLM), 12
Subsidiaries, 2, 50
Sundaram Finance Ltd., 118
Supreme Court Ruling, leasing industry, 180
Survey of Industry Activity (SIA), 1
Swap lease, 41
Sykes, A., 14

TFCIL, 66, 70
Tata Finance Limited (TFL), 118
Tax Deducted at Source (TDS), 196
Tax Saving advantages, 281
Terry, B., 14, 289
Territorial Sales Tax position on lease, 137-41
Thunga Bhadra Hydro Electric (Joint) Scheme, 21
Trade Bills, 195-96
Trade Financing, 16
Transport sector, 32-21
Tripartite agreement, 251-55

United States Leasing Corporation, 43

Van Horne, J.C., 9
Vehicle Leasing, 155-59, 238-41, 310-11
Verma, J.C., 10

Wachowicz, J.M., 9
Wet and dry lease, 41
William, John, 10
World Leasing Conventions, 46
Written Down Value (WDV), 251, 262
 method, 272

Zero tax company, 277